HAPAX LEGOMENA IN BIBLICAL HEBREW

SOCIETY OF BIBLICAL LITERATURE

DISSERTATION SERIES

Robert Wilson, Editor

Jane Schaberg, *The Father, the Son and the Holy Spirit: The Triadic Phrase in Matthew 28:19b*

Daryl Dean Schmidt, *Hellenistic Greek Grammar and Noam Chomsky: Nominalizing Transformations*

Godfrey Nicholson, *Death as Departure*

Eugene V. Gallagher, *Divine Man or Magician?: Celsus and Origen on Jesus*

Bernard H. Brinsmead, *Galatians—Dialogical Response to Opponents*

Frank J. Matera, *The Kingship of Jesus: Composition and Theology in Mark 15*

Rodney Whitacre, *Johannine Polemic: The Role of Tradition and Theology*

Helen A. Kenik, *Design for Kingship: The Deuteronomistic Narrative Technique in 1 Kings 3:4-15*

Toni Craven, *Artistry and Faith in the Book of Judith*

David C. Verner, *The Household of God: The Social World of the Pastoral Epistles*

Gwendolyn B. Sayler, *Have the Promises Failed?: A Literary Analysis of 2 Baruch*

Frederick E. Greenspahn, *Hapax Legomena in Biblical Hebrew: A Study of the Phenomenon and Its Treatment Since Antiquity with Special Reference to Verbal Forms*

Frederick E. Greenspahn

HAPAX LEGOMENA IN BIBLICAL HEBREW

A Study of the Phenomenon
and Its Treatment Since Antiquity
with Special Reference to Verbal Forms

WIPF & STOCK · Eugene, Oregon

Wipf and Stock Publishers
199 W 8th Ave, Suite 3
Eugene, OR 97401

Hapax Legomena in Biblical Hebrew
A Study of the Phenomenon and Its Treatment Since
Antiquity with Special Reference to Verbal Forms
By Greenspahn, Frederick E.
Copyright©1984 by Greenspahn, Frederick E.
ISBN 13: 978-1-4982-8430-1
Publication date 2/16/2016
Previously published by Scholars Press, 1984

Contents

PREFACE vii
ABBREVIATIONS ix

CHAPTERS

    1. The Phenomenon of Hapax Legomena:
       A Survey of Previous Studies 1

    2. Towards a Definition of *Hapax Legomenon* 17

    3. The Distribution of Hapax Legomena
       in Light of Statistical Stylistics 31

    4. The Treatment of Hapax Legomena
       in the Versions 47

    5. The Treatment of Hapax Legomena
       in Rabbinic Literature 61

    6. The Treatment of Hapax Legomena
       in the Middle Ages 71

    7. The Treatment of Hapax Legomena
       in Contemporary Scholarship 101

    8. Summary and Conclusions 171

APPENDIXES

    I. Absolute Hapax Legomena 183

    II. Non-absolute Hapax Legomena 187

    III. Chi-Square Test for Distribution
        of Hapax Legomena 199

    IV. Absolute Hapax Legomena Verbs:
        Index and Glossary 201

BIBLIOGRAPHY 209

Preface

When discussing the meaning of a rare word in the Bible, modern scholars often note that it is a hapax legomenon. Rarely, however, has an effort been made to examine the meaning of this assertion systematically. Other than two dissertations, one limited to the Pentateuch and the other concerned primarily with the relevance of Akkadian and Ugaritic, only relatively brief articles deal with this phenomenon from the perspective of modern biblical scholarship. This study, therefore, explores the various questions pertaining to the existence of hapax legomena in biblical Hebrew. Although such analysis requires a great deal of philological treatment, the ultimate purpose is to treat these words as a class rather than separately in order to assess the significance of their rareness and what qualities some or all of them may have in common.

To establish a list of the Bible's hapax legomena requires more than a quick check in the concordance; indeed, no two of the available lists of hapax legomena are identical. Following a survey of previous discussions and widely held attitudes concerning hapax legomena, this study turns to the various problems which cause such inconsistencies, including homographs, cognates, and parallel passages, in order to establish a definition which can be objectively applied and will exclude all words that might be related to other biblical forms.

The application of this definition produces a list of words which is in itself quite useful. Although little treated in biblical studies, the problems of word frequency in general and hapax legomena in particular have received considerable attention from linguists and statisticians. Their conclusions provide valuable insights regarding the Bible's rare words: why do words appear only once in a particular work or language? Is the list of biblical hapax legomena larger or smaller than might be expected from other experience and statistical probability? Are these words found randomly throughout the Bible? Do they appear in particular contexts such as poetry or genres such as liturgy and wisdom literature? Only after answering such questions can hypotheses be proposed in the light of which specific words can be studied.

A rare word creates a special problem for the exegete, who normally interprets words by their usage in various contexts, a procedure not available in the case of hapax legomena. In order to assess the ways in which these limitations have been overcome, a detailed study of the methods used to deal with these words is presented. Since the purpose of this section is to demonstrate the assumptions and methods applied in various periods rather than to provide an exhaustive description of the treatment of all hapax legomena, the interpretation by the ancient versions, rabbinic tradition, medieval and modern exegesis of the one hundred forty verbal forms among the absolute hapax legomena is provided. From this survey conclusions can be drawn as to the desirable methodology for the treatment of rare forms in general and an assessment made concerning the nature of hapax legomena. In particular, we can hope to be able to assess the relative validity of two opposing attitudes discernible in modern scholarship regarding rare forms. The first treats unique forms as most likely being the result of error in the course of transmission. On the other hand, the precept *lectio difficilior praeferenda est* assumes levelling rather than the creation of strange forms to be the direction of corruption. To what extent these approaches are justified as well as what, if any, importance has been and should be attached to the fact that some words are found only once in the Hebrew Bible are the two focal points of this work.

This study reflects not only the research to which frequent reference is made, but also the assistance of a number of people to whom thanks are due. Lawrence Arend and Ray Jackendoff helped put the problems treated into the context of other literature. Michael Fishbane, Marvin Fox, and Jonas Greenfield read through the material, offering perceptive suggestions on matters of both substance and style. Kent Richards's guidance and advice helped me to negotiate some of the obstacles in publication. Stanley M. Wagner, Director of the University of Denver's Center for Judaic Studies, provided the support necessary for preparation of the manuscript, while Maurya Horgan and Paul Kobelski ensured that the product of that effort would be competent and, indeed, better than it deserves. To Nahum Sarna I owe special gratitude not only for inspiration and guidance throughout this project, but also for the preparation which made it possible. He provided the freedom for me to pursue my own interests, while being generous with both his time and ideas. Of course, ultimate responsibility for the contents must be my own. Finally, thanks are due also to Barbara whose support has never wavered and without whom such efforts would be inconceivable.

Abbreviations

AFD	*The Hebrew-Arabic Dictionary of the Bible Known as Kitāb Jāmiʿ al-Alfāẓ (Agrōn) of David ben Abraham Al-Fāsī the Karaite*
AFP	Solomon L. Skoss, "A Chapter on Permutation in Hebrew from David ben Abraham Al-Fāsi's Dictionary 'Jāmiʿ al-Alfāẓ,'" *JQR* 23 (1932-33) 1-43
Aq	Aquila
Barr	James Barr, *Comparative Philology and the Text of the Old Testament*
Barth	Jakob Barth, *Die Nominabildung in den Semitischen Sprachen*
BHT	Abraham Bedersi, חותם תכנית
BKAT	Biblischer Kommentar Altes Testament
BL	Hans Bauer and Pontus Leander, *Historische Grammatik der Hebräischen Sprache des Sprache des Alten Testamentes*
BM	בית מקרא
BWechter	Pinchas Wechter, *Ibn Barun's Arabic Works on Hebrew Grammar and Lexicography*
BY	Eliezer Ben Yehudah, מלון הלשון העברית

Abbreviations listed in the *Journal of Biblical Literature* 95 (1976) 331-46 have not been included here.

BYP	Abu Ibrahim Isaac ben Barun, יתר הפליטה מן כתאב אלמואזנה בין אלעבראניה ואלערביה
Canaani	Jacob Canaani, אוצר הלשון העברית
CB	The Century Bible (new series)
Cohen	Harold Cohen, *Biblical Hapax Legomena in the Light of Akkadian and Ugaritic*
DLS	Friedrich Delitzsch, *Die Lese- und Schreibfehler im Alten Testament*
DP	Friedrich Delitzsch, *Prolegomena eines Neuen Hebräisch-Aramäischen Wörterbuchs zum Alten Testament*
DST	ספר תשובות דונש בן לברט עם הכרעות רבינו יעקב תם
EA	Jørgen Alexander Knudtzon, *Die El-Amarna Tafeln*
ELB	Elijah Levita, ספר הבחור
ELH	Elijah Levita, ספר ההרכבה
ELT	Elijah Levita, ספר התשבי, לעקסיקאן המבארת לשון התלהוד והמדרשים
EM	אנציקלופדיה מקראית (Jerusalem: Bialik Institute, 1950—)
EMK	Arnold B. Ehrlich, מקרא כפשוטו
ESh	Abraham Even-Shoshan, המלון החדש
Exp	Expositor
EY	ארץ ישראל
GB	Frants Buhl, *Wilhelm Gesenius' Hebräisches und Aramäisches Handwörterbuch über das Alte Testament* (16th ed.)
GHAL	Alfred Guillaume, "Hebrew and Arabic Lexicography, A Comparative Study," *AbrN* 1 (1959-60) 3-35; 2 (1960-61) 5-35; 3 (1961-62) 1-10; 4 (1962-63) 1-18
HTT	*Two Treatises on Verbs Containing Feeble and Double Letters by R. Jehuda Ḥayug of Fez*
HYP	Judah Ḥayyuj, "יתר הפליטה מן כתאב אלנתף", in מספרי הבלשנות העברית בימי הביניים

IBP	Judah ibn Bal'am, "ספר הפעלים שהם הגזרת השמות"
IEM	Abraham ibn Ezra, מאזני לשון הקדש
IES	Abraham ibn Ezra, ספר צחות
IESB	Abraham ibn Ezra, שפה ברורה
IESB*	Michael Wilensky, "ספר שפה ברורה לר' אברהם אבן עזרא", דביר 2 (1923) 274-302
IJOT	Joseph Derenbourg and Hartwig Derenbourg, *Opuscules et Traites d'Abou'l-walid Merwan ibn Djanah de Cordove*
IJR	Jonah ibn Janaḥ, ספר הרקמה
IJSh	*Sepher Haschoraschim, Wurzelwörterbuch der Hebräischen Sprache von Abulwalid Merwan ibn Ganah*
IKSh	*Sharshoth Kesef, The Hebrew Dictionary of Roots by Joseph ibn Caspi*
IPM	Solomon ibn Parḥon, מחברת הערוך
IQR	Judah ibn Quraish, ספר אגרת
Jastrow	Marcus Jastrow, *A Dictionary of the Targumim, the Talmud Babli and Yerushalmi, and the Midrashic Literature*
JE	*The Jewish Encyclopedia*
Kautzsch	Emil Kautzsch, *Die Aramaismen im Alten Testament*
KD	C. F. Keil and F. Delitzsch, *Biblical Commentary on the Old Testament*
KHAT	Kurzgefasstes exegetisches Handbuch zum Alten Testament
KHC	Kurzer Hand-Commentar zum Alten Testament
König	Friedrich Eduard König, *Historisch-Kritisches Lehrgebaude der Hebräischen Sprache*
Lane	Edward William Lane, *An Arabic-English Lexicon*
LCh	Jacob Levy, *Chaldäisches Wörterbuch über die Targumim und einen grossen Theil des rabbinischen Schriftthums*
LESA	Wolf Leslau, *Ethiopic and South Arabic Contributions to the Hebrew Lexicon*

LHC	Wolf Leslau, *Hebrew Cognates in Amharic*
LNHeb	Jacob Levy, *Neuhebräisches und chaldäisches Wörterbuch über die Talmudim und Midraschim*
LS	Carl Brockelmann, *Lexicon Syriacum* (2d ed.)
MA	Wilhelm Muss-Arnolt, *A Concise Dictionary of the Assyrian Language*
Mandelkern	Solomon Mandelkern, *Veteris Testamenti Concordantiae*
MD	Ethel Drower and R. Macuch, *A Mandaic Dictionary*
MEB	Wilhelm Bacher, "לקוטים מספר אבן בחן לר' מנחם בן שלמה הגרן," 4 (1903) 38-58
MM	מחברת מנחם
MM*	David Kaufmann, "Das Wörterbuch Menahem Ibn Saruks nach Codex Bern 200," *ZDMG* 40 (1886) 367-409
MSh	Moses ben Isaac ben Ha-Nesia, ספר השוהם
NJV	*The Torah* (1962); *The Prophets, Nevi'im* (1978); *The Writings, Kethubim* (1982)
NSI	Albert G. Cooke, *A Text-Book of North-Semitic Inscriptions*
OM	Salomon von Urbino, *Ohel Moed, Hebräische Sinonima*
OTL	Old Testament Library
Palache	Jehuda ben Palache, *Semantic Notes on the Hebrew Lexicon*
PD	Profiat Duran, ספר מעשה אפד
Perles	Felix Perles, *Analekten zur Textkritik des Alten Testaments*
Perles*	Felix Perles, *Analekten zur Textkritik des Alten Testaments*, neue Folge
PS	Robert Payne-Smith, *Thesaurus Syriacus*
QG	*Sepher Ha-galuy von R. Joseph Kimchi*
QM	ספר מכלול שחבר דוד קמחי זצ"ל עם נמוקים שהוסיף אליהו אשכנזי

QMChomsky	William Chomsky, *David Ḳimḥi's Hebrew Grammar (Mikhlol)*
QSh	*Rabbi Davidis Kimchi Radicum Liber sive Hebraeum Bibliorum Lexicon cum Animadversionibus Eliae Levitae*
QZ	*Sepher Sikkaron Grammatik der Hebräischen Sprache von R. Joseph Kimchi*
Reuchlin	Johannes Reuchlin, *De Rudimentis Hebraicis*
RG	Arnold B. Ehrlich, *Randglossen zum Hebräischen Bibel*
Ružička	Rudolf Ružička, *Konsonantische Dissimilation in den Semitischen Sprachen*
Sam	Samaritan
SBOT	*The Sacred Books of the Old Testament*
Schulthess	Friedrich Schulthess, *Lexicon Syropalestinum*
ScrH	Scripta Hierosolymitana
SE	*Haʾegron, Kitāb ʾuṣul al-Shiʿr al-ʿibrānī by Rav Sěʿadya Gaʾon*
SO	*Oeuvres Complètes de R. Saadia Ben Iosef al-Fayyoumi*
SS	Nehemiah Allony, "כתאב אלסבעין לפטיה לרב סעדיה גאון", in *Ignace Goldziher Memorial Volume*
Sym	Symmachus
Theod	Theodotion
TSLS	Naphtali Herz Tur-Sinai, הלשון והספר
TSPM	Naphtali Herz Tur-Sinai, פשוטו של מקרא
TY	Tanhum ben Joseph Hayerushalmi, ספר אלמרשד אלכאפי
TY*	Hadassa Shy, "אלמרשד אלכאפי לר' תנחום ירושלמי", *Lešˇ* 33 (1969) 196-207, 280-96
Wagner	Max Wagner, *Die Lexikalischen und Grammatikalischen Aramaismen im Alttestamentlichen Hebräisch*
ZÄS	*Zeitschrift für Ägyptische Sprache und Altertumskunde*

1

The Phenomenon of Hapax Legomena: A Survey of Previous Studies

The term *hapax legomenon* originated among Greek grammarians who used it as an annotation for unique terms in classic works.[1] The earliest counterpart in biblical studies is the Masoretic marginal notation ל, an abbreviation of the Aramaic word לית, which was used to indicate non-recurring forms and constructions in the Bible. For example, למשול (Ezek 19:14) is so marked in the Leningrad manuscript because it is the only case in which this word is spelled plene, while יום שני (Gen 1:8) represents the unique juxtaposition of these two words, even though each occurs elsewhere. True hapax legomena, in the modern sense, should therefore comprise a subcategory of the class of words indicated by the Masoretes.[2] It is consequently surprising to find that a significant number

---

[1] ἅπαξ λεγόμενον is Greek for "once said." A detailed study of its use by Alexandrian grammarians can be found in F. Martinazzoli, *Hapax Legomenon* (Rome: Gismondi, 1953), and is summarized in Cohen, p. 1.

[2] Gérard Weil, *Massorah Gedolah* (Rome: Pontifical Biblical Institute, 1971) xiii, and H. Wheeler Robinson, *The Bible in its Ancient and English Versions* (Oxford: Clarendon, 1954) 29, although G. U. Yule (*The Statistics of Literary Style* [Cambridge: Cambridge University Press, 1944] 8) recognized that the practical value of such an effort is not apparent. Complete lists of the 40,000 unique forms in the Bible arranged according to initial letter can be found in Christian D. Ginsburg, *The Massorah* (New York: Ktav, 1975). The only words here considered hapax legomena which are not included there are the roots שכה (Jer 5:8), the attested form of which is homographic with the hif'il third person masculine singular participle of שכם, and תכה (Deut 33:3) which is homographic with the hof'al second person plural imperfect of נכה (Isa 1:5) and is therefore listed as תריך לישניך (Ginsburg, *The Massorah*, 2. 219).

of hapax legomena are not marked with the Masoretic ל.³ To verify this, two Masoretic editions of the Bible were compared, the Bomberg edition and the Leningrad manuscript represented by *Biblia Hebraica*.⁴ Words with other Masoretic notations were considered to have been recognized, since these notes often explain why a particular form was or was not regarded as unique. Twenty-four of what are here considered absolute hapax legomena are not indicated in either edition.⁵ The assumption that the Masoretes' work was exhaustive seems, therefore, to be without foundation. Yet there is no reason to expect otherwise: interested in avoiding mistaken treatment of the text, they did not point out philological phenomena, but only drew attention to those rare forms which they expected might create scribal confusion.⁶

---

³Chaim Rabin remarks ("מלים בודדות," *EM* 4. 1067): נמצאות רוב המלים הבודדות מסומנות כך [ל].

⁴These editions were used solely becasue of their availability. For the Leningrad manuscript *BHK* and *BHS* were treated together. Regarding problems with the Bomberg edition, cf. Gérard Weil, "Prolegomena," to S. Frensdorff, *The Massorah Magna*, xxii-xxv.

⁵מחוז, כרש, כפה, טמה, דחן, גרד, גלב, גביש, בצל, בזק, אבוי, תפת, שכה, ששה, רזם, צנה, צבת, פג(ה), ערוד, סנסנה, נזק, נבך, נבח, תרגם; here, as elsewhere, references for absolute hapax legomena can be found in Appendix I. That one hundred twenty of our hapax legomena are not marked with a ל by the Masorah in one of the two editions (Bomberg missing a total of fifty-eight and Leningrad one hundred eight) supports Orlinsky's point that there never was an official Masorah or Masoretic text. ("The Masoretic Text: A Critical Evaluation," in Christian D. Ginsburg, *Introduction to the Masoretico-Critical Edition of the Hebrew Bible* [New York: Ktav, 1975] xviii-xx). Not surprisingly both traditions are relatively complete in the Torah where the Leningrad manuscript omits only 10 percent and Bomberg 20 percent of the forty-one absolute hapax legomena, although Bomberg is still more inclusive in the Prophets, missing only 11 percent, and most complete with the Former Prophets and Isaiah where all but two of the respective twenty-eight and forty-seven hapax legomena are marked ל.

⁶C. D. Ginsburg notes (*The Massorah*, 4. lx), "I cannot too emphatically repeat that the Massorah is not a Concordance, that the unique forms of words, the exceptional phrases, the peculiar combinations, &c. which it ranges together under the separate and independent Rubrics are designed to safeguard these and other readings against the variations which have survived in the ancient versions. The Massorah is a controversial corpus."

The Phenomenon of Hapax Legomena

James Kennedy suggests that the Masoretic *paseq* and *legarmeh*, which are orthographically indistinguishable, originated as a sort of asterisk to mark strange forms and constructions; sometimes, he proposes, the mark was placed near the beginning of a verse in which the relevant form actually occurs somewhat later.[7] To support this theory, he claims that the distinction between the two marks is artificial, arguing that it would be odd for one sign to have two names and serve two radically different purposes while noting that the traditional rationales do not apply to many usages.[8]

To test Kennedy's theory, our list of hapax legomena was compared with those for the *paseq* and *legarmeh* published by Ginsburg.[9] Only two *pĕsēqîm* and nine *legarmehs* appear in immediate juxtaposition to a hapax legomenon, while seven and twenty-one respectively appear near the beginning of a verse containing hapax legomena.[10] Such results leave too many unmarked hapax legomena to support Kennedy's argument convincingly.

As a result of these observations, it is clear that the Masoretic notations are not relevant to the phenomenon treated here. They pertain to forms, not words, and reflect scribal, not philological difficulties. Nor do they provide definitive catalogs of phenomena, but draw attention to forms which, by virtue of their uniqueness, might be misunderstood. Finally, even though the lack of exhaustiveness makes absolute certainty difficult, it seems unlikely that the *paseq* and *legarmeh* have any relevance whatsoever; the correlation with hapax legomena is simply not large enough to support such hypotheses, while many instances reveal clearly scribal concerns as characteristic of these signs.

---

[7] James Kennedy, *The Note-Line in the Hebrew Scriptures* (Edinburgh: T. & T. Clark, 1903) 5-9.

[8] *The Note-Line*, 103-10; these problems are similar to those noted above for the ב.

[9] *The Massorah*, 1. 628-44 and 647-52. According to these lists, the Bible contains a total of approximately 1500 *legarmehs* and 500 *pĕsēqîm*.

[10] *Paseq* follows hapax legomena in Deut 27:9 and Jer 49:24; it is found in the same verse as a hapax legomenon in 1 Sam 4:9, Jer 31:39, Ezek 7:11, 41:16, 47:12, Ps 58:7, and Cant 2:3. *Legarmehs* precede hapax legomena in Ezek 17:9, Ps 62:4, 68:17, Cant 4:14, and Esth 1:6. They follow hapax legomena in Jer 2:24, Ps 73:9, Prov 30:15, and 1 Chr 15:27 while occurring in the same verse in Num 11:12, Isa 10:13, 15:5, 27:9, 50:4, Jer 42:6, Ezek 4:9, 5:1, 21:20, Ps 32:9, 48:14, 63:2, 69:21, 101:3, Prov 23:29.

Medieval lexicographers and exegetes frequently point out unique words in the Bible. Among the expressions used for this purpose are אין לו אח/דומה/דמיון/חבר/רע.[11] It is noteworthy that none of these phrases is syntactically equivalent to the modern noun *hapax legomenon*. Nor is any of these Hebrew expressions rigidly fixed: constituent words are often rearranged.[12] Nominal designations such as מלה יחידה and מלה זרה seem more fixed, although these too can be worded differently.[13] A final

---

[11]There is no consistency of usage such that one can readily trace the history of these terms. Menaḥem and Rashi tend to use the phrase אין לו דמיון (for example, MM s.v. גרד and Rashi on Ps 63:2), although Menaḥem also states אין לו חבר (MM s.v. פצם). אין לו דומה is the regular formulation used by Isaiah of Trani (see below, note 15 for references) although he inverts this to דומה אין לו at Isa 33:20 (see also Rashi on Exod 16:14). It is also used by Abraham ibn Ezra (on Cant 8:5), who makes extensive use of אין לו רע (for example, on Isa 33:20 and 44:8, but see also D. Qimḥi on Isa 1:22; this is inverted to אין רע לו on Amos 5:11, Ps 18:46, 60:4, Job 41:14) and אין לו אח (on Exod 32:16, Deut 33:19, Ps 18:46, Lam 3:16). His descriptions אב ואם, אין לו אחות, or משפחה (on Deut 32:34, Isa 11:8, Lam 1:14, see also on Qoh 10:8) seem to play on this latter phrase. The Arabic equivalents of these phrases are ליס לה נט׳יר or אשתקאק (see SS, p. 170), the former corresponding to אין לו דומה while the latter indicates the absence of cognates or an etymology (see Lane, pp. 2813 and 1577).

[12]The extent of these is so large as to preclude complete enumeration in this setting. Examples include לא מצאנו לו חבר (D. Qimḥi on Isa 33:20), בלי רע (Aaron ben Elijah on Deut 27:9), אין לו עוד דומה (ELT s.v. טנף), אין לתיבה זו דמיון (Rashi on 1 Sam 15:33). Note also the inverted phrasings cited in the preceding note. In general, variants are used by the same commentators who most regularly employ the better-known phrases. However, as observed above (note 11), there is not complete consistency. The fluidity of such phrases is illustrated also by Moses Qimḥi's statement אין לשניהם דומה (on Job 33:25) and Rashi's comment ויש דומה (on Lam 3:16, see also below, note 14). Similarly Ibn Ezra notes (on Isa 10:15) that the only רע to משור is found in 2 Sam 12:31, while he mentions several dislegomena (see on Deut 21:14, Qoh 4:10). An extensive catalog of these comments by Rashi, Samuel ben Meir, David Qimḥi, and Ibn Ezra can be found in E. Z. Melamed, מפרשי המקרא (Jerusalem: Magnes Press, 1975) 419, 479, 623-26, 847-49, and supports these remarks.

[13]Moses Qimḥi describes פרשז as רק היא יחידה בעניינה (on Job 26:9). מלה יחידה is used regularly by Ibn Parḥon (IPM s.v. רטפש, רצד, שנס, שקד; see also MM s.v. צנם, D. Qimḥi on Ps 119:131). The Arabic equivalent is مفرد (see Lane, p. 2365). Abraham ibn Ezra uses מלה זרה (for example, on Isa 15:5, 9:17, and Ps 119:103).

The Phenomenon of Hapax Legomena

group of descriptions comprises those which are freely stated, without any indication of fixed formulae.[14] It thus appears that while functionally equivalent to the technical term *hapax legomenon*, these statements were framed by the various exegetes who used them and became more or less standardized only as a result of such usage.

As with the Masoretic ל, such descriptions are not applied to every eligible word. Despite the obvious interest in and extensive terminology for indicating rare forms, many if not most unique words pass unnoticed even by those medieval exegetes and grammarians who seem interested in this phenomenon. Of the one hundred forty absolute hapax legomena verbs checked, Abraham ibn Ezra, who notes such words most often, cites only thirty-seven, too low a proportion to be explained by the assumption that he did not consider all those on our list to be true hapax legomena.[15] Other commentators and grammarians point out significantly fewer. The various authorities do not note the same words, while the relevance of these comments is not always readily apparent.[16]

The function of these notations of uniqueness requires explanation. Menahem observes that:

---

[14]For example, Ibn Kaspi (IKSh, p. 13) לא מצאנו רק and (on Joel 1:17) שם לבדו; ibn Ezra (on Lam 4:8) שרש היה בעברי ולא נמצא רק זה; Moses Qimḥi (on Job 39:23) אין משנה; and Elijah Levita (ELT s.v. חתר) זה השרש לא נמצא במקרא רק פעם אחת. Sometimes these descriptions are combined, for example זה מלה יחידה שאין לה דומה (IPM s.v. רנה), מלה מלה זרה ואין לה חבר (ibn Ezra on Isa 33:19), or זרה אין לה משפחה (Zeraḥya ben Isaac ben Shealtiel of Barcelona on Job 9:26).

[15]Isaiah of Trani also notes a relatively large proportion of the hapax legomena verbs here checked (30 out of 140), and yet both exegetes agree with regard to only thirteen (כמה, יאב, זער, הזה, הדה, בשס, אבך). Ibn Ezra alone notes דוץ, הדך, זהם, מלץ, נוט, פרשז, צען, צפד, רהה. עגן, עגם, עבש, סרף, לעט, כשה, כמס, טפש, חרת, חרג, חספס, חטם, עזק, עשק, פדע, פצם, צנם, רזם, רפק, שפן, and שקד. Isaiah of Trani alone notes בלס, הבר, הכר, נתס, סעה, עתם, צבט, רטפש, רנה, רצד, שקר, תזז, as well as בתק, דהם, קסס, שסף, and ששא which are in books for which no commentary by Ibn Ezra was available.

[16]One is reminded that in modern times the term *hapax legomenon* is often applied freely, but without any indication of its significance. Thus Samuel Terrin remarks (*IB* on Job 9:13), "The verb חתף, 'to prey upon,' is a *hapax legomenon*, but its stem refers elsewhere to human violence." See also E. Dhorme, *A Commentary on the Book of Job* (London: Thomas Nelson, 1967) 638, and KHC where the usage frequently seems gratuitous.

יש בתורה מלין אשר אין להם דמיון
אבל ענינם יורה עליהם ולולא אחיזתם
במחזה ותליית' מענין לא נודע פתרונם.[17]

According to Allony this position reflects a Karaite polemic against Saadia's reliance on rabbinic sources.[18] Several considerations cast serious doubt on this contention. Although Menaḥem is the only one to provide a methodological statement as to the treatment of hapax legomena in general, the approach he presents—reliance on context—is widely and explicitly applied, even by some who would not likely make use of Karaite polemics.[19] In addition, Menaḥem himself uses rabbinic Hebrew to explain several hapax legomena.[20] Although such an approach is found also in the philological work of the Karaite David ben Abraham Al-Fasi,[21] it would certainly be inappropriate in an anti-rabbanite polemic. In fact, Menaḥem never denies the potential usefulness of the comparative method; what he states is that for some words—מלין אשר אין להם דמיון—it will not work. The Hebrew phrase denotes, not hapax legomena, but words without cognates. The observation that a word lacks any parallel must be taken as a methodological assertion. Rather than identifying a particular word as a member of a special class within the biblical lexicon, such comments intend to inform the reader that the word's meaning cannot be determined by comparison with other, related forms inasmuch

---

[17] MM s.v. גלב.

[18] *BM* 7 "ירמיה ב'שבעים מלים בודדות' לרס"ג", Nehemiah Allony ([1962] 47ff) suggests that the Karaites saw the Bible as perfect in every regard (תורת ה' תמימה), including therefore whatever Hebrew had existed in the ancient period. In their view, Mishnaic Hebrew was at best an artificially constructed language which itself relies on interpretation of the Bible and is therefore of no independent value in assessing biblical usage. Menaḥem clearly did not view biblical Hebrew as complete; objecting to the use of consonant interchange to interpret biblical words, he stated (MM, p. 12b): אין קבוצת הלשון מצואה בספר תעודתנו, ואלו היתה הלשון שלמה אצלנו כל אלה המלים אשר ירפאו היינו מוצאים אותם והשגנגן במרחבו. For similar views see below, note 36. Menaḥem's use of rabbinic sources is noted below, note 20.

[19] See below, pp. 94-98.

[20] For example, צבט, סלד, טעה, גרר. The importance of this method is emphasized in a comment pertaining to the recognition of homographs where he states (MM, p. 30a concerning אפל in Exod 9:32): יש מלים הרבה אע"פ שיש להם דמיונות למראה אינם מגזרתם ומצאנו לו דמיון בענין ובמראה בלשון משנה.

[21] See AFD s.v. צפד and חזז.

The Phenomenon of Hapax Legomena

as none exist. Thus, frequently an authority will argue that in contrast to the view of others he finds a specific word unrelated to other biblical words, concluding that it is therefore a word for which אין לו דומה.[22] Such descriptions are occasionally used for words or roots attested twice in a single verse or passage[23] and sometimes for roots which occur several times but in only one form.[24] Rather than confusing the issue, these usages confirm the fact that the Hebrew phrases so applied cannot simply be identified with *hapax legomenon*. The latter refers to the number of times a word appears in a defined corpus, whereas the Hebrew counterparts indicate that the word so designated is the only form based on a given root and so cannot be interpreted with the help of other biblical usages or cognates. Some exegetes explicitly state that a word has no etymology.[25] Still elsewhere it is noted that a word has no parallel except in rabbinic Hebrew or even Arabic, thereby implying that דומה can apply not only to the biblical corpus, but to the entire range of known Semitic texts as well.[26]

Where no additional usages are available, exegesis must rely on context or the interpretations of others, most commonly the Targum.[27]

---

[22]For example, Ibn Ezra on Exod 32:16 (יש אומרים כי חרות כמו חרוש ויש מהפכים אותו חתור), Isa 47:2, Job 29:4 and DST, p. 79 (no. 130) as well as Jacob ben Reuben on Isa 33:20. This is confirmed also by the use of such designations for once-occurring homographs of more common words as by ibn Ezra on Exod 12:9, Isa 44:19, Job 21:32, 40:31 and David Qimḥi on Joel 2:7. So too ibn Ezra regards שקע as unique in Num 11:2 because its meaning is different from that found for other occurrences of this verb (see especially ibn Ezra on Job 40:25).

[23]For example, Ibn Ezra on Gen 30:20, Isa 14:23 and 9:4 (see D. Qimḥi on Isa 9:4) and Lev 26:21 (קרי appears also in vv. 23-41). Concern for words whose occurrences are limited to one section of the Bible is apparent also in his comments to Gen 7:4, 40:12, Isa 24:1, Job 39:16, Qoh 2:16, Est 1:3, 20, Dan 1:3.

[24]For example, Ibn Ezra on Gen 35:16 (כברה occurs also in Gen 48:7), Exod 29:20 (תנוך occurs also in Lev 14:14, 17), Lev 6:14 (מרבכת occurs also in Lev 7:12 and 1 Chr 23:29), Lev 19:19 (שעטנז occurs also in Deut 22:11).

[25]See above, note 11.

[26]For example, Ibn Ezra on Gen 26:20 (ידוע בדברי קדמונינו רק וליס לה נט'יר אלא מן קרב אלערבי) and AFD s.v. עבש (במקרא אין לו ריע אין לו ריע במקרא ואדוני אבי הביא) as well as D. Qimḥi on Isa 1:22 (לו חבר מהערבי). See also Ibn Ezra on Hos 13:1 and Judah ibn Balʿam on Isa 56:10.

[27]For examples, see below p. 93.

In fact the role of context is more pervasive than has often been recognized, extending well beyond the interpretation of hapax legomena. According to Yellin, Saadia considered context more important than even the text itself, leading him therefore to seek methods whereby the text could be effectively altered in order to provide a contextually suitable meaning.[28] Joseph Qara regarded the identification of פדעהו (Job 33:24) as a variant of פדאהו to be proven by its contextual appropriateness,[29] and ibn Janaḥ provided two interpretations of נוט, for one of which he even gives an etymology, with the final choice dependent on whether one regards God or הארץ as its subject.[30] Whatever etymologies you may find, he seems to say, it is ultimately context which must determine the appropriate meaning of an isolated word. This is why context is spoken of not only as מקומו or ענינו, but also כח הפסוק.[31] Nor is its importance limited to hapax legomena—it is just that for these words context is the only criterion available. Only cognates which yield meanings appropriate to a word's biblical context can be accepted as relevant to its etymology. These statements are not, therefore, formulaic assertions of the frequency of particular words in the Bible, but methodological observations reflecting those circumstances in which the exegete is deprived of his normal tools. The added במקרא or בתורה which at first glance seem so casually used are in fact the operative phrases.

The class described by the medievals is not, strictly speaking, hapax legomena but those words for which suitable etymologies were not available either on the basis of biblical material or even from the broader range of then-known Semitic texts. Indeed, the medieval terminology does not imply a class at all, but describes a problem; and the phrases used are intended as methodological assertions for the exegete, not indications of all cases of a particular kind of word or even a claim that such words constitute a "particular kind." The comments are neither gratuitous nor haphazard. They describe the exegete's need to resort to special methods, not the frequency of a specific word. It is therefore clear why these phrases were not identically applied by all who used them. Since

---

[28] David Yellin, תולדות התפתחות הדקדוק העברי (Jerusalem: Qohelet, 1945) 33, 39.

[29] (on Job 33:24) פדעהו כמו פדאהו, אלף מתחלפת בעין, והענין מוכיח.

[30] IJSh, p. 292.

[31] IPM s.v. רצד and שנס; hence ibn Janaḥ's concern with finding a meaning for בשס which יסבול הענין (IJSh, p. 80; see also pp. 12-13 s.v. אדב).

there was not always agreement on the interpretation of specific words, the methods applied or deemed acceptable in an individual case might differ. And so, too, it should be apparent why not all hapax legomena are indicated.

It has been suggested that during the medieval period there were several works in addition to that of Menaḥem which deal specifically with the phenomenon of hapax legomena. The best-known is Saadia's כתאב אלסבעין לפטיה, to which Allony adds three other works as evidence for the existence of a medieval philological debate with ultimately doctrinal roots.[32] In fact, the interrelationship of these various passages (only Saadia's is an independent work) is dubious at best. We have already pointed out the lack of tendentious purpose in Menaḥem's comment to גלב which merely generalizes the approach widely used to treat words presenting a specific methodological difficulty. Ibn Quraish and Ḥayyuj refer simply to words that can be explained only by recourse to rabbinic usage;[33] neither mentions the frequency of these words in the Bible. Even שאלות עתיקות, which does note their rareness, carries the point no further.[34] Thus while these latter works may share a polemical guiding purpose, it is not clear that they pertain to hapax legomena. The debate, if such there was, seems more over the relevance of rabbinic Hebrew than relating to the problem of words which appear only once.

It was Klar who seems first to have recognized the polemical purpose of Saadia's tract.[35] Trying to discredit the Karaite views and demonstrate the importance of rabbinic teaching, Saadia found rare words supportive of his argument from a linguistic point of view, since many words which are not clear in their biblical context can easily be explained

---

[32]Nehemiah Allony, "חיוג' יהודה לר' הקרחה' מ'ספר חדש "קטע in מספרי הבלשנות העברית בימי הביניים (ed. P. Kokovtsov; Jerusalem: Kedem, 1970) 5.

[33]The second section of the Risāla is entitled אלאפאט' אלמוגוד"ה פי אלמקרא מן לשון משנה ותלמוד ("Words Common to Biblical and Rabbinic Hebrew"); Ḥayyuj writes (on Judg 14:9, N. Allony, "קטע חדש," p. 10): ואלפאט' כת'ירה פי אלמקרא כ[דיאך] ליס תפסר באשכאלתא פי אלמשנה לגה אלמקרא אלא מן ("There are many words in the Bible like this one [וירדהו] which cannot be explained as they stand from biblical Hebrew, but only from the Mishna").

[34]Thus it begins אזן מלין תבחן בדמיון (Nehemiah Allony, "המלים", הבודדות ב'שאלות עתיקות'," HUCA 30 [1959] 6).

[35]Benjamin Klar, "הנוסח המקורי של 'פתרון שבעים מלות בודדות'," 1954) 260, הוצאת מחברת לספרות :Tel Aviv) מחקרים ועיונים in.

from rabbinic usage. He was thus able to take advantage of the perception among medieval exegetes that the Bible, a limited corpus, contains only a remnant of ancient Hebrew:

ודלך אן אלמקרא לם יוכתב
לתארץ בהא אללגה...כאנַתָ
אללגה אוסע מן אלכתאב.[36]

Hapax legomena are therefore, from the medieval perspective, those words of which only one attestation happens to be found in the Hebrew Bible. Since the Mishna is relatively close to the Bible chronologically, it stands to reason that it may contain further traces of such words. Allony has supported this contention by observing that the first ten words in Saadia's tract are relatively obvious cases which, he suggests, were placed at the beginning precisely to illustrate that even those who might not resort to rabbinic usage must concede the validity of his approach in these instances.[37] Other characteristics confirm the claim that philology was for Saadia a handmaiden to the doctrinal issue of rabbinic literature's importance. First, not all hapax legomena are mentioned. This should not be surprising since Saadia makes no claim to be writing a definitive work on this subject. Hapax legomena are used solely to illustrate the real point of his work. His concern was doctrinal, with only a linguistic facade. Secondly, several of the words Saadia treats seem to have halachic significance, again reflecting a purposeful selection of material.[38] Finally, some words cited are not strictly speaking hapax legomena. Since

---

[36] SS p. 172; cf. Ibn Kaspi's comment (on Isa 1:22): אין לנו שמוש מזה השרש בספרי הקדש הנמצאים בידינו, ומה נוכל לעשות, אחר שאין בידינו מלשוננו ...... רק מעט. ובכלל רק מה שנמצא כתוב באלה הספרים כי השאר אבדנו בגלותנו (see also IKSh s.v. סרף and עבש, PD p. 41, and MM p. 12b quoted above in note 18). This subject is discussed by A. S. Halkin, "The Medieval Jewish Attitude Toward Hebrew," in *Biblical and Other Studies* (ed. A. Altmann; Cambridge: Harvard University Press, 1963) 245-48; see also David Tene et al., "Linguistic Literature, Hebrew," in *Encyclopedia Judaica* 16. 1361. Ernest Renan remarked (*Histoire Generale et Systeme Compare des Langues Semitiques* [5th ed.; Paris: Calman Levy, 1878] p. 140), "une grade partie des richesses de cette langue [Hebrew] ont perdues pour nous. On en peut juger par le nombre des ἅπαξ εἰρημένα, et aussi par la quantité de racines essentielles que se trouvent en araméen et en arabe, et qui manquent in hébreu."

[37] Nehemiah Allony, "לרס"ג' בודדות מלים ב'שבעים ישעיה ," in ספר טור-סיני (Jerusalem: Kiryat Sepher, 1970) 280.

[38] Nehemiah Allony, "לרס"ג' בודדות מלים ב'שבעים ירמיה ," BM 7 (1962) 46.

the title explicitly refers to מפרדאת, this problem is important. It is possible to argue that Saadia made a mistake, but this seems unlikely in a collection where the choice of material was so carefully made. More likely the term מפרדאת is not to be understood as identical with our own *hapax legomenon*. Indeed, this fits the evidence previously noted with respect to such medieval terms.[39] These descriptions were meant to indicate words to which other biblical forms are not actually related, sometimes despite appearances. Where Menaḥem gathered those cases for which context is the only evidence, Saadia deals with the somewhat less rare group of words for which etymologies from rabbinic Hebrew are possible. Where Menaḥem's concern was philological, Saadia's is doctrinal. He takes those words which must be defined on the basis of rabbinic Hebrew as still further evidence for the importance of the literature which comprises the Oral Law.[40]

In sum, during the medieval period words with etymological problems to which biblical isolation might contribute were recognized and rare words were used for the apparently polemical purpose of illustrating the importance of rabbinic literature. Saadia alone among those making this point seems to have limited himself to words he considered to be hapax legomena, while Menaḥem dealt with the phenomenon of hapax legomena per se. Those who wrote during this period were interested in understanding the Bible itself, not in abstracting from it material for independent study. Word frequency and its impact were simply not considered. In contrast to the treatment of the Masoretes, words without related forms were often noted, doubtless because of the growing grammatical interest which focused on words and roots rather than forms and spelling, and an independent methodology proposed for those without cognates as well as a growing recognition on all sides of the importance of related languages. Still, only one side of the so-called debate has been identified here. Menaḥem and Saadia were not addressing each other. Though both relied on philological methods, in one case this was only a useful basis for justifying a doctrinal position. Where Menaḥem dealt with (some) hapax legomena, Saadia's primary concern was in undermining Karaite ideology.

---

[39] Above pp. 4-5. Saadia's claim is that these words are מפרדאת אלקרא ושרחהא מן תכ'ציץ אלמשנה (SS p. 146), that is, lacking related forms in the Bible, but known from rabbinic usage.

[40] There is no purpose to the work if one accepts Baron's contention that its function was philological (Salo Baron, *A Social and Religious History of the Jews* [Philadelphia: Jewish Publication Society, 1952—] 6. 267). The philological importance of rabbinic literature was conceded from a theoretical point of view even by Karaites (see note 21 above).

Independent examination of the phenomenon of hapax legomena has become more prevalent in the modern period, although only occasionally has such scrutiny been in depth. Most treatments are contained in encyclopedia articles, though there have also been two dissertations and an article on the topic.[41] The most common reference to hapax legomena is in the course of a commentary or its equivalent.[42] Thus the pattern set during the medieval period has persisted: the phenomenon attracts more notice than study.

Perhaps as a result of this lack of inductive scrutiny there has been no consistency of definition for the term *hapax legomenon*. The most inclusive definition is that adopted by Yahuda who accepts words which appear twice with the same form and meaning, roots attested twice by different forms having the same meaning, unique forms of otherwise attested roots, and even unique meanings of otherwise attested words.[43] Cohen and Zelson include words appearing more than once so long as the repeated occurrences are limited to parallel passages or contexts, this latter phrase being taken somewhat loosely, while Rabin excludes all such instances.[44] Consensus can be found in the respect shown to the distinction stated by Casanowicz between absolute and non-absolute hapax legomena, those which are "absolutely new coinages of roots" in contrast to words which "while appearing once only as a form, can easily be connected with other existing words."[45] This distinction and the acceptance

---

[41]Bruno Kirschner, "Hapax Legomena," *Jüdisches Lexikon*, 2. 1429, translated into English for the *Universal Jewish Encyclopedia* (5. 212); H. Torczyner, "Hapax Legomena," *Encyclopedia Judaica* (1931) 7. 997-1000, which seems to have provided the basis for the article in the *Encyclopedia Judaica Castellana* (5. 268); I. M. Casanowicz, "Hapax Legomena —Biblical Data," *JE* 6. 226-28; Chaim Rabin, "מלים בודדות," *EM* 4. 1066-69; J. Blau, "Hapax Legomena," *Encyclopedia Judaica*, 7. 1318-19 (this discussion seems to rely on the enumeration of Casanowicz); L. C. Zelson, "Le *Hapax Legomena* du Pentateuque Hebraique," *RB* 36 (1927) 243-48; Cohen; A. S. Yahuda, "Hapax Legomena im Alten Testament," *JQR* 14 (1902-3) 698-714.

[42]See note 16 above.

[43]For example, גלש (Cant 4:1, 6:5), שמץ and שמצה (Exod 32:25, Job 4:12 and 26:14), הלמות (Job 6:6), קצף (Hos 10:7).

[44]Zelson, for example, includes פיח from Exod 9:8 and 9:10 ("Le *Hapax Legomena*," 245; see Chaim Rabin, "מלים בודדות," 1067 and pp. 25-29 below.

[45]Casanowicz, "Hapax Legomena," 226. Rabin remarks ("מלים בודדות," 1067): רק הסוג של בודדות-שורש ניתן להגדרה מדעית ברורה, although as will become apparent (chapter II below) the application of

it has achieved reflects the important role assigned to grammar and etymology in the study of biblical Hebrew, while continuing as well the medieval perspective which emphasized not the uniqueness of a particular form, as had the Masoretes, but those words for which nothing in the Bible is even similar (דומה).[46]

Modern scholars have made various observations, usually unproven, concerning hapax legomena. Most prominent, and perhaps responsible for the seeming need to point out such words in the first place, is the assumption that their meaning is particularly unclear.[47] From this follows the corollary that the tradition of meaning for hapax legomena is weaker than for other, more common words.[48] While it is difficult to imagine testing this corollary or attempting to measure the strength of the "tradition of meaning" for any word, the basis for the claim of exceptional difficulty is more obvious. Since a word's meaning is determined from its usage in various contexts, there is less information available for a hapax legomenon than for other words.[49] Hence Cohen's willingness to extend the denotation *hapax legomenon* to words which appear in only one context, no matter how often it may recur, since all such words share in the problem of having evidence from only one context available for their interpretation.[50] Having argued, however, that a hapax legomenon is unique because it appears in only one context and is thereby limited with respect to the amount of contextual information available from within the Bible itself, Cohen proposes that the correct evaluation of such words can result only from finding an analogous usage in a cognate language.[51] To

---

even so clear a criterion is not always simple.

[46]See the descriptions cited in note 14 above, as in Elijah Levita's concern with the fact that the *root* חתך is not elsewhere attested.

[47]For example, B. Kirschner, "Hapax Legomena," 1429.

[48]Chaim Rabin, "מלים בודדות," 1067.

[49]Ibid., and H. Torczyner, "Hapax Legomena," 997. This reflects the medieval practice of relating words to similar forms in order to understand their meanings most fully; see IPM p. 74 (s.v. תעה) לא קבלנו
לשון הקדש מן רם אלא מצינו המקרא ודמינו דבריה זה לזה וזה מזה.

[50]Cohen, pp. 6-7.

[51]Cohen, p. 23. We will leave aside his use of non-cognates as evidence for parallel semantic fields, as in arguing that קצף can mean *foam* since the Hebrew חמה, Akkadian *imtu*, and Aramaic רתח mean both *anger* and *soap* (pp. 24-25). While demonstrating the possibility that one word can hold two such meanings, this method does not prove that both meanings were used for the Hebrew word. All Semitic words for *anger* do not mean *foam*. The need to resort to a cognate language is inexplicable. Reuchlin (p. 199) compares the use of חתך (literally *cut*) for *determine* to

be sure, such an approach may be helpful; finding the cognate of any biblical word in a similar non-biblical passage provides a link supporting the validity of comparing these two cognates in the first place. Since this method only confirms the claim of cognate relationship, however, it should apply to non-hapax legomena as well. Furthermore, the value of such an approach is limited to the extent that not all Hebrew words, much less hapax legomena, will have cognates which appear in the same context as their Hebrew counterparts. Cohen himself is able to explain something less than one-third of the hapax legomena he enumerates in this manner, while he often points out that other methods were able to treat these words equally well and much earlier.

This last point is important, for what Cohen's approach achieves most often is the supplying of an etymology rather than a meaning. He points out, for example, that the etymology of תשורה (1 Sam 9:7) was recognized already by Menaḥem. Cohen's only claim is that the analogy with Akkadian *tāmartu* (gift), which is derived from *amāru* (see), proves that a word meaning *gift*, as תשורה is generally recognized to signify, can be derived from a root meaning *see* (i.e. שור).[52] The method is not, therefore, essential for understanding most biblical hapax legomena.

Above all else Cohen's method fails to solve the problem which he himself states as central to hapax legomena, namely their occurrence in only one context. If it is true, as Cohen and others claim, that the difficulty with such words is our lacking a broad enough range of usage to assess their meaning fully, then finding a cognate of the same word in the same context in no way adds to our knowledge. Consider the biblical phrase תנוט הארץ (Ps 99:1). An almost perfect analog occurs in the Ugaritic line *bmt. ʾa* [*rṣ*] *tṭṭn* (*CTA* 4 VII:34-5). The existence of two independent, yet virtually identical usages of these related roots may confirm the validity of each, but it does not provide any new information

---

the use of *incidere* in Horace's phrase "leges incidere ligno" (*Ars Poetica*, line 399, LCL p. 482), and many moderns who relate מהל (dilute) to מול (circumcise) find words with a similar semantic range in various Indo-European languages (for example, English *cut*, see p. 133 below). Arguments from analogy such as these are notoriously weak unless it can be proved that the analogy itself is valid; and it certainly would be hard to show that Hebrew and Akkadian, for example, are analogous in all cases, particularly with respect to the semantic ranges of their vocabulary.

[52]Cohen, p. 24; his point is that this should not, therefore, be regarded as an absolute hapax legomenon.

The Phenomenon of Hapax Legomena

as to the meaning of either word.[53] While scholars will presumably be less inclined to emend the biblical occurrence to a form of the more common root מוט[54] now that the unrelated, but strikingly similar Ugaritic occurrence is in hand, no new evidence for the word's meaning is gained from the parallel. What is truly needed from Cohen's perspective are different usages of the same word so that how it or a cognate functions in other circumstances can be used to understand its semantic range more fully. Cohen should be seeking to find in other languages what the Bible does not provide for hapax legomena, namely additional usages to provide further semantic information, rather than settling for more attestations of the same usage which in no way resolves what he perceives to be the central dilemma concerning these words.[55]

Other modern scholars have suggested that many hapax legomena have been lost in the course of transmission when scribes "corrected" terms that did not occur elsewhere and were difficult to understand;[56] conversely, some would argue that several of the extant hapax legomena are in fact textual corruptions of originally more common words.[57] Many scholars claim that these words were not necessarily rare in the biblical period, but appear only once by accident—as a result of the Bible's own limited interests and size or the unique language of an individual part of it; thus hapax legomena may be dialectic, loan, or even nonce words which were created for stylistic needs by a particular author.[58]

---

[53]The interpretation was recognized already in the medieval period (see Abraham ibn Ezra and Isaiah of Trani on Ps 99:1).

[54]See Rudolf Kittel (KAT) on Ps 99:1.

[55]We will, of course, have to ask to what extent this lack of contextual variety really does create problems for the correct understanding of these words.

[56]For example, Chaim Rabin,"מלים בודדות," 1069.

[57]E. g., H. Torczyner, "Hapax Legomena," 999; thus regarding the hapax legomenon נחץ he remarks: אין 'נחוץ' בלשון המקרא (TSPM on 1 Sam 21:9). Arnold Ehrlich seems very often to argue that forms unattested elsewhere in the Hebrew Bible should therefore be emended (see chapter VII below for specific references).

[58]For example, Torczyner, "Hapax Legomena," 998-99 and Casanowicz, "Hapax Legomena," 226. See also Rabin,"מלים בודדות," 1069 and G. R. Driver's claim ("Hebrew Poetic Diction," VTSup 1 [1953] 28) that "the small bulk and narrow range of the surviving literature has the result that an unduly high proportion of [biblical] words is exceedingly rare, so that their precise sense can hardly be determined." For medieval antecedents of this view see note 36 above. Fannie Chude (*Hapax Legomena: A Linguistic Study of Words Occurring Once*, diss., Radcliffe, 1954, p. 20)

These remain only hypotheses, but it can be seen that with the exception of scribal error, the theories reflect a fundamental continuation of ideas formulated in the medieval period. Hapax legomena are seen as those words which happened into the Hebrew Bible only once such that their meaning is not always clear. However, the implication that their rareness is purely accidental is contradicted by efforts to finds its cause. Only a survey of the words themselves will permit an assessment of the claim that they are especially difficult and an evaluation of the problems created when one has only one context from which to work.[59]

Despite the attention to hapax legomena throughout the ages treated in this survey, the phenomenon has in fact received little careful scrutiny. Hapax legomena were not even recognized as a class prior to the modern period.[60] Masoretic notes point out some unique forms which, even if listed completely which they are not, would comprise primarily non-absolute hapax legomena. The medieval period brought notations referring only to those words for which biblical and then-known Semitic material were insufficient to provide a suitable etymology and treatises on hapax legomena whose concern was more with the nature and importance of rabbinic Hebrew than biblical words of low frequency. Finally, in the modern period hapax legomena seem to have been recognized as a definable class, albeit not consistently so, about which certain generalizations may be inferred. These assertions, however, are offered without support. It remains to analyze unique biblical forms in order to determine whether they are in fact a homogeneous group and to determine what substantial conclusions can be drawn from them.

---

cites, as an example of nonce words, several lines from Christopher Fry's "The Lady is not for Burning": "You bubble-mouthing, fog-blathering,/ Chin-chuntering, chop-flapping, liturgical,/Turgidical, base old man."

[59]One can observe that the value of context with respect to hapax legomena is ultimately dependent on its importance in assessing the meaning of biblical words in general. The methods of modern scholarship suggest that most words are not analyzed in this way. More attention seems focused on etymology and the readings of ancient witnesses. A brief survey of the index in a book such as Barr which deals with modern lexicography or a recent issue of *Elenchus Bibliographicus Biblicus* shows that proportionately more attention is lavished on individual occurrences of relatively common terms which are given new or esoteric meanings than on the more numerous hapax legomena. The trend seems more towards finding rare words behind seemingly common spellings than towards treating obviously unique forms.

[60]Menaḥem treats them as a problem; see pp. 5-6 above.

2

Towards a Definition of Hapax Legomenon

A hapax legomenon is "a word or form of which only one instance is recorded in a literature or an author."[1] With a criterion of such clarity, it would seem simple to enumerate the hapax legomena in a particular text such as the Hebrew Bible; in fact, the seeming clarity of this definition is illusory and any enumeration necessarily arbitrary. This point is best illustrated by a comparison of several purportedly complete lists of hapax legomena based on generally similar definitions of that term. A glance at the samples given below for entries beginning with *aleph* and those from the book of Genesis will suffice to show that the definition is not so clear as to ensure even two identical lists.[2]

Several factors enter into the decision as to which words are hapax legomena: the corpus from which they must come, that part of the corpus' vocabulary to be checked for words appearing once, and the criteria defining "one-ness" which are applied to that vocabulary. None of these is without problems.

---

[1] *Oxford English Dictionary*, p. 3984.
[2] Sources for the following lists are Nehemiah Allony, "כתאב אלסבעין לפטה," in *Ignace Goldziher Memorial Volume* (ed. S. Löwinger; Jerusalem: Rubin Mass, 1958) 2. 173-77 for Saadia (abbrev. "S"); N. Allony, "השקפות אוצר יהודי ספרד ''קראיות ב'מחברת' מנחם והמלים הבודדות בערך 'גלב'," 5 (1962) 51-54 for Menaḥem (abbrev. "M"); N. Allony, "שבעים מלים בודדות ספר שמואל ייבין in ב'רסאלה' ליהודה אבן קריש" (Jerusalem: Kiryat Sepher, 1970) 15 for ibn Quraish (abbrev. "Q"); N. Allony, "המלים הבודדות ב'שאלות עתיקות'," in *HUCA* 30 (1959) 13-14 (abbrev. "SA"); I. M. Casanowicz, "Hapax Legomena," *JE* 6. 226-28; L. C. Zelson, "Le *Hapax Legomena* du Pentateuque Hebraique," *RB* 36 (1927) 243-48; Cohen, pp. 108-26; Chaim Rabin, "מלים בודדות," *EM* 4. 1068.

HAPAX LEGOMENA LISTS: GENESIS ENTRIES

Casanowicz	Medieval
אברך	בטנים (SA)
בטנים	גפר (M, SA)
גפר	זבד (M, SA)
טחה	ימם (SA)
ימם	לוז (SA)
להלה	עשק (M, Q)
לוז	פצל (M)
לעט	צנם (M, SA)
מכרה	שחט (M)
משק	שערים (S)
סלם	
צנם	
שחט	
שאה	
שפיפון	

Greenspahn	Cohen	Zelson		
דגה	אברך	עשק	יזם	אבק
טחה	זבד	פצל	ימם	אברך
יזם	טחה	פרת	כפר	בטנים
ימם	לעט	צהב	לוז	בכר
לעט	סלם	צנם	לעט	גמא
עשק	עשק	שוח	מכרה	גפר
צנם	פצל	שחט	מנה	דגה
שוח	צנם	שאה	משק	ולד
שחט	שוח	שכל	נפתל	זבד
שפיפון	שחט	שער	נשה	זבל
	שפיפון	שפיפון	סות	זעה
	תלה	תלה	סלם	טחן
		תליך	עדנה	טען
			עקד	

A Definition of Hapax Legomenon

HAPAX LEGOMENA LISTS: ALEPH ENTRIES

Casanowicz		Medieval
אבה	אמון	אביונה (S)
אבחה	אנס	אח (SA)
אבטחים	אנקה	אטון (M)
אבי	אפדן	אנס (S)
אבך	אפנין	אנקה (SA)
אברך	אפע	אלי (Q)
אגוז	אפריון	אקדח (SA)
אגל	אקדח	אקו (SA)
אגם	אקו	ארה (S)
אדב	ארשת	אשך (Q)
אהל	אשד	אשפה (M)
אזן	אשיה	
אח	אשך	
אחשתרנים	אשמנים	
אלץ	אשש	
אלקום		

Greenspahn		Cohen	Rabin		
אבוי	אלקום	אביונה	אפסים	אזן	אבה
אנחה	אלץ	אבך	אפע	אחים	אבוי
אבטחים	אנו	אבעבעות	אפריון	אטון	אבחה
אבך	אנס	אברך	אצל	אטים	אבטחים
אברך	אפדן	אגוז	אקדח	אישון	אביונה
אגוז	אפע	אגל	אקו	איתון	אבך
אגל	אפריון	אגרטל	אראל	אכל	אבעבעות
אדב	אקו	אחשתרנים	ארוז	אלה	אברך
אדש	ארן	אטון	ארן	אלה	אבק
אורות	ארשת	אלץ	אשדת	אלקום	אגוז
אטון	אשיה	אפדן	אשיה	אמן	אגורה
איתון	אשך	אפע	אשתממ	אמר	אגל
		אפריון	אשויות	אנס	אגרטל
		אקו	אשמנים	אנקה	אדב
		ארנבת	אשש	אפדן	אהלים
		אשיה	אתרים	אפנים	אול
		אשך			

That we must eliminate Aramaic portions of the Bible from consideration is obvious; as a distinct language, none of its vocabulary can be strictly speaking identical with that of Hebrew, but only potentially cognate.[3]

Some Hebrew hapax legomena such as אנס, בטל, and רשם are attested in biblical Aramaic; that these words appear only once is due to our having excluded Aramaic passages from consideration. Treating such words which do after all appear elsewhere in the Bible as hapax legomena may seem to trivialize that category; criteria intended to exclude irrelevant words seem to have allowed some inappropriate words to enter into consideration. But their use in Hebrew is unique and prima facie no different from that of a word with Aramaic cognates in non-biblical texts. Ezra 4:7 provides a more ambiguous instance. The sentence is Hebrew, yet both of its hapax legomena (תרגם and כנת) are known from Aramaic. These may reflect late Aramaic influence on the Hebrew language, or they might be a sort of "spillover" from the Aramaic passage which follows and, as such, poor evidence as to the nature of Hebrew itself.

As a general rule the contextual language, that in which the sentence itself is framed, will be judged to be the language of a passage, thereby allowing for the elimination of the admittedly isolated sentence in Jer 10:11 as well as Dan 2:4-7:28, Ezra 4:8-6:18 and 7:12-26. These sections are not, of course, to be ignored, but used with other non-Hebrew sources to interpret those words that are examined. Furthermore, the ambiguities indicated above necessitate considering the possibility that some hapax legomena are in fact Aramaisms and their isolated appearance evidence of their recent entry into the language.

A second exclusion which is both obvious and problematic is that of proper nouns. John Stuart Mill pointed out that such words denote rather than connote.[4] Of course, names do have meanings; but such etymologies explain their origin rather than their function in a particular usage. Some proper nouns seem to connote.[5] Names such as *Black Sea* and ים סוף appear to have meanings that are intentionally conveyed by the language

---

[3] One could study hapax legomena in biblical Aramaic; however, the small size of the corpus provides little opportunity for words to recur, artificially inflating the number of rare forms. Rabin ("מלים בודדות," 1070) counts 291 Aramaic hapax legomena in the Bible; for the relationship between corpus size and word frequency see pp. 32-33 below.

[4] John Stuart Mill, *A System of Logic Ratiocinative and Inductive* (8th ed.; New York: Harper & Brothers, 1890) 36.

[5] On this subject see John Stuart Mill, *A System of Logic*, 36.

A Definition of Hapax Legomenon

which uses them. However, names come to function independently of their origin. The Black Sea could be so-called even long after its "color" had changed. Nor should the components of a name like *Black Sea* or ים סוף be treated separately, since they function as one unit with no meaning other than the body of water they identify. One might argue that to ignore such words would lead to the loss of useful data about the language being studied. It is not, however, the concern of this study to recover possible entries for the lexicon of ancient Hebrew, but simply to determine which attested words occur only once in the Bible. Since names do not function within the language according to their meanings, they need not be included nor are they generally considered in studies of this kind.[6]

A serious problem results from the need to identify proper nouns in a text which lacks capitalization, leading inevitably to ambiguity, cases in which one cannot be certain whether a particular word is a proper or a common noun. The following list includes once-occurring words which were judged to be proper nouns, but in light of the preceding deemed problematic.

PROBABLE PROPER NOUNS

Amos 4:3	הרמון	1 Sam 20:19	אזל
Ps 42:7	חרמונים	Gen 46:21	אחי
Amos 5:26	כיון	Num 21:1	אתרים
Amos 5:26	סכות	Josh 15:28	בזיות
2 Sam 23:8	עצן	2 Sam 20:14	ברים
Gen 49:12	שילה	Ezek 37:16	המונה

Having limited our corpus and the components of its vocabulary from which hapax legomena must come, we can now deal with problems pertaining to the determination of which words appear only once. The best known sign of such cases is the Masoretic ל.[7] However, inasmuch as its use includes unique constructions and phrases, what might be called syntactical hapax legomena, and since such a category is theoretically limitless, only those deemed problematic were so indicated. While this served the Masoretic concern to ensure the correct preservation of the text, it does not serve the lexicographic purposes here addressed.

---

[6]A resultant anomaly is the inclusion of the verb עשק in our list of hapax legomena, since it appears alongside the purportedly related place name עשק in Gen 26:20, while we exclude words which appear twice or with a related form in the same verse (see p. 27 below).

[7]For a full treatment see pp. 1-3 above.

Christian D. Ginsburg's list contains "upward of forty thousand [unique] forms," consisting only of words, rather than constructions, and claiming at least approximate inclusivity.[8] His purpose, however, was to evaluate the purpose and worth of the Masoretic lists with which he worked. The list contains what might be called morphological hapax legomena--all the unique forms in the Bible, even where this uniqueness is the result of the definite article, a pronominal suffix, or the unique use of plene or defective spelling. Although this may be the only type of list which can claim complete objectivity,[9] it deals with forms and not words.

It is clear then that any list and the criteria which generate it must be designed to fulfill the needs for which it is produced. To understand the underlying reasons for rareness requires an analysis of those words which appear only once in the Bible and whose sole occurrence may provide insufficient information to the lexicographer and cause the text critic to ponder their authenticity. A unique phrase may be perfectly explicable from an understanding of its constituents alone; an isolated form may be generated from common components inflected in an ordinary way. The attempt will be to locate, insofar as is reasonable, the most isolated words in biblical Hebrew.

To achieve this, one must seek not simply unique words, but more importantly those which derive from unique roots. Just as a known word which appears only once with a particular suffix cannot be counted as truly rare, so too a form which is attested only once, but derived from a frequently used root is not totally isolated. There is no intention here to enter the debate concerning the reality and significance of roots. The Semitic root may well be a hypostatization or theoretical construct.[10] But even if a word does not equal its etymology, words from known roots, although themselves attested only once in the Hebrew Bible, can hardly be considered isolated in the sense here intended; they will, however, be included where necessary for comparison with other material and their infrequency will be discussed.[11] The existence of related forms makes

---

[8] Christian D. Ginsburg, *The Massorah* (New York: Ktav, 1975) 4. 4.

[9] Such a list has the drawback of excluding homographic forms even where syntax shows a clear distinction; thus Ginsburg omits משכים (Jer 5:8) which we treat as an absolute hapax legomenon under the root שכה.

[10] Chaim Rabin, "התיתכן סמנטיקה מקראית?," *BM* 7 (1962) 23 and James Barr, *The Semantics of Biblical Language* (London: Oxford University Press, 1961) 100-108.

[11] For example, p. 33; a list of non-absolute hapax legomena (excluding homographs) can be found in Appendix II.

A Definition of Hapax Legomenon

them that much less isolated, providing at least a first step in their interpretation. This study will deal with the so-called absolute hapax legomena, those words which occur only once and seem unrelated to otherwise attested roots.

Even with a working definition of the term *hapax legomenon*, it can be surprisingly difficult to determine how many times a given word appears. A first problem stems from the possibility of corruption within the biblical text; it might be argued that accepted emendations, where unique, should also be included. The flaw in this proposal is that consensus is frequently lacking and the possibilities for emendation are endless. As a methodological principle, therefore, the text in *BHK* has been accepted as the sole basis for judging inclusion in the list.[12] Some implications of this method are critical. Since פח-בג appears several times in Daniel with a *maqqeph*, בג in Ezekiel 25:7 can be included only as a questionable hapax legomenon. Also excluded is בלי-מה (Job 26:7) which is printed as two words although other manuscripts and editions treat it as one.[13] In accepting a Masoretic text, we are bound also to consider both *kĕtîb* and *qĕrê*, even if one may sometimes be judged a corruption which the other corrects. While objections to this approach are easily conceived, the implications of any other would be worse still; refinement and subjective modification are possible only after a rigorously defined methodology has been applied and its results analyzed.

A more difficult problem is that of homographs.[14] With the burgeoning of philological treatments of the biblical text and the concomitant rise in the number of proposed homonyms in Hebrew, the problem of

---

[12] See Yehudah Radday, *The Unity of Isaiah in the Light of Statistical Linguistics* (Hildesheim: H. A. Gerstenberg, 1973) 50. *BHS*, which was only partially completed at the time this study was initiated, has also been consulted along with Ginsburg's and the Baer-Delitzsch editions.

[13] This procedure preserves בלם (Ps 32:9) which might be related to a form בלימה and therefore not an absolute hapax legomenon by our criteria.

[14] The term "homonym" is generally avoided when referring to Hebrew since it implies the identical sound of two words, while in some cases of biblical Hebrew it is not at all certain that identically spelled words were pronounced the same (see pp. 24-25 below). Although cited material does not always make this distinction, reference is to the same problem. The existence of homographs in Hebrew was recognized by Menaḥem (MM s.v. אפל); see Israel Efros, "Maimonides Treatise on Logic," *PAAJR* 8 (1937) 59-60.

determining validity, as in the case of emendation, becomes virtually impossible.[15] This is complicated by the fact that languages are not rigid, unchanging entities amenable to strict, mathematical analysis. Individual words may have more than one meaning, while homonymous words of separate origin can in the course of time become virtual synonyms.[16] Hence Muller's comment that "historiquement, on peut distinguer la polysémie et l'homonymie. Du point de vue synchronique, cette distinction n'existe pas."[17] Even historically such a distinction is not always certain.[18] Because of the hopelessly confusing nature of this issue and to avoid including possibly inappropriate forms, homographic roots are treated here as if identical while the previously stated dictum regarding the *BHK* text has been extended so that its orthography is regarded as normative as well. Thus words which can be traced by known patterns of Hebrew word development to roots exemplified elsewhere in the Hebrew Bible have been excluded as have words which might be explained in this manner (e.g., אקדח, אברך, אבטח). Although no judgment is intended as to the certainty of these interpretations, such forms are indicated as possibly absolute hapax legomena where deemed appropriate. In general, then, the printed consonants are taken as the basis for decisions with respect to homographs and homographic roots, although in this setting perhaps more than elsewhere allowance should be made for atypical phenomena.

The fact that several letters in the Hebrew alphabet are used for more than one Semitic phoneme may mask genuine distinctions among words and roots. To assess the relative importance of this phenomenon the material provided in KB was tested. This resource lists 113 forms as

---

[15] Barr (pp. 125ff) cites nine supposedly independent meanings claimed by scholars for עיר and points out (pp. 151ff) that this approach imputes to Hebrew a greater proportion of homonyms than is found in other, even closely related languages.

[16] Elise Richter, "Über Homonymie," *Festschrift für Universitäts-Professor Hofrat Dr. Kretschmer* (Beiträge zur Griechischen und Lateinischen Sprachforschung; Vienna: Verlag für Jugend und Volk, 1926) 176.

[17] Charles Muller, "Le MOT, unité de text et unité de lexique en statistique lexicologique," *Travaux de Linguistique et de Litérature* I (1963) 165.

[18] Gustav Herdan, *Quantitative Linguistics* (London: Butterworths, 1964) 7. Moshe Held ("Studies in Biblical Homonyms in the Light of Akkadian," *JANESCU* 3 [1970] 47) suggests that the question of homonyms in biblical Hebrew needs careful investigation.

A Definition of Hapax Legomenon

absolute hapax legomena (by the definition here used) which are derived from roots having claimed homographic counterparts in the Bible. Seventy of these include one of the graphemes which could mask such etymological divergence, namely ז (for Semitic d̲ and z), ח (for ḥ and ḫ), ע (for ʿ and ġ), צ (for ṣ, ḍ, and ẓ), and שׂ (for š and t̲). Because this lexicon provides etymological information to justify its entries, it is possible to assess the extent to which the orthographic convergence of these letters is responsible for the separate listing of these roots. In only twenty-one cases was this the basis for the claim of a distinct root,[19] while for twenty-three words the "Proto-Semitic" roots of the two words are identical with respect to the letters here discussed, the separate entry being based on homonymy, metathesis, or the like.[20] In other words, whereas fully seventy out of 113 claimed cases of homographic roots yielding hapax legomena could have been explained on the basis of the orthographic convergence in Hebrew of originally distinct consonants, such an argument was put forward for only twenty-one. Less than nineteen percent of the claimed homographic hapax legomena are therefore attributed to this phenomenon.[21] It is thus clear that the existence of relatively few hapax legomena has been obscured by the nature of the Hebrew alphabet. To accept Hebrew orthography as the basis for decision is not to lose a large number of words, but to avoid introducing yet another element of subjectivity into the analysis. Minimizing potential sources of subjectivity and thereby error in the compilation of a list ensures its usefulness for assessing the nature of this class even if it may as a result be somewhat incomplete.

---

[19] אהל (Job 25:5), אל (1 Sam 27:10), אלה (1 Sam 17:39), אלה (Joel 1:8), אמה (2 Sam 8:1), אנקה (Lev 11:30), ארן (Isa 44:14), זבח (Isa 19:6), זרה (Ps 139:3), חב (Job 31:33), חבב (Deut 33:3), חטב (Prov 7:16), חפף (Job 40:17), חרט (Isa 24:6), חשׂף (Ps 29:9), טען (Gen 45:17), טען (Isa 14:9), לוז (Gen 30:3), לקשׁ (Job 24:16), מורשׁ (Job 17:11), מחה (Num 34:11), עמם (Lam 4:1), עמר (Ps 129:7), פצח (Mic 3:3), צב (Lev 11:29), צהל (Ps 104:15), צוץ (Cant 2:9), רצא (Ezek 1:14), שׁלל (Ruth 2:16).

[20] For example, נוח (Hab 3:16) and גזר (Isa 19:19). Lexical data for the remaining 26 cases were insufficient to categorize the justification for KB's claiming a separate root.

[21] Cohen (pp. 126-43) provides a long list of homonymic hapax legomena, analysis of which yields similar results although he does not provide the lexical data to justify his claim in most instances.

A final problem to be treated is that of a word which would be an absolute hapax legomenon but for a second occurrence in a passage identical with or extremely similar to its original occurrence, or one with multiple occurrences in close proximity to one another.[22] Zelson accepts words which appear several times in one verse (e.g. פורה in Gen 49:22) or in "passages parallèles [sic] composés de phrases à peu près identiques."[23] As can be seen from the comparative list above, these seemingly minor modifications dramatically increase the relative length of his list. Cohen attempts to provide a theoretical justification for this approach, arguing that a hapax legomenon is any word which occurs in only one context, regardless of how often that context and thereby the word itself is attested; he then tries to find a similar context elsewhere in Semitic literature in order to interpret the biblical passage.[24] As noted above, definitions are often shaped by the purpose to which they will be put. Cohen's concern is with words for which limited lexicographic information can be derived from their context. Words appearing several times, but in only one usage would seem appropriate for such study; they are not, however, hapax legomena. Some words may occur in only one context because of the nature of the corpus in which they are found. It might be determined, for example, that in non-medical circles the word "aspirin" tends to be used primarily with reference to headaches; this does not, however, make it a hapax legomenon. Similarly it should not be surprising to find that many rare animal names recur in biblical lists pertaining to dietary laws, though they would undoubtedly appear in more varied contexts were the biblical canon to include an ancient zoological treatise.[25] This phenome-

---

[22] Chaim Rabin ("מלים בודדות," *EM* 4. 1067) excludes all such cases.

[23] Zelson, "Les *Hapax Legomena*," 244.

[24] Cohen, pp. 22-24; his philological methods are discussed above, pp. 13-15.

[25] Cohen's belief (p. 22) that these must have been common names in antiquity because the people had to understand which animals were designated by the Bible as unclean ignores an obvious modern parallel. Traditional Jews today may not and need not understand the name of every species forbidden to them so long as they recognize the basic principles involved or have access to a suitable authority. Law codes need not use everyday terminology, even when dealing with everyday situations. Modern decisions as to an animal's *kashrut* need not be rendered by the housewife at the butcher's shop; and although the institutions have changed, there is no reason to assume that the lists of Leviticus 11 and Deuteronomy 14 were intended for use by the ordinary populace.

non is of interest, but not for the study of hapax legomena which are by definition words that occur only once.

A prototype for the kind of definition Zelson and Cohen accept which illustrates both the strengths and flaws of utilizing contextual frequency is the treatment of hapax legomena in Plato by Fossum who includes words attested more than once so long as their multiple appearances are limited to a space of no more than seven pages, suggesting that words which appear in only one part of Plato's writing and no where else in prior Greek literature are apt to have been coined by Plato.[26] Though his choice of seven pages is clearly arbitrary, the justification for such a procedure is the purpose for which his material is to be used--identifying Plato's contribution to Greek and the evolution of his style. The multiple appearances of one word or related forms in a single passage is a result of the author's style; such repetition is therefore of great importance. Our concern, however, is with word frequency regardless of style; to treat such words as occurring only once is to modify the definition of hapax legomena so as to contradict itself and to include cases where repetition not only exists but is intentional. Furthermore, such a category is itself not homogeneous. Some words appear in repeated images (for example, גלש in Cant 4:1 and 6:5), while others appear twice in a single verse or within adjacent verses. Moreover, there are roots attested by different derivatives in only one verse of the Bible as well as those unique words which appear many times, but in only one context or passage.[27]

DISLEGOMENA

within one verse		within adjacent verses		common root within one verse	
Ezra 1:9	אגרטל	Exod 9:9-10	אבעבעות	Nah 2:11	בוק
Isa 59:10	גשש	Ps 68:16-17	גבנן	Gen 30:20	זבד
Amos 5:16	הו	Job 40:21-25	צאלים	Num 11:8	דוך
1 Chr 26:18	פרבר			Isa 14:23	טאטא
				Isa 9:4	סאן

---

[26] Andrew Fossum, "Hapax Legomena in Plato," *American Journal of Philology* 53 (1931) 207.

[27] Lists in this section are not intended to be comprehensive, but to provide examples of the phenomena described. The roots טוה (Exod 35:25-26) and גבח (Lev 13:41-55) are borderline cases between the two major categories here listed.

MULTIPLE USE IN ONLY ONE PASSAGE

Lev 21:20, 22:22	ילפת	Hos 13:10-14	אהי
Dan 1:11, 16	מלצר	Esth 8:10, 14	אחשתרנים
Lev 16:8, 26	עזאזל	Ezek 40:16-36	אילמה
Job 30:3, 17	ערק	Genesis 44	אמתחת
Jonah 4:6-10	קיקיון	Amos 7:7-8	אנך
Isa 28:25, 27	קצח	Jer 38:11-12	בלו(א)י
Ezek 37:6, 8	קרם	Lev 2:14, 16	גרש

While appropriate for Fossum whose interest lay in the area of Plato's style, the inclusion of such words when dealing with a document as heterogeneous as the Bible not only ignores the frequency-defined nature of the category, but also obscures stylistic differences within the Bible by treating several distinct phenomena as if they were one.

The existence of parallel passages in the Bible raises a somewhat more subtle problem. The argument for including words which appear twice, but in identical passages, is that the second occurrence is wholly dependent on the first from which it was copied and ought not therefore to be counted. The argument against doing so proceeds from a statistical rather than philological posture. Since this category is circumstantial to begin with, defined by its constituents' frequency of appearance rather than reflecting any inherent unity among them,[28] the reason for repetition is irrelevant. To decide which bases of repetition will be accepted or ignored is to assume that some are more or less valid than others and thereby beg the question as to the factors responsible for word frequency. It is this latter position which is adopted here, albeit with some regret and an exposition of those words thereby omitted.[29] The primary reason for this decision is the intention to provide a statistical evaluation of the data compiled. To which book should a word such as שנהב in 1 Kgs 10:22, which is quoted by 2 Chr 9:21, be credited when assessing the distribution and concentration of these words, or should it be ascribed to both? And how then are we to count the apparent removal of a rare word such as ועָר (Isa 15:5) in a parallel passage (Jer 48:5)? The problem of defining "parallel passages" as well as the other categories described above complicates rather than alleviates the difficulty. Whatever their importance, such words are not hapax legomena, and including them may bias our data and obscure the uniqueness of true hapax legomena.

---

[28] Whether such an intrinsic unity can be discerned will be explored empirically (for example, p. 45 below).

[29] These words will be considered wherever they may constitute a possible source of bias (for example, p. 41 below).

A Definition of Hapax Legomenon

DISLEGOMENA IN PARALLEL PASSAGES

Job 13:27, 33:11	סד	Lev 11:6, Deut 14:7	ארנבת
Lev 11:13, Deut 14:12	עזניה	2 Sam 6:19, 1 Chr 16:3	אשפר
1 Kgs 10:22, 2 Chr 9:21	קוף	Isa 18:2, 7	בזא
2 Sam 22:37, Ps 18:3	קרסל	Cant 4:1, 6:5	גלש
1 Kgs 10:22, 2 Chr 9:21	שנהב	Lev 11:19, Deut 14:18	דוכיפת
Num 24:3, 15	שתם	Exod 28:19, 39:21	זחח
Exod 28:32, 39:23	תחרא	Exod 27:5, 38:4	כרכב
Exod 28:19, 39:12	שבו	Prov 18:8, 26:22	להם
1 Kgs 10:22, 2 Chr 9:21	תוכי	Exod 28:19, 38:12	לשם

Having evaluated the various factors affecting a definition of hapax legomena, we have arrived at criteria which, however arbitrary, meet the requirement of defining their category "so precisely that different analysts could apply them to the same body of content and secure the same results."[30] An absolute hapax legomenon will be any word other than a proper noun which is the only exemplification of its root within the Hebrew sections of the received text as represented in *BHK*. The possibilities of corruption and homographs will be ignored, while frequency will be judged on a strict basis of apparent occurrence, with problems to be collected and categorized for later evaluation. Application of these criteria yields 289 hapax legomena.[31]

While the decisions which produced the definition and thus the resulting list may well be arbitrary, as any available choice would be,[32] they have been governed by an attempt to reflect the nature of the phenomenon under study and will be reconsidered in the course of analysis to determine any bias which may result. Thus, for example, whether the exclusion of proper nouns and dislegomena attested only in parallel passages has artificially lowered the relative standing of a book like Chronicles which abounds in both will be examined again when the concentration of hapax legomena in particular parts of the Bible is assessed.

---

[30] J. Arthur Baird, "Content-Analysis and the Computer," *JBL* 95 (1976) 256.

[31] See Appendix I.

[32] Muller notes ("Le MOT," 172), "On admettre qu'il n'y a pas de norme parfaite, parce que le caractere complexe et mouvant du langage n'obéit jamais parfaitement à la quantification"; see Gustav Herdan, *Quantitative Linguistics*, 76.

3

The Distribution of Hapax Legomena in Light of Statistical Stylistics

A question which necessarily pervades this study is why there are hapax legomena at all. One possible explanation for the existence of unique forms is that errors have evolved in the course of transmission creating ghost words, terms which, as a result of lexicographers' failure to recognize textual corruption, exist only in the dictionary.[1] This hypothesis can be tested by comparing the proportion of hapax legomena in the Bible to that in other bodies of linguistic material. If it is relatively high, textual error may be suspected as one cause.

The question of word frequency has been considered in some detail for various kinds of linguistic material. Statisticians have analyzed the distribution of word frequency within a given text or literature,[2] and it is clear beyond doubt that when words in a text are arranged according to the frequency with which they occur, the hapax legomena are always the largest group, followed by dislegomena and so on.[3] Several factors affect

---

[1]The term "ghost word" seems to have originated with W. W. Skeat, "Report upon 'Ghost-Words,' or Words Which Have No Real Existence," *Transactions of the Philological Society* (1885-7) 350-74.

[2]The study of the problem is reviewed by Richard W. Bailey, "Statistics and Style: A Historical Survey," in *Statistics and Style* (ed. R. W. Bailey and L. Dolezel; New York: American Elsevier, 1969) 217-36.

[3]It is important to recognize that the term "hapax legomenon" as used in such studies refers to non-absolute hapax legomena (see p. 12 above). G. Udny Yule (*The Statistics of Literary Style* [Cambridge: Cambridge University Press, 1944] 45-47) points out that such tables are not actually complete, since they omit at least theoretically the largest category of all, those words which do not occur even once in the given text;

the specific proportion of a work's vocabulary which occurs only once. The first is the nature of the language in which it is written: a highly inflected language will necessarily have a greater variety of forms than one which is less inflected and has, consequently, fewer occurrences per form.[4] A second factor is style: some authors may for a variety of reasons use a more abstruse vocabulary and thus a greater proportion of rare words than others.[5] A final factor influencing the exact proportion of hapax legomena is the length of a work. A small text provides little opportunity for words to repeat themselves and contains therefore a large proportion of hapax legomena; as the length increases, there is a growing probability that these words may recur even as new hapax legomena are introduced.[6] Although the percentage is, for these reasons, not subject to absolute precision, the following table reveals that hapax legomena consistently comprise one-third to one-half of the vocabulary in any given

---

thus he speaks of such frequency-distribution tables as "decapitated." Studies in word frequency have generally been for one of two purposes, either to identify the number of words in a foreign language text which a student must master in order to read that text easily or to ascertain whether the distribution of words of differing frequencies within a text is a characteristic of individual style. Assuming this latter possibility, statisticians have tried to devise a mathematical formula which can yield a numerical index of any author's style. Yule's study, the pioneering work in this field, arose out of an effort to determine mathematically whether Thomas à Kempis was the author of the *De Imitatione Christi*.

[4]This is how G. K. Zipf explains the high proportion in Chinese (*Selected Studies of the Principle of Relative Frequency in Language* [Cambridge: Harvard University Press, 1932] 23).

[5]This phenomenon is responsible for the fact that, as Yule notes (*The Statistics of Literary Style*, 9-10, 26) only 24.3 percent of the nouns in the Basic English version of John's Gospel occur once whereas 42.8 percent do in the Revised Version; it is the intention of Basic English to restrict its usage to a vocabulary of under one thousand words, thereby requiring greater repetition. It is remarkable that the proportion of hapax legomena nouns in this sample is still so high.

[6]Since the vocabulary of any language is theoretically finite (with the exception of nonce words), one would expect the resources of the language eventually to be depleted so that the number of hapax legomena repeated will be larger than the number added. Yule suggests (*The Statistics of Literary Style*, 55, note 4) that there should be a point at which dislegomena outnumber hapax legomena; in point of fact, this hypothesis has not been confirmed.

body of linguistic material--oral or written, long or short, homogeneous or diverse.[7]

Since the sources on which these conclusions are based do not differentiate between absolute and non-absolute hapax legomena, a proper comparison for the Bible will have to be with the combined lists of Appendices I and II, containing 289 absolute, 1,179 non-absolute, and 33 ambiguous hapax legomena for a total of 1,501. The Bible contains a vocabulary or between five and eight thousand words.[8] In such a context, 1,501 hapax legomena, representing less than one-third of the total, constitutes the lowest proportion of all the samples noted. Such evidence alone should suffice to counter the argument that the correct transmission of a particular word can be doubted solely because it occurs only once in the Bible. The Bible contains fewer such words than one would expect according to the distribution found in other corpora; indeed, the

---

[7] Gustav Herdan, *Quantitative Linguistics*, 83 and Yule, *The Statistics of Literary Style*, 273. The table is based on material in Zipf, *Selected Studies*; Paul E. Bennett, "The Statistical Measurement of a Stylistic Trait in *Julius Caesar* and *As You Like It*," in *Statistics and Style*, 32-45; Herdan, *Quantitative Linguistics*, 87; and Charles Muller, "Lexical Distribution Reconsidered: The Waring-Herdan Formula," in *Statistics and Style*, 44-50. The examples have been arranged according to the proportion of hapax legomena in each. The diversity of material is intentional--so as to show that the proportion of hapax legomena is not dependent on the language, date, or style of the corpus. According to Zipf (p. 22), the sample of Chinese material is colloquial. "Aucassin et Nicolette" is characterized by Muller (p. 48) as a *chantefable*. His figure of "345" as the number of hapax legomena in *L'illusion Comique* (p. 45) must be regarded as a misprint, since it would not otherwise support his figures or the use he makes of it.

[8] Chaim Rabin, "מלים בודדות," EM 4, 1069. *Theologisches Handwörterbuch zum Alten Testament* (ed. Ernst Jenni and Claus Westermann; Munich: Chr. Kaiser Verlag; Zurich: Theologische Verlag, 1976) counts a total vocabulary of 8,250 words of which 2,500 are proper nouns (2. 542). Although the argument here is only general, precise comparison (which would be inappropriate for the radically dissimilar materials compared) requires that hapax legomena be presented as a percentage of occurrences (total number of words appearing) rather than vocabulary (Yule, *The Statistics of Literary Style*, 97-103). Jenni and Westermann's data result in hapax legomena as 18.2 percent of the vocabulary and 0.5 percent of all occurrences in the Bible.

SAMPLE PROPORTIONS OF HAPAX LEGOMENA

	Sample Size		Hapax Legomena		
	Occurrences (words used)	Vocabulary	Numb.	Percent of	
				Vocab.	Occur.
Plautus	33,871	8,437	5,439	64.3	16.0
Peking Chinese	13,248	3,332	2,046	61.4	15.4
As You Like It	3,609	1,231	729	59.2	20.2
"A Polybe" (Seneca)	5,688	1,430	822	57.5	14.5
"A Helvia" (Seneca)	6,755	1,856	1,046	56.4	15.4
Julius Caesar	2,919	965	534	55.3	18.3
Captain's Daughter (Pushkin)	28,591	4,783	2,384	49.8	8.3
Newspaper English	43,990	6,001	2,976	49.6	6.8
Gospel of Mark (Greek)	11,229	1,345	634	47.1	5.6
"Aucassin et Nicolette" (Old French)	9,870	1,073	483	45.0	4.9
L'illusion Comique (Pierre Corneille)	16,586	1,906	845	44.3	5.1
Paul's Epistles (Greek)	32,303	2,648	1,140	43.1	3.5
English telephone conversations	80,000	2,240	819	36.6	1.0
Basic French conversations	312,135	7,995	2,700	33.8	0.9

proportion is so low that the question must be reversed: Why are there so few hapax legomena in the Bible when, in light of the proportion in other material, one would have expected closer to forty or fifty percent?[9]

Several facets of the methodology here utilized as well as the nature of Hebrew may account for this deviation. First, it will be recalled that the criteria used were intentionally very strict so as to remove as many cases of non-hapax legomena as possible even at the risk of excluding some legitimate words. A second factor was the exclusion of homographs. Since there is every reason to presume that Hebrew, like other languages, tolerates the existence of such words, their omission has undoubtedly lowered the proportion still further. A final consideration can be traced to the character of Hebrew as a rather heavily inflected language which can, therefore, generate numerous related words. Although this factor has been minimized by the inclusion of non-absolute hapax legomena, it is not always clear whether variant forms of similar words are to be counted together or separately;[10] furthermore, one sizable component of the vocabulary has definitely been left out. Hebrew verbs are regularly ascribed to roots; the various conjugations of one root —not to mention participles, infinitives, and the like—are then treated as categories of the same word. Where other languages might use different verbs, Hebrew can therefore generate separate meanings out of one "word" by conjugating it differently.[11] A truly equivalent count of hapax legomena would have to treat each conjugation as a separate word, multiplying the number of non-absolute hapax legomena (as well as words) ascribed to Hebrew.[12]

If the total number of hapax legomena encountered in the Hebrew

---

[9]According to Richard E. Whitaker's *A Concordance of the Ugaritic Literature* (Cambridge: Harvard Univesity Press, 1972), 44.6 percent of the 919 words and names beginning with the first five letters of the Ugaritic alphabet are non-absolute hapax legomena although a more thorough analysis would be necessary before such data could be validly compared with the other examples here provided.

[10]Thus Rabin ("מלים בודדות," 1068) points to the uncertainty as to whether plurals in ־ים and ־ות should be counted as based on the same or different words.

[11]For example, למד can mean "learn" (qal) or "teach" (piᶜel).

[12]Rabin ("מלים בודדות," 1069) finds 2440 hapax legomena in KB, which is closer to what one would expect. Word counts for other languages do not specify their criteria and may include proper nouns.

Bible is not surprising in light of the comparative data such that their authenticity cannot be suspect on these grounds alone, we have yet to explain the reasons for their isolation.

Some hold that hapax legomena result only from the chance frequency of words in a limited text. Therefore, they suggest, a word's being unique is merely accidental; words which appear only once may in fact have been common in the language as a whole.[13] Herdan has shown, however, that the majority of hapax legomena in a small sample are also rare in the whole from which it is taken;[14] thus he claims that most hapax legomena are inherently rare, that is, that part of their nature within a particular language is to be uncommon.

The relatively small size of the Bible and the fact that it is uniquely well studied permits further exploration into this question. We can, of course, no longer ask why there are words which appear only once. This is inherent in the way language is used and reflects the kind of random process which word selection and distribution tend to be.[15] But we can ask *which* words are rare and whether their single appearance is due to chance or rather any identifiable characteristics of hapax legomena.

If the choice of hapax legomena is purely random, resulting solely from the nature of word-frequency distribution, then they should not be found concentrated in any identifiable part(s) of the Bible. To assess distribution, one cannot simply point out which books have more than others; the three hapax legomena in a short book such as Joel are surely more telling than the four in a book as long as Exodus.[16] Nor will it suffice to compute the ratios of hapax legomena to words actually used. Such a method can neither distinguish among books which lack hapax legomena altogether, all of which have the same proportion, namely zero,

---

[13]Joshua Whatmough (*Poetic, Scientific and Other Forms of Discourse* [Berkeley: University of California, 1956] 43) cites the morphological normality and brevity of many Greek hapax legomena in support of this position.

[14]Gustav Herdan, "The Hapax legomena: a real or apparent phenomenon?" *Language and Speech* 2 (1959) 26-36.

[15]Yule (*The Statistics of Literary Style*, 42) considers it analogous to cases of personal accidents.

[16]This discussion does not pertain to the number of hapax legomena in each book treated as an isolated unit (How many words appear only once in Joel?), but to the distribution of the Bible's hapax legomena (How many words which appear only once in the Bible are found in Joel?).

The Distribution of Hapax Legomena 37

regardless of length, nor can it reveal whether the distribution as a whole is random.

The appropriate method for measuring the probability that an existing distribution can be considered random is the chi-square test. It is based on a comparison of the actual number of a particular phenomenon per unit of text with that which would result from a perfectly even distribution; this difference is squared and divided by the number one would have expected in an even distribution.[17] The resulting figure—here called "D" for "deviation from expected"—is an index of the difference in the rate of occurrence from what would have been expected were it completely even throughout the Bible that takes relative size into account without being biased by it. Thus a twenty-four chapter work such as Joshua appears as more "deviant" than the one chapter Obadiah although neither contains any hapax legomena, while the "D" for these books can be fairly compared with that of other books as well. The sum of "D" for all books of the Bible yields chi-square[18] which can be measured against that found in standard tables for random distribution. In the case here treated entailing thirty-five books of the Bible, these tables show that for such a distribution to have better than a 0.3 percent probability of being random, its chi-square must total less than 58.91.[19] Our data yield a chi-square of 419.05 for the distribution of absolute and 1187.93 for that of all hapax legomena in the Bible.[20] Such a distribution could not possibly be random, although it remains to explore the factors responsible for this.

---

[17] These calculations are based on the word count in the statistical appendix of Ernst Jenni and Claus Westermann's *Theologisches Handworterbuch zum Alten Testament*, 2. 539-40.

[18] $\chi^2 = \sum \frac{(\text{expected occurrences - actual occurrences})^2}{\text{expected occurrences}}$

[19] Catherine M. Thompson, "Table of Percentage Points of the χ^2 Distribution," *Biometrika* 32 (1941-42) 187-91; the proper method of interpolation is described on page 190. Probabilities less than 5 percent are considered unlikely although Herdan notes (*Language as Choice and Chance* [Groningen, Holland: P. Noordhoff, 1956] 95) that 0.3 percent may be a better figure for linguistic phenomena. Because of their original unity, pairs of books such as 1 and 2 Samuel, 1 and 2 Kings, Ezra and Nehemiah, and 1 and 2 Chronicles are treated as one book each; see p. 40 below.

[20] For complete data, see below Appendix III; all figures have been rounded off.

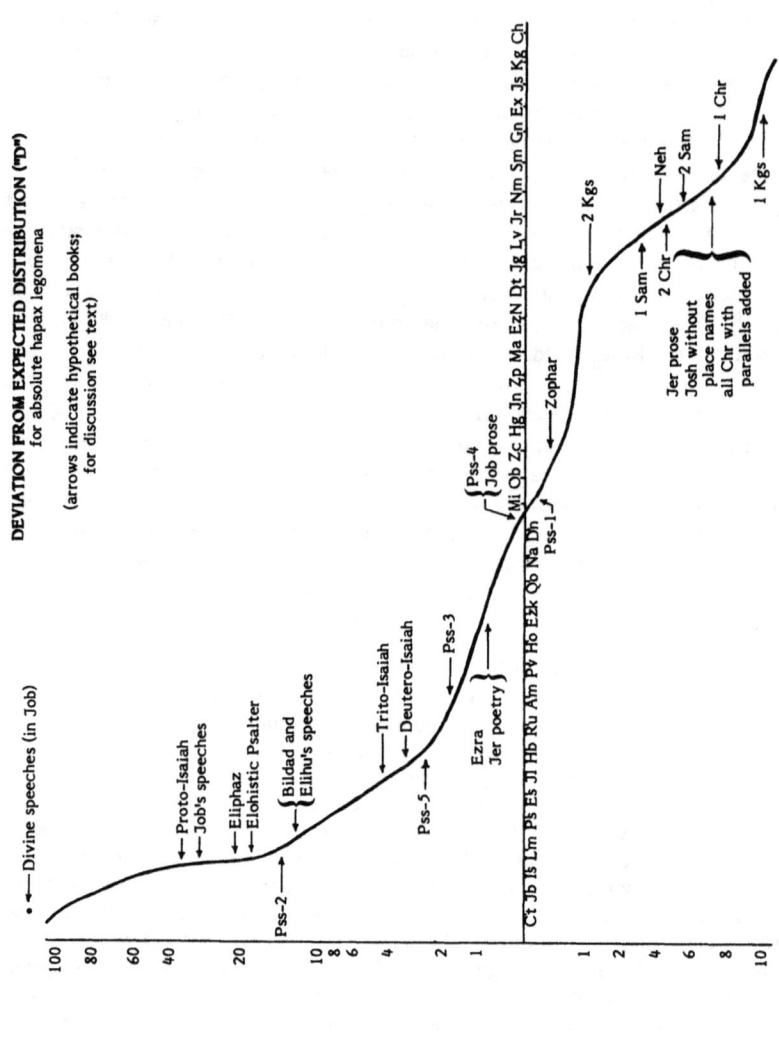

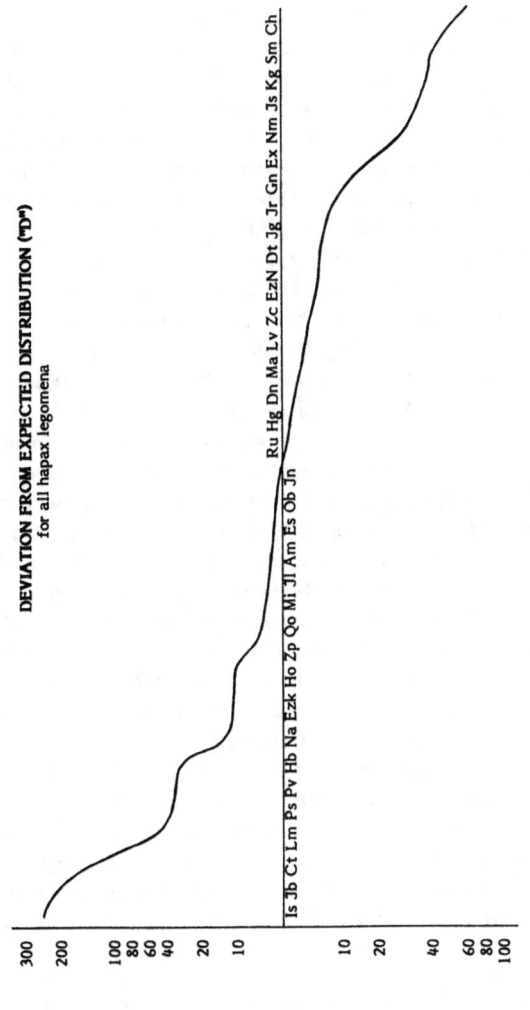

The index of deviation (D) for each book is presented in the graphs on the following pages according to relative magnitude, with those caused by a surplus of hapax legomena indicated as positive while those resulting from a deficit are shown as negative.[21] So arranged, the two graphs present a strikingly similar sequence of books, one which is based on an easily recognized pattern: books with a large surplus of hapax legomena are poetic, those with a deficit are narrative prose. While the middle range on the chart cannot be so neatly divided—an area of overlap is to be expected—the two extremes make the point most clearly.

This observation can be further explored. Several books are artificially divided in our editions of the Bible; their two halves can be tested separately to see how the measure here applied responds. Since all are narrative prose, the sample of hapax legomena is small; yet in all cases each of the components into which the book has been artificially broken appears generally close to the location of the "original" book on the graph.[22] By contrast, when the prose and poetic sections of Jeremiah are separated (a less artificial distinction according to our hypothesis) and the measure of deviation (D) calculated for each, the prose is much closer to the original book, reflecting more of a deficit while the poetic portions contain more of a surplus of hapax legomena than Jeremiah as a whole. It becomes clear that even though Jeremiah's poetry is no more than average in its use of such words, the reason the book as a whole lies among the narrative books on the graph is that it contains a significant amount of prose.[23] The distinction between Jeremiah's prose and poetry seems, therefore, to reflect a real stylistic difference in contrast to the intentionally artificial distinctions previously tested.

Other possible differences are not readily distinguished. The graph does not separate more specific genres or dates of authorship. While the texts here examined were not so analyzed because of the lack of scholarly consensus on such matters, we can observe that with respect to a given genre there is great variation: within wisdom literature, for example, Job ranks high, while Proverbs and Ecclesiastes are in the middle range—all of

---

[21] This distinction is obscured when the Deviation is squared during the test. The graphs use a modified logarithmic scale in order to spread out differences near the center range and flatten both ends; differences in the middle have thus been exaggerated and those at the ends minimized.

[22] The apparent divergence between Ezra and Nehemiah and 1 and 2 Kings is exaggerated by the manner in which the scale has been constructed (see note 21 above).

[23] 61 percent by our measure.

which fit where they are by virtue of their use of prose or poetry; among the prophets, Isaiah is high while Jeremiah, even in its poetic sections, is moderate, thereby reflecting apparent stylistic differences between the two. As for dates of authorship, one can see that Samuel and Kings on the one hand are not readily distinguishable from Ezra, Nehemiah, and Chronicles on the other through this technique.[24] Only the prose-poetry distinction is consistently reflected in the results presented here.

There is, of course, the possibility that these numbers have been affected by the definition of hapax legomenon here employed, notably the exclusions of parallel passages and proper nouns. To check the former, those words in Chronicles which were excluded because they appear in parallel passages were reintroduced into the list and the measure of deviation recalculated with them.[25] As can be seen on the graph, what change there is tends merely to moderate the relative extremeness of the measure. A second exclusion, that of proper nouns, could be the decisive factor for a book such as Joshua, half of which contains little else. Chapters twelve through twenty-one which are mostly proper nouns were therefore excluded and "D" recalculated; again the effect was merely to alleviate the extremeness of Joshua's position.

Two observations emerge from this analysis. The first is that the nature of the criteria previously stated and the prose-poetry distinction do have a real impact on the proportion of hapax legomena in a text; on the other hand, this influence is not sufficient to account for all the distribution figures. There must be additional factors.

A logical possibility is the style of a particular author; this would explain, for example, why even the poetic portions of Jeremiah rank so much lower than Isaiah.[26] To investigate this, a modified form of the previous test was performed. Instead of separating parts of books known to be of common origin, the books of Isaiah and Psalms, which are widely believed to be composite, were split into what scholars regard as distinct sections.[27] The measure of deviation was then calculated for each of

---

[24]For a different view, see S. Morag, רובדי קדמות, עיונים" לשוניים במשלי בלעם," in *Tarbiz* 51 (1981) 4-7.

[25]See p. 28 above; data on hypothetical books are also in Appendix III.

[26]This accords with Yule's expectation (*The Statistics of Literary Style*, see above note 3) that the proportionate usage of words of differing frequencies by a given author is characteristic of his style.

[27]Isaiah was divided into chapters 1-39, 40-55, and 56-66; and the five books of Psalms as indicated in the Hebrew text. The book of Zechariah was also checked but, because of its size and middle-range position, did not yield useful information.

these hypothetical books; since virtually all of these texts are poetic, any deviation would have to be the result of stylistic peculiarity. The results were striking: the "D" of most components in these books are similar, with a relatively small surplus of hapax legomena as would befit poetic works, except that First Isaiah and the second book of Psalms contain significantly more than the rest of these works, suggesting that they almost alone may be responsible for the high rank of these books in our overall chart. In the case of Psalms this analysis can be carried still further. The second book of Psalms is, in large part, co-extensive with the Elohistic Psalter (Psalms 43-83). Analysis shows that the "D" for this unit is slightly higher than that of even the second book of Psalms. The proportion of hapax legomena in a work does seem to be an index of its style, reflecting most likely the general use of a rarified vocabulary. An additional test dramatically illustrated this point.

A master writer will provide each of his characters with a different style. So the book of Job was divided according to speaker and the measure of deviation calculated for each. Here the position previously proposed was remarkably confirmed. Job, it will be recalled, includes the second highest proportion of hapax legomena among all biblical books. Yet most components would fit into the middle and upper-middle range on our graph with two exceptions—Job's speeches which would, if treated separately, be the fourth highest book in the Bible and God's which would rank higher than any book, including Job itself.[28] It is these components then which are largely responsible for the high rank of the entire book! Use of hapax legomena, while not alone sufficient to support an argument relative to authorship, is nonetheless an important indicator of style.

A second approach casts new light on this problem while corroborating the conclusions here proposed. Although less mathematically precise than the procedure heretofore used, examining those chapters and verses which contain several of these words will permit us to determine those sections within biblical books that contain a high proportion of hapax legomena.[29] That some sections have more than others is not

---

[28] Prof. Cyrus Gordon has drawn my attention to the fact that in other cultures, too, deities were believed to use a vocabulary different from that of ordinary mortals; see J. Friedrich, "Göttersprache und Menschensprache im hethitischen Schrifttum," *Sprachgeschichte und Wortbedeutung, Festschrift Albert Debrunner* (Bern: Francke, 1954) 135-39.

[29] For the purposes of this section, forms marked questionable have been included. The lowered precision results from the fact that chapters and verses are not all of equal length.

surprising; the nature of random distribution could lead to such a possibility. What is of interest is determining which chapters have more than others and why; if the distribution is purely random, interpreting these data should be virtually impossible. Such is not the case.

It would be desirable also to treat those chapters and verses lacking in hapax legomena; this is the "head" of our decapitated data, to use Yule's terminology.[30] The sheer quantity of these passages makes such a proposal impractical. We can, however, cite those books which have no hapax legomena and attempt to explain why. In the case of Obadiah, Jonah, Zephaniah, Haggai, and Malachi this is not difficult: each is exceedingly short, with an expected number of occurrences that is less than one. Furthermore, all contain non-absolute hapax legomena and, according to our measure of deviation, rank in roughly the same relative position for that category as for absolute hapax legomena. The absence of hapax legomena in these books is the result of their brevity.[31] As for Joshua, it is in a similar position on both graphs, the extremity of which has already been shown to result from the abundance of geographical names in the book's latter half.

There are several verses which contain more than one hapax legomenon apiece. In four of these, the unique forms are found within a list of some sort;[32] such rare forms occur in a context which treats a particular topic more in depth than would normally be the case. Ezra 4:7 also contains two hapax legomena, both of which are to be counted as Aramaisms. The fact that this verse lies adjacent to one of the Bible's Aramaic sections suggests several explanations.[33] Whichever one adopts, the phenomenon is a result of the passage's stylistic uniqueness. Such may also account for the two entries from Jer 5:8, though their occurrence in

---

[30] Above p. 31, note 3.

[31] The similarity of results using these two categories confirms the validity and value of having applied the chi-square test.

[32] Lev 11:30, Num 11:5, Cant 1:17, Esth 1:6; significantly both verses containing three hapax legomena (Num 11:5 and Esth 1:6) are found under this heading.

[33] Later Hebrew was influenced by Aramaic or this author's writing may have been colored by the language of the following verses; see Max Wagner, *Die Lexakalischen und Grammatikalischen Aramaismen im Alttestamentlichen Hebräisch* (BZAW 96; Berlin: Alfred Töpelmann, 1966) 65 and 81.

sequence might be counted as a rudimentary list. This leaves the concentration in only three verses unexplained.[34] Perhaps it is due to a less readily charcterized uniqueness in their style or more likely to random distribution.

In isolating those chapters which contain more than one hapax legomenon, cases due to the concentration in a particular verse will be excluded since they have already been treated. Overall the data corroborate previous conclusions. The heaviest concentrations fall in poetic books, with numerous occurrences from Job, Isaiah, and less obviously Song of Songs and Lamentations whose smaller size obscures this fact. Internal style also plays a part; the only chapter in the Bible with five hapax legomena, Job 41, is part of God's speech which also includes the high ranking chapters 38 and 40 with three and two respectively, while Job's speeches are also well represented.[35] Most of the Isaiah chapters with more than one are from First Isaiah.[36] Stylistic uniqueness is obvious in the case of Deuteronomy 32, the only chapter with four hapax legomena, while Psalms 68 and 119 have three apiece; the latter case is to be attributed to length.[37]

As noted, these results coincide with those previously suggested: hapax legomena occur most often in specialized contexts such as lists; their frequency is a function of style—some writers tend towards a more rarified vocabulary while some genres lend themselves to this kind of writing. The obvious case of the latter is that of poetry, two reasons for which can be suggested. Poetry requires a much broader vocabulary for its imagery and description than does prose writing; as such, it is bound to contain a higher proportion of rare forms.[38] Semitic poetry, with its emphasis on parallelism, carries this need still further: the demands of such a medium force the poet to reach deeper into his vocabulary to find a synonym than would otherwise be the case.

Since the discovery that biblical Hebrew shares many parallel pairs

---

[34] Prov 29:21, 30:31; 2 Chr 2:15.

[35] Job 6, 16, 17, 19, 26, 30; see p. 42 above.

[36] Isaiah 3, 5, 27, and 33 have three apiece as does chapter 44, while Isaiah 9, 10, 11, 19, and 28 as well as chapters 43 and 64 have two; see pp. 41-42 above.

[37] Of those chapters containing two or more hapax legomena only Judges 5 and 16, 2 Kings 17 and 23, Ezekiel 2, 7, 23, and 47, Hosea 10 and 13, Habakkuk 2, Psalm 140, Canticles 4 and 7, Ruth 2, and Lamentations 4, which contain two apiece, have not been explicitly mentioned.

[38] But not necessarily, see p. 38 above.

with Ugaritic poetry, this last point has been greatly amplified through the suggestion that in such fixed pairs the second word should be less common.[39] Our list of the rarest words in the Bible permits an interesting test of this hypothesis based on the way in which they appear in poetic passages. This can be hard to quantify. For the most part words must have some approximate counterpart in the other half of a poetic verse in order to be counted, so that instances of "staircase" parallelism have been disregarded when the unique word is the one that does not recur. Some verses restate the same thought several times; the unique word is here counted as "A" only if it is in the first statement, but is ascribed to "B" even if it is third or fourth. A few prose passages have been included where symmetry seemed sufficient to suggest a poetic style.[40] As a result, our conclusions can be only tentative; a definitive examination of this question is beyond the scope of this study. Still the results are quite convincing, especially since nothing in our selection, whatever its shortcomings, should bias the results in either direction. A total of 154 absolute hapax legomena lend themselves to being categorized in their existing contexts. Of these, 98 (64 percent) are B words, supporting the hypothesis previously described.

Having subjected the data to various kinds of statistical analysis without recourse to the specific meanings or problems of any word, we have been able to reach several conclusions. First, rareness alone is not surprising and therefore an inadequate basis for suggesting emendation. There is no evidence that the distribution of word frequency in the Bible is significantly different from that in other languages and corpora; in fact, the only uniqueness here noted was the relative paucity of rare words, the explanation for which was felt to lie in our own methodology and the nature of Hebrew lexicography which treats conjugations of the same root as one word. Secondly, those words which do occur only once seem to do so because they are less mundane, reflecting a more abstruse style, or as a result of their being specialized vis a vis the text in which they are found; zoological and architectural terms are rare in the Bible, but liturgical and cultic words are not, though in another corpus they might be. Finally, evidence has been collected to show that the use of rare words does constitute a stylistic criterion. Poetry uses more hapax

---

[39] For a survey of this issue, see Mitchell Dahood and Tadeusz Penar, "Ugaritic-Hebrew Parallel Pairs," in *Ras Shamra Parallels* (ed. Loren R. Fisher; AnOr 49; Rome: Pontifical Biblical Institute, 1972) 71ff.

[40] For example, Num 32:24.

legomena than prose, and some poets do so to a greater degree than others. This does not, however, seem a refined enough criterion to apply in order to differentiate various strata with any degree of certainty.[41] Concentration of rare forms in general and hapax legomena in particular is therefore a characteristic of style, but not a useful test of authorship.

---

[41] A better approach is to assess style according to the most common features of a language, such as particle frequency or sentence length, the measures of which, since based on larger and more homogeneous samples, are far better indicators of stylistic peculiarity than is the use of rare forms. See Frederick Mosteller and David L. Wallace ("Inference in an Authorship Problem," *Journal of the American Statistical Association* 58 [1963] 275-309) who use the frequency of selected prepositions and the like to analyze disputed authorship of various of the *Federalist Papers*; the various methods proposed for such distinctions are discussed in the survey by R. Bailey (see note 2 above).

4

The Treatment of Hapax Legomena in the Versions

The ancient translations are too valuable a resource to be ignored in treating the history of any facet of biblical interpretation, for they contain the first post-biblical interpretation of the material with which we are concerned. From their treatment of hapax legomena one ought to be able to determine the problems, if any, that these words presented to the translators of the period. Furthermore, we can begin to assess the uniformity of tradition, or lack of same, for these words in antiquity, possibly even tracing the interdependencies among the different versions. Yet the use of this material presents serious, probably insuperable difficulties, for although a translation is necessarily comprehensive, dealing with every passage in some way or another, the lack of explanation often renders the significance of any individual rendering unclear.[1] Several explanations may be proferred for an unexpected treatment: Many assume that the translators had before them a Hebrew text different from our own, leading to proposals of emendations in our own reading; but it is equally conceivable that the ancient text was the same as ours, only interpreted differently whether through the ascription of an unusual meaning to the attested word or by some form of philological modification.[2] To understand how hapax legomena were dealt with in this period,

---

[1]Barr, pp. 238-72. Even straightforward translations may not reflect our own text, although in the absence of other information they must be assumed to do so. The limitations inherent in using this material are responsible for those translations not included, specifically renderings which appear to rely on context or immediate recognition of the root (for example, בתק, גרד).

[2]Similar problems exist for attempts to interpret the significance of biblical parallels attesting early variants for hapax legomena. (For variants implicit in the kĕtîb and qĕrê, see chapter VII s.v. ידן, יחר, ימש, נדא, and שאס.) The use of ויחגרו in 2 Sam 22:46 where Ps 18:46 has

47

we will restrict ourselves here to examples of these latter possibilities.[3]

INTERPRETATION OF HAPAX LEGOMENA

The problems of drawing conclusions from the versions can best be understood with a few examples. The Septuagint's rendering נדהם as ὕπνων (sleep) is often taken as evidence for the contention that the Hebrew text used by the Greek translators read נרדם at this point.[4] There is, however, absolutely no confirmation for this hypothesis. No Hebrew manuscript reads נרדם, nor does any other version so render the passage. Indeed, the Greek word used here does not translate any of the other thirteen biblical occurrences of the Hebrew root רדם. Those responsible for this translation may have taken "sleep" to be a meaning of the root דהם.[5] Even more ambiguous is the case of נוט. The Greek translation σαλευθήτω is used several times for מוט as are the corresponding translations in the Targum and Vulgate.[6] But it can also render the Hebrew נטה (see LXX Ps 73:2), which might have been related to נָגוּט through a biliteral theory of roots, as well as the root נוד (e.g. LXX 2 Kgs

---

ויחרגו, if not corrupt, may be the result of scribal "correction"; and a similar motivation has been proposed for the Chronicler's use of מכרבל where 2 Sam 6:14 has מכרכר (p. 130 below; note that the root כרכר in v. 16 is replaced by רקד in 1 Chr 15:29, supporting the likelihood that difficult forms were replaced with better known words). Isa 15:5 is parallel to Jer 48:5 which reads שמעו instead of the former's difficult יעערו. The only other hapax legomenon verb in a passage with a biblical parallel is צנס which is omitted altogether in Gen 41:6, leading some commentators to view this word, which has Aramaic cognates, as a late gloss (p. 154 below). The more numerous cases of rare forms supported by parallel passages have been treated as dislegomena (see pp. 28-29 above).

[3]Evidence for the existence of variant readings will be used later to assess the words themselves; for now, our interest is not to establish the best reading, but to study how the ancients handled rare words in their text.

[4]See p. 108 below; biblical citations for hapax legomena verbs treated in these chapters can be found in Appendix IV. All passages, including those in ancient translations, are cited according to the standard numbering of the Hebrew text.

[5]The same interpretation is provided in IPM, s.v. דהם and MSh, p. 61, neither of which emends the attested reading.

[6]The Targum also uses זעזע at Ps 38:17, 46:7, and 66:9; *moveatur* is used by the Vg. to render מוט at Isa 54:10, Ps 10:6, etc.

Hapax Legomena in the Versions   49

21:8, Ps 36:11), which could be connected with נוט through the interchange of dentals, a view held by the rabbis and medieval grammarians.[7]

Some assistance in this regard can be garnered from the tendency of the Aramaic versions to render the Hebrew original with apparent cognates.[8] The possibility that these renditions are Hebraisms, copied into the translation, is minimized by the fact that most of the words so treated occur also in Aramaic. In the case of זער, for which this is not the case, both the Peshitta and Targum use what would be an appropriate Aramaic equivalent—דְעֵר;[9] and כסס is related to the Aramaic כסא by *Pseudo-Jonathan* and one manuscript of the *Samaritan Targum*,[10] evidencing again the effort to etymologize rather than blindly copy Hebrew readings into their versions. This is illustrated also by רזם which is "corrected" to רמז and the whole array of renderings for צנם which seem simply to be sound-alikes; this tendency may also have crept into Symmachus' translation of the root מוק with καταμωκωμενοι to which the Targum's יתמקמקון should be compared.[11]

Even if a consciousness of etymology is not responsible for all such cases, the tendency to use cognates does aid in assessing the basis for a particular rendering. From such information and evidence elsewhere as to the *Textwort* which corresponds to a specific rendering, one can see that several hapax legomena were equated with other biblical forms.

אדב - Jonathan's נפח is also used by *Onqelos* for דוב (Lev 26:16) and דאב (Deut 27:65); the Peshitta uses the root דוב.

---

[7]See pp. 67-68 and 82 below.

[8]The Peshitta so treats 26 of the 140 words checked (אלץ, אדב, כסס, כחל, יהד, יאה, טעה, טמה, טנף, טוש, זער, דוץ, דוב, גרד, בטל, לעז, נבח, סאסא, סלק, עשק, פנק, פשח, צפד, רשם, שתר, תרגם (see also אנס, בטל, פרשז, רהה, and רזם); *Tgs. Onq., Neb.*, and *Ket.* 21 words (בטל, אנס, סמן, סלק, סאסא, נבח, מוק, יסך, טפש, טעה, טנף, טוש, זער, דוץ, עשק, פנק, צנם, רטה, קאם, שתם; see also רזם, פרשז), while less extensive targumim do so proportionately (*Tg. Ps.-J.* עשק, צנם, שיה; *Tg. Neof.* דוב, עשק; *Sam. Tg.* דוב, יסך, כסס, עשק, שיה; *Frg. Tg.* עשק, שיה; and *Pal. Tgs.* צנם).

[9]The Peshitta's rendering of צפד with ܡܦܣ may be suggested by the correspondence of Hebrew צ (representing Semitic *ḍ*) to early Aramaic ק; note Jer 10:11 ארקא. For other explanations see p. 79 below.

[10]Abraham Tal, *The Samaritan Targum and the Pentateuch, A Critical Edition* (Tel Aviv: Tel Aviv University, 1980-81) 266; for the rabbinic comparison with Aramaic see p. 64 below.

[11]The validity of this comparison is still maintained. See p. 133 below.

אדש - all versions treat similarly to דוש.¹²

בטה - the use of אמר by the Targum and Peshiṭta presumably link this form to בטא.

בשׂט - the Targum treats this as if it were a form of שׂטט preceded by the preposition ב (בְּשָׂטְכֶם instead of בּוּשָׁשְׂכָם).

דגה - all targumim refer to fish (דג) as prolific;¹³ the Peshiṭta, Vg., and LXX translate simply as "multiply."

דוב - variants in both the *Sam. Tg.* and *Tg. Neof.* use דבא; *Onqelos'* נפח is also used for דאב at Deut 28:65.

הבו - the Latin *adferre* is also used for יהב at Prov 30:15, Ps 29:1, and 96:7.

הדך - the Vg. *contere* and Sym καταθλων suggest the roots דכא/דכך (see Sym Job 19:2, Vg. Job 6:9, etc.); the Targum's דעדק may have been chosen for its similar sound, while 11QtgJob הטפי seems to assume a form based on דער.¹⁴

הלא - the Vg. *laboraverat* seems to derive this from לאה.

התת - Aq's unusual επιβουλευετε (plot) may be based on a comparison such as that made by ibn Ezra with הוות.¹⁵

חספס - *Onqelos'* מקלף is comparable to the treatment of מחשף (Gen 30:37); the Peshiṭta translates similarly. *Tg. Neof.* and the *Frg. Tg.* מפספס seem intended to sound like the Hebrew.

טחח - all versions relate this to טוח.

יזן - according to Giesebrecht the Vg. derives the attested form from זנה.¹⁶

ימש - translated by all versions as if from מוש or משש.¹⁷

---

¹²Compare *Tg. Neb.* Isa 28:27, LXX Job 39:15, and Isa 25:10, and Vg. Isa 28:28, etc. Note that the Aramaic versions use forms similar to those rendering ידושנו in the same verse.

¹³This would appear to be true for only one tradition of the *Samaritan Targum* which reads וינון, whereas the more dominant version reads ויפתון and related forms (A. Tal, *The Samaritan Targum*, 208-9). For the rabbinic interpretation, see p. 65 below.

¹⁴Michael Sokoloff, *The Targum to Job from Qumran Cave XI* (Ramat-Gan: Bar-Ilan University, 1974), xxiv.

¹⁵See p. 73 below.

¹⁶HKAT on Jer 5:8 (see Vg. Hos 2:7); *amare* is in fact rarely used for the Hebrew זנה (see Vg. Jer 3:1).

¹⁷This more likely reflects the qĕrē.

Hapax Legomena in the Versions 51

- יסך – translated by all versions as if from סוך or נסך.
- יעז – Jonathan and the Vg. treat this as a form of עזז (compare Isa 56:11).
- יעט – Jonathan also uses עטף for עטה (Ezek 24:17, 22, Mic 3:7, Jer 43:12).
- כמה – the LXX ποσαπλῶς may be based on a comparison with כַּמָּה; note also Vg. multipliciter.
- נוש – Targum Jonathan translates אנש similarly at Jer 17:9, 30:12; the Vg., at 2 Sam 12:15 and Mic 1:9.
- נלה – the Vg. (cum fatigatus) seems to assume the root לאה which is actually used by Jonathan (כד תלאי).
- נצא – Vg. floriens suggests comparison with נוצה,[18] while Jonathan's מגלא may be based on an etymology relating this form to יצא.
- עוש – Rashi explains the Targum's יתכנשון (compare the Peshiṭta's ܠܝ ܚܘܫ) as relating this form to עשת in Cant 5:15 and עשות in Ezek 27:19.
- פסג – the Targum's רמן is likely based on a comparison with פסגה (Deut 34:1).
- פרשז – all versions seem to equate this form with פרש (note the Peshiṭta and Targum's use of פרס; the LXX often uses ἐκπετάζειν and the Vg. expando for פרש).
- צות – all versions treat this form as if it were from the root יצת, although the Targum does so only by implication.
- רנה – the Vg. sonavit could apply equally to רנן.
- רשם – Biblical Aramaic רשם is treated identically by the LXX.
- שוח – Tg. Onq., LXX, Aq, Sym, and the Vg. all concur in the rabbinic comparison of this form with שיח.[19]
- שקד – the Targum's reference to burning may be based on comparison with the root יקד of which this is seen either as a šaf‛el or verbal form with added relative ש.[20]
- שיה – this form is often ascribed to the root נשה (Tg. Onq., Frg. Tg., Tg. Ps.-J., Vg.; see also LXX).[21]

---

[18] See p. 81 below.
[19] See p. 66 below.
[20] For the treatment of ש as שׂ see p. 53 below.
[21] Sam has תשא in place of MT אֶשִׁי.

שכה - Sym (ἑλκόμενοι), Theod and Aq (ἕλκοντες) consider the root of משכים to be משך (see Sym and Aq Cant 1:4, Aq Judg 4:7, and Theod Job 28:18).

תזז - LXX "cut off"[22] may reflect an identification with נתז.

תכה - Aq ἐπλήγησαν follows the same logic as the later view which sees in אֻפּוּ a hof‛al-like form of the root נכה (see Aq Gen 4:15, 14:17, etc).[23]

תרגל - *Targum Jonathan* (באורחא . . . דברית) apparently considers this to be related to רגל as does LXX (συνεπόδισα).

Where a word cannot be immediately identified with other biblical usages, various techniques are used to provide such a connection. One possibility is metathesis. Hence רזם is translated by רמז in both the Targum and Peshiṭta, the latter of which renders חרג with חגר, exactly as it does the parallel form (ויחגרו) in 2 Sam 22:46.[24] Elsewhere, too, parallel passages are used as an aid in interpretation. The difficult הלא parallels נדח in Mic 4:6; both are translated with the same word by the Septuagint (ἀπωθεῖν) and Targum (גדר). The Peshiṭta's rendering of ערר is virtually identical with that of the parallel עור in Jer 48:5.[25]

Additional relationships can be asserted on the assumption that similar consonants interchange. This conclusion must be attended with much caution. An equally sound methodological presumption is that the translator's Hebrew text actually had the alternate letter and either it or the Masoretic reading is the result of scribal error. Alternatively, these treatments could have resulted from orthographic confusion (such as ס and שׂ) or similar pronunciation (for example, ע and א) at the time of the translation as well as out of philological interpretation.

The evidence must be carefully assessed. The Peshiṭta's translating ܬܚܕܝܠܠ for תרהו is more likely an effort to find a similarly-sounding Syriac word for the Hebrew original than a case of interchange, although it might be taken as evidence supporting emendation were the contextual meaning of the biblical word not so clear. 11QtgJob renders רוץ by תרוט; in light of the Septuagint's προτρεχει/τρεχει (run) and the orthographic

---

[22] ἀποκόψει or κατακόψει.

[23] See p. 83 below.

[24] In such cases the possibility that the translator's Hebrew text had the same word in both passages cannot be dismissed.

[25] ܣܚܓܘܗܝ and ܣܚܙܘܗܝ respectively, one of which is undoubtedly a corruption of the other.

Hapax Legomena in the Versions   53

similarity of ר and ד, that some ancient texts read תרוץ is more likely than the medieval view of a ד-ר interchange.[26]

Sibilant interchanges are still widely recognized. שׁ is especially often regarded as equivalent to ס.[27] Thus שׂוט is rendered by the Aramaic טוס in both the Targum and Peshitta, which also appears to translate עמשׂ as if it were עמס.[28] עסק renders עשׂק in several Aramaic versions. שׂתם is apparently understood as equivalent to סתם by all the ancient versions, and שׁשׁה is clearly equated with ששׂה by Aramaic and Greek translations.[29] Similarly סרף is treated by the Targum (מיקידא) and Vulgate (conburet) as if it were שרף. Aquila treats שׂ like ס when rendering פשׂח as "make lame" (ἐχώλανε),[30] while the Septuagint's translation of שׁקד (ἐγρηγόρηθη) is used often for שׂקד.[31] Finally, Aquila's ἀπόθετος for שׂפן may indicate that שׂ and צ were also related.[32]

A bilabial shift is explained by Ibn Janaḥ as the basis for the Targum's treatment of עבשׁ (אתמסיא) and of כפשׁ (כנע יתי) according to Naḥmanides.[33]

---

[26] See p. 83 below; Nahum Sarna has suggested (review of M. Sokoloff, *The Targum to Job from Qumran Cave XI*, IEJ 26 [1976] 152) that these translations can be explained as based on the Masoretic text as we have it.

[27] Orthographic confusion of these consonants is known already for the biblical period; see S. Har-Zahav, דקדוק הלשון העברית (Tel Aviv: הוצאת מחברות לספרות, 1950-55) 2.20 and BL §14d. Joshua Blau (*On Pseudo-Corrections in Some Semitic Languages* [Jerusalem: Israel Academy of Sciences and Humanities, 1970] 23) rejects the claim that this has any bearing on the date of a biblical text although it is well known in later Hebrew including the Qumran scrolls (see E. Y. Kutscher, *The Language and Linguistic Background of the Isaiah Scroll* [Leiden: E. J. Brill, 1974] 185) and the Mishna (see J. N. Epstein, מבוא לנוסח המשנה [Jerusalem, 1948] 1233ff.). Rabbinic tradition preserves a reference to such a variant in the Severus scroll according to which Gen 27:27 read סדה where our texts have שדה [מדרש בראשית רבתי ed. H. Albek; Jerusalem: Mekize Nirdamim and Mossad Harav Kook, 1940] 210). The Masorah (ed. Ginsburg, 2. 586) lists several hapax legomena verbs the uniqueness of which is there ascribed to this kind of spelling, (עשק, עמש, סרף, טוש, שתר, שתם, שקר, שקד, שחט, שוח).

[28] ܡܣܐܠ; for Vg. *imponentium* see 2 Chr 10:11.

[29] Tg. בזית, Peshitta ܟܠܠ, LXX προνομεύσω. For שׂתם cf. Tg. אסתתים, Peshitta ܣܟܪ ܢܗܕܘ, LXX ἀπέφραξε, and Vg. *exclusit*; the word is spelled with a *samek* in several manuscripts (see BHK Lam 3:8).

[30] See Aq Isa 33:23.

[31] For example, Jer 5:6 and 31:28.

[32] See Aq Isa 33:23.

[33] IJSh s.v. עבש and Naḥmanides on Lam 3:16.

The dentals ט and ת were often regarded as equivalent. The Septuagint uses the common translation of תעה for טעה,[34] and צבט is rendered "pile up" in accord with צבת.[35] A ט-ת interchange may also explain the Septuagint's understanding of עָשִׁי as "leave behind" (ἐνκατέλιπες): with the loss of *nun*, such a form could have been related to נטש.[36] נוט may be related to the root נוד by the Septuagint, although other interpretations are possible.[37] A final possible use of assumed dental interchange depends on the Targum's propensity for using cognates. At Exod 32:16, one manuscript of the *Samaritan Targum* translates חריד which may have been connected with חרת by a ת-ד shift.[38]

Guttural interchanges were accepted by the rabbis and medieval grammarians. *Targum Jonathan* and the Septuagint treat גדא as if it were נדח and all versions treat יחר like אחר.[39] *Videntes* (Isa 56:10 for הזה) is often used by the Vulgate for חזה.[40] Finally the Peshitta translates טמה by ܠܗܐ while the Targum uses טמע. Many of these are susceptible to other interpretations as has been noted, but should not be ignored in light of subsequent acceptance of guttural interrelationships.

Several final examples are highly speculative, but may also show that ancient translators, uncertain as to the meaning of rare words, relied on a theory of interchanges or the similarity of some consonants. Targum Jonathan treats מחק as if it were מחץ, and the Vulgate's *contriti sunt* for נתע is suggestive of נתץ.[41]

---

[34] πλαναν; note Ezek 14:11, 44:10, 15.

[35] βουνιζειν, see LXX Ruth 2:14.

[36] See LXX Deut 32:15, *Tg. Neof.* שבקתון; for the loss of *nun* compare those versions which relate this form to the root נשה as noted on p. 51 above.

[37] See LXX 2 Kgs 21:8, Ps 36:11 and pp. 48-49 above. An נ-מ interchange could also be inferred from the Aramaic (Tg. יזעזע, Peshitta ܢܘܙܠ) and Vg. (*moveatur*) usages, although scribal error seems more likely as in the case of כמס which LXX treats like כנס (συνῆκται, see LXX Isa 28:20, Ps 12:44, 1 Chr 22:2; however, Sam reads כנס, regarding which see p. 127 below), but note the Targum's translation of עגן in Ruth 1:13 by עגימין.

[38] A variant reading is עירד.

[39] These more likely reflect the *qĕrê*.

[40] Aq and Sym render similarly; see 1QIsa[a] חוזים.

[41] *Tg. Neb.* תברת (Judg 5:26), see also Deut 33:11 and Ps 68:21. On Hebrew צ corresponding to Aramaic ע and ק, see above p. 49; note also the medieval theory regarding the interchange of alphabetically adjacent consonants (p. 79 below).

Hapax Legomena in the Versions 55

There are a few cases of reliance on non-biblical cognates. We have already noted that the *Samaritan* and *Jonathan* Targumim seem to relate כסס to Aramaic. *Jonathan's* על סימנין for the Masoretic נסמן relates the biblical word to its apparent rabbinic counterpart, while the Greek and Aramaic translations "wink" for שׂקר seem to rely on the later סקר.[42]

As indicated above, it is unlikely that all the examples adduced support the hypotheses here presented. There are alternative explanations in several cases, while the evidence itself can by its very nature never be decisive. It is, however, to be hoped that the quanitity of material and the correlation of methods here proposed with those known to be used in approximately contemporaneous Jewish settings does at least indicate the likelihood that these methods were in fact employed. Certainly the general trend of this material illustrates the primary method of dealing with hapax legomena: every effort was made to equate such theoretically unique words with other known forms, both biblical and otherwise. While the philological equations may not always be acceptable today, there can be no doubt as to the emphasis placed on etymology. Thus the treatments here noted do not relate to the words as isolated.

When hapax legomena are perceived as totally isolated, translators are forced to rely on the two least certain methods available. One is context which, though crucial, is inherently subject to error and imprecision. When the context is clear, this is not a particular problem. Thus the Septuagint, Vulgate, and Peshitta are unanimous in translating דגה as "multiply" although there is no certain proof that they derived this from the tradition explaining the form as related to דג (fish).[43] David Qimḥi observes that the Targum's translation of רהה by תיתברון is based on the contextual parallelism of אל תפחדו ואל תרהו (Isa 44:8) with לא תירא ולא תחת (Deut 31:8) which *Onqelos* translates similarly.[44] The other possible technique is to appeal to authority, translating in the same manner as do others. Because of the ultimately Jewish roots of these translations, similarities with rabbinic interpretation are not surprising. *Targum*

---

[42]*Tg. Neb.* ומסרבקן, Peshitta ܣܟܘܡ, LXX νεύμασιν.

[43]The same likely holds for the *Samaritan Targum*. The meaning "multiply" must have been universally derived from context and only the qualification "like fish" based on comparison with דג since there is no reason to expect a denominative from דג to mean "be prolific."

[44]D. Qimḥi on Isa 44:8. This latter phrase occurs several times in the Bible, see especially Josh 10:25 and the Targum there.

Jonathan's translation of the difficult phrase בולס שקמים (Amos 7:14) as ושקמים לי בשפילתא is mentioned in *b. Ned.* 38a.⁴⁵

INTERRELATIONSHIPS AMONG VERSIONS' TREATMENT OF HAPAX LEGOMENA

Where there is insufficient information available for interpreting a particular word such that the versions must resort to context and the authority of tradition, it ought to be possible to use this reliance to detect the interrelationships among the various ancient translations. The most important result of examining the evidence from this perspective is the versions' unanimity with respect to the meaning of a very large number of these words. Thus Greek, Latin, Aramaic, and Syriac versions all agree on the meaning of thirty-four out of the one hundred forty hapax legomena verbs checked, constituting the largest such category of words.⁴⁶ Three of the four major versions agree on twenty-one more,⁴⁷ and agreement of two versions is predictably also quite common.⁴⁸ While interrelationships

---

⁴⁵The reference to the שפילתא is apparently based on its use with שקמים in 1 Kgs 10:27, 2 Chr 1:15 and 9:27. Other similarities between interpretations in the versions and rabbinic literature are noted when relevant or can be found from the page references cited for each hapax legomenon verb in Appendix IV.

⁴⁶The Targum, Peshiṭta, LXX, and Vg. agree with respect to אדש, ימש, יחר, טעה, טנף, טחח, טחה, הדה, דוב, גרד, בטל, אלץ, שקר, שחט, פרשז, סלק, נחץ, נוט, נדא, נבח, מלץ, מהל, לעב, כרבל, שתם, שנס, ששה; the Greek translations of Aq, Sym, and/or Theod agree with versions in the other three languages for יזם, סכת, ספף and סאסא. The Aramaic "tradition" is represented by *Tg. Ps.-J.* and *Tg. Neof.* for חרת (a variant of *Onqelos* agrees), while VL is closer than the Vg. to translations in the other languages for לעט.

⁴⁷Targum, Peshiṭta, and LXX agree for כסס, עוש, קוש, and שתר (Aq and Theod concur with the Aramaic versions for חספס). Targum, Peshiṭta, and Vg. agree with respect to אנס, יעט, פנק, and פשח. Targum, LXX, and Vg. concur on חלט, יאב, לעז (all use forms based on βαρβαρου!), קאם, עגם, and שוח. Sym and Aq agree with the Targum and Vg. for כפה, while the *Tg. Neof.* agrees with the LXX and Vg. for שיה. Peshiṭta, LXX, and Vg. translate similarly for מוק, כחל, טפש, בשס, אדב, רפק, and שקד. Sym concurs with Peshiṭta and Vg. for כמס, while the VL agrees with Syriac and Greek translations of עגן.

⁴⁸The common translations are found as follows: Targum-Peshiṭta: פון, פדע, עשק, עזק, יבב, חשל, חפא, זער, התת, דוץ, דגה, בטה and

Hapax Legomena in the Versions   57

among the various ancient renderings are probable, either through direct dependence or reliance on a common tradition, such claims require more evidence than can be provided from a study of how they treat only hapax legomena and is neither necessary nor particularly appropriate in this setting. Whatever the cause, it seems that these words were for the most part understood from context or tradition; and thus the appropriate conclusion is simply that hapax legomena were not as difficult as one might suspect, calling into question as well the claim that the tradition of meaning for such words is particularly weak. While, as noted above, it is impossible to put this kind of assertion into objective terms, only thirteen words are treated so differently by the various versions as to suggest widespread uncertainty concerning their meaning in antiquity.[49]

As difficult as it is to ascertain why a particular version renders as it does, it is still harder to correlate philological interpretations among versions in different languages with any certainty. In comparing the several Aramaic translations, this problem is minimized since one need not speculate as to "shared intent," but can seek instead identical translations as the basis on which to posit interrelationships.

The Peshiṭta is unique among the Aramaic versions in that it encompasses the entire biblical text, although the translation itself is not always uniform.[50] The frequency with which it uses the same root as does the Targum, excluding those cases in which only the meaning is similar, lends dramatic support to the oft-propounded position that the Peshiṭta's origins are to be traced back to Jewish tradition.[51] This is not

---

[49] רזם. Targum-LXX: עתם and שאס (compare Targum with Sym for בלס and מוק, as well as with Aq for עלע; compare LXX with 11QtgJob דוץ, and the Sam. Tg. with Aq for תכה). Targum-Vg.: בלם, נלה, and סרף. Peshiṭta-LXX: עות, צען, רנה, רשם, and תרגם (compare Peshiṭta with Aq and Theod for יאה as well as with Vg., and with Sym for סעה). Peshiṭta-Vg.: אבך, טמה, רטה, and שאס (compare Peshiṭta with VL for צבט, with Targum, Aq, and Sym for עלע). LXX-Vg.: בלס, בתק, דגה, חפא, חרג, צנם, צבט, פצם, פסג, עשק, עזק, סמן, סכת, נוש, כשה, יזן, חשל, תזז (compare Vg. with Sym for הדך, Theod for חתך, Sym and Aq for שפן). ערע, סלד, סלא, נתע, נצא, ירט, יעז, יבב, זרב, הכר, דהם[49], מחק, יהד, הזה, הבר; the translations of six other words (תרגל, רצד, נתס, רטפש) are generally similar enough so as to seem to be the result of deduction from context.

[50] Otto Eissfeldt, *The Old Testament, An Introduction* (New York: Harper and Row, 1965) 699-700.

[51] See J. H. Hospers, "The Present-Day State of Research on the Pešiṭtā," in *Verbum* (H. W. Obbink Festschrift; Utrecht: Drukkerij en Vitgeuerig V/H Kemink EN Zoon, N.V., 1964) 148-57, for a survey of this

58   Hapax Legomena in Biblical Hebrew

to suggest that there are no significant differences. We have already
noted some cases where the Peshiṭta does not concur with the targumim,
as in its omission of "fish" in the translation of דגה. But overall there can
be little doubt from the material here collected that the Peshiṭta is
properly treated as having a place within the tradition represented by the
Targum.

For the Pentateuch alone there are several targumim to be compared. Because of this and the limited number of hapax legomena contained in it, definitive conclusions are hard to draw. The following chart
delineates the translations of each of these twenty-one hapax legomena
by the various Aramaic translations.[52]

In a large proportion of these cases there is sufficient unanimity to
illustrate the validity of the phrase "targumic tradition." Versions which
deviate from the prevalent translation are especially significant. The
slight variations of the Peshiṭta's treatment of דגה has already been
noted; for צנם it alone translates in a manner not assonant with the
Hebrew (קטינן), while it is the only Aramaic version not to treat שוח as
meaning "prayer" in accord with rabbinic tradition.[53] The other "individual" among these translations is the *Samaritan Targum*.[54] Although it
does accord once with *Neofiti* (טחן) and once with *Onqelos, Neofiti,* and
the Peshiṭta (כסס), it is unique in its treatment of ידם, כשה, לעט, and
תכה.[55] Other conspicuous commonalities are in the translations of חספס
and כמס by *Neofiti* and the *Fragment Targum,*[56] and of ירט by *Neofiti* and

---

problem. Twenty-eight of the hapax legomena verbs are translated with
the same Aramaic root as in the Targum (הדה, דוץ, בטל, בטה, אדש,
לעב, יעט, ימש, יחר, יבב, טעה, טנף, טוש, חרת, חפא, חספס, זער,
ששה). שסף, רזם, פרשז, פנק, פדע, עוש, נוט, נדא, גבח, מלץ).

[52]Because it is impractical to include all variants in such a setting,
the best attested reading has been selected for inclusion in this chart.

[53]See p. 66 below.

[54]On problems with determining the text of the *Sam. Tg.* see A. Tal,
The Samaritan Targum and Lea Goldberg, *Das Samaritanische Pentateuchtargum* (Bonner Orientalistische Studien XI; Stuttgart: W. Kohlhammer, 1935). John W. Nutt (*A Sketch of Samaritan History, Dogma,
and Literature* [London: Trübner and Co., 1874] 109) considers its treatment of hapax legomena to indicate a relationship with *Tg. Onq.*, but see
L. Goldberg, pp. 28ff.

[55]Regarding its translation of חרת see p. 54 above.

[56]The translation of כמס by *Tg. Neof.* and *Tg. Ps.-J.* is likely to be
explained from rabbinic tradition, see *Sifre* האזינו 324.

TRANSLATION OF HAPAX LEGOMENA IN THE ARAMAIC VERSIONS

Hebrew	Tg. Onq.	Peshitta	Tg. Neof.	Sam. Tg.	Tg. Ps.-J.
דגה	כנוני יסגון	ונכברון	ויסגון היך נוניא	ויפתון	דכורי ימא סגי
דוב	ומפחן	ומדיב	ומדיבה	ומדביאן	ומסייפא
חספס	מקלף	מתקלף	מפספס	מנצנץ	מסרגל
חרת	מפרש	רשם	חקיק	חריד	חקיק
חשל	מתאחרין	דפש	הרהר	שליטיה	
טחה	כמגד	משדא	כמרמי	כמרמי	כ- מיגד
יזם	דחשיבו	אתחשבו	די חשבו	דיזמנון	דחשיבו
יסך	יתסך	נתשיף	יתמשח	יתנסך	יתמרק
ירט	גלי... למיזל	דתרצת	סטת	בישה	סטט
כמס	גלו	נטיר	כסא דפורענותא	כערוק	גלין
כסס	תתמנון	תמנון	תתמנון	תמנו	תיכסון
כשה	קנא	קנא	קנון	אשפרת	קנון
	נכסין	נכסא	נכסין		נכסין
לעט	אטעימני	אטעמיני	איכל	אסגי	אטעם
סכת	אצית	צות	אציתו	אצית	ציתו
עשק	אתעסקו	דאתעסקו	אתעשקו	אתעשקו	אתעסקו
צנם	נצן	קטינן	צנינן	צלילן	נצן
שוח	לצלאה	למהלכו	למצלויה	למצלאה	לצלאה
שחט	ועצרית	ועצרת	ועצרת	ועצרת	ועצירית
שפן	יתגלן	יאלפא	יתגליון	ושפעים	גלא
שיה	אתנשיתא	טעית	שבקתון	תשף	אתנשיתין
תכה	מדברן	מדברין	מדברין	יכנען	מדברין

Fragmentary Targum

חספס – מפספס
חשל – הרהר
כמס – כסא דפורענותא
כשה – וקנון נכסין
עשק – דאתעסקו
שפן – יסימתא
שיה – אנשיתון
תכה – מדברין

Palestinian Targum

דגה – ויסגון מא דסגי נונא
סכת – ציתו
צנם – צנימים
שחט – ועתרת

Pseudo-Jonathan, שיה by Onqelos, Pseudo-Jonathan, and the *Fragment Targum*, and כשה by all Aramaic versions except the *Samaritan Targum*.

In all, while no decisive claim for dependence can be made from this evidence, the general commonality of approach is in itself significant, showing not only the broad cohesion of the targumim but also the general consensus with regard to these rare words in contrast to what many would expect.[57] It should, however, be restated that the treatment of hapax legomena alone is not a sufficient basis from which to discuss the interrelationships of any of the versions. Rather a comparison must be made of their treatments of an entire section of the Bible.

The evidence of the versions has provided some broad hypotheses, detailed examination of which must be made in other contexts. First, we have seen that there is general agreement as to the interpretation of most hapax legomena. Whatever explanation may be offered for this, it will not suffice to assert without proof that these words were perceived as uniquely difficult; it seems doubtful that they as a group caused more trouble for these translators than did other words. We have also noted hints of the development of exegetical and even philological methods. Although the possibility of variant readings cannot be ignored, one must not assume that wherever an ancient translation differs from the modern view there was a different reading before the translators. There can be no doubt that they took an active approach to the text, attempting to find interpretations even where it seemed problematic. Finally, the treatment of hapax legomena has been used to explore some potential interrelationships among the versions. In this regard, however, such a method is plainly only tentative and further examination from other perspectives is bound to have more validity.

---

[57] Although the *Frg. Tg.* agrees in almost all its attestations with *Tg. Neof.*, there are only eight instances on which to rely.

5

The Treatment of Hapax Legomena in Rabbinic Literature

Although rabbinic literature does contain some exegesis, it is not primarily philological; nor are the methods used to explain those words which are described always obvious. Moreover, because they predate the flowering of systematic Hebrew grammar, rabbinic interpretations frequently betray a rather unsophisticated view, not always in accord with the modern understanding of Hebrew philology. Of course, much that is seemingly philological may have been intended as dĕrash; yet it will be shown that the methods used by the rabbis set the pattern to a remarkable degree even to the present day.[1]

There is no evidence to indicate that the rabbis recognized the phenomenon of hapax legomena. Word frequency was not important to them. Nor is there any indication that hapax legomena were treated differently than more common words. Many of the words so-identified are not discussed or interpreted at all in the corpus of rabbinic literature. Others are treated with a rather unashamed familiarity, as if there were nothing particularly unusual about them. Sometimes a word is used almost to explain itself, suggesting that it was still a part of the contemporary language and thus neither surprising nor difficult.[2]

---

[1]Because of the limited amount of material relevant to this study, no effort has been made to separate out homiletic interpretations, but special note should be made of those cases where the result is a "moral" which does not fit smoothly into the word's biblical context (for example, regarding חרת as noted on p. 65 below). Taken as the crystallization of prior Jewish tradition, this material can also be understood as providing the justification for many interpretations found in the ancient versions (for example, p. 56 above).

[2]Rabbinic passages in which biblical hapax legomena are so treated include t. Sanh. 4:7 (תרגם); b. ʿErub. 54a (חרת); this word was apparently

RELIANCE ON COGNATES AND RELATED FORMS

That these words were not necessarily difficult is further proved by the fact that some hapax legomena are themselves used to explain rabbinic terms. עגן is compared with עוגין (anchor),[3] while צבט provides the origin for the term בית צביטה (handle).[4] Similarly, the place name בית יעזק is explained according to the ascribed meaning of עזק.[5] Thus no clear line was drawn to separate biblical from rabbinic Hebrew, as is confirmed by the story according to which the meaning of a difficult biblical word was discovered from colloquial usage.[6] A word which might appear to be rare, were one to treat biblical Hebrew alone, thus ceases to be unusual in the light of rabbinic usage. This approach shows an awareness on the rabbis' part of both the comparative method's importance and the basic continuity between their own language and that of the Bible. However, since they were not always in a position to assess phenomena such as semantic change or homonymy, reliance on rabbinic Hebrew occasionally led to what are now recognized as inappropriate interpretations. Thus בלם is compared to the rabbinic root meaning "kick," which fits the contextual

---

familiar enough for R. Eliezer to infer from it a connotation of permanence, although this may have been based on earlier exegesis), b. Ketub. 10b (עפד); b. B. Bat. 9b (כפה); Gen. Rab. 22:6 (פנק), 31:12 (נתע), 61:2 (רשב); Exod. Rab. 25:8 (יעץ); Num. Rab. 9:1 (שיה); it is likely that שָׁי is ascribed to the root נשה, for evidence supporting this position see p. 51 above), 9:7 (יזן), 4:20 (כרבל); ʾAbot R. Nat. A 34 (כרסם); Mek. Shim. b. Yoḥ. יתרו 20:19 (לעב); Pesiq. R. 30:4 (אבר); Pesiq. Rab. Kah. 141b (דוץ), 147b (יעט); Sifre האזינו 324 (כמס); Midr. Tanḥ. בחקתי 2, p. 237b (חפא); Yal. Shim. 1.98 (טנף), 750 (יסן), 2.547 (חתר).
[3] b. B. Bat. 73a עוגין תני רבי חייא אלו עוגינין שלה וכן הוא (הוא...הלהן תעגנה....).
[4] b. Ḥag. 22b מאי בית הצביטה א"ר יהודה אמר שמואל מקום שצובטו (וכן הוא אומר ויצבט לה קלי).
[5] Although a meaning "cultivate" seems intended by y. Roš. Haš. 2:3 מהו בית יעזק ששם היו עוזקין את ההלכה כמה דאת אמר ויעזקהו (ויסקלהו) the commentary Qorban Ha'edah (on y. Sukk. 4:6, p. 18a) notes also a meaning "encircle" or "fortify" (see also b. Roš. Haš. 23b).
[6] Gen. Rab. 79:7. The rabbis did recognize that the language had changed (לשון תורה לעצמה לשון חכמים לעצמו, b. ʿAbod. Zar. 58b) although the very fact that such statements had to be made demonstrates a sense of general continuity.

Hapax Legomena in Rabbinic Literature 63

reference to horses but not its intent.[7] The form מטחוי is ascribed to a form of the root טוח meaning "reproach," yielding a reinterpretation of the biblical passage, as well as with טָוָח which results in a more felicitous understanding of the verse;[8] similarly כמס is recognized as the root of the post-biblical כֻּמְסָה.[9] Other comparisons with rabbinic vocabulary are noted below.

אנס – Esth. ,אין אונס באנפקא רב אמר אין אונס ביין נסך) "compel" – אנס
Rab. 2:13)

זרב – "be hot" (מה טעמא לחולטנות זריבתן עיקר אמר לוי בן יהושע ר'
נצמתו יזורבו בעת, y. Sanh. 10:3, p. 38b; see also Qoh. Rab. 9:2)

יאה – "befit" (יאה מלכותא לך יאתה לר, Midr. Pss. 93:1)[10]

כמה – "long for" (למים מצפין שהן הללו ככמהות איבו א"ר לך כמה, Gen. Rab. 69:1)[11]

לעט – "gulp down" (כגמל הרשע אותו פיו פער זעירה א"ר .... כהדא), Gen. Rab. 63:12, see b. Šabb. 155a) מלעיטין אבל דורסין ולא הגמל את אובסין אין דתנינן,

מהל – "dilute" (במים מהול סבאך, למה לסיגים היה כספך ד"הה ליה המהיל ביתיה לבר אמר, Pesiq. Rab. Kah. 122b)[12]

עגן – "be an עגונה" (לאיש היות ,בלתי לבלתי עגונות יושבות אתם יכולות תעגנה הלהן", Ruth. Rab. 2:17)

עלע – "(bleed from) side" (דמא ואתי מיניה גדפא שמיט מכי אביי, כשרים יונה בני מאימתי קרחה יעקב תני דם יעלעו אפרוחיו לה אמר והוא לה תני הוָא משיעלעו אימת אמר), b. Ḥul. 22b)[13]

---

[7]Pesiq. Rab. Kah. 24ab (את הזה הסוס כפרד תהיו אל בולם והוא בולם שעורים מאכילו בולם והוא מקשטו בולם והוא מכשכשו בולם והוא ממתגו בולם והוָא לגניה לאקריב בולם והוא).

[8]Gen. Rab. 53:13 (מעלה כלפי דברים כמטחת ברכיה א"ר). טוייחים קשת שני כמטחוי יצחק א"ר

[9]y. Pe'a 5:7, p. 19b (עמדי כמוס הוא הלא). דתימר כמה מלרע אמר אבינא רבי לכומסאות

[10]The less acceptable comparison with נאה (Yal. Shim 2.847) persisted through the Middle Ages; see Rashi on Jer 10:7.

[11]This root is ascribed to כמהות (mushrooms) which "long for" water.

[12]The "cognate" is questionable since it is used only with regard to this verse. For the purposes of this chapter, the possibility that rabbinic words were based on biblical occurrence is not relevant; it will have to be borne in mind in determining the original meaning of each word (see pp. 176-77 below).

[13]The comparison is with the Aramaic עלע which corresponds to Hebrew צלע ("rib"); on the lack of a strict distinction between Hebrew and Aramaic see note 16 below.

פנק - "indulge self" (אמר ר' אבין כל מי שמפנק את יצרו בנערותו
סופו להיות מנון עליו בזקנותו, Gen. Rab. 22:6)
פשח - "split" (דרכי סורר ויפשחני תילהי כדאמרינן אילו שנפשח קושרין
אותו, Lam. Rab. 3:4, see m. Šeb. 4:6)
רטה - "wring out" (וכדי שלא יצאו ישראל רשעים בדין לכך הרטה אותי
בידו הוי וע"י רשעים ירטני, Exod. Rab. 21:7)
שקד - "be mistaken" (נשקד עול פשעי בידו שקודה הייתי מעוונותי
סבורה הייתי שימחול לי על כל עונותי, Lam Rab. 1:42)[14]
שיה - "be weak" (צור ילדך תשי התשת כחו של יוצר, Pesiq. R. 25:2)[15]

When Hebrew did not supply related words, recourse was made to more removed dialects. For the rabbis, of course, only Aramaic was available.[16] In a frequently repeated treatment, יבב is explained on the basis of the Targum's translation of תרועה and a mishnaic cognate as meaning "sigh."[17] כסס is related to the Syriac כוס which means "kill,"[18] and פדע is taken as if it were the Aramaic cognate of Hebrew פצע.[19]

Other words seem to have been understood from the context in which they are found. The importance of this approach can best be illustrated by the interpretation of נסמן which has often been related to the rabbinic סימן. One would expect such a view to be especially popular in the rabbinic period in light of the frequency with which the rabbis interpret biblical words in terms of their own vocabulary. But here the demands of context led them in a different direction. Since the word occurs in a list of grains, they treat it as the name for another such species.[20] Other words apparently taken from context are רפף and

---

[14] According to Jastrow (p. 1620), but this is the only passage cited.
[15] The attested form שַׁשִּׁי is ascribed to the root תשש.
[16] In this regard we can rely only on their explicit statements as to the source of information; it is not clear that Hebrew was always distinguished from Aramaic passages in what we know as rabbinic literature. Saul Lieberman notes comparisons also to Phoenician, Syriac, and Coptic (*Hellenism in Jewish Palestine* [New York: Jewish Theological Seminary, 1950] 51).
[17] b. *Roš. Haš.* 33b (יום תרועה יהיה לכם ומתרגמינן יום יבבא
יהא לכון וכתיב באמימה דסיסרא בעד החלון נשקפה ותיבב אם סיסרא מר
סבר גנוחי גנח ומר סבר ילולי יליל); see also *Tg. Onq.* Num 29:1.
[18] b. *Pes.* 61a (ר' אמר לשון סורסי הוא [תכוסו] כאדם שאומר
לחבירו כוס לי טלה זה).
[19] *Pesiq. Rab.* 10:9 (מהו פדעהו אלא אותו המלאך שמלמד עליו זכות
אמר להקב"ה פדעהו ביסורים).
[20] y. *Ḥal.* 1:1, p. 1b (נסמן זה השיפון).

שסף.²¹ So too בלס is taken as "own," the simplest possible interpretation in light of the contextual reference to the fact that it was something Amos did with respect to trees just as he cared for cattle.²² Aside from its obvious relationship to יהודי, the verb התיהד was understood to mean "converted" from the fact that the people were afraid of the Jews.²³ The best contextual aid for understanding a word would be a parallel in the same verse.²⁴ Among words which may have been understood in this manner are כמה and פצם.²⁵

In all these cases the fact that the words are hapax legomena is clearly unimportant to the rabbis. Whether obvious from contemporaneous usage or implicit in the context, these words are in no way treated as especially difficult or unique. In all cases the interpretation proceeds in a manner applicable to other words which require elucidation. In fact, several words were explained from within the Bible itself.²⁶ These do not, therefore, constitute absolute hapax legomena as judged by the criteria of rabbinic etymology.

דג - דגה "be like fish" מה דגים שבים מים מכסים עליהם ואין עין רעה
שולטת בהם, b. Ber. 55b)

חרת - חירות²⁷ "be free" אל תקרי חרות אלא חירות, Exod. Rab. 41:7)

סוך - יסך "pour" ת"ר הסך בשמן המשחה וכלים פטור ... דכתיב)
על בשר אדם לא ייסך, b. Ker. 7a)

מכסה - כסס "number" יכול שחטו שלא למנויו יהא כעובר על המצוה)
. . . . וכשר ת"ל במכסת תכוסו הכתוב שנה עליו, b. Pes.
61a)

---

²¹Cf. b. Ḥag. 12a and Esth. Rab. 7:13 respectively.

²²b. Ned. 38a (כדמתרגם רב יוסף ארי מרי גיתי אנא ושקמין
בשפלתא לי). The passage refers to R. Joseph's "translation," and indeed this exact translation is found in Tg. Neb. Amos 7:14.

²³ʾAg. Ber. 5 (. . . אף האומות מבקשין לבא תחת כנפי השכינה
וכן בימי מרדכי ורבים מעמי הארץ מתיהדים).

²⁴That this was the basis for the interpretation is obviously not always certain.

²⁵Gen. Rab. 69:1 רבנן אמרי כשם שנפשי צמאה לך כן רמ"ח אברים)
הרעשה ארץ) and 59:11 (שיש בי צמאים לך היכן בארץ ציה ועיף בלי מים
בימי אברהם פצמתה בימי אליעזר רפה שבריה בימי יעקב כי מטה בימי
ישבי בנוב).

²⁶Saul Lieberman (Hellenism, p. 57) compares this use of the גזרה שוה to the Greek δὶς λεγόμενα.

²⁷This word is not attested in the Bible.

סאה - סאסא	"measure" (תריבנה בשלחה בסאסאה שנאמר מדה כנגד מדה, b. Šabb. 105b)	
סלת - סלא	"fine flour" (כפז המסולאים דתימא כמה סלת, Num. Rab. 13:14)	
עת - עות	"time" (לאורו שייאותו עד הנר על מברכין אין תנינן תמן רב אמר יאות ושמואל אמר יעותו . . . מאן דאמר יעותו, y. ʿErub. 5:1, p. 26a)[28] לדעת לעות את יעף דבר	
יצת - צות	"ignite" (נשרף העולם היה מיד יחד אציתנה, Midr. Tanḥ. Bub. 4, p. 42a) משפטים	
שיח - שוח	"pray" (בשדה לשוח יצחק ויצא שנאמר תפלה אלא שיחה אין, b. ʿAbod. Zar. 7b)	
תוך - תכה	"amid" (הצדיקים וכל האבות מן למעלה מיסב כביכול, Exod. Rab. 25:8) לרגליך תכו והם שנאמר בתוכו	
רגל - תרגל	"train" (ארכובותיו על ונתנו בכח בן לו שהיה למלך משל, Lam. Rab. 2:2) לאפרים תרגלתי ואנכי כך . . בכח	

This provides what has become the basic approach utilized by the rabbis and all subsequent students of the Bible for the elucidation of rare forms. This principle is simply to find some way in which to relate the difficult forms to other known words.[29] As noted, primary recourse was made to other biblical forms as well as contemporary (rabbinic) usage. Some words cannot be resolved in this manner, and for these cases other measures must be found to broaden the possibilities for comparison; however, the purpose remains the same—to find further attestations of the same or a related word.

RELIANCE ON WORD MODIFICATION

A first method which was to achieve substantial prominence during the medieval period and is still used, although not always overtly, is that of consonant interchange.[30] To the extent that one of its consonants can under varyingly explicit conditions be equated with another, a seemingly isolated word may be related to other biblical forms. Sibilants are a prime focus of such methods, and there is no more fertile ground than the relationship between שׁ and ס which are often orthographically confused,

---

[28] Here the biblical word is used to explain the interpretation of a rabbinic dictum (לאורו שיעותו עד הנר על מברכין אין) although another opinion holds that the relevant word of that statement is יאותו. For the use of other biblical hapax legomena to explain rabbinical terms see p. 62 above.

[29] ממפורש סתום ילמד (b. Tem. 16b).

[30] The existence of this exegetical technique within rabbinic literature and the targumim is forcefully defended by AFP, pp. 1-12.

particularly in this period.[31] Thus כשׂה is understood as "cover" (כסה), a comparison which is "confirmed by the apparently similar usage of the latter root in Job 15:27.[32] שׂתם is apparently taken as "close" (סתם).[33] עשׂק is understood as identical with the rabbinic עסק which means "engage in," although that meaning has nothing to do with the biblical context and results in a midrashic interpretation of Gen 26:20.[34] Finally, various interpretations of שׂקר use this method, according to which it refers either to the process whereby women color their eyes with סיקרא or to their roving eyes.[35] A broader attitude toward sibilant interchange is reflected in those passages which suggest that a שׂ be understood as שׁ.[36] Using this approach, שׂקר is taken as "lie" (שׁקר).[37] This method also results in the treatment of שׂקד as if it were שׁקד (consider carefully).[38]

A shift between the dentals ת and ט is responsible for the interpretation of חטם as "sealed."[39] Elijah Levita suggests that guttural interchange underlies the common interpretation of אלץ as referring to Delilah's withdrawing herself (חלץ) from under Samson during intercourse

---

[31] Jacob N. Epstein, מבוא לנוסח המשנה, pp. 1233ff.

[32] *Yal. Shim.* 1. 945 (כאדם ששמנו בפנים עושה[!]) שמנת עבית כסית
(כסלי' מבחוץ כן הוא אומר כי כסה פניו בחלבו ויעש פימה עלי כסל).

[33] *b. B. Meṣ.* 59a (נגעלו שערי בית המקדש שנחרב מיום אלעזר א"ר
תפלתי שתם ואשוע אזעק כי גם שנאמר תפלה).

[34] *Gen. Rab.* 64:8, according to which the spring was so-named in honor of the book of Genesis which describes God's being "engaged in" the creation of the world (נתעסק שבו בראשית ספר כנגד עשׂק שם ויקרא הבאר
הקב"ה וברא את העולם).

[35] *b. Šabb.* 62b (לעינייהו כוחלא מלאן דהנה עינים ומשקרות) and *Midr. Tanḥ. Bub.* וישלח 17, p. 86b (בורא אני אם הקב"ה אמר ומרמזן
סוקרנית אדם [של] מעניניו . . . [חוה]).

[36] Although such interpretations may be based on the similarity of שׂ and שׁ, the possibility that they are due to the orthographic confusion of the one sign used for these two letters is somewhat mitigated by the fact that other interpretations previously noted clearly recognize the letter as שׂ (see above). An additional interpretation of this type concerning שׂתם is on p. 69 below.

[37] *Midr. Tanḥ. Bub.* נשא 1, p. 13b (שהיא שקר לשון עינים ומשקרות
[סוטה] נואפת עם איש אחר ומתעברת ממנו ומשקרת ואומרת לבעלה ממך אני
מעוברת); the word thus refers to what an adulterous woman must do in order to explain resulting pregnancies to her husband.

[38] *Lam. Rab.* 1:42 (עלי להביא איך הקב"ה שקד כתוב שי"ן נשקד
את הרעה).

[39] *Num. Rab.* 5:6 (הקב"ה) של שמו יתחלל שלא כדי לך אחטם ותהלתי
בהם יביא להם קץ הגאלה החתום).

in order to upset him.[40] This may also explain the enduring comparison of
פדע with פדה (save) as is implicit in several rabbinic and subsequent treatments.[41] In this regard it should be noted that one cannot assume consonantal interchange to have been a linguistic theory during the rabbinic period as it became in the Middle Ages.[42] The discussion of עות refers to a confusion of sounds,[43] and such confusion is likely responsible for other such treatments as well.

A hint of another approach can be discerned in the treatment of רפק through a pun on פרק;[44] metathesis too can be used to "normalize" rare words, although this also should be considered an aural rather than linguistic approach to the extent that other evidence from rabbinic philology supports such a contention.

A still more esoteric way to wrest a common expression from the abnormal is by *notarikon*, whereby a word can be broken down into smaller parts, even individual letters, which are taken as initials for an entire phrase.[45] Thus ירט is explained as יראתה ראתה נטתה,[46] while פרשז is understood to represent פרש רחום שדי זיו.[47] More commonly words are treated as compounds.

חספס - "melt on palm" (דק מחוספס אמר ר"ל דבר שנימוח על פיסת היד", *b. Yoma* 75b)

סאסא - "measure for measure" (תני היה רמ"א מנין שבמדה שאדם מודד בה, מודדים לו שנאמר בסאסא בשלחה תריבנה, *Num. Rab.* 9:24)

סכת - "make yourselves into groups" (הסכת עשו כתות ועסקו בתורה, לפי שאין התורה נקנית אלא בחבורה, *b. Ber.* 63b)

צען - "leave and move" (תני רבי אליעזר בן יעקב אהל בל יצען בל יצא ובל ינוע, *Cant. Rab.* 1:5)

רצד - "appease judgment" (דרש בר קפרא מאי דכתיב למה תרצדון הרים

---

[40]In QSh, p. 424; see *b. Soṭa* 9b (מאי ותאלצהו אמר רבי יצחק דבי רבי אמי בשעת גמר ביאה נשמטה מתחתיו).

[41]For example, *b. Šabb.* 32a (ואלו הן פרקליטין של אדם תשובה ומעשים טובים ואפי' תשע מאות ותשעים ותשעה מלמדים עליו חובה ואחד מלמד עליו זכות ניצול).

[42]See pp. 79-84 below.

[43]P. 66 above.

[44]*Cant. Rab.* 8:5 (מתרפקת על דודה א"ר יוחנן שהיא מנחת פרקי תורה ופרקי מלכות לעתיד לבא).

[45]H. L. Strack, *Introduction to the Talmud and Midrash* (New York: Harper & Row, 1965) 97.

[46]For example, *b. Menaḥ.* 66b.

[47]For example, *Exod. Rab.* 42:4.

גבנונים יצתה בת קול ואמרה להם למה תרצו דין עם סיני כולכם בעלי מומים, b. Meg. 29a); also interpreted as:
"run and quarrel" (רצים ומדיינים אלו עם אלו בסיני היו תורה ליתן הקב"ה שבא בשעה, Gen. Rab. 99:1)
שתם כתיב לפי שתמו הצבור תפלתהון, Lam Rab. 3:3)[48] – "because finished" שתם
ואנכי תרגלתי . . . תרתי ריגלתי ברוח הקודש) "seek and send" – תרגל לברך אפרים אימתי קחם על זרועותיו, Pesiq. R. 3:4; see also ʾAg. Ber. 5)

Gematria can also be divided into two parts.[49] The first relies on the calculation of a word's numerical value; in this case מחספס which has a value of 248, the number of tendons in the body, is taken to imply that manna was absorbed by the entire body.[50] Another form of substitution is that in which each letter of the original word is replaced with another letter as determined by a specific principle. In ʾatbash the first letter of the Hebrew alphabet is replaced with the last (ת-א), the second by the next to the last (ש-ב), and so on. So treated, the root ירט emerges as equivalent to מגן.[51]

The rabbis did not treat hapax legomena any differently than other words; the methods on which they relied are those which can be found throughout the material of this kind. Most hapax legomena seem to have posed no problems whatsoever; others were related to elements of rabbinic and cognate vocabulary in often effortless fashion. The rabbis assumed that their own language was fundamentally the same as that of the Bible. For words which were not easily interpreted, various approaches were applied in order to make the hapax legomenon comparable to known words through metathesis, interchanges, and sometimes more elaborate, if linguistically dubious, procedures.

Through all this, two fundamental attitudes can be recognized. The first is the familiarity with which the rabbis treat most such words, despite their willingness to apply variously exotic methods. Equally important is the effort to find a way of relating those words which did need elucidation to other known forms, whether we judge the result to be successful or naive, gentle or abrasive. These two characteristics of the treatment of hapax legomena continue throughout the history of biblical lexicography.

---

[48]Regarding ש-ש see p. 67 above.
[49]H. Strack, *Introduction*, 97.
[50]b. *Yoma* 75b (מחספס כתיב . . . לחם שנבלע במאתים וארבעים ושמנה אברים).
[51]*Num. Rab.* 20:15 (כי ירט הדרך יראה ראתה נטתה ד"א ירט בא"ת ב"ש מגן).

6

The Treatment of Hapax Legomena in the Middle Ages

The many methodological uncertainties encountered when dealing with earlier periods are fortunately not applicable to medieval Hebrew grammarians and exegetes. Thorough by necessity—a dictionary or commentary should not be selective in the material it treats—medieval scholars were intentionally explicit as to their reasoning, enabling us to avoid the kind of speculation which has inevitably permeated the treatment of earlier interpretations.

It was in this period that the phenomenon of hapax legomena was first truly recognized.[1] Every effort was made to find a way in which rare words could be related to other, better attested forms. Words were split, analyzed for "hidden" roots, and compared with the vocabulary of related languages in order to find some analog. Only after all else had failed was a word described without qualification as אין לו דומה with the necessary recourse to previous interpretations or the demands of context (כח הפסוק).[2] Although the resources used by medieval exegetes were obviously more limited than those available today, their approaches are fundamentally identical with our own and basically the same as those already treated for the versions and rabbis. There was, of course, no more unanimity as to the meaning of a specific word in the Middle Ages than in antiquity or our own time.

---

[1] Pp. 4-11 above.
[2] This is not to say that these considerations were otherwise ignored; see p. 8 above.

HAPAX LEGOMENA RELATED TO OTHER BIBLICAL FORMS

The first method was to find a corresponding word in the Bible itself. Several words are even correlated with proper nouns, although the value of such comparisons is not always apparent.[3] David ben Abraham Al-Fasi compares זהם to זַחַם (2 Chr 11:19), נבח to לֹבַח (Num 32:42) and עזק to עֲזֵקָה (Josh 10:10).[4] Saadia Gaon connects כמס with מִכְמָס.[5] Other such relationships are more helpful. התיהד is recognized as a denominative from יהודי, meaning "join Jews"[6] or "claim to be Jewish."[7] פסג, which is seen as the root of פִּסְגָה (Deut 3:27), is variously explained as "fortify,"[8] "look high,"[9] or "look at buildings."[10] On the basis of סִכּוּת (Amos 5:26), which was understood to refer to idolatrous images, סכה was explained as "accept (idolatry)"[11] or "picture in mind."[12]

Uncertainty as to the exact nature of Hebrew roots led to comparisons of forms which are today regarded as not directly related. מַשְׁכִּים (Jer 5:8), which we have ascribed to a root שכה on the basis of its singular subject, is widely viewed as a hifʿil form of שכם (do early).[13] Menaḥem takes אֲפוּ from תוך (midst).[14] That הלא pertains to distance is ascribed to its derivation from הלאה.[15]

So-called weak roots retain only some consonants in all forms. For such words some medievals proposed the existence of one and two letter roots. Hapax legomena with weak letters were often equated with other such biblical forms. Examples are given below.

---

[3] See pp. 20-21 above.
[4] AFD, 1. 477 and 2. 249 and 380-84.
[5] SE, p. 238.
[6] For example, MM p. 378.
[7] For example, SE, p. 238. יהודי is in turn traced to הדה by ibn Janah (IJSh, p. 191, see IJR, p. 21) and to جاه by ibn Barun (BWechter, p. 95).
[8] For example, IJSh, p. 405.
[9] For example, MM, p. 400.
[10] For example, IBP, p. 148; for this view the verb and its context seems to have been the basis for interpretation.
[11] For example, IJSh, p. 339; see QSh, p. 240.
[12] Obadiah Sforno on Deut 27:9.
[13] For example, QSh, p. 386, although Qimḥi also notes ibn Ezra's derivation of this form from משך meaning "attracted to female" (QSh, p. 202).
[14] MM, p. 184; such a position is rejected by Aaron ben Elijah on Deut 33:3.
[15] See David Qimḥi on Mic 4:7 and QSh, p. 80.

Hapax Legomena in the Middle Ages   73

HAPAX	RELATED ROOT/FORM	EXEGETE
הדה	היד(ד)	Rashi on Isa 11:8
התת	הוות	Rashi, Abraham ibn Ezra, Isaiah of Trani and others on Ps 62:4
טחה	טחות (Ps 51:8, Job 38:36)	MM, p. 97[16]
טחח	טוח	AFD, 2. 10 and others
יעט	עטה	IPM, p. 27a (s.v. יעט)
ירט	רטה	MM, p. 163
כסס	כסה (Ps 81:4, Prov 7:20) מכס(ה) (Ex 12:4, Lev 7:23, Num 31:28-41) כוס	See IJSh, p. 225 IJSh, p. 225 and QSh, p. 166 Aaron ben Elijah on Exod 12:4
כפה	כפף [17] אכף (Mic 6:6)[18]	Abraham ibn Ezra on Prov 21:14 MM, p. 208 and HTT, p. 83 as well as others
מוק	מקק [19]	MM, p. 119 and OM, p. 146
נוט	נטה (Ps 73:2)	Rashi on Ps 99:1, see SE, p. 331
עוש	עש (Job 38:32)	IQSh, p. 258 and Eliezer of Beaugency on Joel 4:11
עות	עת	MM, p. 139
ערר	ערער [20]	David Qimḥi on Isa 15:5
פון	פן [21] פנה	IJSh, p. 397 and QSh, p. 289 MM, p. 143 and IJR, p. 355

---

[15] See David Qimḥi on Mic 4:7 and QSh, p. 80.
[16] See AFD, 2. 9-10.
[17] Ibn Ezra cites the pairs משגה-שגג and מחוקה-חקק as evidence for the semantic relation between geminate and middle weak roots.
[18] This comparison is rejected by IJOT, p. 147.
[19] Isaiah of Trani (on Ps 73:8) rejects the comparison.
[20] Although the comparison is actually with an occurrence in rabbinic sources (m. Soṭa 3:3), the form occurs also in biblical Hebrew (Jer 51:58).
[21] This opinion is rejected by Moses ibn Ezra, Kitab al-Muḥaḍara (ed. A. S. Halkin; Jerusalem: Mekize Nirdamim, 1975) 212-13.

	אפן (Prov 25:11)[22]	Rashi on Ps 88:16
צות	יצת[23]	IPM, s.v. ציח and QM, p. 78a
קוש	יקש	Abraham ibn Ezra on Isa 29:21
	קשה (2 Sam 19:44)	Eliezer of Beaugency on Isa 29:21
	קשש (Zeph 2:1)	QSh, p. 326
רטה	ירט	MM, p. 163
	רטט (Jer 48:9)	Moses Qimḥi on Job 16:11
רנה	רנן	Abraham ibn Ezra on Job 39:23
רפף	רפה	Abraham ibn Ezra, Moses ben Naḥman and Joseph Qara on Job 26:11

The fact that י, נ, and ל can assimilate provided the possibility for additional correlations. Loss of *yod* is used to relate הֲבִי to the root יהב by many in this period.[24] יאב is equated with אבה,[25] יאה with אות, יבב[26] with בבה (Zech 2:12),[27] ידם with דמם,[28] יסך with סוך,[29] יעז with עזז,[30] and יצע with צען[31] Recognition of *nun*'s weak characteristics—that it can assimilate or be added as a conjugational preformative—is responsible for relationships perceived between יבב and נוב,[32] נדא and ידד (Joel 4:3,

---

[22] Concerning prosthetic *aleph* see below p. 76.
[23] Forms of יצת are considered middle weak; QMChomsky (p. 9) ascribes all such forms to the root נצת.
[24] For example, Rashi on Hos 4:18.
[25] IPM, s.v. יאב; see IKSh, p. 16 where a relationship with אוה may also be implied.
[26] HTT, p. 26 (Hebrew p. 23); the attested form יאתה is ascribed to a root יאת.
[27] For example, Rashi on Judg 5:28.
[28] AFD, 1. 489, although ibn Ezra (on Gen 11:6) considers these to be separate roots.
[29] QM, p. 94; ibn Ezra (on Exod 30:32) cites an opinion according to which ייסך is equivalent to יוסך and thus a form of סוך (compare וַיִּישֶׂם Gen 50:26), anticipating thereby the view of many moderns (see p. 124 below). Regarding the possibility of an "i—u" shift, see ibn Ezra on Mic 1:7 and E. Y. Kutscher, *The Language and Linguistic Background of the Isaiah Scroll*, 452-94.
[30] David Qimḥi on Isa 33:19 and QSh, p. 143.
[31] See MM, p. 151 and AFD, 2. 519-20.
[32] Rashi on Judg 5:28.

Hapax Legomena in the Middle Ages   75

Obad 11, Nah 3:10),[33] נחץ and חוץ,[34] צות and נצת,[35] סלק and נשק,[36] נתע and תעה,[37] נצא and יצא.[38] סעה was considered to derive from the root נסע by Rashi among others,[39] while נתע is explained by ibn Janaḥ as nifʿal of לתע with the *lamed* assimilating.[40] Rashi and Eliezer of Beaugency explain ששא as a reduplicated form of נשא (Gen 3:13).[41]

Some consonants generally considered radicals today were treated as prefixes by the medievals. Thus roots beginning with ה were often considered to be hifʿil: הדך is traced variously to the roots דוך and דכא,[42] התת to the root הבר,[43] הזה to נזה,[44] הכר to נכר, [45] הדה to ידה,[46] and apparently to אתה or חיו.[47]

Mem too can serve as a conjugational prefix. Joseph Qara ascribes מחק to חקק.[48] By treating מ as a radical, מלץ is seen as underlying מליצה.[49]

---

[33] Gersonides on 2 Kgs 17:21.
[34] IJSh, p. 298 who compares the use of חוץ in Qoh 2:25 to which is ascribed the meaning "fast"; see also Ps 119:60.
[35] QM, p. 78a (see note 23 above).
[36] Abraham ibn Ezra on Ps 139:8; the root was commonly taken to be נסק (compare Dan 6:24) although medieval scholars recognized a root סלק and were aware of the possibility that ל can assimilate (see p. 76 below). Ibn Ezra's position is rejected in IQR, p. 16.
[37] For example, QSh, p. 547 and Moses Qimḥi on Job 4:10.
[38] Joseph ibn Kaspi on Jer 48:9; compare HYP, p. 36.
[39] On Ps 55:9.
[40] IJR, p. 258; regarding Saadia's observation (on Job 4:10) of a ל-נ interchange see p. 82 below.
[41] On Ezek 39:2.
[42] Rashi on Job 40:12 and IPM, s.v. הדך.
[43] MM, p. 48; see also AFD, 1. 418 and 421. MEB, p. 50 compares ברו (1 Sam 17:8).
[44] Zeraḥyah ben Yiṣḥaq on Isa 56:10; see also Rashi there.
[45] AFD, 1. 435.
[46] MM, p. 62.
[47] Rashi on Ps 62:4 and MM, p. 68b; regarding the weakness of *aleph*, see below.
[48] On Judg 5:26, see also Rashi there.
[49] For example, PD, p. 43. This relationship is denied by ibn Ezra who insists instead that מלץ is a מלה זרה ("hapax legomenon," see p. 7 above). In a similar manner Yeḥiel Altschuler (on Isa 1:22) derived מהולל (Qoh 2:2) from מהל (see Rashi on Isa 1:22).

Initial *aleph* was frequently regarded as prosthetic. אבך is thereby related to בכא and בוך,[51] אדב to דוב,[52] אדש to דוש,[53] and אלץ to ליץ.[54] This mode of reasoning also seems responsible for Saadia's translation of טמה by נאטמנו.[55] The loss of *aleph* provides still more correlations. הַבוּ is described variously as the imperative or perfect of אהב;[56] חפא is equated with חוף (Gen 49:13),[57] and יחר with אחר.[58] אנושה is derived from *אאנושה through the assimilation of one *aleph*.[59] Medial *aleph*, too, was sometimes regarded as weak.[60] Isaiah of Trani explains כנלתך as derived from the root לאה.[61] while David Qimḥi sees the medial *aleph* of שאס as replacing a *ḥolem*.[62]

In addition to these relatively common phenomena, the medievals were aware of processes of root development recognized today as dissimilation and consonantal infixing. Added liquids were used to trace אלץ to אוץ,[63] כרוב to זרב,[64] זוב to זרב,[65] and כסם to כרסם.[66] Final *mem* in כרסם is considered a suffix by some who relate it thereby to כרש (Jer

---

[51] For example, MSh, s.v. אבך (p. 42) according to which the verb is privative ("destroy" "בכאים) and Eliezer of Beaugency on Isa 9:17. MM, p. 4 compares forms such as נבכים (Exod 14:3).

[52] IJSh, pp. 12-13.

[53] The form itself is described variously as a verb or noun. Ibn Gabirol regards it as an infinitive (ענק), line 87 in שני שירים לר' שלמה "בן גבירול" in *Jubelschrift zum Neunzigsten Geburtstag des Dr. L. Zunz* [ed. J. Egers; Berlin: Louis Gerschel, 1884] p. 196. MM p. 87 equates it with a hif'il (הדרוש). Jacob ben Reuben (on Isa 28:28) considers it a noun of agent on the pattern of אדון, and ELH, p. 3 considers it a composite of infinitive and nominal forms.

[54] AFP, pp. 36-38.

[55] On Job 18:3.

[56] For example, IJSh, p. 14 and IJR, p. 277.

[57] MM, p. 92.

[58] HTT, pp. 16-17.

[59] For example, Rashi and David Qimḥi on Ps 69:21.

[60] QG, p. 82; ELH, p. 15a finds in the unique form קאם evidence that other forms of קום have lost an original middle radical.

[61] On Isa 33:1.

[62] The proper root, therefore, is שסה; see HYP, pp. 30-31 and David Qimḥi on Jer 30:16.

[63] AFD, 1. 92 and 106.

[64] QM, p. 134a; the cherubim were thus understood as those angels who guard the *wrapping*.

[65] This opinion is noted by David Qimḥi on Job 6:17.

[66] QG, p. 24.

41:34).⁶⁷ Ibn Ezra cites an opinion that the ת in עתם is infixed, relating it to יגעם in Lam 4:1,⁶⁸ and several authorities view תרגל as derived from the root רגל.⁶⁹ Saadia mentiona an opinion relating זער to forms based on עוז, implying that *kaf* may have been considered a suffix.⁷⁰

Metathesis was recognized already in the earliest periods of biblical interpretation.⁷¹ Formally described in the Middle Ages, it continued to play a significant role. Among the most notable of such cases are those which rely on the claimed interrelationship of initially and middle weak verbs. Relying on perceived closeness between forms such as טוב and יטב,⁷² the medievals equated also יזן with זון,⁷³ קוש with יקש,⁷⁴ and ימש with מוש.⁷⁵ אדב was considered a metathesized form of דאב.⁷⁶ חשל, which seems clearly to mean "weak," was related to חלש.⁷⁷ רזם was equated with רמז,⁷⁸ and the difficult forms based on עלע and ערע resolved as metathesized from לעע and רעע respectively.⁷⁹ Aaron ben Elijah was thus able to relate the root כשה to the form משׂכיות attested in Ps 73:7.⁸⁰

Several examples yield unique interpretations of the biblical words they treat. חרת was deemed by some to be a metathesized form of חתר.⁸¹

---

⁶⁷QM, p. 134a, but see DST, p. 33 (no. 57). On a potentially similar interpretation of צנם see AFD, 2. 517.

⁶⁸Abraham ibn Ezra on Isa 9:18.

⁶⁹Menaḥem (MM, p. 43a) and David Qimḥi (on Hos 11:3) view it as analogous to the hifʿil through a ה-ת interchange (see p. 83 below). Qimḥi cites the opinion of his brother Moses that the form is nominal, on the pattern of תפארת. Ibn Janaḥ (IJR, pp. 82 and 112) considers תפוגות (Jer 25:34) to be similarly derived and cites an equivalent form in Arabic (IJSh, p. 468).

⁷⁰SE, p. 214. Later, Yeḥiel Altschuler (on Job 26:9) so regarded the ז in פרשז (see Jacob ben Reuben on Job 26:9).

⁷¹Pp. 52 and 68 above.

⁷²QM (p. 94) notes the following additional examples: קוץ-יקץ, שים-ישם, עוף-יעף.

⁷³Isaiah of Trani on Jer 5:8; MM* (p. 378) ascribes both to the biliteral root זן.

⁷⁴Jacob ben Reuben on Isa 29:21.

⁷⁵David Qimḥi on Judg 16:26.

⁷⁶For example, QG, p. 82; compare Deut 28:65.

⁷⁷IJR, p. 352, Abraham ibn Ezra and Aaron ben Elijah on Deut 25:28.

⁷⁸For example, Moses Qimḥi on Job 15:12.

⁷⁹QM, p. 108a and IJSh, p. 361.

⁸⁰On Deut 32:15.

⁸¹See Ezek 12:5; IJR, p. 353.

Moses Qimḥi related רפף to פרר (Isa 24:19),[82] and Isaiah of Trani treated רפק as equivalent to פרק in b. Pesaḥ. 85a which he interpreted as "cling."[83] Other such treatments seem less necessary for understanding the relevant word's meaning than simply to point out textual relationships. Moses ben Isaac ben Ha-Nesia related כחל to חכלילי,[84] and Al-Fasi compared כמס to כסם in Ezekiel 44:20.[85] It is possible that Ibn Parhon's definition of כפה by הפך may also be based on this principle.[86]

Several hapax legomena were considered portmanteau words. In addition to those so-described in previous periods,[87] the following new cases were proposed:

נדהם — גד + הם "fled from worrisome thought"
(QG, p. 83, see also J. Qara on Jer 14:9)[88]

נועז — נכרי + עז "foreign and strong"
(Jacob ben Reuben on Isa 33:19)

יכרסמנה — יכרש + מנה "fill (his) belly from it" (AFD 2. 131)[89]

יעלעו — על + על "more, more" (Rashi on Job 39:30)

פרשז — פרש + אז "then spread" (Joseph Qara on Job 26:9)

רטפש — רטוב + פש "very moist" (Joseph Qimḥi on Job 33:25, QG, p. 45)
רפש + טיט "muddy mire" (IPM, s.v. רטפש)

Similarly, נתעו is considered to reflect two forms of the verb תעה—the

---

[82] On Job 26:11.
[83] On Cant 8:5.
[84] MSh, p. 81.
[85] AFD, 2. 109-10.
[86] IPM, s.v. כפה. In a similar vein, Elijah Levita compares לעב to Aramaic עלב (in QSh, p. 431, see Tg. Onq. Gen 29:32).
[87] The treatments of סאסא by ibn Barun (BYP, p. 71), תרגל by Jacob ben Reuben (on Hos 11:3), and בשׁס by Menaḥem (MM, p. 49; see also Jacob ben Reuben on Amos 5:11) were first noted in antiquity (see pp. 68-69 above). According to Profiat Duran all quadriliterals are composite (PD, p. 85).
[88] According to I. Abrabanel (on Jer 14:9) this interpretation relies on the Arabic meaning of הם.
[89] מנה is understood as a shorter form of מננה; compare מִמֶּנִּי > מִמֶּנִּי in Ps 18:23.

nif'al participle and imperfect by ibn Janaḥ, nif'al perfect and imperfect by ibn Ezra, and nif'al and hitpa'el by Moses Qimḥi.[90]

The previously described principle of consonantal interchange was widely used.[91] Besides the earlier method based on ʾatbash,[92] some held that alphabetically adjacent letters could interchange.[93] Thus בתק was treated as בתר,[94] מחק equated with מחץ,[95] and רצד deemed a by-form of רקד.[96] Most importantly it was during the Middle Ages that relationships among similarly articulated consonants (ממוצא אחד) were noted.[97] While not always acceptable today, this approach comes remarkably close to the modern reliance on scribal error and dialectic variation. Although the explanation that similarly articulated consonants were confused refers to oral rather than written corruption, the implication that under appropriate circumstances one letter may be substituted for another is fundamentally the logic of emendation;[98] indeed, some of the interchanges

---

[90]David Qimḥi's apparent statement (on Gen 11:6) that יזמו is a *forma mixta* based on זמם and יזם is "corrected" by the editor to assert that these two roots are to be considered separate. Regarding נתעו see IJSh, p. 457, IEM, p. 19b, and Moses Qimḥi on Job 4:10. Igal Yannay discusses the phenomenon of portmanteau words ("Augmented Verbs in Biblical Hebrew," *HUCA* 45 [1974] 93); there is little evidence in its behalf for biblical Hebrew except with regard to particles.

[91]Note AFP and David Yellin, תולדות התפתחות הדקדוק העברי (Jerusalem: Qohelet Ltd., 1945) 16 and 44; note also QZ, p. 71 and Adolphe Neubauer, "Abraham Ha-Babli, 'Appendice a la Notice sur la Lexicographie la Hébraique,'" *JA* 6th Series, 2 (1863) 210-16.

[92]See p. 69 above. ELH (p. 28a) notes an opinion according to which רטפש is derived from רטוב, the last two letters of which have been subjected to ʾatbash (yielding פש) and joined to it.

[93]This may have tended to support the common interpretation of לעב with לעג (for example, MM, p. 113).

[94]IPM, s.v. בתק.

[95]For example, AFP, p. 42.

[96]MSh, p. 127; for an alternative explanation see p. 83 below.

[97]AFP. A less sophisticated aproach to the same method relies on the general similarity of two words' sounds rather than specifically defined consonantal shifts. This may be the basis for Gikatilla's translation of הכר by עכר (on Job 19:3) as well as Joseph Qara's treatment of סלא as analogous to צהל (on Lam 4:2). Ibn Kaspi rejects the possibility of interchange (on Isa 61:6, see IKSh s.v. עבש); for Menaḥem's position see p. 6 n. 18 above.

[98]The premise is that similarly articulated consonants may have been confused, which amounts to a theory of oral corruption.

proposed is this period are clearly not similar-sounding, but rather orthographically based.[99]

The largest such group of consonants are the sibilants (זסשר"ץ).[100] The interchange of שׂ and ס is used to explain several words as equivalent to other biblical roots:[101] כשׂה,[102] שׂרף,[103] עמשׂ,[104] עשׂק,[105] שׂחט,[106] שׂפן,[107] שׂקר,[108] שׂחם,[109] שׂתר,[110] and שׂשׂה.[111] ס and שׂ were equated with שׁ[112] for בשׂ which Rashi and Joseph Qimḥi considered to be a polel of בוס, פשׂח[113] which Jacob ben Reuben suggested may be related to פסח,[114] and שׂקד which Al-Fasi proposed to relate to שָׁקֵד.[115] Judah ibn Quraish equated תזז, which was ascribed to the root נתז, with נתס;[116]

---

[99] This is stated explicitly by MSh, p. 7.

[100] Although the components of each group here listed are those mentioned by the medievals, the names applied are the modern ones which most closely approximate the group intended.

[101] Concerning Masoretic recognition of this see p. 53 above.

[102] For example, Rashi on Deut 32:15.

[103] Eliezer of Beaugency considered it to allude to a prostitute's fires (on Amos 6:10), while MSh (p. 99) and Rashi (ed. Maarsen, p. xvii) relate it to the practice described in Jer 34:5. Ibn Ezra (on Amos 6:10) would translate "save from fire" with Tg. Neb. See also Jacob ben Reuben and Isaiah of Trani on Amos 6:10.

[104] IJSh, p. 375.

[105] Elijah Levita (in QSh, p. 435) notes the correlation of שׂ and ס in ארשׁ and יחשׁ.

[106] QSh (p. 441) identifies this with rabbinic סחט.

[107] IPM s.v. ספן (p. 46a); Aaron ben Elijah (on Deut 33:19) relates it to ספינה (Jonah 1:5).

[108] IPM and OM (s.v. שׂקר) compare rabbinic סקר (be curious); compare AFD, 2. 346-48 and Judah ibn Balʿam on Isa 3:16.

[109] See Rashi and Abraham ibn Ezra on Lam 3:8.

[110] Aaron the Karaite on 1 Sam 5:9 explicitly states the equivalence of ס and שׂ in this instance.

[111] Isaiah of Trani (on Isa 10:13) compares this to the use of שׂסה in 1 Sam 23:1.

[112] Concerning this interchange see pp. 53 and 66-67 above.

[113] Rashi on Amos 5:11 and QG, p. 33.

[114] On Lam 3:11, see p. 53 above.

[115] AFD, 2. 346ff. compares also שׂריון-סריון as well as פלשׂתים which he apparently ascribes to the root סתם.

[116] IQR, p. 185 (note m. Sanh. 7:3 התיז "remove") and David Qimḥi on Isa 18:5. Yeḥiel Altschuler later equated these with נתץ (on Job 30:13).

Hapax Legomena in the Middle Ages   81

Al-Fasi identified קסט with קצץ and שפן with צפן.[117] Such reasoning may also underlie the relationship often proposed between צען and נסע.[118] Isaiah of Trani proposed that צבט and שבט be correlated.[119]

A second group of consonants includes the gutturals and semi-vowels (אהוחי"ע). It is this latter group which enabled correlations between הדה and ידה,[120] יזן and זון,[121] יחר and אחר,[122] יסך and סוך,[123] קאם and קום,[124] שאס and שסה.[125] Final ה and א were also deemed interchangeable[126] so that נצא may be a denominative of נוצה,[127] סלא from סלה,[128] בטא from בטה,[129] חפא from חפה,[130] and ששא from ששה.[131] Similarly, תרהו which could be derived from ירה was seen as a variant of תיראו.[132] Among the gutturals, interchanges of א, ה, and ע with ח enabled various authorities to equate אלץ with חלץ,[133] הבר with חבר,[134] התת with חתת,[135] עוש with חוש,[136] and עתם with חתם.[137] The phenom-

---

[117] AFD, 2. 185 and 344.
[118] The final *nun* was regarded as energic by Joseph Qimḥi (cited by Solomon ibn Parḥon on Isa 33:20).
[119] On Ruth 2:14.
[120] HTT, p. 93 (Hebrew p. 80); see Abraham ibn Ezra on Isa 11:8. Menaḥem had ascribed both to the uniliteral root ד (see p. 75 above).
[121] David Qimḥi on Jer 5:8.
[122] HTT, p. 19 (Hebrew p. 16), IESB*, p. 297.
[123] QM, p. 94; ייסך is thus to be equated with יוסך* from the root סוך; see also IJOT, pp. 31-32 and 369ff.
[124] For example, IEM, p. 15a, QG, p. 82; see IJR, pp. 36, 105, and 346.
[125] For example, HTT, p. 13 (Hebrew p. 11), IJR, p. 78, IES, p. 1a and IESB*, p. 297.
[126] This relation was recognized also by ben Asher (cited in David Yellin, תולדות התפתחות הדקדוק העברי, p. 10).
[127] For example, Ezek 17:3, Isaiah of Trani on Jer 48:9.
[128] For example, IJSh, p. 340 and ISh, p. 241.
[129] For example, IJSh, p. 61 and AFD, 1. 212-14.
[130] For example, IJSh, p. 164.
[131] "Six." IES, p. 406 (see MSh, p. 128 which compares Ezek 45:13) David Qimḥi on Ezek 39:2. For a discussion of various issues pertaining to this word, see QSh, p. 362.
[132] This is the reading of 1QIsaᵃ; see AFP, p. 38.
[133] "Withdraw." MSh (p. 48) and Naḥmanides (on Gen 32:25) add metathesis so as to equate this root with לחץ.
[134] IJSh (p. 116) cites Deut 18:11, although this interpretation is rejected by ibn Balaʿam on Isa 47:13.
[135] "Fear," MM, p. 68b.
[136] For example, Rashi on Joel 14:11.
[137] For example, QZ, p. 71.

enon of guttural interchange also seems to provide the necessary theoretical basis for the previously implied correlation of פדע with פדה.[138]

A third group of related consonants comprises the dentals and nasals (דטלנ"ת). Particularly common interchanges from this group are ת-ט[139] and נ-ל.[140] Thus נועז was equated with לועז,[141] while an opinion comparing נחץ with לחץ is cited by ibn Janaḥ.[142] Ibn Ezra also mentions the possibility of equating צנם with צלם.[143] ר and ל were regarded as interchangeable in Joseph Qimḥi's identification of מלץ with מרץ.[144] Less common correlates from within this group are used to identify ירט with ירד[145] and סכת with סכן.[146]

Bilabial relationships, in fact only פ-ב,[147] are cited to equate בתק with Arabic فتق ("slit") by Al-Fasi,[148] כבה with כפה,[149] כבש with כפש,[150] and עבש with rabbinic עפש.[151]

---

[138] For example, Moses Qimḥi (on Job 33:24, citing התגלע from Prov 17:14, which he derives from גלה as proof), QZ (p. 71), and AFP (p. 41). The interchange is actually ע-א since the "normalized" form would be פְּדָאֵהוּ.
[139] חתם=חטם (Jacob ben Reuben on Isa 48:9), חרט=חרת (Rashi on Exod 32:16), צבט=צבת (for example, Isaiah of Trani on Ruth 2:14), and טעה=תעה (QSh, p. 129; however Elijah Levita, in QSh, p. 428, distinguishes the forms by meaning, arguing that טעה means "err," whereas תעה means "be lost"). MSh (p. 114, see also IPM, s.v. ירט) ascribes מטחוי to the root מתח.
[140] This is justified by the observed correlation between לשכה and נשכה (Neh 13:7-8) as well as the roots נטש and לטש.
[141] Rashi (on Isa 33:19, Ps 114:1) considers both to refer to unintelligible language, whereas Reuchlin (pp. 218 and 271) treats both as "barbarous" on the basis of יעז which he views as a metathesized form of עזי.
[142] IJSh (p. 298) ascribes his recognition that the nun is a radical to the payyetanim who, he explains, based their interpretation on the Targum; see also Abraham ibn Ezra on 1 Sam 21:9 and MSh, p. 94.
[143] On Gen 41:23.
[144] QZ, p. 71.
[145] IPM, s.v. ירט (p. 27b); as is often the case, this interpretation applies also to רטה.
[146] Aaron ben Elijah on Deut 27:9.
[147] A מ-ב interchange may underlie Moses Qimḥi's interpretation of זרב as having the same meaning as זרם (on Job 6:17).
[148] AFD, 1. 281-82.
[149] Jacob ben Reuben on Prov 21:14; see also ELT, p. 39b.
[150] Naḥmanides and Jacob ben Reuben on Lam 3:16.
[151] E.g., SS, p. 167 (citing b. Pesaḥ. 7a) and Rashi on Joel 1:17 although the possibility of such an interchange is vehemently denied by Ibn Kaspi (on Joel 1:17). See also Isaiah of Trani's equation (on Job 6:17) of זרב with צרף as well as those who relate רטפש with רטב (p. 78 above).

Hapax Legomena in the Middle Ages   83

The palatals (גיכ"ק) were related in the treatments of כרסם as equivalent to rabbinic קרסם,[152] גרד as related to tannaitic קירוד,[153] and כשה as a by-form of גסה.[154]

What modern scholarship recognizes as dialectic characteristics in which originally identical sounds came to be represented by different consonants in separate Semitic languages and dialects were used to provide the basis for still more interchanges.[155] Thus Hebrew צ can appear in Aramaic as ט.[156] Having observed such correlations, Al-Fasi treated חלט as related to חלץ,[157] while Rashi seems to have taken ירט and רטה, which were generally ascribed to a common root, as equivalent to רצה.[158] The correlation of ז and ד enabled David Qimḥi and Rashi to treat זער as equivalent to דער.[159] The recognition that Hebrew שׁ may correspond to Aramaic ת explains the interpretation of חרת as related to חרש.[160] Finally, the grammatical insight that non-radical ה and ת can be equivalent is responsible for the identification of תרגל and תכה as the hifʻil of רגל and hofʻal of נכה respectively.[161]

Two last categories of interchange would today be ascribed to orthographic confusion. Rashi pointed out the close relationship of גרד to the Talmudic usage of גרר,[162] and Al-Fasi suggested that פדע may be related to פרע.[163] There are two instances of נ-מ shifts according to the

---

[152] See p. 87 below.
[153] MSh, p. 60, citing m. Beṣa 2:8.
[154] IPM, s.v. כשה (p. 31b); see SO, 1. 302 and IQR, p. 70.
[155] See pp. 24-25 above.
[156] It may also appear as ק (see p. 49 above) which may explain the correlation noted above with regard to the interchange of alphabetically adjacent letters (p. 79 above).
[157] AFD, 1. 546-52.
[158] On Num 22:32.
[159] On Job 17:1, see also the Aramaic versions cited on p. 49 above.
[160] QSh, p. 120 and AFD, 1. 581-91, although this position is rejected by Abraham ibn Ezra (on Exod 32:16) who maintains that the word is אין לו דומה (see p. 7 note 22 above).
[161] For example, IESB*, p. 302 and QG, p. 56. Ibn Ezra conjectures that the similar shapes of these two letters may be responsible for this (see p. 79 above); he also relates עות to עוה (IESB*, p. 302).
[162] Rashi on Job 2:8 noting the usage in b. Šabb. 22a, 29b, 46b, etc.; Ružička (p. 35) makes the same observation regarding this root which constitutes his only evidence for an r-d shift in Semitic.
[163] AFD, 2. 447-48.

medieval view: Saadia Gaon related נוט to מוט,[164] while Profiat Duran treated עגן as related to עגם.[165]

The effect of all these treatments is to find ways by which apparent hapax legomena are related to existing forms so that they cease to be unique, thus alleviating that widely ascribed difficulty, the lack of multiple contexts. But some words do not lend themselves to equation with other biblical forms, and for these different techniques had to be found.

HAPAX LEGOMENA EXPLAINED BY COGNATES

The most productive direction which the medievals took was to seek cognates in related languages, and what they lacked in diversity of resources they more than made up in resourceful thoroughness. Reference is made to rabbinic Hebrew, Aramaic, Arabic, and even Berber as detailed in the following list.[166]

אדב — Arabic جدب ("become emaciated") is compared by BYP, p. 28.

אנס — this root, meaning "force," occurs in Aramaic (for example, Dan 4:6, Tg. Onq. Lev 19:13) and throughout the rabbinic Hebrew as noted by SS (p. 149), IQR (pp. 16 and 51), and IJSh (p. 40).

בטה — TY (p. 51) compares שבועת בטוי ("false oath") in m. Šebu. 3:9 which is also ascribed to the root בטא.

בטל — Aramaic (Ezra 4:24) and tannaitic Hebrew (m. Ber. 2:5); cognates are widely noted (for example, MM, p. 45 and QSh, p. 39). Arabic بطل ("be corrupted") is cited by BWechter, p. 74.

בלם — Talmudic usage (for example, b. Ḥul. 89a, b. Giṭ. 67a) is noted by Isaiah of Trani (on Ps 32:9) and QG (p. 75) who mentions a related use in ספר יצירה.[167]

---

[164]SE, p. 331.

[165]PD, p. 82; see Tg. Ruth 1:13 (cited above on p. 54). Orthographic similarity is cited by Ibn Ezra as the basis for ת-ה interchange (see note 161 above), and it may also underlie Menaḥem's claim of a ת-מ interchange to justify his comparison of עתם with עֲמֵמֻהוּ in Ezek 31:8 (se MM*, p. 380).

[166]Rabbinic Hebrew was not always conceived as a separate language (see p. 10 above). Concerning Aramaic, Elijah Levita remarks: מתורגמן [Isnae: 1541] intro., p. 1).

[167]The discussions there pertain to בלימה (Job 26:7) which is also ascribed to this root (cf. MM, p. 45 and QG, p. 75); this is the case also with regard to b. Ḥul. 89a.

Hapax Legomena in the Middle Ages 85

בלט — Rashi (on Amos 7:14) compares Aramaic בלש ("search," in *Tg. Onq.* Gen 31:35, for example).
rabbinic Hebrew בלוסה ("mixed," for example *b. Šabb.* 76b) is noted by IJSh, p. 66.

בתק — Arabic اِنْبَتَق ("slaughter") is noted by IJSh, p. 81. IQR (p. 109) ascribes the meaning "split" to this word's Arabic cognate.

גרד — a rabbinic cognate is noted by SS, p. 167 and MM, p. 59 (see *b. Šabb.* 141b and *b. Roš. Haš.* 27a).[168]
Arabic לגיּרד נפסה is noted by IQR, p. 114.

דהם — Joseph Qimḥi compares Arabic مَدْهُوم (cited in QSh, p. 68).

דוץ — *Tg. Neb.* Isa 66:10 is mentioned by QSh, p. 70.

הבר — QSh (p. 76) compares Arabic أَلْهَبَرَم ("cutter").[169]

הדה — Arabic هَدَا ("take rest") is noted in BWechter, p. 79.

הדך — BWechter (pp. 55, 79) compares Arabic هتك ("rend").

הזה — *b. Ber.* 24a is cited by AFD, 1. 431.
Arabic هَاذِيَان ("sleep") is cited by QSh, p. 78; ibn Balʿam (on Isa 56:10) compares הזה.

הכר — Joseph Qimḥi (on Job 19:3) compares Arabic هكر ("be insolent") which ibn Janaḥ defines as "surprise" (IJSh, p. 118).

התת — Arabic هت الرجل means "speak too much" according to IJSh, p. 124.

זהם — cognates meaning "despise" in rabbinic Hebrew (as in *b. Ber.* 46b), Aramaic (see *Tg. Ezek.* 24:6), and Arabic are noted by IQR, pp. 31, 56, and 119.

זרב — Talmudic הזדרב ("be cold," for example, *b. Yoma* 78a) is compared by IJSh, p. 136.
rabbinic מרזב ("gutter," see *b. B. Bat.* 58b) is mentioned by QSh, p. 90; see also Naḥmanides on Job 6:17.

חטם — חוטם ("nose") is widely compared from both Hebrew and Judeo-Aramaic (as by Abraham ibn Ezra on Isa 48:9).
Hebrew and Arabic cognates meaning "bridle" are mentioned by IQR, pp. 58 and 165 (see *m. Šabb.* 5:1); BWechter (pp. 83-84) notes that خَتَمْتُ غَنْظِى means "I curbed my anger."

---

[168] For the correlation with *m. Beṣa* 2:8 see above p. 83.
[169] Note the semantic parallel of גזר in Dan 4:4 (BWechter, p. 78).

חלט — *Tg. Onq.* Lev 25:23 (חלוטין) is cited by Rashi (on 1 Kgs 20:33) and QSh (p. 104) who explains the biblical usage as "snatch speech," thus talk fast (see *Tg.* 1 Kgs 20:33).
BWechter (p. 84) compares Arabic حلط ("hurry").

חספס — mishnaic חפיסא ("wineskin") is compared by Rashi at Exod 16:14.

חפא — *Tg. Onq.* Exod 10:15 חפא ("cover") is cited by QSh, p. 113 (see IPM s.v. חפה).

חרג — *Tg. Onq.* Deut 32:25 חרגת ("fear") is compared by Rabbenu Tam in DST, p. 62 and Rashi at Ps 18:46.
Ibn Janaḥ, relying on metathesis (see the parallel 2 Sam 22:46), compares the use of חגר to translate פסח in the Targum (IJSh, pp. 143 and 168).

חרת — *Tg. Onq.* Lev 19:28 חרת ("engrave") is compared by IJSh, p. 173.
Arabic محروث ("plow") is cited by BWechter, p. 91.

חשל — Dan 2:40 חשל ("grind") is compared by MM, p. 96 and QSh, p. 122 (see *Tg. Sam*'s rendering שליטיה).

חתך — mishnaic חתיכה ("piece," found in *m. B. Meṣ.* 2:1, *m. Nid.* 3:1) is widely compared (see SS, p. 156, AFD, 1. 596-98).

טוש — *y. Taʿan.* 4:5 (p. 22a) is cited by AFD, 2. 16.
QSh (p. 126) compares *Tg. Hab.* 1:8.
Syriac (Peshiṭta 1 Kgs 10:22 ܛܘܫ) is compared by TY, p. 175.
BYP (p. 57) compares Arabic طوش ("be light-headed").

טחה — *b. Sanh.* 46a (הטיח) "shoot") is noted by Rashi at Gen 21:16.

טמה — SS (p. 158) compares tannaitic טמם ("fill up," *b. Šabb.* 73b); QSh (s.v. טמה) notes also טמיון (as in *b. Sukk.* 29b), describing the root meaning of all these forms as "close, seal."

טנף — various rabbinic usages (for example, *t. Ber.* 2:17, *b. Ber.* 24b) are compared by SS (p. 162), IQR (p. 67), IJSh (p. 181) and QSh (p. 129).

טעה — *m. Ber.* 5:3, *b. Ber.* 34a, *Tg. Onq.* Gen 21:14, *Tg. Isa* 21:4 are compared by IJSh, pp. 181-82 and QSh, p. 129.

טפש — *b. Tem.* 16a and *Tg. Isa* 6:10 and Deut 28:28 are cited to justify the meanings "fat" and "fool" by AFD, 2. 18-20 and TY, p. 185; see also IPM, s.v. טפש, IQR, p. 41, and QSh, p. 130.
Arabic طفس is noted by BYP, p. 58.

יבב — Aramaic and rabbinic use of יבבא ("shout," see *Tg. Onq.* Lev 23:24, *b. Roš. Haš.* 33b) is widely compared (as by QSh, p. 132).

Hapax Legomena in the Middle Ages 87

יזן — BWechter (p. 95) compares Arabic مُزَيَّنَة ("adorned").

יסך — m. *Yoma* 8:1 includes יסיכה in some editions, which is deemed cognate to this root by IJSh, p. 197.

ירט — Arabic الورط ("circumvent") is compared by BWechter, p. 97; IQR (p. 199) notes that ورط ("fall") may be related (see AFD, 2. 606-7).

כחל — כחל ("antinomy," see *b. Ketub.* 17a) is noted by QSh, p. 161.
an Arabic cognate (كحل — "anoint eyes with colyrium") is noted by BWechter, p. 100 and IBP, p. 142.

כמה — Rabbenu Tam compares rabbinic כמהות ("mushrooms," in DST, p. 72).[170]

כמס — IQR (p. 197) cites the Berber أكمش أفو سيك ("clench fist") in support of the meaning "bind up."[171]

כפה — various rabbinic usages of כפה are used to to derive meanings including "appease," "overturn," and "coerce" (see *m. Šabb.* 16:7 and 18:2, *b. Šabb.* 127b, *b. Giṭ.* 41b, *m. Ketub.* 7:10 and 7:20, *t. Ketub.* 5:5, *b. Qid.* 50a, cited by IJSh, p. 227,[172] IPM, p. 31a s.v. כפה, and QSh, p. 168).
Arabic نكفه ("afflicted") is noted by IJSh, p. 227.

כפש — Rashi (on Lam 3:16) and QG (p. 111) compare מדה כפושה (hence "overturn," *b. Yebam.* 107b).

כרבל — Dan 3:21 כרבלתא ("cloak") is noted by IPM, s.v. כרבל and QSh, p. 169.

כרסם — *m. Peʾa* 2:7 and *Frg. Tg. Deut* 28:38 קרסם are widely cited (for example, SS, p. 157 and DST, p. 33).

לעב — *Tg. Onq. Gen* 27:12 and *Tg.* 2 Chr 36:16 are cited by IJSh, p. 246 and QSh, p. 182.
IQR (p. 129) notes an Arabic cognate لعب ("jest").

לעז — SS (p. 169), IJSh (p. 246), and QSh (p. 182) compare rabbinic usage in *m. Meg.* 2:1, 8, *b. Meg.* 17a and 18a which they explain as "speak a foreign tongue" or "speak poorly, stutter."
Arabic لغز ("defame") is noted by IQR, p. 169.

---

[170]See p. 63 above.
[171]Judah ibn Quraish, רשאלה, ed. J. J. L. Barges and D. B. Goldberg (Paris: B. Duprat and D. Maisonneuve, 1857) 121.
[172]Or "suffer" as he interprets the usage in *b. Pesaḥ.* 112b.

לעט — rabbinic לעט ("eat fast" as in *m. Šabb.* 24:3, *b. Šabb.* 155b) is noted by IJSh, p. 240, Rashi on Gen 25:30, David Qimḥi on Gen 25:30, and QSh, p. 182.

מהל — the homographic Aramaic form of Hebrew מול ("circumcise") is cited by AFD, 2. 190-91 (noting *Tg. Onq.* Exod 4:25), MEB, p. 45, and Joseph ibn Kaspi on Isa 1:22 (as well as a Syriac usage).
Solomon ibn Parḥon (on Isa 1:22) compares the Arabic مهل ("mix").

מוק — מקק(*m. Ketub.* 7:10 and *b. Ketub.* 77a, hence "melt with words") is widely noted (as by IJSh p. 260 and Jacob ben Reuben on Ps 73:8).

מחק — rabbinic מחק ("remove," see *b. B. Bat.* 89a) is noted by IPM, s.v. מחק and MSh, p. 88.

נבח — IJSh (p. 280) and QG (p. 121) compare the Targum's use of a cognate for this passage.
Abraham ibn Ezra (on Isa 56:10) and BWechter (p. 103) compare Arabic نبح.

נלה — Arabic نال ("achieve") is cited by AFD, 2. 273 (see QMChomsky, p. 334).

סאסא — Arabic سوا ("be uniform, the same") is compared by BWechter, p. 104.

סכת — SE (p. 367) mentions an opinion comparing אסתכי ("look") in *Tg. Onq.* Deut 26:15.
Arabic أسكى ("keep quiet") is noted by BWechter, p. 166.

סלד — *b. Giṭ.* 57b (ביצה סולדת) is noted by MM, p. 127.

סלק — Dan 6:24 and *Tg.* Isa 14:13 are noted by IJSh, p. 309 and IQR, p. 685; see also AFD, 2. 347.

סמן — tannaitic סימן is considered cognate by all medievals, beginning with Saadia (SE, p. 155, see *m. B. Meṣ.* 2:7) and Al-Fasi (AFD, 2. 331-33).[173]

סעה — *Tg.* 2 Sam 2:25 and *b. Šabb.* 13b (סיעה) are noted by ELT, p. 57.

עבש — Arabic عبس ("dry, shrivel") is compared by AFD, 2. 360-65, IJSh, p. 352, and BYP, p. 76.

---

[173]David Qimḥi (on Isa 28:25) supports this view with what he construes to be the semantic parallel חטה שורה in the same verse.

Hapax Legomena in the Middle Ages 89

עגם — *m. Meg.* 4:4 עגמת נפש is noted by QSh, p. 251 and Moses Qimḥi on Job 30:25.

עגן — עגונה ("deserted wife," e.g. *b. Giṭ.* 3a) was compared already by SS, p. 159; QSh (p. 250) notes also עוגין ("anchor").
עוגיה (*m. Moʿed Qaṭ.* 1:1) is compared by IJSh, p. 353.

עות — Arabic غتّ is noted by BWechter (p. 58)[174] who explains the meaning as "talk incessantly" and by ibn Balʿam (on Isa 50:4) with the meaning "instruct."
Aramaic כענת is noted by Jacob ben Reuben (on Isa 50:4) to justify his interpretation of the form as derived from the root ענה.

עזק — the meaning "dig" is justified on the basis of rabbinic usage in *m. Ohol.* 18:5 and *b. Menaḥ.* 85b (Maimonides on *m. Ohol.* 18:5 and Solomon ibn Parḥon on Isa 5:2).
Aramaic עזקא ("ring") is widely compared (for example, QSh, p. 260).
Arabic عزق ("dig earth") is also compared by IQR (p. 136), BWechter (p. 111), and Maimonides (on *m. Ohol.* 18:5).

עלע — citing Aramaic עלע ("rib"), ibn Ezra and Moses Qimḥi (on Job 39:30) explain this verb as meaning "break rib."

ערר — QSh (p. 257) compares ערער ("break") in *m. Soṭa* 3:3.

עשק — citing *m. ʾAbot* 4:10, AFD (2. 413-15) explains this word as "circle."
rabbinic עסק ("trouble," as in *b. B. Qam.* 9a, *b. Šebu.* 31a) is related to this by ibn Ezra and David Qimḥi (on Gen 26:20) and QSh, p. 282).

עתם — Arabic عتم ("dark") is widely compared (as by ibn Ezra on Isa 9:18 and BWechter, p. 113).

פון — Arabic فينة is cited by IJSh (p. 397) to justify the meaning "at every time"; BWechter (p. 71) also compares فنيت ("perish").

פנק — SS (p. 149) compares פנק ("delicate," *Mek.* משפטים 8 end; see also Jacob ben Reuben on Prov 29:21).
Tg. Onq. Gen 49:20 תפנק ("delight") is widely cited (for example, MM, p. 143).

פצם — *m. Šabb.* 8:7 פצים ("board") is compared by SS, p. 169.
Tg. Jer 22:14 is noted by QG, p. 141 (see Rashi on Ps 60:4).
Arabic אפצים ("idol") is noted by AFD, 2. 474 and Dunash ben Labraṭ (cited by Rashi at Ps 60:4).

---

[174] Hebrew final weak verbs are compared to Arabic geminates.

פשח — b. B. Bat. 54a and m. Šeb. 4:6 פשח ("split") are cited by Rashi at Lam 3:11 and Maimonides on m. Šeb. 4:6.
Tg. 1 Sam 15:33 פשח is noted also by Rashi on Lam 3:11.[175]
Arabic فسك is compared by IJSh, p. 415.

צבט — m. Ḥag. 3:1 בית צביטה ("handle") is cited by MM, p. 148 and QSh, p. 306.
Joseph Qimḥi compares Arabic ضبط ("grasp," cited in QSh, p. 306).

צנם — b. Ber. 39a פת צנומא is noted by IJSh (p. 433) and QG (p. 145) to justify the meaning "small, thin."
b. B. Bat. 18a and 89b צונמא ("rock") is noted by Rashi (on Gen 41:23) who, relying on the Targum's rendering, interprets this word as "dry" (see QSh, p. 315).

צעו — Arabic ظغن ("be moved") is noted by ibn Balᶜam (on Isa 33:20, see also Saadia's translation of Isa 33:20).

צפד — mishnaic צפודה is interpreted by Al-Fasi as supporting the meaning "cling" (AFD, 2. 521-23, see QSh, p. 316).[176]

קוש — IJSh (p. 446) and ibn Balᶜam (on Isa 29:21) ascribe the form to the same root as rabbinic קושי (as in m. Nid. 4:6), קושיא, and other forms of קשה.

קסס — m. B. Bat. 6:2 קסס ("sour") is noted by SS, p. 167.
Arabic وقس is compared by IJSh, p. 450.

רהה — Arabic تورّه ("be unskilled") is noted by BWechter, p. 117.

רזם — universally considered a form of רמז, this verb is related to rabbinic, Aramaic, and Arabic verbs (IQR, pp. 91 and 149, BWechter, p. 118, QSh p. 350) with specific citations to m. Giṭ. 5:7, b. B. Qam. 24b, Tg. Prov 10:10, Tg. Hos 3:5.

רטה — t. Dem. 1:25 רטיה ("plaster") is related according to an opinion mentioned by MSh, p. 154.
Arabic ورط ("hurl into abyss," cf. وَرْطة "abyss") is compared by IQR, p. 200 and BWechter, p. 97; see Saadia on Job 16:11.

רטפש — b. Ḥul. 49b טרפש ("pericardium"?) is noted by TY (p. 188) who cites also the usage by Maimonides (הלכות שחיטה 6:10).

רנה — Arabic رنّ ("twang bow") is mentioned by BWechter, p. 59.

---

[175] IJSh (p. 415) translates this as "plunder."
[176] The word is in fact not attested, regarding which see S. Skoss in AFD, 1. lv-lvi.

Hapax Legomena in the Middle Ages 91

רפף — rabbinic usage of רפפות, רפרף and הריף עין are widely cited in support of the meaning "shake" (as by Hai Gaon according to IJSh, p. 475 and QSh, p. 349).[177]
Arabic رفرف ("flutter") is noted by BYP, p. 90.

רפק — Gersonides (on Cant 8:5) notes the rabbinic מרפק ("elbow").
Arabic رفق is used to justify the meaning "friend" by QSh (p. 358) and "join" by IJSh (p. 484, see also Rashi and ibn Ezra on Cant 8:5); BWechter (p. 121) compares مُترَفِّقة to derive the meaning "act gently."

רצד — Arabic رصد ("hope") is noted by Hai Gaon (cited in QSh, pp. 358-59, see D. Qimhi on Ps 68:17); BWechter (p. 121) notes that ترتصدون means "lie in wait."

רשם — cognates in Dan 6:9, 13, 5:25 and Tg. Ezek 9:4 and Tg. Onq. Lev 19:28 are noted by MM, p. 167 and Elijah Levita in QSh, p. 440. QSh (p. 361) implies that the occurrence in Dan 10:21 is an Aramaism.
Arabic رسم ("write") is cited by BYP, p. 95.

שוח — IBP (p. 144) refers to an Arabic cognate which means "walk among trees."

שחט — b. Šabb. 22b and 143b סחט ("squeeze") is compared by Rashi at Gen 40:11 and several others.

שקד — SS (p. 167) cites a cognate (סקדא) in b. B. Qam. 22a;[178] Rashi compares מסקדא ("goad") in Pesiq. Rab. Kah. 153a to derive the meaning "teach" (at Lam 1:14).

שקר — comparing rabbinic סקר ("paint eyes," "look around"), Rashi, ibn Ezra (on Isa 3:16), and David Qimḥi (QSh, p. 404) note appropriate meanings; IJSh (p. 534) suggests the derived meaning "shine." David Qimḥi (on Isa 3:16) cites Tg. Job 30:9 in support of a possible meaning "wink" or "nod."

ששא — AFD (2. 710) compares Arabic شوش ("confuse").

תזז — m. Ḥul. 2:3 התיז ("remove") is cited by SS, p. 165.

---

[177] Yeḥiel Altschuler (on Job 26:11) compares מתרפין in Tg. Job 9:6.
[178] Saadia cites b. B. Qam. 22a as reading כלבא בסיקדא וגדיא בסירכא whereas our editions have בזקירא in place of his proposed cognate. Louis Ginzberg ("Beiträge zur Lexicographie des Jüdisch Aramäischen II," MGWJ 78 [1934] 30) accepts Saadia's reading which he regards as a secondary formation from עקד ("bind") meaning "dance."

תרגל — Arabic ترجل ("put onto feet") is compared by Yapheth ben Ali (in Hartwig Hirschfeld, *Literary History of Hebrew Grammarians and Lexicographers* [London: Oxford University Press, 1926] 34 and 104).

תרגם — *Tg. Onq.* Gen 42:33 and Exod 4:16 are cited by ELT (p. 92a) to support his interpretation "explain."

From this sampling of comparative material, included here because of its relevance to hapax legomena, there can be little doubt as to the deep roots of the now common philological method. For the medievals it was but an extension of their concern to find forms related to biblical words in as close a body of material as possible. To a large extent this was achieved from within the Bible itself. Where this was insufficient, the search was extended to rabbinic Hebrew, Aramaic, Arabic, and beyond. Unanimity was not always achieved, either with respect to a word's meaning or its etymology. The final arbiter was always context, requiring inevitably subjective judgment.[179]

מלין אשר אין להם דמיון

There remain words for which no cognates were known. These are cases in which the exegete stated without qualification אין לו דומה, and it is to these that Menaḥem alluded when he emphasized the importance of context.[180]

One source for such support may derive from an analysis of similar contexts.[181] This method was applied already to words with known etymologies. האריך אף parallels חטם (Isa 48:9) which was commonly related to the Aramaic and rabbinic חוטם ("nose"),[182] so that it was not a difficult inference to suggest that it may be used in a manner similar to that preceding phrase. The semantic development of חתך from its known meaning "cut"[183] to "decide, determine" is analogous to that of גזר.[184]

---

[179] See David Yellin, תולדות התפתחות הדקדוק העברי, 39 and p. 8 above.

[180] See p. 6 above.

[181] For a modern example of the use of parallel semantic fields see pp. 13-14, note 51 above.

[182] See p. 85 above.

[183] See p. 86 above.

[184] MM, p. 96; for a similar semantic development in Latin see pp. 13-14 note 51 above.

Hapax Legomena in the Middle Ages   93

This method was applied also to words whose backgrounds were obscure. On the basis of the Arabic هبر ("cut"), ibn Barun connected הברי שמים (Isa 47:13), which refers to astrologers, with גזרין in Dan 2:27.[185] The isolated צפד was explained by several authorities on the basis of the similar usage of דבק in Ps 102:6, thus effectively creating a parallel passage to illustrate a difficult verse.[186]

For those situations in which no additional information was available regarding a particular word, the medievals had either to infer the appropriate contextual meaning or rely on the interpretation of another authority. For them, as for modern scholars, the ancient versions offered advantages of perspective and authority. Ancient translators may have known the biblically rare word from contemporary usage; they certainly had better access to an early tradition of its meaning.

As with cognates, the modern variety of resources relating to ancient versions was not available to medieval authorities; however, the Targum was widely used.[187] Occasionally this approach is reflected in an interpretation that differs from the more prevalent view. Joseph Qara and David Al-Fasi rely on the Targum's interpretation of יבב being the same as is used elsewhere for השקיף,[188] and ibn Janaḥ treats עוש as "gather" on the basis of the Targum.[189]

---

[185] BWechter, p. 78.
[186] IJSh, p. 435, IJR, p. 315.
[187] Reuchlin (pp. 133 and 245) does note both LXX and Vg., and even Sym. Interestingly, MSh (s.v. דהם) observes the similarity of נדהם to נרדם as a basis for his suggested interpretation "sleep," an interpretation close to that of many moderns for explaining the LXX reading (see also IPM, p. 14b s.v. דהם and p. 48 above).
[188] Joseph Qara on Judg 5:28 and AFD 2. 37; they may also rely on comparison with בבה (see p. 74 above).
[189] IJSh (p. 361). QSh (p. 258) provides the necessary etymology by comparing the verb with עש (Job 4:19, 9:9) "constellation," which is explained as a *gathering* of stars. Other interpretations based on the Targum are: Saadia for שחט (SE and commentary); AFD, s.v. שסף and שחט; Maimonides for שסף (on m. Šeb. 4:6); IJSh, s.v. הזה, חלט, עוש, עשק, עתם, and שסף; Rashi for בתק, הדה, כמס, כסס, נחץ, עשק, סכת, שפן, שאס, and שסף; Solomon ibn Parḥon for עתם and שקר, and IPM s.v. חלט and שסף; QG (p. 36, no. 76) for דגה; David Qimḥi for בתק, הלא, סלק, שתר, שסף, and ששא and QSh s.v. עוש, שסף, and ששא; Samuel ben Meir for טחח and שחט; BHT (p. 141) for יזם; MSh, s.v. חלט; OM for בתק, חלט, כמה, מלץ, נחץ, שנס, רזם, צפד, פדע, עוש, and שסף. See also Yeḥiel Altschuler for אלץ, בתק, and נחץ; Elijah Levita (in QSh, p. 424) for אלץ; Reuchlin, s.v. חלט;

A similar appeal to authority is to be understood in those interpretations which rely on rabbinic interpretations. Since such traditions may be long-lived and similar meanings can be provided by different exegetical methods, it is not always clear when there is complete reliance on rabbinic sources. The best indication is the exegete's own statement; other clear evidence can be found in the reliance on a typically rabbinic method applied exactly as it is known to have been used from earlier sources.[190]

The final resort is to context alone. It is this above all else which characterizes the treatment of a word for which it is literally true that אין לו דומה, and not just for Menaḥem but most, if not all medieval exegetes.[191] The following treatments are presented as derived from context.

אבך — become thick (Saadia on Isa 9:17)
    rise (for example, IJSh, p. 10, OM, p. 254, ibn Ezra on Isa 9:17)
    be proud (David Qimḥi on Isa 9:17 and QSh, p. 2)
    destroy, detest (IKSh, pp. 6-7)[192]

אלץ — bother, press (Judah ibn Balʿam on Judg 16:16)

בלס — shake (MM, p. 45, IJSh, p. 66)
    work with (Isaiah of Trani on Amos 7:14)
    dwell ("in shadows"; Eliezer of Beaugency on Amos 7:14)

בשס — bother (IJSh, p. 80)

בתק — thrust (MM*, p. 384)
    pierce (Eliezer of Beaugency on Ezek 16:40)
    cut (Isaiah of Trani on Ezek 16:40)

גרד — peel (MM, p. 58)

---

and MEB (p. 52) for הזה. Unspecified references are to the appropriate comment (see Appendix IV for biblical citations) or the appropriate entry in dictionary-format works.

[190] See Rashi on Gen 21:16, 48:16, and Isa 1:22; PD, p. 123 and ELB, p. 516 regarding פרשז, and virtually all exegetes regarding סאסא. Equally obvious, though non-explicit reliance can be seen in Rashi and Joseph Bechor Shor's reference to *notarikon* in dealing with ירט (on Num 22:32), see p. 68 above.

[191] Thus אין לו דומה ופתרונו לפי מקומו.

[192] See Eliezar of Beaugency (on Isa 9:17) who takes it as a privative of בכא, that is, "destroy the בכא tree" (p. 76 above).

דהם — weak (MM, p. 62 and Isaiah of Trani on Jer 14:9)[193]

הבר — astrologer (Eliezer of Beaugency on Isa 47:13)

הדה — extend (Isaiah of Trani on Isa 11:8)

הדך — tread (Zeraḥyah ben Yiṣḥaq on Job 40:12)

הזה — sleep (DST, p. 24, no. 32)

הלא — fat (Joseph Qimḥi cited in QSh, p. 80)

זהם — despise (MM, p. 78)

זער — cut (MM, p. 80 and Isaiah of Trani on Job 17:1)

זרב — be hot (MM, p. 83 and Moses Gikatilla according to QG, p. 93)

חטם — forgive (MM, p. 86, Eliezer of Beaugency on Isa 48:9)

חלט — snatch (MM, p. 88)

חספס — scattered (Samuel ben Meir on Exod 16:14)

חפא — deceive (Rashi on 2 Kgs 17:9)

חרג — weakly girded (MM, p. 94)

חתך — cut, decide (MM, p. 96)

טוש — fly (Abraham ibn Ezra on Job 9:26)
hurry (Zeraḥyah ben Yiṣḥaq on Job 9:26)[194]

טפש — fat (MM, p. 99)

יאב — desire (for example, IJSh, p. 186; David Qimḥi and Isaiah of Trani on Ps 119:131)

כמה — melt (MM, p. 106)[195]
(DST, p. 72, no. 113; Isaiah of Trani on Ps 63:2)

כמס — seal (MM, p. 106, Aaron ben Elijah on Deut 32:34)

---

[193]Yeḥiel Altschuler (on Jer 14:9) derives the meaning "be afraid" from this word's context.
[194]See *Tg.* Hab. 1:8.
[195]The text of Menaḥem's comment is not certain. Filipowski notes that readings include תמס, תמה, and תאב, although he prefers חמס; Dunash cites it as תמס (DST, p. 72).

כפש — invade (MM, p. 109)
   be dirty (Isaiah of Trani on Lam 3:16)

כשה — be fat (Saadia Gaon on Deut 32:15)

לעט — eat a little (Aaron ben Elijah on Gen 25:30)

מהל — mix (MM, p. 115)

מלץ — sweet (Isaiah of Trani on Ps 119:103)

נוט — shake (IJSh, p. 292)[196]

נלה — finish (Rashi on Isa 33:1)

סכת — receive (IJSh, p. 339)[197]
   listen (David Qimḥi on Deut 27:9)

סעה — stir up (QSh, p. 242)
   blow (Isaiah of Trani on Ps 55:9)

סרף — maternal uncle (QSh, p. 246 and Joseph ibn Kaspi on Amos 6:10; see IJSh, p. 134 and ibn Balʿam on Amos 6:20)[198]

עבש — contain (MM*, p. 189)

עגם — worry (Abraham ibn Ezra on Job 30:25)

עוש — hurry (MM, p. 139)

עות — teach (DST, p. 79, no. 130)

עזק — clear (MM, p. 132)
   hoe (Eliezer of Beaugency on Isa 5:2)

עלע — eat (Joseph Qara on Job 39:30)

---

[196]This interpretation applies only if הארץ is the subject in which case ibn Janaḥ compares Ps 60:4 (see p. 8 above).

[197]At issue is the logical sequence of סכת and שמע —whether one can obey before having heard or whether the syntactic sequence must be the logical order.

[198]Although Ibn Ezra (on Amos 6:10) rejects this interpretation as without basis, B. Felsenthal ("Zur Bibel und Grammatik," *Semitic Studies in Memory of Rev. Dr. Alexander Kohut* [Berlin: S. Calvary, 1897] 135-36) suggests that ibn Quraish from whom it derived may have based it on cognates (see pp. 142-43 below).

Hapax Legomena in the Middle Ages 97

עטם — dark (MM*, p. 380, Isaiah of Trani on Isa 9:18)
fall (Eliezer of Beaugency on Isa 9:18)

פדע — save (MM, p. 141)

פצם — destroy (MM*, pp. 400-402)

פרשז — pour (MM, p. 146)
spread (Isaiah of Trani on Job 26:9, see also Zeraḥyah ben Yiṣḥaq on Job 26:9)

צבט — reach (MM*, p. 402)

צנם — dry (MM*, p. 412)
hard (Samuel ben Meir on Gen 41:23)
cut (Aaron ben Elijah on Gen 41:23)

צען — move (Isaiah of Trani and Jacob ben Reuben on Isa 33:20)

צפד — black (MM, p. 151, MM*, p. 402)
cling (DST, p. 92, no 147; Isaiah of Trani and others on Lam 4:8)

קסס — cut (MM, p. 156, Isaiah of Trani on Ezek 17:9)

רהה — fear (Rashi and David Qimḥi on Isa 44:8)

רטה — appease (Isaiah of Trani on Job 16:11)[199]

רטפש — soften (OM, p. 259; see ELT, p. 28a)

רפק — long (QSh, p. 358, see Gersonides on Cant 8:5)

רצד — be jealous (Isaiah of Trani on Ps 68:17)
lower yourselves (QSh, pp. 358-59)
choose (IPM, s.v. רצד)

שפן — hide (Abraham ibn Ezra on Deut 33:19 and OM, p. 186)

שקד — bind (MM, p. 180)
see (Isaiah of Trani on Lam 1:14)

שקר — look, wink (MM, p. 180, Isaiah of Trani on Isa 3:16)

שנס — gird (MM, p. 177)

---

[199]Since this word and ירט (Num 22:32) are regularly ascribed to the same root, this is actually a case of determining the meaning of a dislegomenon according to its contexts.

ששא — destroy (QSh, p. 362)
seduce, mislead (Isaiah of Trani on Ezek 39:2)

תזז — throw (MM, p. 184)

תכה — cling (OM, p. 52)

Because the authorities here cited considered these words to be the purest hapax legomena, lacking additional attestation even in related or cognate forms, these treatments permit us to see the methods of biblical scholarship as applied to extreme cases.[200] It is obvious that some words were so difficult to understand that a whole array of meanings was offered; אבך and בלס are extreme examples of this. But other words were understood by those who used context in a way that is virtually identical to that achieved by those who cited related forms or words. Thus there is little diversity of interpretation for the word בתק while Menaḥem's treatment of זהם, זרב, חטט, טפש, מהל, עתם, פדע, and צבט, ibn Ezra's rendering of טוש, David Qimḥi's of יאב, and Isaiah of Trani's interpretation of עתם and פרשז are identical with those derived from contemporary data. In several cases these exegetes seem to have been aware of the same material as their "colleagues," but found it inadequate, presumably on philological grounds.[201] Moses Gikatilla defined זרב as צרב, Menaḥem defined עוש with חוש, Isaiah of Trani defined פרשז with פרש, and he and Menaḥem defined קסס with קצץ although none seems to accept these pairs as having a common origin as others had claimed. The difference is therefore based not on ignorance of other interpretations or a rejection of their conclusions, but the inability to accept the underlying logic. This explains also the occasional comments rejecting alternative interpretations with the assertion that אין לו דומה, followed by a contextual interpretation which need not differ substantially from the views previously cited.

Context alone is not, of course, always sufficient to ensure a complete understanding of isolated words. Alongside cases such as בתק and שנס which seem clearly understood, one can note others in which the correct nuance of a word was lost as a result of inadequate data. Cohen has pointed out that כמס has a root meaning of "gather,"[202] although this is

---

[200] See pp. 6-9 above.

[201] Recall those instances in which a medieval exegete listed interpretations (usually etymologies) he could not accept, concluding as a result that for the word in question אין לו דומה (p. 7 above).

[202] Cohen p. 39; this observation is based on the Akkadian cognate, which was obviously not available to the medievals.

hardly crucial for understanding its biblical occurrence, even if it does add a further dimension to the word itself. While Aaron ben Elijah recognized the basic thrust of לעט ("eat"), his not using rabbinic parallels led to understanding the passage as meaning "eat a little" when the opposite was more commonly accepted.[203] The "debate" between ibn Janaḥ and David Qimḥi as to whether סכת means "receive" or "listen" may have little ultimate impact, but this ambiguity too can be traced to the lack of external data. Even Joseph Qimḥi's treatment of עלע as simply "eat" seems somewhat colorless in comparison with לוע. Finally, one must examine סרף. Comparative philology led to a purported link with שרף and the translation "burn." Recognized as a parallel to דוד, it was explained as meaning "maternal uncle." Ultimately these two views were reconciled by Jacob ben Reuben who explained that it is this relative who ישרף לבם עליו.[204]

It should be noted that there are many words considered hapax legomena and therefore to be interpreted according to context for which the result of this interpretation is not given by the exegete.[205] Perhaps the contextual significance was felt to be so obvious as not to need stating, or the dictionaries and commentaries in which these observations occur were deemed inappropriate for such speculation. Most likely, however, contextual interpretations were left to the individual and possibly even recognized as inadequately precise to merit stating. If so, this further illustrates the point that hapax legomena were not deemed an actual class of words but simply those for which the tools of biblical exegesis were inadequate and the interpretation of which was therefore left in abeyance.

It must be noted in conclusion that some interpretations from this period are surprisingly prescient. Although the medievals did not propose emendations as such, they did suggest that the text should not always be understood as written, arguing contextually for the interpretation of a word as if it were another, similar form.[206] The widespread comparison

---

[203] See p. 88 above.
[204] On Amos 6:10.
[205] For example, Joseph ibn Kaspi on Amos 5:11, Eliezer of Beaugency on Isa 11:8, Joseph Becher Shor on Exod 16:14, and Moses Qimḥi and Abraham ibn Ezra on Job 17:1.
[206] Note especially the principle of substitution (IJR, pp. 307-35); see the general discussion of this problem by Nahum Sarna, "Hebrew and Bible Studies in Medieval Spain," *The Sephardi Heritage* (ed. R. D. Barnett; New York: Ktav, 1971) 1. 347-48 and p. 79 above.

of תאב to יאב (Ps 119:174), Menaḥem's reference to הדוש regarding אדש, Rashi's mention of ככלותך when dealing with נלה, David Qimḥi's reference to תיראו for רהה —all these interpretations correspond to readings found in the Qumran scrolls.[207] Even those medieval authorities who did not accept the probability of certain interchanges often relied on similar interpretations.

There is no evidence that hapax legomena were treated differently from other words during this period.[208] Criteria of context, cognate and related biblical forms were applied to all words. For those adjudged to be hapax legomena by the medievals themselves, fewer of these tools were available. Context was necessarily the ultimate criterion. Alone it often seems adequate for a clear, if incomplete understanding of rare words; but there are cases for which it cannot suffice.

Generalizations as to the difficulty of interpretation of hapax legomena are simply not supported by the facts. While diversity of opinion has been obvious, as it might for many more common words, consensus can also be frequently found. Even where different methods were applied, similar results seem often to have emerged. The experience of the medievals offers littls support for any effort to isolate hapax legomena as a unique class of words.

---

[207] See the relevant discussion in chapter VII. This is not to claim that the medievals had access to such texts, but that their philologically-based interpretions correspond to Qumran readings.

[208] The fact that many words which receive special attention are hapax legomena is not equivalent to the assertion (here denied) that all hapax legomena require such attention. This probably explains Allony's observation that such studies often deal with the same words (see p. 9 note 32 above).

7

The Treatment of Hapax Legomena in Contemporary Scholarship

Although generally less tolerant of perceived peculiarities in the received text than earlier exegetes and blessed with a greater array of resources with which to evaluate difficult forms, modern scholarship has not created new techniques for the evaluation of hapax legomena. The basic goal remain the same—to find, wherever possible, a way in which to equate rare words with other, known terms; and the primary methods—metathesis, cognates, consonantal shift (however explained), and the like — are those already described. Indeed, many modern interpretations can be traced back to the views of earlier, most often medieval exegetes.[1]

There is little reason therefore to restate the basic approaches employed. Instead a discussion of the solutions proposed for the words here studied now follows, accompanied by observations where relevant.[2] The methods and conclusions of research into these words are presented in the concluding chapter.

אבך **(Isa 9:17)**

BHK emends ויתאבכו to ויתאכלו on the basis of the Septuagint's συγκαταφαγεται. There is, however, no support for such a reading; the root אכל is not attested in the hitpaᶜel even once throughout the Bible, while συγκατεσθω occurs nowhere else in the Septuagint. Many have noted the similarity of התהפך with respect to both form and meaning; there is,

---

[1]For treatment of earlier interpretations see references listed in Appendix IV.

[2]Since our primary concern is historical, the exegetes who cite a particular cognate are here noted rather than sources for the cognate itself although such sources have been sought and pertinent observations provided where relevant.

however, no need for emendation.³ Driver compares the similar meaning of Akkadian *abâku*, Aramaic אפך and Arabic أفك, arguing that Hebrew evolved two forms from the same original root.⁴ With such etymological support for the word's contextual meaning "whirl up," Duhm's assumption of a nonce form is unnecessary,⁵ although Isaiah's choice of an existing word may have been influenced by its assonance with the nearby סבך.

אדב (1 Sam 2:33)

This passage cannot be understood apart from the parallel phrases in Lev 26:16 and Deut 28:65 which use forms of דוב and דאב respectively.⁶ In light of the semantic parallels, these three roots must be related. Some would emend ולאדיב to yield a form of דאב, as through metathesis of the א;⁷ others prefer a reading based on דוב, itself possibly related to דאב,⁸ in which case the *aleph* would be prosthetic.⁹ Whether related to דוב or even a corruption of דאב,¹⁰ אדב can hardly be considered a truly isolated usage; the meaning "languish" is not in question.¹¹

---

³Against T. K. Cheyne, SBOT on Isa 9:17.

⁴G. R. Driver, "Some Hebrew Words," *JTS* 29 (1928) 390ff. הפך would correspond more directly to Aramaic אפך and Arabic أفك. Driver translates the biblical form as "and they are carried away as in. . . ." Some relationship with בוך also seems likely, but there is no evidence to include אבק in this group as proposed by Otto Procksch (KAT on Isa 9:17) and others.

⁵Bernard Duhm in HKAT on Isa 9:17.

⁶See also Jer 31:24 and Sir 4:1.

⁷For example, H. P. Smith in ICC on 1 Sam 2:33.

⁸Thus H. Wiener, "The Text of 1 Samuel II 33," *JPOS* 8 (1928) 63.

⁹Barth p. 73; compare אָדֹשׁ (Isa 28:28) and the use of *aleph* as a prefix for the causative conjugation in Aramaic.

¹⁰There is no evidence that this form is corrupt.

¹¹The Bible does reflect a root אדב in the proper name אדבאל (Gen 25:13) which is usually explained by the Arabic أذب ("invite," see Lane p. 34), but this does not suit the passage here treated. Akkadian *adâbu* ("bind, oppress") will not serve to explain the other passages noted (against G. R. Driver, "Some Hebrew Roots and their Meanings," *JTS* 23 [1922] 70). The same must be said for the seeming Ugaritic root ᵓdb (implied in CTA 14.8, see also line 24), which is usually emended to ᵓbd. According to Mandelkern (p. 11) there are those who would emend אדב similarly.

אדש (Isa 28:28)

Although some see אדש as a by-form of דוש,[12] Bergstrasser argues that infinitive absolutes of one verb are not coupled with finite forms of another, even related root.[13] The absence of evidence for a root אדש meaning "thresh" in post-biblical Hebrew coupled with the fact that modern Hebrew has taken over a distinct root אדש ("be quiet") from Aramaic—an unlikely development were a root אדש available within the Hebrew vocabulary—reinforces the notion held since antiquity that this should be derived from דוש. Many suggest the elimination of this form altogether[14] or that it be modified to some form of דוש.[15] Most, however, ascribe the *aleph* to a specialized infinitive pattern. Barth sees it as an infinitive for the hif'il of middle weak verbs, comparing the Aramaic 'af'el infinitive pattern אֲקָמָא.[16] Although there is precedent for an infinitive absolute's being used with finite forms of a different conjugation,[17] there is no other biblical evidence for a hif'il of דוש. This, coupled with the apparent lack of a subject for the following finite verb (ידושנו) led Luzzatto to see אדוש as a noun of agent on the pattern of אדון.[18]

אלץ (Judg 16:16)

There is no question as to the meaning of this root. Contextually paralleled by הציק, it is well-known from throughout Aramaic to mean

---

[12]DP, p. 188; F. Böttcher (*Ausführliches Lehrbuch der hebräischen Sprache* [Leipzig: Johannes Ambrosius Barth, 1868] 227) explains it as emphatic lengthening.

[13]GKB 2. 64.

[14]Thus T. K. Cheyne, SBOT on Isa 28:28.

[15]RG on Isa 28:28; see 1QIsa^a הדש.

[16]Barth p. 73, where he compares אסף (Jer 8:13, Zeph 1:2). E. Hammershaimb ("On the so-called *infinitivus absolutus* in Hebrew," in *Hebrew and Semitic Studies Presented to Godfrey Rolles Driver* [Oxford: Clarendon Press, 1963] 85) remarks in another context that "one can expect to find nominal types which, sporadically, may adopt infinitive functions."

[17]See Lev 19:20, Jer 51:58; most such cases involve the qal infinitive which GKB (pp. 63-64) ascribes to the relative antiquity of that form as compared to the infinitive absolute of other conjugations.

[18]On Isa 28:28; Procksch (KAT on Isa 28:28) proposes reading אָנוֹשׁ.

"press, urge."[19] For just this reason Tur-Sinai rejects the word's authenticity, arguing that Aramaisms are possible only in late Hebrew and proposing instead a form of the similar-meaning אוץ.[20] His assumption that rare forms are inauthentic is without basis, while many other "Aramaisms" are to be found in early Hebrew texts.

אנס (Esth 1:8)

This word, meaning "compel," is well-known from later Hebrew as well as Aramaic, although its implication is this passage has not met with consensus.[21] Guillaume's comparison with Arabic نس ("urge") is thus unnecessary.[22] The word is well-attested in Aramaic and in the Hebrew of Ben Sirah and the Damascus Document.[23] While these facts alone are insufficient to prove an Aramaism, the word's isolated occurrence in a late biblical text makes such a conclusion probable.[24]

בטה (Prov 12:18)

On the basis of the contextual reference to speech and acknowledged cases in which final ה and א forms are used interchangeably, this is almost universally equated with the root בטא as meaning "speak (rashly)."[25]

---

[19] Cognates cited in KB; see G. F. Moore, ICC on Judg 16:16.
[20] TSPM on Judg 16:16.
[21] The issue is whether the people were not forced to drink (thus, L. Paton, ICC on Esth 1:8) or not restricted from drinking (TSPM at Esth 1:8, where he compares Dan 14:6). The use of an active participle suggests the former although G. Gerleman (BKAT on Esth 1:8) would read the nominal אָנָה.
[22] GHAL 1. 6.
[23] It is identified with הנס in the ZKR and Nerab inscriptions by J. Barth ("Zur altaramäischen Inschrift des Königs Zkr," OLZ 12 [1909] 11) although this interpretation is not commonly accepted (see KAI 2. 210 and 275). See Sir 20:4, 34:21, and CD 16:13.
[24] G. Wildeboer, KHC on Esth 1:8. Kautzsch's claim (p. 22) that a pure Hebrew root with this meaning would have occurred more often is an argument from silence (see Wagner p. 27).
[25] For example, C. H. Toy, ICC on Prov 12:18. בטא is used for oaths in Lev 5:4 and Num 30:7-9, regarding which see A. Ahuviah, "כל אשר יבטא האדם - שבועה," BM 28 (1983) 107-10. HALAT (s.v. בטא) notes a possible relation with בדא.

Some manuscripts actually read בוטא at this point.[26] Forms of this root with final ה occur as early as Ben Sirah.[27] This is the root's only biblical occurrence in the qal which may account for the atypical form, although בטא is not common enough to permit any well-based conclusions.

בטל (Qoh 12:3)

Well-known from Aramaic and rabbinic sources, this root is attested also in Arabic, Ethiopic, and Akkadian.[28] It is hard to be certain that it is pure Aramaic as Barton maintains, although its isolated presence in the late Ecclesiastes does lend credence to Nöldeke's suggestion that it is an Aramaism.[29]

בלם (Ps 32:9)

The recognized meaning "restrain" is supported by the Peshiṭta's use of this root to render the Hebrew חסם.[30] Presumably because of the word's rareness in the Bible and its correlation with Aramaic, Duhm considers it a gloss;[31] Ehrlich proposes the reading לכלוא.[32] In fact, the true difficulty of this verse lies more in עדיו than בלם.

בלס (Amos 7:14)

The interpretation of this word has almost invariably followed the patterns set early in the history of biblical exegesis. Some relate it to the

---

[26] See *BHK* and *BHS* on Prov 12:18; others read בוטח, regarding which see Theod πεποιθως (Prov 11:15).
[27] Sir 9:18 and especially 5:13 where one manuscript has בוטא and another בוטה.
[28] Cognates are cited by KB and BDB s.v. בטל; note especially the usage in Ezra 4:21-24, 5:5, and 6:8.
[29] G. Barton, ICC on Qoh 12:3; T. Nöldeke, review of Kautzsch, *ZDMG* 57 (1903) 412. Gordis's argument (*Kohelet* on Qoh 12:3) that Hebrew would use חדל and שבת pays inadequate attention to the possibilities of synonymy.
[30] Peshiṭta at Deut 25:47, see also 1 Cor 9:9 and H. Gunkel, HKAT on Ps 32:9. D. Yellin ("הוראות נשכחות לשרשים," *Leš* 1 [1928] 19) compares the usage in *b. Ḥul.* 88b.
[31] KHC on Ps 32:9.
[32] *Die Psalmen* (Berlin: M. Poppelauer, 1905) on Ps 32:9.

mishnaic בלס ("mix")[33] or בלש ("collect");[34] others cite Arabic بلس ("mulberry fig"), according to which this is a denominative meaning "own" or "tend" trees.[35] But most attention has derived from the Septuagint and Vulgate references to one who nips or slits fruit in order to make it edible, with any number of botanical justifications for this procedure offered along with the necessary citations to show that it was practiced in antiquity.[36] There is, however, limited etymological justification for this position. It seems unlikely that the denominative of a kind of tree would refer to such an isolated part of its treatment. Because of the lack of any satisfactory connection between the Hebrew word and the practice reflected in the Septuagint as well as the contextual inadequacies of the supposed rabbinic cognates, one must conclude that the evidence is not sufficient to permit a convincing treatment of this word.

בשס (Amos 5:11)

Widely connected with בוס, this form is explained as having dissimilated from the pôlēl בוסס,[37] or resulted by error from בוסכם which was

---

[33]Thus "mix food for livestock," see T. J. Wright, "Amos and the 'Sycamore Fig,'" *VT* 26 (1976) 366.

[34]Hence "collect harvest from trees," as by N. H. Torczyner, "בשולי המלון של אליעזר בן-יהודה," *Lešʹ* 13 (1944) 107-8; this interpretation may underlie Aquila's ερευνων.

[35]P. Humbert ("בולס שקמים [Amos VII,14]," *OLZ* 20 [1917] 297), noting the use of this word for a ripening stage of the fruit, suggests that the Hebrew verb refers to one who brings the fruit to ripeness; see also Joseph Braslavi, "עמוס - נוקד, בוקר ובולס שקמים," *BM* 12 (1967) 97ff. E. Ullendorff (*Ethiopia and the Bible* [London: British Academy, 1968] 128) compares the denominative כורם (as in 2 Kgs 25:12).

[36]See Pliny, *Natural History*, XIII.14 (LCL pp. 130ff.); Athenaeus, *The Deipnosophists* II.51 (LCL p. 223); *The Greek Herbal* of Dioscorides, I.127 (ed. R. Gunther [New York: Hafner, 1959] 66); Theophrastus, *Enquiry into Plants*, IV.ii.1 (LCL, p. 282). P. Humbert argues that the LXX is the only source which knows the sense of the word, but even its translation could be based on an educated guess relying on the botanical practice with regard to such trees in the translators' environment ("בולס שקמים," 269-70); see also George Henslow, "Egyptian Figs," *Nature* 47 (Dec. 1, 1892) 102.

[37]See Ružička, p. 178; compare Arabic شمس and شرس. BDB (s.v. בשס) regards the form as an error for בוסכם.

Hapax Legomena in Contemporary Scholarship 107

mistakenly written בושכם and then corrected without the removal of the extraneous ש.[38] Fenton points out that בוס is never used with על, arguing instead for the reading בְּשָׂכְכֶם.[39] Relying on the Akkadian phrase *šabašu šibša ina eqli* ("take rent from a field," as in ARM III 17.27), Tur-Sinai proposed that the text should be שבסכם, which Ginsberg compared with the Ugaritic *tšm ʿl dl* (CTA 6.6.48) through an elaborate phonetic shift followed by metathesis.[40]

בתק (Ezek 16:40)

Although Tur-Sinai has proposed reading ובתרוך,[41] there is no reason to question this root whose various developments are discussed extensively by Greenfield.[42] Its primary meaning is "split."

גרד (Job 2:8)

The meaning "scrape" is clear from context. Cognates are found in post-biblical Hebrew, Aramaic, Arabic, and Phoenician.[43]

דגה (Gen 48:16)

The meaning "multiply" is universally recognized and usually explained as deriving from דג ("fish"), an interpretation used since

---

[38]נפיססים and ועמססי (Neh 7:52 and 11:13) are similarly explained by J. Wellhausen (*Skizzen and Vorarbeiten* [Berlin: Georg Reimer, 1893] 5. 18) and others.
[39]Terry L. Fenton, "Ugaritica-Biblica," *UF* 1 (1969) 65-66; see *Tg.* Amos 5:11 (במיבזבון).
[40]H. Torczyner, "Presidential Address," *JPOS* 16 (1936) 6-7. Ginsberg's view is described by Cohen (p. 94 note 262 on the basis of "oral communication") where he cites Akkadian *lawû>lamû>labû* as an example of the needed phonetic shift.
[41]TSPM on Ezek 16:40.
[42]J. C. Greenfield, "Lexicographical Notes 1," *HUCA* 29 (1958) 220-22; compare mishnaic פתק, Addakian *batâqu* (Cohen, pp. 116-17, considers *Enuma Eliš* IV.101-2 especially pertinent), Arabic بتق and even Hebrew בדק. LESA (p. 13) lists an Ethiopic cognate as well.
[43]Cognates are cited in BDB and HALAT (s.v. גרד). Ružička (p. 35) refers to גרר as a result of dissimilation from this root (see p. 83 above) although it could more easily be explained as a scribal error.

antiquity.[44] However, all forms related to דג, including the true denominative דיג (Jer 16:16), point to a middle weak root;[45] furthermore, there is no evidence that fish were considered uniquely prolific. Ehrlich emends to ויחיו,[46] while Ball prefers וירבו on the basis of the Septuagint and Peshiṭta;[47] but these are more easily explicable as contextual interpretations of the existing text than is the corruption he assumes. Guillaume cites نجا ("spread") which fits the meaning required and corresponds to the Hebrew more easily than the alternatives.[48]

דהם (Jer 14:9)

Many emend נדהם to נרדם on the basis of the Septuagint although that evidence is hardly convincing.[49] Tur-Sinai prefers נדם;[50] and Del Olmo would read נדה הם, equating the verb with Ugaritic *ndy* and Akkadian *nadû* ("throw").[51] The root דהם has been compared with Arabic ادهمand Akkadian *da'âmu*, both referring to darkness,[52] as well as Arabic دهم ("attack by surprise") which fits the biblical passage quite well.[53] Its presence in the Yavneh-Yam inscription is now deemed unlikely;[54] there is no reason, however, to question its biblical authenticity, nor is its meaning obscure. Luzzatto suggested it is an Aramaized form of דום meaning "silenced (by fear)."[55]

---

[44] See pp. 50 and 65 above.
[45] T. Nöldeke, *Neue Beiträge zur Semitischen Sprachwissenschaft* (Strassburg: Karl J. Trübner, 1904) 123. Ugaritic texts include the title *dgy*, usually translated as "fisherman" (*CTA* 3.6.10 and 4.2.31).
[46] RG on Gen 48:16.
[47] SBOT on Gen 48:16.
[48] GHAL 1. 8; see also جد (Lane, p. 851).
[49] Thus RG on Jer 14:9, see p. 48 above.
[50] TSPM on Jer 14:9, see Jer 49:26 and 50:30.
[51] "Notas Criticas al Texto Hebreo de Jr 14-17," *Claretianum* 11 (1971) 298-99.
[52] Hence "misfortune"; thus S. E. Loewenstamm and J. Blau, *Thesaurus of the Language of the Bible* (Jerusalem: Bible Concordance Press, 1957-) 2. 285.
[53] *HALAT* s.v. דהם.
[54] *KAI* 200.14 which was read ולא תדהם ("do not be helpless") by Amusin and Heltzer ("The Inscription from Meṣad Ḥashavyahu," *IEJ* 14 [1964] 154), but corrected to ולא תדחני ("do not drive him away") by Cross ("Epigraphic Notes," *BASOR* 165 [1962] 46).
[55] On Jer 14:9; could such an interpretation underlie the LXX rendering ὑπνῶν?

דוב (Lev 26:16)

This is generally related to אדב, as either a variant or a corruption of דאב.[56] Some compare זוב ("melt, flow").[57] Schulthess compares Syriac ܕܘܒ ("languish") to Hebrew דאב,[58] while Guillaume notes Arabic دوب ("in a bad state").[59] Along with אדב and דאב this root is probably to be traced to an originally biliteral root.

דוץ (Job 41:14)

Opinions are split between those who would emend this form to תרוץ[60] and those who rely on cognates in Aramaic and Arabic meaning "jump," here manifest as "dance."[61] In either case the meaning is fundamentally the same.[62]

הבו (Hos 4:18)

The root of this word is so uncertain that even its inclusion among hapax legomena must be deemed tentative. Several scholars omit it as dittography.[63] Others see it as an abbreviated form of אהבו[64] or "correct" it with the preceding אהב to אהבו אהב אָהֹב.[65] And some would combine

---

[56] See p. 102 above.
[57] Thus Wagner p. 62; compare Arabic ذوب.
[58] F. Schulthess, *Homonyme Wurzeln im Syrischen* (Berlin: Reuther & Reichard, 1900) 173-74.
[59] GHAL 1. 8.
[60] Thus N. H. Tur-Sinai, *The Book of Job* (Jerusalem: Kiryat Sepher, 1957) on Job 41:14, see LXX and 11QtgJob renderings (discussed on pp. 52-53 above).
[61] Such as Palache, p. 13; Wagner (p. 43) counts this word as an Aramaism. DP (p. 65) includes Akkadian $dâṣu$, but see *CAD*, D, p. 118.
[62] See Nahum M. Sarna, review of M. Sokoloff, *The Targum to Job from Qumran Cave XI*, in *IEJ* 26 (1976) 152. The ostensibly more common דאבה is more problematic in this context (Frank M. Cross, "Ugaritic Db'at and Hebrew Cognates," *VT* 2 [1952] 162).
[63] Thus DLS, p. 81.
[64] König, p. 395; note Gen 44:20, 2 Sam 12:29, Isa 20:17 and 48:14. For a similar view, see F. I. Andersen and D. N. Freedman, *Hosea* (AB; Garden City: Doubleday, 1980) 379.
[65] For example, J. L. Mays, OTL on Hos 4:18.

the two forms to yield a p^e^al^c^al אהבהבו.[66] Alternatively it is ascribed to
יהב.[67] Comparisons have also been made with Arabic هَبّ ("desire")[68]
and the attested הבהב ("burn")[69] as well as post-biblical הוב ("guilt"), a
softened form of חוב.[70] Emendations include הבל and הנחלו.[71] The preceding infinitive absolute construction (הזנה הזנו) makes some relation
of הבו to אהב syntactically attractive; but this is hardly necessary, and
the possibility that the prophet chose a form of הבב for its assonance with
אהבו cannot be ignored.

הבר (Isa 47:13)

There is no question that הברי שמים means "astrologers"; only its
derivation has been uncertain. Various philological methods have been invoked for this purpose. A common comparison has been with ברר and the
Akkadian barû.[72] Others rely on the Arabic هبر ("cut") to interpret the
phrase as alluding to those who divide up the sky; this meaning of the
Arabic root is, however, secondary and therefore likely an internal Arabic
development.[73] The emendation to חקרי is ascribed to G. F. Moore;[74]
others have preferred reading חוברי, now supported by 1QIsa^a.[75] The discovery of Ugaritic hbr ("bow down"), which parallels kbd, supports both

---

[66] Thus H. S. Nyberg, *Studien zum Hoseabuche* (UUÅ 1935.6; Uppsala: Almquist & Wiksells Boktryckerie-AB, 1935) 35.
[67] Wilhelm Rudolph, "Hosea 4,15-19," in *Gottes Wort und Gottes Land* (H. W. Hertzberg Festschrift; ed. H. G. Reventlow; Göttingen: Vandenhoeck & Ruprecht, 1965) 195; compare Vg. *adferre*.
[68] J. J. Glück, "Some semantic complexities in the book of Hosea," *Studies on the Books of Hosea and Amos* (1964-65) 57.
[69] Hos 8:13; see Barr, p. 325.
[70] C. Rabin, "Etymological Miscellanea," *ScrH* 8 (1961) 384; note also CD 3:10.
[71] D. Nowack, HKAT and TSPM on Hos 4:18.
[72] F. Hommel ("The Word הברו in Isaiah xlvii,13," *ExpTim* 12 [1900-1] 239) compares the Š stem *šabru* in its meaning "magician."
[73] J. Blau ("Hōḇərē šāmājim," *VT* 7 [1957] 183-84) points out that the Arabic verb is a denominative from هبر ("piece of meat") and, like Luzzatto (on Isa 47:13), argues that the oft-compared גזרין (Dan 2:27) does not mean "astrologer."
[74] BDB s.v. הבר.
[75] See also Isa 47:12. Ehrlich (RG on Isa 47:13) compares Arabic خبر and rabbinic חָבָר ("warning").

the consonantal text and its vocalization.[76]

הדה (Isa 11:8)

The meaning "extend" seems clear enough from context, and an etymology based on Arabic and Syriac *hdy* ("lead, guide") is commonly espoused.[77] But the perfect tense is difficult in this context, while Gray notes that the commonly noted cognates do not yield the desired nuance.[78] For these as well as metrical reasons, Tur-Sinai combines הדה with ידו, reading instead ידהדה, which he compares with Arabic نهده ("roll/throw stones").[79]

הדך (Job 40:12)

Because of the parallel הכניעהו, the meaning of this form is not in doubt. Emendations have been proposed to הֲדֹך, הדק, and הדרוף.[80] Dahood repoints the entire phrase to read וְהֹדְךָ רְשָׁעִים תְּחִתָּם ("and by your majesty destroy the wicked")[81] The simplest aproach is to compare the Arabic هدم ("tear down").[82]

---

[76] See *CTA* 6.1.37. E. Ullendorff ("Ugaritic Marginalia II," *JSS* 7 [1962] 340) suggests this may be derived from South Semitic *kbr* by means of spirantization.

[77] Thus BDB s.v. הדה. The root occurs also in Palmyrene (Comte du Mesnil du Buisson, *Inventaire des Inscriptions Palmyreniennes des Doura-Europos* [Paris: Librarie Orientaliste Paul Geuthner, 1939] 21) and Sabaean (Joan Copeland Biella, *Dictionary of Old South Arabic, Sabaean Dialect* [Chico: Scholars Press, 1982] 105). M. Noth *(Die Israelitischen Personennamen im Rahmen der gemeinsemitischen Namergebung* [BWANT 3:10; Stuttgart: W. Kohlhammer Verlag, 1928] 196) ascribes the name יהדי (1 Chr 2:47) to this root.

[78] ICC on Isa 11:8, but see GHAL 3. 2. One would expect an imperfect form, but see S. R. Driver, *A Treatise on the Use of the Tenses in Hebrew* (3d ed.; Oxford: Clarendon Press, 1892) 20-21.

[79] TSPM on Isa 11:8 and J. Reider, "Etymological Studies in Biblical Hebrew," *VT* 2 (1952) 115.

[80] See N. H. Tur-Sinai, *The Book of Job*; K. Budde, HKAT; and E. P. Dhorme, *A Commentary on the Book of Job* (London: Thomas Nelson, 1967) on Job 40:12.

[81] M. Dahood, "The Phoenician Contribution to Biblical Wisdom Literature," in *The Role of the Phoenicians in the Interaction of the Mediterranean Civilizations* (ed. W. A. Ward; Beirut: American University of Beirut, 1968) 125.

[82] Thus BDB s.v. הדך.

הזה (Isa 56:10)

Those who would emend this word to חוזים have gained support from the reading of 1QIsa^a although Kutscher sees this as a substitution of a well-known root for the unclear, but authentic hapax legomenon.[83] Others relate the form to Arabic هذى and Syriac ܗܓܐ, both of which pertain to confused speech.[84] The form has been emended to הנם, גהרים, and הוגים.[85]

הכר (Job 19:3)

Finding an appropriate cognate or reading has been most difficult; thus the lower-critical and philological methods have gone hand in hand, but with no truly satisfying results. A significant proportion of the discussion about the word centers on identifying the first radical as ה or ח, each of which has some manuscript support.[86] The latter would justify comparison with Arabic حكر ("act unjustly").[87] Otherwise one must consider هكر ("be astonished") and possibly even הכרת פנים (Isa 3:9) which is usually ascribed to the root נכר.[88] Although حكر seems to provide a better meaning, the Hebrew text tends to support the not impossible هكر, with no criterion to lend certitude to either. Emendations include תכרו, תהכרו and תרהבו, תכרהו, תתחברו, תחברו, תחרפו.[89]

---

[83] E. Y. Kutscher, *The Language and Linguistic Background of the Isaiah Scroll*, p. 235; see DLS p. 164.

[84] *HALAT* s.v. הזה.

[85] RG on Isa 56:10 see also GB and Mandelkern s.v. הזה.

[86] See *BHK* on Job 19:3; *BHS* notes also some evidence of a reading תחברו.

[87] *GHAL* 2. 12; *HALAT* compares also Akkadian ḫakâru ("dash to pieces").

[88] *HALAT* s.v. הכר. S. Grünberg, "Exegetische Beitrage," *Jeschurun* 10 (1923) 385, compares also Arabic ركى which in the fourth form can mean "reprove."

[89] See *BHS*, RG, and TSPM on Job 19:3, BDB s.v. הכר, and TSLS 2. 146.

הלא (Mic 4:7)

Generally regarded as corrupt, this form is emended either to הנלאה or הנחלה.[90] The meaning is determined by the similarly used נדחה in the preceding verse. Aramaic forms of הלי ("labor") are usually judged to have been metathesized from לאה.[91] The modern Hebrew verb הלא is derived from the adverb הלאה.[92]

התת (Ps 62:4)

Although emendations to תהוללו and תקותכם have been noted,[93] the general tendency has been to find appropriate etymologies for the attested form. Tur-Sinai derives a contextual meaning of "rely on" by comparison with Ps 42:9 and 90:1.[94] A meaning "assault" has been supported by comparison with Arabic هتّ and Ugaritic ht.[95] Alternatively, "speak" is derived from Ugaritic hwt ("word")[96] and Damascus Arabic هوّت ("threaten, cry out").[97] A choice from among these must be made on the basis of perceived contextual demands.

זהם (Job 33:20)

Although its suffix is problematic, there is no doubt as to the meaning ("loathe") or appropriateness of this root in which virtually no one has

---

[90] As by DLS, p. 96 (note Vg. Mic 4:7 laboraverat discussed on p. 50 above) and G. R. Driver, "Linguistic and Textual Problems: Minor Prophets, II," JTS 39 (1938) 267, who notes the use of final aleph for ה in 2 Chr 16:12 which limits the corruption here to the mistaken copying of א for ה.

[91] PS p. 1011 and MD p. 148.

[92] ESh s.v. הלא, see also p. 72 above.

[93] See BDB s.v. הות.

[94] N. H. Torczyner, review of GB, ZDMG 70 (1916) 557.

[95] Thus KB s.v. התת. A. Ehrlich (Die Psalmen on Ps 62:4) compares also هتّ ("fall"). The Ugaritic form is found in CTA 3.E.28; see U. Cassuto, האלה ענת (Jerusalem: Mossad Bialik, 1951) 88.

[96] This is equivalent to Akkadian awātu; see Mitchell Dahood, Ugaritic-Hebrew Philology (Rome: Pontifical Biblical Institute, 1965) 56.

[97] Like התת, هوّت is used with the preposition على. See GB s.v. הות. Kittel (KAT on Ps 62:4) compares also هذّ. Briggs (ICC on Ps 62:14) notes also هتّ ("utter").

proposed any substantive changes.⁹⁸ Nichols notes the similar thought in Ps 107:18.⁹⁹ Cognates are cited from tannaitic Hebrew, Aramaic, Arabic, and even Coptic.¹⁰⁰

זער (Job 17:1)

Despite a diversity of proposed readings, including נזעכו, נעזבו, נתעבו, and even נָזְעַ בִּי,¹⁰¹ the overwhelming tendency of critical research has been to relate this word to דעך ("extinguish") as either a dialectical form or corruption.¹⁰² דעך, however, occurs throughout Hebrew, including four times in Job itself.¹⁰³ Job's earlier statement that he still has some time to live (Job 16:22) seems to render a statement "my days are extinct" inappropriate although the nuance "becoming extinct" is possible. The meaning "short" fits the context best, and Arabic has provided a possible cognate.¹⁰⁴

זרב (Job 6:17)

Proposed emendations include חרב, שרב, and זרח.¹⁰⁵ This root is usually considered a by-form of צרב or שרף.¹⁰⁶ Szold compares the rabbinic מרזב ("gutter tube") as the basis for the meaning "flow."¹⁰⁷ Most comparisons, however, are to the Syriac زُڤ ("narrow, compress").¹⁰⁸ Driver has found a similar nuance in the Akkadian *zarâbu*; thus he explains

---

⁹⁸Budde (HKAT on Job 33:20) cites Voigt's proposal to read וחמדה.
⁹⁹"The Composition of the Elihu Speeches," *AJSL* 27 (1911) 157.
¹⁰⁰*HALAT* s.v. זהם. C. J. Ball (*The Book of Job* on Job 33:20) sees this word as an Aramaism, but the evidence is not conclusive.
¹⁰¹C. J. Ball (*The Book of Job*), G. Hölscher (HAT), and *BHK* on Job 17:1. DLS (p. 119) compares the reading אחז for אחד in 1 Chr 24:6.
¹⁰²Mitchell Dahood, "Northwest Semitic Philology and Job," in *The Bible in Current Catholic Thought* (ed. John L. McKenzie; New York: Herder and Herder, 1962) 72. Such a reading is attested in several manuscripts (see *BHK* at Job 17:1).
¹⁰³Job 6:17, 18:5-6, 21:17.
¹⁰⁴GHAL (4. 15) notes أرعكنّ meaning "short."
¹⁰⁵C. J. Ball (*The book of Job*) and E. P. Dhorme (*A Commentary on the Book of Job*) on Job 6:17.
¹⁰⁶The relationship between זעק and צעק or עלז and עלץ is often cited; see S. R. Driver (ICC on Job 6:17).
¹⁰⁷*The Book of Job* on Job 6:17; compare NJV "thaw."
¹⁰⁸G. R. Driver ("Some Hebrew Medical Expressions," *ZAW* 65 [1953] 261) compares the phrase سلام ذو مصل ("torrent").

the verb in šīnatešunu uzarrabu (OIP II 47.vi.31), which refers to an involuntary discharge of urine, as deriving from the meaning "squeeze> flow."[109] Further evidence of this root has been detected in 3Q15.9.[110]

חטם (Isa 48:9)

Although various emendations have been put forth (אחמל, אחום, אחתם, אחסם, אמחה חטאים),[111] the general view of this word as relating to the later חוטם ("nose") has not changed. Verbal forms of this root meaning "muzzle" in Akkadian, Arabic, and Mandaic confirm the likelihood of the meaning "restrain oneself."[112]

חלט (1 Kgs 20:33)

The reading of this root is not generally challenged.[113] Ehrlich relies on the Targum for the meaning "snatch," hence "catch the meaning of words."[114] Although Keil considers it a by-form of חלץ,[115] the verb is usually explained from the tannaitic Hebrew and Aramaic root חלט meaning "to state positively," hence Gray's "take as definite indication."[116] It has also been compared with the Arabic خلص ("extract the best from").[117]

---

[109]"Some Hebrew Medical Expressions," 255-57 against CAD (Ṣ, p. 103) which reads uṣarrapu and explains the verb as referring to the passing of hot urine. Lambert (*Babylonian Wisdom Literature* [Oxford: Clarendon Press, 1960] 287) proves the consonants ṣrp, but not for the passage in question. The meaning "hold back (urine)" there proposed is wholly inappropriate to the context as noted by Luckenbill (*Ancient Records of Assyria and Babylonia* [Chicago: University of Chicago Press, 1926-27] 2. 128 note 1).
[110]DJD 3. 239-40 and 245-46.
[111]See T. K. Cheyne (SBOT), B. Duhm (HKAT), O. Procksch (KAT), and Gesenius according to S. D. Luzzatto on Isa 48:9 as well as H. Oort, "Kritische Aanteekeningen op Jez 40-66," *Theologisch Tijdschrift* 25 (1891) 468.
[112]See *HALAT* s.v. חטם.
[113]The word division is usually repaired to ויחלטוה מננו.
[114]EMK on 1 Kgs 20:33 and virtually all English versions.
[115]KD on 1 Kgs 20:33, see also J. Montgomery in ICC on 1 Kgs 20:33.
[116]OTL on 1 Kgs 20:33.
[117]GHAL 1. 8 and 23.

חסּפס (Exod 16:14)

Although the tendency to relate the verb חשׂף has persisted from antiquity, there is no evidence for a $p^{e\,c}ala^c$ conjugation anywhere else in Semitic, a difficulty which applies equally to KB's comparison with Arabic حشف ("crackle").[118] Some have therefore described it as derived from an equally unattested *חספּס.[119] The form in not adequately understood.

חפא (2 Kgs 17:9)

Although a variety of emendations have been offered,[120] the mainstream of biblical exegesis has related this isolated form to the more common חפה ("cover"), usually by inferring a meaning "do secretly" or the like.[121] As recognized by the Targum and Peshiṭta, however, the appropriate meaning is "said." According to G. R. Driver, this is now supported by an Akkadian-Sumerian syllabary which includes the entry ḫapû under the listing BI.[122] Haupt preferred to compare Akkadian ḫepû ("destroy").[123]

חרג (Ps 18:46)

The text of this passage is subject to some question on the basis of the earliest possible evidence: the parallel 2 Sam 22:46 reads here

---

[118] s.v. חספס. TSPM (on Exod 16:14) prefers to repoint the form as a noun (דק מ-חספס), "thinner than חספס"; compare 1QEx כהספס, and LXX and Vg.) although he is unable to explain the resultant noun. Already Dunash (DST, p. 67, no. 109) recognized that reduplication is always of two letters; Yannay ("Augmented Verbs in Biblical Hebrew," HUCA 45 [1974]87-88) cites two additional examples of forms such as this from modern Hebrew.
[119] GKB I §20e; disappearance of the final letter in this format is equally unknown.
[120] Such as יפיחו (TSPM on 2 Kgs 17:9), וירפאו (see B. Stade, SBOT on 2 Kgs 17:9), ויחטיאו (Grätz cited by Stade), ויחפשו (KB s.v. חפא).
[121] See BDB s.v. חפה; this may be the basis for the LXX ἠμφιέσαντο (see LXX 2 Chr 3:5-9) and the Vg. operuerunt (see at 2 Sam 15:30, Jer 14:3-4, and Esth 6:12, 7:8).
[122] G. R. Driver, "The Modern Study of the Hebrew Langauge," in The People and the Book (ed. A. S. Peake; Oxford: Clarendon Press, 1925) 89; the observation apparently originated with V. Scheil. This verb is not cited in the CAD.
[123] In SBOT on 2 Kgs 17:9.

ויחגרו. The meaning "gird" is not appropriate at this point while all Hebrew text witnesses, including Origen's second column, confirm the Masoretic reading.[124] The similar phrase in Mic 7:17 (ירגזו ממסגרותיהם) suggests that the verb ought to mean "tremble" or "fear,"[125] as is known from the Aramaic חרגתא.[126] Others compare the Arabic خرج ("come out of").[127]

חרת (Exod 32:16)

There are two mutually exclusive etymologies cited for the widely accepted meaning "engrave." One, comparing חרושה על לוח (Jer 17:1), holds this to be an Aramaized form of חרש.[128] The other points to Ugaritic ḥrt ("cemetery").[129] The two are not compatible because the former implies the last radical to be t which does not accord with the Ugaritic evidence. Gordon, however, has shown that Ugaritic ḥrt belongs to the root ḥry.[130] In light of its biblical occurrence in a relatively early passage and the fact that similar forms are found in Punic and Arabic as well as post-biblical Hebrew, the form is most probably a dialectical variant of חרש rather than an Aramaism.[131]

---

[124]The Peshitta's ܘܣܝܩܘ leads TSPM (on Ps 18:46) to interpret the Hebrew word as meaning "gird sackcloth for mourning."

[125]On this basis Gunkel (HKAT on Ps 18:46) suggests that a better reading would be ויחרדו.

[126]BDB (s.v. חרג) cites Tg. Onq. Deut 32:25; KB (s.v. חרג) compares also Arabic خرج. S. Lieberman and Y. Kutscher ("חרגיו, חרמיו, וחגריו", Leš 27 [1962] 34-39) discuss a possible South Arabic origin for the rabbinic occurrence of this root which appears in CIS II.350 where in a Nabatean text it clearly refers to "sacred" (NSI, p. 243).

[127]KB s.v. חרג.

[128]For example, Wagner, p. 59.

[129]KB s.v. חרת.

[130]He compares the Akkadian ḥiritu (RS 15.85:17 in PRU III); C. Gordon, "Ugaritic ḤRT/ḤIRITU 'Cemetery,'" Syria 33 (1956) 102-3.

[131]See Mark Lidzbarski, Ephemeris für Semitische Epigraphik (Giessen: J. Ricker'sche Verlagsbuchhandlung, 1900-1915) 1. 170; Lane pp. 541 and 717. Hebrew usages occur in Sir 45:11, 1QS 10:6, 8, 11, 1QM 12:3, and 1QH 1:24. W. Nauck ("Lex insculpta [חוק חרות] in der Sektenschrift," ZNW 46 [1955] 138) compares the phraseology of Jub. 5:14, 6:21, 31, 16:9, and 24:33. S. Gevirtz ("The Issachar Oracle in the Testament of Jacob," EY 12 [1975] 108*) relates חרט to this root as well (see also Palache, p. 45).

חשל **(Deut 25:18)**

The meaning "stragglers" is clear enough from context. While some have argued that this is metathesized from חלש, Joüon prefers reading נכשלים,[132] and Kohn suggests נמשלים on the basis of the Samaritan Targum (שליטיה).[133] Otherwise the search for cognates has yielded roots meaning "crush," "forge," and even "drive cattle violently."[134] Guillaume, on the basis of a ف-ث interchange, proposes comparison with Arabic حفل ("assemble").[135]

חתך **(Dan 9:24)**

There is no dispute as to the interpretation of this word which exemplifies the evolution of a meaning "decide" from "cut."[136] Cognates are known from tannaitic Hebrew, Aramaic, and possibly Arabic.[137] Although some consider this to be an Aramaism, it is attested also in Akkadian.[138]

טוש **(Job 9:26)**

This is another form about which there is virtually no disagreement nor any reason to expect debate.[139] The word is equivalent to Aramaic

---

[132] "Notes de Lexicographie Hebraique," *Bib* 6 (1925) 423; see GB s.v. חשל.
[133] Samuel Kohn, *Samaritanische Studien* (Breslau: Schletter'schen Buchhandlung, 1868) 41.
[134] Akkadian ḫašâlu (F. Delitzsch, *The Hebrew Langauge Viewed in the Light of Assyrian Research* [London: William and Norgate, 1893] 62), note also Biblical Aramaic חשל, Syriac ܚܫܠ (S. R. Driver, ICC on Deut 25:18); *HALAT* cites Arabic حسل (s.v. חשל) suggesting that the biblical usage pertains to those animals left behind (i.e. ḫasīl).
[135] "A Contribution to Hebrew Lexicography," *BSOAS* 16 (1954) 6, 10.
[136] Palache (p. 19) compares Hebrew חרץ and גזר, rabbinic פסק, Syriac ܣܕܡ, ܓܕܡ, and ܦܣܩ, Arabic قطا, جزم, and قض, Akkadian parâsu, and Latin *decidere*.
[137] J. Barth (*Etymologische Studien zum Semitischen insbesondere zum Hebräischen Lexicon* [Berlin: H. Itzkowski, 1893] 23) cites Arabic هتك.
[138] ḫatâku; E. Ullendorff ("Ugaritic Marginalia II," *JSS* 7 [1962] 341) cites also Ugaritic htk ("father/offspring").
[139] KD (on Job 9:26) notes Grätz's recommendation to read ישוט.

טוס ("soar") which occurs also in later Hebrew.[140] Wagner considers it an Aramaism.[141]

טחה (Gen 21:16)

The meaning "(bow)shot" is generally recognized from context and confirmed by the Arabic cognate طحى ("spread").[142] Emendations usually gravitate towards noun forms, although the attested participle is readily understood as "those who shoot (bows)."[143]

טחה (Isa 44:18)

Were it not for the vocalization טָח, this form would be ascribed to the common root טוח. Luzzatto considers טחה to be an intransitive form corresponding to such a root,[144] but most emend this form to טָחוּ. GKB prefers to see in this the root טוח pointed on the pattern of a geminate verb.[145] The possibility that weak verbs of one type can be conjugated acording to the pattern of another is especially important in that it emphasizes the possibility that apparent verbs may in fact be variants of other, more common roots.

---

[140]G. R. Driver ("Once Again: Birds in the Bible," *PEQ* 90 [1958] 57) compares Arabicطح and sees this root as likely to be found also in Num 11:31 where our text reads ויטש. See J. Blau, "Etymologische Untersuchungen," *VT* 5 (1955) 342.

[141]Wagner pp. 59-60; he suggests that this is true also of the Arabic word cited.

[142]*HALAT* (s.v. טחה) also cites Akkadian *ṭeḫû* ("adjoin") and Pehlevi טחי ("reach"). Others note Arabic طَحَّ ("spread") which, in the fourth form, means "throw" (thus O. Procksch, KAT on Gen 21:16). Luzzatto (on Gen 21:16) compares רומי קשת (Ps 78:9). TSPM (on Job 38:36) notes that in Arabic طوح and طحو refer to birds of prey.

[143]EMK (on Gen 21:16) would read כִּמְטוּחֲי from the noun מָטָח; he compares also the talmudic phrase הטיח דברים (as in *b. Meg.* 22b).

[144]On Isa 44:18; see DLS, p. 27. T. K. Cheyne (SBOT on Isa 44:18) notes the preference of some for טָחוּ.

[145]GKB §28p; compare the Arabic root cited in note 142 above. It is conceivable that an Arabic geminate could occur in Hebrew as middle weak.

טמה (Job 18:3)

The meaning of the verse is not in question, but the definition of this word cannot be fixed with certainty from context. Ehrlich calls it "unhebräische."[146] Some would emend it to נדמינו or נטמנו;[147] others relate it to טמא.[148] However, the consonants may also be interpreted as deriving from a cognate of the Aramaic and rabbinic Hebrew root טמם ("be stupid") which Palache suggests is itself to be related to טמא.[149] The fact of several distinct etymologies, each of which adequately suits the attested context, illustrates the limits of modern methodology. It is unlikely, however, that additional attestation would be of assistance in resolving this uncertainty. Debate would most likely persist as to whether this is the same root as is found in such a text. Perhaps an identical context using this root in some other language or dialect would be helpful in identifying it.[150]

טנף (Cant 5:3)

There is no difficulty with this word; both context and cognates point clearly to the meaning "soil."[151] In light of its widespread occurrence, the evidence does not justify calling it an Aramaism.[152]

טעה (Ezek 13:10)

This root is well attested in Aramaic, Arabic, and tannaitic Hebrew,[153] and its meaning is not in doubt; however, only the related

---

[146] RG on Job 18:3.
[147] E. Dhorme, *A Commentary on the Book of Job*, on Job 18:3 and Anton Blommerde, *Northwest Semitic Grammar and Job* (Rome: Pontifical Biblical Institute, 1969) 83. (See *HALAT* s.v. טמה where the reading נְטַמֹּנוּ is proposed.)
[148] G. Fohrer, KAT on Job 18:3; see also Lev 11:43.
[149] BDB s.v. טמה and Palache p. 35 (see also Sir 10:16).
[150] See pp. 13-14 above.
[151] For example, Akkadian *ṭanāpu* and forms throughout Aramaic; on Arabic طنب see S. Fraenkel, *Die Aramäischen Fremdwörter* (Hildesheim: Georg Olms, 1962) 23; GB (s.v. טנף) notes also a Coptic form.
[152] Against BDB s.v. טנף.
[153] For Akkadian see MA s.v. *ṭiʾu*; an Ethiopic cognate is noted by E. Ullendorff in *Ethiopia and the Bible*, 122.

form תעה occurs in the Bible, including several times in Ezekiel, leading to the suggestion that it is an Aramaism.[154]

טפש (Ps 119:70)

The meaning "fat" is recognized from several languages and developed naturally a connotation of "stupid" in which it is attested as a gloss to Ben Sirah 42:6.[155] Ehrlich considers this a by-form of תפש, which was needed to start this line of the acrostic psalm.[156]

יאב (Ps 119:131)

Some would read תאב on account of the semantically similar verses 20 and 40.[157] Most, however, compare Aramaic יאב ("desire"), often concluding that the biblical usage is an Aramaism, occurring as it does only in this one, late text.[158] Palache compares also the weak verbs אבה and תאב in support of an apparently biliteral theory of this word's origin.[159]

יאה (Jer 10:7)

This root, which means "be fitting," is well known from sources external to the Hebrew Bible, including Aramaic, Arabic, Punic, Ethiopic, and rabbinic Hebrew.[160] Gevirtz suggests that a cognate may also be found in the Amarna correspondence.[161] As he did with יאב, Palache

---

[154]Kautzsch, pp. 34-35; see Ezek 14:11, 44:10, 15, 48:11. A possibly related form would result if כעטיה (Cant 1:7) were emended to כטעיה (Kautzsch, pp. 34-35).

[155]The root occurs also in Aramaic, Arabic, and Akkadian. Palache (p. 37) compares the semantic development of שמן, כסל, אול, and Latin brutus; note also Greek παχύς and Latin pinguis.

[156]Die Psalmen, on Ps 119:70.

[157]See HALAT s.v. יאב; this is supported now by the reading of 11QPs[a] 119:13.

[158]Thus BDB s.v. יאב.

[159]Palache, p. 4.

[160]See HALAT s.v. יאה.

[161]"On Canaanite Rhetoric," Or 42 (1973) 176. The passage is in EA 147:38 which states, "If the king, my lord, says 'Stand before the army,' thus says the servant to his master—'ia-a-ia-ia.'" Albright equates it with Egyptian y?, meaning "yes" (Gevirtz, p. 176). The form is preceded by the glossenkeil, suggesting that it is not pure Akkadian.

compares יאה with several other weak verbs with similar roots and meanings— אוה, אות, תאה, and תוה.[162]

יבב (Judg 5:28)

The treatment of this word has barely advanced beyond the evidence available since antiquity. On the one hand, context suggests a meaning similar to the parallel נשקפה as is supported by the Septuagint's κατεμανθανεν; some therefore propose reading ותבט.[163] It is difficult, however, to ignore the oft-cited Aramaic יבבא which means "make a sound" and thus often leads to an interpretation "lament, bewail."[164] Interestingly, the root was used in the *qal* by ibn Gabirol with the meaning "look" even while its pi'el was taken as "wail."[165] Guillaume compares Arabic أَبَّ ("cry loudly").[166]

יהד (Esth 8:17)

Universally accepted as a denominative from יהודי,[167] this verb may fit the letter, but hardly the spirit of the definition here utilized for absolute hapax legomena. The force of the hitpa'el for this root is not,

---

[162] Palache, p. 2.
[163] For example, RG on Judg 5:28; see Prov 7:6. *BHK* (on Judg 5:28) suggests alternatively ותתבונן.
[164] Moore (ICC on Judg 5:28) points out that the Targum does not use this root, which is regularly applied by the Targum for תרועה where it refers to a cry of anguish or terror (as at Isa 15:4 and Mic 4:9), rejecting therefore the importance of y. *Yebam* 16:5 (p. 78a). Note Vg. *ululabat*. The various cognates are listed by *HALAT* s.v. יבב. The seeming conflict between context and etymology is made particularly acute by the obvious possibility for fitting the cognate-derived meaning into the biblical context. Where etymological information yields a meaning appropriate to the context, there is little justification in pressing for emendation solely to provide a "more perfect" parallel. Context is the ultimate check, but comparative philology necessarily provides the raw data in such cases.
[165] Cited in Canaani, s.v. יבב.
[166] GHAL 2. 17.
[167] Bardtke (KAT on Esth 8:17) cites several manuscript variants— מתיהבים, מתיהודים, מתיחדים. A similar usage in Syriac is to be traced to the impact of this passage; see Julius Grünthal, *Die Syrische Uebersetzung zum Buche Esther* (Breslau: H. Fleischmann, 1900) 50.

however, certain. Some see in it a reference to conversion "in the more or less strict sense."[168] Others prefer to translate "pretend to be a Jew."[169]

יזם (Gen 11:6)

The meaning ("intend") is not in doubt, only the etymology. Some have preferred to revocalize יָזְמוּ from זמם, while others accept the unique vocalization but consider it nonetheless to be a form of זמם.[170] Sperber proposes instead that יזם is a by-form of זמם.[171] The similar phrase יבצר ממך מזמה (Job 42:2) along with the absence of cognates[172] makes a derivation from זמם, however achieved, virtually certain.

יזן (Jer 5:8)

That this root is attested only in the qĕrê does not obviate the need to explain it, although some do therefore view it as corrupt.[173] Since the verse in which it is found contains two hapax legomena, it is difficult to ascertain the contextual requirements of the passage.[174] Schultens justified this word as equivalent to the Arabic وزن ("weigh") which, in keeping with those who regard משכים as shortened from *מאשיכים, he took as an allusion to large testicles.[175] As with other initial yod roots here noted, one must recall the possibility that they may be correlated with middle weak roots, sharing the same strong radicals, so that even if the form is

---

[168] John Gray (CB on Esth 8:17). According to ESh (s.v. יהד) it is primarily in this sense that the word has functioned in subsequent Hebrew.
[169] C. Gordon, *Introduction to Old Testament Times* (Ventnor, NJ: Ventnor Publishers, 1953) 279.
[170] BL §58p'.
[171] "Hebrew Based upon Biblical Passages in Parallel Transmission," *HUCA* 14 (1939) 195.
[172] In modern Hebrew this root is used for "initiate."
[173] This is the only reading in the Eastern tradition (see *BHK* on Jer 5:8).
[174] See p. 164 below, s.v. שכה.
[175] Cited in GB, pp. 195-96. חנות מיוזנת (*b. Giṭ.* 67a) is textually uncertain (see Tosaphot there); Jastrow (s.v. יזן) views it as a denominative from מזון. The verb's occurence in Sir 36:6 (Joseph Marcus, "A Fifth Ms. of Ben Sira," *JQR* 12 [1931] 231) is pure conjecture, resting on that passage's similarity to Jer 5:8.

unique it need not be totally isolated.[176] Tur-Sinai prefers to read זונים.[177]

יחר (2 Sam 20:5)

There is no question that the meaning of this word is "be late."[178] Some suggest that an *aleph* has been assimilated; others emend the form to conform better to standard patterns for the root אחר.[179] The form has had no subsequent impact on Hebrew, nor are there any cognates.[180]

ימש (Judg 16:26)

This form could be viewed as an error by metathesis or even a by-form of מוש.[181] The only other view commonly held is that which on the basis of the root משש would read instead הַמְמַשֵּׁנִי. Only Guillaume finds evidence to support a prima-*yod* root here.[182] There are no other possible cognates nor any subsequent evidence for such a root in Hebrew itself.

יסך (Exod 30:32)

As with most of the prima-*yod* verbs here treated, יסך is understood easily from context and conforms well to the meaning of what would be the corresponding middle weak verb.[183] Barth prefers to see in יִיסָךְ a

---

[176] See p. 77 above.
[177] TSPM on Jer 5:8. This interpretation, although not necessarily this reading, may be shared by the Vg. (*amatores*), see p. 50 above.
[178] Otto Boström (*Alternative Readings in the Hebrew of the Books of Samuel* [Rock Island, IL: Augustana, 1918] 55) prefers to see ויחל in the *kětîb*.
[179] Budde (SBOT on 2 Sam 20:5) suggests reading ויאחר, and RG (on 2 Sam 20:5) וייחר. BL §53r suggests ואחר*>ואאחר. The *qěrê* (ויוחר) is easily understood on the basis of the comparison with וַתֹּהַן (v. 9, see S. R. Driver, *Notes on the Hebrew Text and Topography of the Books of Samuel* [2d ed.; Oxford: Clarendon Press, 1913] on 2 Sam 20:5).
[180] However, compare Sabaean *wḥr* (J. C. Biella, *Dictionary of Old South Arabic*, p. 126).
[181] See p. 50 above.
[182] GHAL 2. 17 where Arabic ومس ("rub against, polish") is compared.
[183] See the versions' interpretation on p. 51 above.

qal passive of סוך, comparing also וַיִּישֶׂם (Gen 50:26, see also 24:33) and suggesting a phonetic shift *yusyam> *yuysam>yiysam.[184] The Samaritan יוסך supports those who would emend the second yod to a waw, yielding a derivative of סוך in that way.[185] There is limited evidence for a root סוך in Phoenician and rabbinic Hebrew.[186]

יעז (Isa 33:19)

The nearby phrases עמקי שפה and נלעג לשון as well as the fact that this is a hapax legomenon are used to justify the preference of some to read לעוז here.[187] GB then explains the present text on the basis of an נ-ל interchange as proposed in the Middle Ages.[188] BDB finds instead an appropriate etymology in Arabic وعز ("give sign, command").[189] Some see in יעז a parallel to the more common root עזז, with occasional suggestions to read נָעַז from that root.[190]

יעט (Isa 61:10)

Were the text unvocalized, there would be no basis to interpret this as anything other than a form of עטה, a fitting parallel to הלבישני. Many

---

[184]"Das passive Qal . . ." in Jubelschrift . . . des Dr. Israel Hildesheimer (Berlin: H. Engel, 1890) 150-51. Concerning "u-i" changes see William Chomsky, "Some Irregular Formations in Hebrew," JQR 38 (1947-48) 415; BL §17k, and Kutscher, The Language and Linguistic Background of the Isaiah Scroll, pp. 452-54, who cites Bergsträsser's assertion that i and u belong to the same phoneme.

[185]RG (on Exod 30:32) calls the present text "eine unform."

[186]KAI 89.1, although a radical nun could have assimilated; for the mishnaic form יסיכה (m. Yoma 8:1) see p. 87 above. Jonas Greenfield has pointed out (written communication) the possibility of corresponding meanings for initial yod and nun verbs, for example, נצב-יצב, נגג-רגג. For further discussion, see Moshe Bar Asher, "צורות נדירות בלשון התנאים," Leš 41 (1977) 85-87.

[187]Thus RG (on Isa 33:19) despite the fact that לעז is also a hapax legomenon.

[188]s.v. יעז.

[189]s.v. יעז.

[190]DLS, p. 40 (note 1QH 6:25 ונעוז בחומה נשגבה) GB (s.v. יעז) suggests the possibility of a cognate in the Sabean surname אועֿז.

therefore revocalize the consonants appropriately.[191] *BHS* prefers to delete the word altogether.[192] Other than Aramaic יעט (= Hebrew יעץ), such a root is attested only in forms dependent on its biblical usage.[193]

ירט (Num 22:32)

This form has usually been considered along with the apparent root רטה (Job 16:11) although the two are here treated separately on the basis of the Masoretes' pointing. Because the passage in which it is found can be understood in several different ways, context does not provide adequate guidance in this case: one cannot determine whether the subject is דרך or Balaam and whether דרך refers to Balaam's behavior or the road on which he travels.[194] Despite various emendations, many prefer a form based on Arabic ورط ("throw").[195] Paterson ascribes to Gesenius a comparison with ירד.[196] Noth describes the entire clause as "incomprehensible."[197]

כחל (Ezek 23:40)

Although a hapax legomenon in the Bible, this root is now confirmed for ancient Hebrew through the discovery of a jug inscribed יין כחל.[198] There is no question as to its meaning or correctness. Cognates are

---

[191] יַעְטֵנִי (*HALAT* s.v. יעט); others prefer עָטָנִי (Duhm, HKAT on Isa 61:10). EMK (on Isa 61:10) explains the tense confusion as due to scribal confusion with respect to הלבישני.

[192] On Isa 61:10; this is on the basis of LXX although reference is made to all the versions.

[193] See BY s.v. יעט.

[194] דרך can be masculine (as in 1 Kgs 18:6).

[195] Thus יָרַטָה. RG (on Num 22:32) would read רע (Sam has הרע); DLS (p. 63) suggests יָרֵט.

[196] SBOT on Num 22:32.

[197] OTL on Num 22:32.

[198] N. Avigad, "Two Hebrew Inscriptions on Wine-Jars," *IEJ* 22 (1972) 1-9. A. Demsky ("'Dark Wine' from Judah," *IEJ* 22 [1972] 233-34) compares חכלילי (Gen 49:12) which he regards as a metathesized form of the same root; see Moses ben Naḥman on Gen 49:12. Cognates include Akkadian *ekêlu* and Arabic حلك and حكل (see Palache, p. 3 and GHAL 1. 23).

attested throughout Semitic; the word has even reached English in *alcohol*.[199] The meaning is "to paint the eyes with antimony."[200]

כמה (Ps 63:2)

Its context makes a meaning "long for" inevitable for this word. The only appropriate cognates mean "be weak, pale," supporting KB's "be faint with longing."[201] Tur-Sinai proposes reading כמר ("burn").[202]

כמס (Deut 32:34)

The parallel חתום as well as general context make a meaning "sealed" or "stored" obvious. There has been some tendency to emend this form to כנס on the basis of the Samaritan (כנוס) and Septuagint (συνῆκται).[203] Driver points to the use of כנס as parallel to באוצרות נתן in Ps 33:7, noting that נ could easily be confused for מ in Paleo-Hebrew.[204] The Samaritan reading could as easily be the corruption (or correction), and a suitable root is now recognized from Akkadian *kamâsu* (A) "gather, collect."[205] Van Zijl's claim to find a cognate in the Ugaritic *ktmsm* (CTA

---

[199] Semitic cognates are noted in KB s.v. כחל; others can be found in Karl Lokotsch, *Etymologisches Wörterbuch der Europäischen Wörter Orientalischen Ursprungs* (Heidelberg: Carl Winter's Universitätsbuchhandlung, 1927) 98. W. Vycichl ("Ägyptisch-Semitische Anklänge," *ZÄS* 84 [1959] 146) notes not only an Egyptian form, but also Greek κολλυρίου, Latin *collyrium*, and French *kuhl*.

[200] Concerning this custom see R. J. Forbes, *Studies in Ancient Technology* (2d ed.; Leiden: E. J. Brill, 1965) 3. 17ff.

[201] S.v. כמה; note Arabic كمَس, Syriac ܟܡܗ ("pale, blind"); concerning rabbinic כמה ("mushroom") see p. 63 above. GB (s.v. כמה) notes also Akkadian *kamû* ("bind").

[202] TSPM on Ps 63:2.

[203] LXX uses συναγω also at Ps 33:7, Neh 12:44, and 1 Chr 22:2.

[204] ICC on Deut 32:34; Mandelkern (s.v. כמס) points out a general phonological similarity with גנז and כנס (initial palatal and final sibilant).

[205] Cohen (p. 39) notes especially one occurrence in which it parallels *kanāku* and refers to a storehouse (STT I 38:85-86, cited in *CAD* K, p. 115). For a similar interpretation see RG on Deut 32:34.

6.I.51) creates unique problems, and other treatments are more likely.[206] Fortunately, it is not essential for an adequate understanding of the biblical כמס which is attested in Aramaic as well as Akkadian.[207]

כסס (Exod 12:4)

This form has been related to the noun מכסה in the same verse although that is more likely to be derived from a root מכס.[208] Comparisons with other Semitic languages have pointed to a basic meaning "cut up" for the root כסס.[209] Guillaume compares Arabic تكسّس ("take great trouble in") to justify his interpretation "compute."[210]

כפה (Prov 20:14)

Context suggests a meaning "avert" or "subdue." Although there are those who read instead יכפר,[211] comparisons with כבה are most common.[212] Some rely on evidence of a פ-ב interchange which, for example, Dahood uses to explain this word as a dialectic variant of כבה; others prefer to emend the text to a form of that verb.[213] Comparisons have

---

[206] Peter van Zijl (*Baal* [AOAT 10; Neukirchen-Vluyn: Verlag Butzon & Bercker Kevelaer, 1972] 193-94) summarizes various interpretations of this passage; objections to his conclusions are presented in Cohen, pp. 63-64, note 92.

[207] *HALAT* s.v. כמס; the word means "hide" or "store" in Syriac and Mandaic as well as in rabbinic usage; see Cohen, "Studies in Hebrew Lexicography," *AJSL* 40 (1924) 153-85.

[208] Compare Akkadian *makâsu* (*AHW* p. 588); this view was anticipated in IJR, p. 23.

[209] Thus KB s.v. כסס (meanings include "chew," "pulverize," "break small," "gnaw," and "count"). Geez *käsäyä* ("diminish") and *käsäkkäsä* ("cut in small pieces") are compared by LHC (p. 49). A possible attestation in line 11 of the Yavneh Yam inscription (S. Yeivin, "The Judicial Petition from Meẓad Ḥashavyahu," *Bib Or* 19 [1962] 5) is to be rejected on epigraphic grounds (*KAI* 3.201).

[210] GHAL 1. 10.

[211] Frankenberg (HKAT on Prov 21:14) compares Prov 16:14; RG (on Prov 21:14) objects that כפה is elsewhere unattested.

[212] Such interpretations usually require revocalizing the verb into the piʿel; for the evidence of the versions see BHS.

[213] M. Dahood, "Hebrew-Ugaritic Lexicography III," *Bib* 46 (1965) 320, 331; for emendation see C. H. Toy (ICC on Prov 21:14) and the versions (Tg. and Sym use the same rendering as at 1 Sam 3:3).

also been made with the rabbinic כפה ("overturn") and Syriac ܟܦܐ ("lean") as well as Arabic كفأ and even Akkadian *kapû* ("bend").[214] The nuance of the Hebrew depends on the specific cognate which is emphasized.

כפש (Lam 3:16)

Ehrlich considered this word to be meaningless; proposed emendations include הפלישני, האכילני, and הכשיפני.[215] Comparison has been with rabbinic כפש ("overturn"), Akkadian *takpuštu*, and Arabic كفس ("have crooked feet," hence, "make cower").[216] However, the most common view is that this form is a variant of the more common כבש ("tread"), and indeed forms of *kapāšu*, equivalent to the more common *kabāšu*, are known from the Amarna letters.[217] Ugaritic *kpt* would be particularly appropriate if its meaning "earth" were certain. RS 252.7-8 refers to Anat as b'lt.šmm.rmm / b'lt kpt, "mistress of the lofty heavens, mistress of the *kpt*" for which "earth" seems an appropriate meaning.[218] However, this explanation relies on much the same evidence as is applied to כפש which makes using it to support an interpretation of that verb a form of circular logic. Furthermore, the cognates considered here point to a Semitic *š* which does not acord with the *t* attested as the third radical of the

---

[214] *HALAT* and BDB s.v. כפה as well as KD on Prov 21:14.

[215] RG on Lam 3:16. Comparing the use of פלש in *b. Yebam.* 107b, Praetorius ("Threni III, 5.16," *ZAW* 15 [1895] 326) interprets the word as "roll." *BHK* relies on the LXX ἐψώμισεν for the second proposal, and H. Wiesmann (*Die Klagelieder* [Frankfurt: Philosophisch-theologische Hochschule Sankt Georgen, 1954] 177) derives the third emendation cited from Akkadian *kušapu*.

[216] See page 53 above and F. E. Peiser ("Miscellen," *ZAW* 17 [1897] 350) who notes that the interpretation of rabbinic passages may have been influenced by this biblical usage and that *takpuštu* is in fact based on an original form *takpuru* (see *AHW* s.v. *kapâru*). See also R. Gordis, *The Song of Songs and Lamentations* (New York: Ktav, 1974) on Lam 3:16.

[217] F. Buhl, *Die Sprache der Amarnabriefe* (Leipzig: August Pries, 1909) 21.

[218] The text is from *Ugaritica* V, p. 555. The comparison is rejected by J. Blau and J. C. Greenfield ("Ugaritic Glosses," *BASOR* 200 [1970] 13). Dietrich, Loretz, and Sanmartin ("Zur Ugaritischen Lexikographie XIII," *UF* 7 [1975] 162) compare Akkadian *kubšu* ("turban"). On "heaven" and "earth" as a fixed pair in West Semitic texts, see Y. Avishur, "Word Pairs Common to Phoenician and Biblical Hebrew," *UF* 7 (1975) 42-43.

Ugaritic word. To use this word therefore to broaden the understanding of biblical כפש is both ill-advised and unnecessary.

כרבל (1 Chr 15:27)

Context alone makes it obvious that this word means "clothed."[219] The parallel passage in 2 Sam 6:14 has the fundamentally different and yet orthographically similar מכרכר בכל עז לפני יהוה, which Bertheau saw as the original and 1 Chr 15:27 as a corruption, although a surprisingly coherent one appropriate to the Chronicler's interests.[220] Although likely included because of its similarity to 2 Sam 6:14 this phrase is not to be regarded as a corruption of it.[221] The verb is commonly regarded as a denominative from the Aramaic noun כרבלא ("mantle," as in Dan 3:21) while Ružička sees the root rather as a dissimilated form of כרבר from the root כבר meaning "braid."[222] Rabin argues that it could not have dissimilated from כבל ("tie, fetter") since such a meaning is inappropriate for a מעיל בוץ, tracing it instead to the Hittite *kariya* ("cover, wrap") and thence *kariulli* ("hood").[223]

כרסם (Ps 80:14)

That this root refers to the damage caused to a plant which is eaten by a wild boar is confirmed by the parallel ירענה. Comparison with the rabbinic קרסם is therefore quite appropriate.[224] An etymology is offered by the observation that dissimilation of a lengthened second radical often

---

[219] For a homographic root in rabbinic Hebrew see LNHeb 2. 395; an Arabic form means "march slowly" (Lane s.v. كربل).

[220] See E. L. Curtis and A. Madsen, ICC on 1 Chr 15:27.

[221] W. Rudolph, HAT on 1 Chr 15:27.

[222] For the Aramaic see Dan 3:21; the word is known also in Akkadian (*karballatu*) on which see *CAD* K, p. 215. It could have entered Hebrew through Persia (J. C. Greenfield, written communication). In any case, it may be the sole example of a loan-word, albeit Hebraized, among the verbal forms here discussed. Ružička (pp. 20 and 120) compares גדיל for an example of the semantic shift from "big" to "braid."

[223] C. Rabin, "Hittite Words in Hebrew," *Or* 32 (1963) 123; see also I. Yannay, "Augmented Verbs," *HUCA* 45 (1974) 91-92.

[224] M. Peʾa 2:7 and *Tg. Ps.-J.* Deut 28:38, cited by BDB s.v. כרסם and H. Vogelstein, *Die Landwirtschaft in Palästina zur Zeit der Mishnah* (Berlin: Mayer & Müller, 1894) 53. LESA (p. 27) notes also Ethiopic *qärsämä* ("cut dry wood").

takes the form of a liquid, especially ר, so that this word might be compared with כסם ("cut hair").[225] Proposed emendations include יהרסנה and ירמסנה.[226] The verb has also been proposed for 1QM 14:7.[227]

כשה (Deut 32:15)

As it follows שמן and עבה, this word can reasonably be expected to refer to obesity. Among those cognates adduced to suit this meaning are Arabic كشئ ("fill with food"), vulgar Arabic كشى ("be stubborn"), and Akkadian kissatum ("food").[228] Ehrlich considers حش ("fill") also related.[229] A more apt comparison would be with Akkadian kašû ("increase").[230] Proposed emendations include עָשָׁה and כָּשִׁית.[231] Driver explains the versions' "enlarge" as due to comparison with Syriac ܟܫܐ ("pile up").[232]

לעב (2 Chr 36:16)

That this word means "mock" is recognized from cognates in Aramaic and Arabic as well as later Hebrew.[233] According to Kautzsch it is common Semitic only in the meaning "play, jest" attested for Arabic, but was displaced in Hebrew by שחק, only to be restored as an Aramaism by

---

[225] Ezek 44:20, also Akkadian kasâmu ("cut to pieces"). Ružička (p.185) compares כסמח. Other examples of such dissimilation are שרביט and דרמשק (GKB 1. 110).

[226] C. A. Briggs, ICC and William Oesterley, The Psalms on Ps 80:14.

[227] Yigael Yadin, The Scroll of the War of the Sons of Light Against the Sons of Darkness (Oxford: University Press, 1962) 326-27.

[228] GB and BDB s.v. כשה; see A. S. Yahuda, "Bagdadische Sprichwörter," in Orientalische Studien Theodor Nöldeke (Giessen: Alfred Töpelmann, 1906) 413.

[229] EMK on Deut 32:15.

[230] R. Giovanni, "Nota," Bibbia e Oriente 8 (1966) 306. KB (s.v. כשה) notes also Pehlevi כשון ("grow") and conjectures a related form for the Masoretic ויכש (Hos 14:6). Driver (ICC on Deut 32:15) objects that the Arabic كشئ would appear in Hebrew as כשא.

[231] Bertholet (KHC) and TSPM (on Deut 32:15); see also Jer 5:28.

[232] ICC on Deut 32:15; Vg. dilatatus may also suggest כסה (see Vg. Deut 12:20).

[233] BDB s.v. לעב. Regarding the possibility of this verb's occurrence in Sir 30:13 see APOT and Moshe Katz in IQR p. 129, note 4.

the Chronicler with the attested connotation.[234] Tur-Sinai proposes reading מעליבים although this word too is unattested in the Bible and often regarded as a transposition from the biblical לעב.[235]

לעז (Ps 114:1)

The certainty of the meaning and accuracy of this root is probably due to its prominent place in subsequent Hebrew usage, which Kutscher ascribes to its use by Rashi.[236] Although occasionally emended, it is usually understood as alluding to the foreign nature of Egyptian language.[237] The word is not limited to languages subject to Jewish influence; cognates are found also in Arabic and Syriac.[238]

לעט (Gen 25:30)

On the basis of Syriac ܠܥܛܐ ("jaw"), Akkadian laʾātu ("consume"), and tannaitic usage, it has long been recognized that this word means "eat voraciously."[239] Comparisons with Arabic have focused on لغط ("utter indistinct sounds, speak confusedly") although Guillaume notes ألغط ("make gurgling noise").[240]

מהל (Isa 1:22)

The meaning "dilute" is obvious from context. Tannaitic Hebrew (מהול) and Arabic (مهل) attest words referring to "diluted juice" and "liquid pressed from olives" respectively.[241] However, there has been a

---

[234] Kautzsch, pp. 46-47.
[235] TSPM on 2 Chr 36:16; see HALAT s.v. לעב.
[236] מלים ותולדותיהן (Jerusalem: Kiryat Sepher, 1965) 63.
[237] A. A. Anderson (The Book of Psalms [London: Oliphants, 1972] on Ps 114:1) notes that foreign languages are regarded with hostility in Isa 28:11 and Jer 5:15. Gunkel (HKAT on Ps 114:1) suggests לעג, whereas Dahood (AB on Ps 114:1) would read לעז ("strong") , regarding the lamed as emphatic.
[238] Arabic لعز ("talk enigmatically," Lane, p. 2664) and Syriac ܠܚܕ ("speak indistinctly," PS, p. 1961).
[239] HALAT s.v. לעט and F. Perles, "Babylonisch-biblischen Glossen," OLZ 8 (1905) 128. CAD (L, p. 6) regards laʾātu as a variant of alātu.
[240] GHAL 2. 20; see KB and BDB s.v. לעט.
[241] BHS even proposes reading מוהל here (on Isa 1:22); see G. B. Gray (ICC on Isa 1:22). GHAL (1. 11 and 27) compares Arabic مهين which means "vitiated."

persistent fascination with seeing מהל as the Aramaization of biblical מול ("circumcise"). Scholars have compared the Latin *vinum castrare* as well as other Indo-European phrases describing dilution metaphorically.[242] This equation is not without problems. Procksch notes that castration (as in the Latin) is hardly the same as circumcision.[243] Ehrlich points out that wine was always mixed with water among Israelites, while Haupt remarks that from the biblical point of view circumcision symbolized purification and would be an unlikely metaphor for weakening.[244] He compares Syriac ܢܚܠ and Hebrew נהל ("rest, subside") to justify his definition "dreggish."[245]

מוּק (Ps 73:8)

Despite occasional emendations, this verb is well attested in various dialects of Aramaic, where it means "mock," and as "be foolish" in Arabic.[246] A relationship with Greek μωχαω is often noted.[247] Briggs considers the form to be an Aramaism.[248]

מחק (Judg 5:26)

A contextual meaning "smash" or the like is obvious. Often compared with Aramaic מחק ("rub off, erase") which is deemed cognate to the nearby Hebrew מחץ, the meaning is closer to Arabic محق ("annihilate").[249]

---

[242] Pliny, *Natural History* XIX.53; Procksch (KAT on Isa 1:22) compares the reference to uncircumcised fruit in Lev 19:23. See also English *cut*, German *verschneiden*, Latin *jugulare falernum*, etc., as cited by Wildberger (BKAT on Isa 1:22).
[243] KAT on Isa 1:22.
[244] RG on Isa 1:22, but cf. Gen 34:24-25.
[245] "The Etymology of Mohel, Circumciser," *AJSL* 22 (1906) 252-53; he considers מים to be a gloss.
[246] *HALAT* and BDB s.v. מוּק and GHAL 1. 11. H. Torczyner (review of Schlögl, *Die Heiligen Schriften*, in *Gottingische Gelehrte Anzeigen* 178 [1916] 328) compares Ps 78:6. KB (s.v. מוּק) proposes the reading יעמיקו, while Gunkel (HKAT on Ps 73:8) cites Grätz's suggestion to read יקמו.
[247] LCh (2. 17) regards the Aramaic as original, while H. P. Chajes ("Notes de Lexicographie Hebraique," *REJ* 44 [1902] 228) suggests the opposite.
[248] ICC on Ps 73:8.
[249] See C. F. Burney, *The Book of Judges* (on Judg 5:26) and C. Rabin, "Judges V,2 and the Ideology of Deborah's War," *JJS* 6 (1955) 133 as

מלץ (Ps 119:103)

Context suggests the meaning "be sweet" which can be supported by cognates in Arabic.[250] Some relate also מרץ (Job 6:25).[251]

נבח (Isa 56:10)

This word illustrates well the weaknesses in the proposition that hapax legomena are necessarily difficult or obscure. The context alone makes the meaning "bark" clear, while cognates can be found in rabbinic Hebrew, Akkadian, Mandaic, Arabic, Syriac, and Ethiopic.[252] The meaning is universally recognized and accepted.[253]

נדא (2 Kgs 17:21)

The meaning of this word can be seen in the qĕrē וידח. Several contend that the kĕtîḇs א is merely a textual corruption for the more correct ח.[254] Thus Montgomery compares the use of נדח in Deut 13:6.[255] Perles regards וידא as a mixed form of the qĕrē (וידח) and וישא on the basis of the preceding verse.[256] Others see it as a parallel form of נדה ("drive away").[257] One should note also Arabic ندا ("throw") and Syriac ܢܘܥ ("spring forth").[258] The root has had no place in subsequent Hebrew use.

---

well as Y. Kutscher, מלים ותולדותיהן, 50 and W. F. Albright, "The Earliest Form of Hebrew Verse," *JPOS* 2 (1922) 80 note 2.

[250] *HALAT* (s.v. מלץ) compares also Ethiopic lāmāsā.

[251] H. Gunkel (HKAT on Ps 119:103); see also A. Fitzgerald, "The Interchange of *L, N,* and *R* in Biblical Hebrew," *JBL* 97 (1978) 485. This position is disputed in KD (on Isa 56:10). KB (s.v. מלץ) proposes that עמלץ also be related to this root.

[252] See BDB and GB s.v. נבח.

[253] W. von Soden ("n als Wurzelaugment im Semitischen," *Wissenschaftliche Zeitschrift Martin-Luther-Universitat Halle* 17 [1968] 176) includes this among examples of initial *nun* verbs which are from possibly biliteral roots and pertain to sound.

[254] This seems to be the interpretation of the versions; LXX and *Tg. Neb.* use translations commonly applied to נדח. For manuscript evidence see *BHK*.

[255] ICC on 2 Kgs 17:21; see also DLS, p. 94.

[256] F. Perles, "A Miscellany of Lexical and Textual Notes on the Bible," *JQR* 2 (1911-12) 82.

[257] Thus BDB and KB s.v. נדא.

[258] PS (p. 2291) compares this with Hebrew נזה; LS (p. 415) with Akkadian nazû.

נוט (Ps 99:1)

We have already alluded to the lessons one can learn from an evaluation of this word.[259] The evidence of the versions is ambiguous. The contextual meaning "shake" was for a long time justified by emendation to the more common root מוט (as in Ps 93:1) on the basis of the orthographic similarity of מ and נ in Paleo-Hebrew script.[260] Alternative emendations include תמוג, תנוס, and תנוע.[261] Others have preferred to see a by-form of נוד or the Arabic نط.[262] BDB cites both the Targum's נוט ("scare") and Arabic نوط ("hang").[263] A conjectural, but striking parallel emerges from the Ugaritic root ntt ("shake") and is now widely considered to confirm the textual validity of this Hebrew passage.[264] נוט and ntt are thus presented as by-forms from the same originally biconsonantal root.[265] So reliable is this conclusion held to be that Judg 5:4 is understood by some to include an attestation of the same verb.[266] The history of this word's interpretation thus vividly illustrates the shift in exegetical styles: where a hapax legomenon was once assumed to be textually corrupt, given some cognate support it is accepted and in turn used to reassess the vocalization and word division of another passage.[267]

נוש (Ps 69:21)

It is not clear that this is the root intended by the attested form ואנושה. GB and BDB compare the Syriac ܢܫ ("weak").[268] Others note

---

[259] Pp. 14-15 and 48-49 above.
[260] DLS, p. 116.
[261] See GB s.v. נוט, H. Gunkel (HKAT), R. Kittel (KAT), and J. Wellhausen (SBOT) on Ps 99:1.
[262] For example, A. Ehrlich (*Die Psalmen* on Ps 99:1) and L. Kopf ("Arabische Etymologien und Parallelen zum Bibelwörterbuch," *VT* 8 [1958] 183). KD (on Ps 99:1) cites Arabic نود ("bend").
[263] S.v. נוט.
[264] E. Lipinski, "Juges 5,4-5 et Psaume 68:8-11," *Bib* 48 (1967) 191-93.
[265] Although some regard תנוט as a form of נטט, Loewenstamm ("Ugarit and the Bible I," *Bib* 56 [1975] 107) notes that middle weak and geminate verbs often have interchangeable forms.
[266] נטפו is interpreted by Lipinski ("Juges 5,4-5," 193-94) as a combination of conjunctive פ and a form of נט ("shake").
[267] Although Ugaritic provides a parallel usage, the Semitic root was already known from Arabic.
[268] S.v. נוש; the verb is a geminate in Syriac (see PS p. 2471).

the Akkadian nâšu ("shake," a meaning found also for Arabic نوس) which could fit this context.[269] Many prefer to derive this word from the common root אנש ("weak, sickly"). Thus Dahood describes the attested form as a feminine noun meaning "disease," while Gunkel prefers the adjectival reading אֲנֻשָּׁה,[270] Tur-Sinai emends it to אֲבוּשָׁה, and Oesterley would omit the word altogether so as to create a better reading.[271]

נחץ (1 Sam 21:9)

The context clearly requires a meaning "urgent" for נחוץ. Emendations proposed to suit this include נאוץ and נחוש although Budde notes that none of these roots occurs in the nifʿal.[272] Klostermann has suggested reading נחרץ ("decisive").[273] Comparison with Arabic نحض ("urge") is common, as is the ascribed relationship to לחץ through a ל-נ interchange.[274] Stoebe mentions the possibility of reading בְּחוּץ.[275]

נלה (Isa 33:1)

The structure of the verse in which this root appears is quite transparent, and כנלתך is clearly equivalent to כהתמך, meaning "finish." The proposed reading ככלתך suits this meaning well and is supported by one Hebrew manuscript and now 1QIsa^a,[276] as well as the complete absence of the root נלה in other Semitic languages, including post-biblical Hebrew, although some have compared Arabic نال ("obtain") and others the

---

[269]DP, 64, note 3.
[270]AB and HKAT on Ps 69:21. D. Wetzstein ("Ueber אנושה Ps 69,21" in *Biblischer Kommentar über die Psalmen* [ed. Franz Delitzsch; 4th ed.; Leipzig: Dorffling und Franke, 1883] 890) notes also Mic 1:9.
[271]TSPM and William Oesterley, *The Psalms* (London: SPCK, 1955) on Ps 69:21.
[272]TSPM, H. P. Smith (ICC) and K. Budde (KHC) on 1 Sam 21:9.
[273]Cited by H. P. Smith, ICC on 1 Sam 21:9 (see Dan 9:26).
[274]S. R. Driver, *Notes on the Hebrew Text and Topography of the Books of Samuel* and E. P. Dhorme, *Le Livre de Samuel* (Paris: Librairie Victor Lecoffre, 1910) on 1 Sam 21:9.
[275]KAT on 1 Sam 21:9.
[276]Duhm (HKAT on Isa 33:1) notes the occurrence of כלה in the similar context of Isa 16:4; TSLS (2. 130) lists several other cases in which כ was mistaken for נ. For manuscript evidence, see C. D. Ginsburg's edition of the Hebrew Bible.

obscure מגלם (Job 15:29).[277] The claimed occurrence of a related word in the Tabnit inscription is generally regarded as an error and in any case does not seem to provide a meaning which can adequately resolve the Hebrew context.[278]

נצא (Jer 48:9)

Böttcher ascribes this verb to the root נצץ, spelled as it is to resemble the following תצא; Bergstrasser, however, rejects the accuracy of all passages in which a finite verbal form is joined to the infinitive absolute of a similar root.[279] Some therefore prefer to read נֵצָא; others retain the consonants by revocalizing this and the following verb to נִצָּה הִצָּה.[280] Bright considers the present text to be the result of a conflation of both these texts.[281] The root has had no place in Hebrew until the modern period when it has been used for "fly."[282]

נתס (Job 30:13)

This root is most often regarded as a variant of נתץ, which is actually attested in nine manuscripts, and to conform with which Duhm would emend this passage.[283] Tur-Sinai prefers נָסֹתוּ, claiming that the

---

[277] König 1. 575 and M. Dahood, "Northwest Semitic Philology and Job," 61.
[278] The inscription reads (line 7) אל יגל; see C. C. Torrey ("New Notes on Some Old Inscriptions," ZA 26 [1912] 81) and S. Gevirtz ("West-Semitic Curses and the Problem of the Origins of Hebrew Law," VT 11 [1961] 149) who equates this with the noted Arabic word. KAI (13.7) presents the phrase as אל <כ>י <ל>ג<ך>.
[279] Friedrich Böttcher, Ausführliches Lehrbuch der Hebräischen Sprache, p. 227 and GKB 2. 64.
[280] W. L. Moran, "Ugaritic ṣiṣuma and Hebrew ṣiṣ," Bib 39 (1958) 71 and Friedrich Schwally, "Die Reden des Buches Jeremia gegen die Heiden," ZAW 8 (1888) 197. Dahood ("The Linguistic Position of Ugaritic in the Light of Recent Discoveries," Sacra Pagina [Gembloux: Editions Duculot, 1959] 1. 274) interprets the attested form as "shine" on the basis of yṣ' in Ugaritic and Arabic.
[281] AB on Jer 48:9.
[282] Canaani s.v. נצא. ESh compares יצא (s.v. נצא); for examples of similar verbs with initial yod and nun see note 186 above.
[283] B. Duhm, KHC on Job 30:13 and KB s.v. נתס; Driver (ICC on Job 30:13) remarks on the slightly difference nuance of נתץ which is applied elsewhere to the pulling down of buildings, whereas the present context

present text has been influenced by the following נחיבתי, although Szold argues that the assonance is intentional.[284] One should also note Arabic نتش ("pull forth").[285]

נתע (Job 4:10)

The simplest explanation for this obscure form is that it is an Aramaized or even corrupt form of the common Hebrew root נתץ. The former position is, however, considerably weakened by the absence of such a verb with the same meaning in Aramaic.[286] Several better-supported etymologies have therefore been proposed. Eitan notes the Ethiopic nateʿa ("flee") which yields a meaning fundamentally similar to that intended by the medievals who saw in this word a nifʿal form of מחה.[287] Šanda compares Akkadian naṭû ("crush"), which may also provide the etymology for attaʾu ("fang") for which Guillaume compares the modern Egyptian Arabic تعتح ("pull out," especially a tooth).[288] Moran

---

refers to breaking up a path; to relieve such concerns, the kind of semantic parallel Cohen proposes would be helpful (see pp. 13-15 above) See also *BHK* on Job 30:13.
[284] N. H. Tur-Sinai, *The Book of Job* and Benjamin Szold, *The Book of Job* (Baltimore: H. F. Siemers, 1886) on Job 30:13.
[285] Lane, p. 2762.
[286] Syriac ܢܬܥ means "pull, outweigh" (PS, p. 2482). Fitzmyer finds this root in *KAI* 222:B.29 which he reads ותנתע לי יקפי יקף ותקף (if I am attacked, "you must surround those who surround me and draw for me," *The Aramaic Inscriptions of Sefire* [BibOr 19; Rome: Pontifical Biblical Institute, 1967] 68), although Dupont Sommer reads ותנת עליה קפי קפי (cited in *KAI* 2. 255); but much of the line is damaged and the word division is quite uncertain. Dhorme (*A Commentary on the Book of Job*, on Job 4:10) notes the contextually similar use of נתץ in Ps 58:7; the root appears also in Job 19:18.
[287] "Biblical Studies," *HUCA* 14 (1939) 12 and p. 78 above. LESA (p. 35) notes also natʿe ("be split").
[288] A. Šanda, "Zu Job 4,10," *BZ* 2 (1904) 121 and GHAL 3. 5. AHW (p. 768) compares naṭû to Hebrew נטה ("extend"). Attaʾu occurs several times, but only in *Enuma Eliš*. (For citations see *CAD* A-2, p. 511; note the parallel use of sinnu as in II.83.) That the root begins with n is supported by variants which read an-ta-ʾu (S. Langdon, *The Babylonian Epic of Creation* [Oxford: Clarendon Press, 1923] 86-87). Harri Holma (*Die Namen der Körperteile im Assyrisch-Babylonischen* [Leipzig: Otto Harrassowitz, 1911] 151) correlates this with the root ltʿ, although this is not necessary for the biblical נתע. Landsberger considers attaʿu more likely an indefinite pronoun (see W. von Soden, "Zum Wortschatz des hymischepischen Dialekts," *ZA* 41 [1933] 172). Dahood ("The Etymology of

finds support for this interpretation in the reading of 1QIsa[a] 19:18 נתעם which he interprets as a scribal correction of the "meaningless [sic]" form נהעם.[289] Obviously this view assumes the meaninglessness of נהעם, at least to the scribe of the Qumran scroll, as well as his willingness to make corrections in a biblical text. Scribal error by transposition seems a more suitable explanation—whichever text one judges to be corrupt.[290]

סאסא (Isa 27:8)

The interpretation of this word has been dominated by the rabbinic view of it as a reduplicated form of סאה referring to the fairness of retribution.[291] The form is beset with difficulties which make any interpretation uncertain. The correct text is not clear—whether the word is to be read as בסאסאה or בסאה, with or without a *mappiq*.[292] Its sequential relationship with בשלחה suggests that it be treated as an infinitive with the third person feminine singular suffix. This approach would support a meaning "drive away" on which basis some compare שאשא › ששא.[293] Ehrlich treats the form as basically equivalent to בשאה.[294] Others compare זעזע or טאטא.[295] Proposed cognates include Arabic سوس ("scare away"), Syriac ܣܐܣܐ ("drive away with cry of *sa*ʿ"), and rabbinic סאסאה ("top of ear of corn").[296]

---

*Malta*ʿ*ot* [Ps 58,7]," *CBQ* 17 [1955] 301-3) suggests that the root occurs also in the Ugaritic text *CTA* 4.VIII.19-20 and 6.II.24 where instead of b<u>t</u>brn qn ... he would read b<u>t</u>br ntʿn ..., explaining ntʿn as a noun meaning "teeth."

[289] W. M. Moran, "The Putative Root ʿtm in Is. 9:18," *CBQ* 12 (1950) 153. The root's occurrence in Sir 3:14 is certainly to be judged as a misspelling of the corrected form of תנטע, although the parallel with תמחה is striking.

[290] See s.v. עתם (p. 148 below).

[291] See p. 66 above; the word is thus translated in the *KJV*, *RV*, *RSV*, and *JPSV*.

[292] See *BHK*, *BHS*, and Ginsburg edition on Isa 27:8.

[293] J. Herrmann, "סאסא Jes 27₈ and שאשא Hes 39₂," *ZAW* 36 (1916) 243 and p. 166 below.

[294] EMK on Isa 27:8; see J. Herrmann, KAT on Ezek 39:2.

[295] F. Feldmann, EHAT and O. Kaiser, OTL on Isa 27:8; note also Arabic زَاجَل ("push away"). Buchanan (ICC on Isa 27:8) would read בטאטא. KB regards the form as possibly onomatopoeic, and Driver ("Some Hebrew Verbs, Nouns, and Pronouns," *JTS* 30 [1929] 372) compares English *shoo-shoo*.

[296] For example, TSLS 3. 399. S. Daiches ("An Explanation of Isaiah 27,8," *JQR* 6 [1915-16] 402) considers Akkadian *sassu* equivalent to this rabbinic form (see *AHW*, p. 1032).

סכת (Deut 27:9)

Context requires a meaning close to "pay attention." Several apparent cognates, including Arabic سكت, Akkadian *sakâtu*, and Old South Arabic שכת, have the appropriate meaning "be silent."[297] Albright, relying on the usual correspondence of Arabic س to Hebrew שׁ and the fact that הסכת is followed by a *paseq* which, he claims, often indicates a textual corruption, as well as the dubious status of a hapax legomenon, prefers to read התכנס.[298] The root occurs in Sir 13:23.[299]

סלא (Lam 4:2)

On the basis of סלה (Job 28:16, 19) which also occurs in the puʻal followed by ב and in context with "gold," this word is usually understood to mean "as valuable as."[300] Cognates are found in the Arabic سلا ("pay") and Sabean סלא ("consecrate").[301] Rudolph's emendation הממלאים is based on the Vulgate's *amicti*, which would itself be more easily explained as based on a derivation from סלל.[302] The apparently opposite meaning of rabbinic Hebrew's homographic root is to be traced to Aramaic.[303]

סלד (Job 6:10)

The most obvious cognate to this word is in rabbinic Hebrew where סלד seems to mean "recoil" (as in *b. Šabb.* 40b) leading to the meaning "jump" for the biblical occurrence.[304] Others prefer the Arabic سلد ("beat the ground in running").[305] Driver objects to both these compari-

---

[297] KB s.v. סכת; Nöldeke (*ZDMG* 29 [1875] 327) questions Stade's effort to include שׁקט in this group.

[298] "The Assumed Hebrew Stem *skt*, "be silent," *JBL* 39 (1920) 166-67. On his claim regarding the *paseq*, see p. 3 above.

[299] For the meaning of this passage see Qoh 9:16 (*APOT* on Sir 13:23). Regarding the fact that this occurrence is in the nifʻal, see p. 177 note 22 below.

[300] Thus H. Wiesmann, *Die Klagelieder*, 219; D. Hillers, AB on Lam 4:2; GB, BDB, and KB s.v. סלא.

[301] GB and BDB s.v. סלא.

[302] KAT on Lam 4:2, citing also Cant 5:14, Exod 28:17 and 39:10; see also Wiesmann on Lam 4:2.

[303] LCh 2. 165.

[304] BDB s.v. סלד; NJV translates "writhe."

[305] KB s.v. סלד; according to Dhorme (*A Commentary on the Book of Job*, on Job 6:10) this word can be traced to the Indo-European base *sal* from which derive also Latin *salire* and Greek ἅλλομαι.

sons. With regard to the latter, he points out that Arabic س does not normally correspond to Hebrew ס and that the meaning adduced is actually secondary in Arabic; as for rabbinic usage, he claims that the usual interpretation is influenced by the biblical passage.[306] This leaves only Grätz's emendation ואעלזה or the similar ואעלסה.[307]

סלק (Ps 139:8)

This verb can hardly be considered a mystery. Not only is its meaning clear from context, but the same word is attested often in biblical Aramaic as well as throughout Aramaic and Arabic.[308]

סמן (Isa 28:25)

We have already alluded to the medieval opinion which interpreted this word as "marked" on the basis of rabbinic סימן.[309] Since סימן is generally taken to be a loanword from the Greek σημαινω and so inappropriate for the period at which Isaiah 28 was composed, BHS would omit the form altogether, citing numerous ancient versions in support; others regard the verb as a corrupt dittography of the following כסמת.[310] Theodotion, Aquila, and the Vulgate equate נסמן with דחן which stands in a similar place in the list of Ezek 4:9 and is appropriate for the list of

---

[306] S. R. Driver, ICC on Job 6:10.
[307] Cited by S. R. Driver, ICC on Job 6:10.
[308] The root is סלק although the dagesh and nasalized form הנסקה have often led to the assumption of נסק (see W. von Soden, "n als Wurzelaugment im Semitischen," *Wissenschaftliche Zeitschrift Martin-Luther-Universität Halle* 17 [1968] 178). According to AHW (p. 1014), Akkadian *salâqu* is an Aramaic loanword. For semantic parallels to the biblical passage see Amos 9:2 and EA 264:15.
[309] Pp. 55 and 88 above.
[310] BHS on Isa 28:15, citing LXX, VL, Syro-Hexapla, Peshiṭta, Arabic, and Ethiopic translations; see KB and BDB s.v. סמן (for כ-נ confusion, see note 27 above). RG (on Isa 28:25) considers this to be an Aramaized plural form of כסמת (hence כסמין) which was added as a gloss. N. Allony ("ספר טור-סיני in "ישעיה ב'שבעים מלים בודדות' לרס"ג] [Jerusalem: Kiryat Sepher, 1960] 285) rejects the derivation of rabbinic סימן from Greek σημεῖον, arguing that were this the case the word would have been spelled סימיון.

grains of which it is a part.[311] McPherson emends the word to נסמר ("bristly").[312]

סעה (Ps 55:9)

The interpretation of this word is in many ways illustrative of the fate of hapax legomena. It was often emended to various similar-looking words which might pertain to wind— סערה, סער, סופה[313]—or compared to appropriate cognates such as Arabic سعى ("hurry"), Syriac ܣܥܐ ("attack"), and even Akkadian seʾu.[314] More recently attention has turned to the tannaitic root סוע ("sweep")[315] and Ugaritic sʿy ("sweep") which is equated with Arabic ساع.[316] The form סעה is thus derived from a middle, rather than final, weak verb.

סרף (Amos 6:10)

Little scholarly progress has been made in dealing with this word. There are still those who would see in it an orthographic variant of שרף ("burn") although interpretations must be such as to avoid violating ancient Israel's disdain for the practice of cremation.[317] Hammershaimb, for example, holds that the burning may have been of fragrance in honor

---

[311] The translations are κεγχρον and milium respectively; see the rabbinic interpretation (cited on p. 64 above).

[312] W. B. McPherson ("The Words Sorah and Nisman in Isaiah xxviii, 25," *Johns Hopkins University Circulars* 22 [1902] 88) notes that the word is used also in y. Ḥal. 1b.

[313] C. A. Briggs, ICC and H. J. Kraus, BKAT on Ps 55:9.

[314] BDB and KB s.v. סעה; KB notes also Arabic ساع and Syriac ܣܥܐ ("calumny").

[315] Saul Liebermann, *Tosefta Ki-fshutah* (New York: Jewish Theological Seminary, 1955) 2. 629, and Hanoch Yalon, מבוא לנקוד המשנה (Jerusalem: Bialik Institute, 1964) 83-84 regarding m. Kil. 5:7 and t. Kil. 3:12 where the subject is also wind. The word may also occur (albeit derived from the biblical usage) in 1QH 3:6] רוח סוע, although the lacuna could have held a ר.

[316] Jonas C. Greenfield, review of ספר חנוך ילון in *JAOS* 87 (1967) 70 and "Some Glosses on the Keret Epic," *EY* 9 (1969) 63; see also John Gray, *The KRT Text in the Literature of Ras Shamra* (2d ed.; Leiden: E. J. Brill, 1964) 13 and 46-47.

[317] Tacitus, *The Histories* V, 5 (LCL pp. 182-83) and m. ʿAbod. Zar. 1:3.

of the dead, and Sellin sees the word as a gloss added to explain this atypical use of cremation, here required on account of the multitude of deaths.[318] Since the time of Ibn Quraish, Jewish tradition has emphasized the preceding דודו, inferring thereby that מסרף must be a relative ("maternal uncle"), a view echoed by Mays.[319] Felsenthal points to Samaritan texts to justify this derivation,[320] while Robinson compares Arabic سراف ("husband of wife's sister").[321] Driver prefers "anoint with resin" on the basis of rabbinic שָׂרָף.[322] Various emendations of the entire phrase would replace סרף with ומסרפים, מספדו, מספר, משרתו, ומספיד, or ומספרו.[323]

עבש (Joel 1:17)

The opening phrase of this verse is difficult; as exegetes are fond of noting, three of its four words are hapax legomena.[324] Although our particular interest is the first word, it should by now be abundantly clear that the meaning of any word is dependent on its context. Bewer professes the entire clause corrupt and meaningless, arguing that the correct reading is to be found in the last part of the verse.[325] Most commonly cited among potential cognates are the Arabic عبس ("dry out, shrivel")

---

[318] *The Book of Amos* (Oxford: Basil Blackwell, 1970) and KAT on Amos 6:10; see 2 Chr 16:14, 21:19, and Jer 34:5.
[319] OTL on Amos 6:10.
[320] He translates ומסרפו as "or his maternal uncle" ("Zur Bibel und Grammatik," in *Semitic Studies in Memory of Rev. Dr. Alexander Kohut* [Berlin: S. Calvary & Co., 1897] 135-36). The Samaritan texts cited are שאר יהודה 32a and 69b and Joshua ben Ali Halevi on Lev 18:18 as cited in S. Pinsker, לקוטי קדמוניות (Vienna: A. Della Tarre, 1960) Anhänge p. 67.
[321] HAT on Amos 6:10.
[322] "A Hebrew Burial Custom," *ZAW* 66 (1954) 314-15.
[323] K. Budde, "Zu Text und Auslegung des Buches Amos," *JBL* 43 (1924) 127 (noting Arabic شارف "wine jar"); BHS on Amos 6:10 (noting LXX); Joseph Reider, "Contributions to the Scriptural Text," *HUCA* 24 (1952-3) 96; TSPM on Amos 6:10; Mandelkern s.v. סרף; and RG on Amos 6:10 (noting Arabic سفر "remove" and Job 37:20), respectively. See also Georg Hoffman, "Versuche zu Amos," *ZAW* 3 (1883) 114-15 and N. H. Torczyner, "דביר", למחקר הלשון והמקרא 2 (1922) 65-66.
[324] For example, EMK on Joel 1:17.
[325] ICC on Joel 1:17.

and the rabbinic עפש ("rot, be moldy").³²⁶ Others emend, usually according to the versions: עכש עכס, בשו, פשו פרות, or עששׁ, ענשו.³²⁷ Schulz is credited with relating the form to יבש on the basis of an א-ע exchange after which א became י.³²⁸

עגם (Job 30:25)

The application to נפש makes comparison with אגם probable (compare Isa 19:10) as well as with rabbinic נפש עגימה (as in b. Ber. 55b) and עגמת נפש (b. Šabb. 116a).³²⁹ The word has been judged both an Aramaism and an Akkadian loanword although these two views seem incompatible and the evidence cited for each renders the other improbable.³³⁰ Akkadian *agâmu* would suggest a Hebrew אגם; however, Dhorme notes the nominal *tegimtu* ("anger") in support of a first radical ע.³³¹ KD also compares Arabic عجم ("disgust").³³² עגם means "grieve for."

עגן (Ruth 1:13)

Context as well as the syntactically parallel שבר suggest the meaning "wait." Comparisons with rabbinic עגונה are common but problematic.³³³ The fact that עגונה, although a tempting cognate, also refers to women

---

³²⁶BDB s.v. עבש and M. Sprengling, "Joel 1,17a," *JBL* 38 (1919) 132. Note Vg. *conputruerunt* and J. Ziegler, "Beiträge zum griechischen Dodekapropheton," in *Sylloge, Gesammelte Aufsätze zur Septuaginta* (Göttingen: Vandenhoeck & Ruprecht, 1971) 97.
³²⁷See E. Nestle, "Miscellen," *ZAW* 20 (1900) 164.
³²⁸H. Holzinger, "Sprachcharakter und Abfassungszeit des Buches Joel," *ZAW* 9 (1889) 116.
³²⁹S. R. Driver, ICC on Job 30:25; H. H. Rowley (CB on Job 30:25) regards the *aleph* a a weakened form of the guttural.
³³⁰C. J. Ball, *The Book of Job* on Job 30:25 and Josef Scharbert, *Der Schmerz im Alten Testament* (BBB 8; Bonn: Peter Hanstein Verlag, 1955) 60. Although an Akkadian word could enter Hebrew via Aramaic (see s.v. תרגם below), it would not then be called an Akkadian loanword.
³³¹E. Dhorme, *A Commentary on the Book of Job* on Job 30:25.
³³²On Job 30:25.
³³³For example, A. Bertholet, KHC on Ruth 1:13. The root of the biblical form is not entirely certain. עגן should have a dagesh in the *nun*, since the radical נ has assimilated to the suffix -נה, while a root עגה would be expected to have a *yod* in the same place (W. Rudolph, KAT on Ruth 1:13).

unable to remarry makes it so similar as conceivably to have been derived from this passage.[334] Other cognates avoid these difficulties. BDB notes עוגין ("anchor") and the Targum's עגן ("imprisoned").[335] GB cites Arabic عجم ("lock up" in the fourth form) and Syriac ܥܓܢ.[336]

עוש (Joel 4:11)

The uniqueness of this root has led several to propose emendations, including עורו, חושו, and גשו.[337] In fact, it occurs in rabbinic Hebrew and has been explained on the basis of Arabic غاث ("aid") and Old South Arabic עוֹי ("restore") and עוֹתֿ ("help").[338] Holzinger views it as a by-form of חוש.[339]

עות (Isa 50:4)

The meaning of this word is not certain, nor is its context adequate to determine which, if any, etymology is most acceptable. One possibility is that the verb is the Aramaized equivalent of the preceding.[340] Some still accept the medieval comparison with עת.[341] Ehrlich interprets the consonants (לעות) as the infinitive of לעה (= Arabic لغا, "speak a thought").[342] Volz compares also the Talmud's עות ("be accommodat-

---

[334] Edward Campbell, AB on Ruth 1:13.
[335] S.v. עגן.
[336] S.v. עגן; on n-m relationships see p. 54 note 37 above.
[337] J. Wellhausen, Skizzen und Vorarbeiten 5. 212; B. Duhm, "Anmerkungen zu den Zwölf Propheten," ZAW 31 (1911) 188; T. K. Cheyne, "A New German Commentary on the Minor Prophets," Exp series V, vol. 6 (1897) 365.
[338] See b. B. Bat. 9a. Cognates are noted by A. Guillaume, "A Contribution to Hebrew Lexicography," BSOAS 16 (1954) 5, 9, and KB and BDB s.v.עוש. Note the personal name יעוש which occurs in Akkadian as Ia-ḫaš-šu (Maurice Birot, "Textes Economiques de Mari," RA 49 [1955] 26). Rudolph (KAT on Joel 4:11) prefers غوث ("sprint") or عشاشن ("hastily") for a meaning "hurry."
[339] H. Holzinger, "Sprachcharakter und Abfassungszeit des Buches Joel," ZAW 9 (1889) 117.
[340] BDB s.v. עות.
[341] TSPM on Isa 50:4.
[342] EMK on Isa 50:4.

ing").³⁴³ It has even been treated as a by-form of עוד.³⁴⁴ But the most common view is that the text is to be emended—to לענות, להחיות, להות, לרעות, or לעות.³⁴⁵ However, the present reading is supported by all Hebrew texts as well as the allusion in 1QH 8:36.³⁴⁶ Even the Septuagint (εἶπειν) cannot be taken as decisive evidence against the received text in light of the possibility that it reflects an early effort at etymologizing.

עזק (Isa 5:2)

Interpretation continues to focus on the meaning "dig," with comparisons made to tannaitic Hebrew, Arabic, Akkadian, and Ethiopic.³⁴⁷ The word occurs in this sense also in 1QH 8:22.³⁴⁸ The sole dissenter from this interpretation is Rabin who compares Himyaritic ʻazīqa ("plain") as well as the town עזקה to derive the meaning "level."³⁴⁹

עלע (Job 39:30)

On the testimony of the versions as well as the logic of its context this word is understood as referring to "swallow." In the absence of cognates, emendations have been proposed: ילעו, ילעלעו, יעלעלו, ילעעו, or יבלעו.³⁵⁰ Others see in יעלעו a form derived from one of the

---

³⁴³P. Volz, KAT on Isa 50:4.

³⁴⁴A. Bartura, "לשון למודים לדעת לעות את יעף דבר," BM 28 (1982) 72.

³⁴⁵Günther Schwarz, "Jesaja 50₄₋₅ₐ Eine Emendation," ZAW 85 (1973) 357; T. K. Cheyne (SBOT), B. Duhm (HKAT), BHK and BHS on Isa 50:4. Support is drawn from LXX (εἶπειν, which is used for forms of ענה at 1 Kgs 25:10 and Job 2:2 etc.) and Tg. Neb. (לאלפא).

³⁴⁶לחיות רוח כושלים ולעות לעאף דבר נאלם.

³⁴⁷See m. Ohol. 18:5 and references in KB and BDB s.v. עזק as well as G. R. Driver and John C. Miles (The Babylonian Laws [Oxford: Clarendon Press, 1960] 2. 263) regarding Akkadian ezêqu. Others derive the meaning "encircle" from this evidence, compare Aramaic עזקתא ("ring").

³⁴⁸בהניפי יד לעזוק ופלגיו יכו שרשיו בצור חלמיש.

³⁴⁹Chaim Rabin, Ancient West-Arabian (London: Taylor's Foreign Press, 1951) 28.

³⁵⁰The only "exact" correspondence is with Aramaic עלעא which is cognate to Hebrew צלע (see Ezra 4:9, Dan 7:5). For emendations, see BHK, G. Hölscher (HAT) on Job 39:30, and KB and GB s.v. עלע as well as C. J. Ball, The Book of Job on Job 39:30.

above.³⁵¹ The simplest view is that the text is in error; the attested form is anomalous with respect to Hebrew phonology.³⁵²

עמש (Neh 4:11)

At first glance this would appear to be simply an orthogrphic variant of עמס, the spelling of which is supported by the personal names עמשי and עמשה.³⁵³ On the basis of the Septuagint's ἐν ὅπλοις ("armed") several scholars prefer to read חֲמֻשִׁים, which as Batten notes also avoids the apparent redundancy of עמשים.³⁵⁴ Conjectural readings include Ehrlich's נשאים and Batten's עשים.³⁵⁵

עער (Isa 15:5)

Like עלע, this root is phonologically dubious and has no known cognates.³⁵⁶ Emendations are to read יערו or יערערו although the present text may be construed as having developed from either of these.³⁵⁷ The parallel Jer 48:5 reads שמעו suggesting perhaps that the word was deemed problematic quite early.

עשק (Gen 26:20)

It is difficult to separate this root adequately from עסק and עשׂק—the former because of the inconsistent distinction between ס and שׂ in the Bible and subsequent Hebrew texts, the latter because most ancient

---

³⁵¹KD (on Job 39:30) describes the form as derived by assimilation from יעלעלן.
³⁵²See p. 174 below.
³⁵³Several manuscripts read עמסים (*BHK* on Neh 4:11), an interpretation supported by the Massorah (ed. C. D. Ginsberg, 2. 586). M. Held ("The Root zbl/sbl . . . ," *JAOS* 88 [1968] 94) compares the proximity of עמס with נשא in Isa 46:3. See Joshua Blau, *On Pseudo-Corrections in Some Semitic Languages* (Jerusalem: The Israel Academy of Sciences and Humanities, 1970) 121-22.
³⁵⁴RG and ICC on Neh 4:11. (Regarding ס-שׂ see p. 53 above).
³⁵⁵ICC on Neh 4:11 and BDB s.v. עמס.
³⁵⁶See p. 174 below.
³⁵⁷RG, B. Duhm (HKAT), KD, and H. Wildberger (BKAT) on Isa 15:5. For a discussion of the relevant kind of assimilation, see König 2. 497.

scripts do not preserve a distinction akin to that represented in Hebrew.[358] The meaning "contend" is justified by both the general demands of context and the meaning of the name שטנה in the following verse. The word is usually related to the Aramaic עסק ("quarrel") although some compare its later Hebrew homograph which means "to be occupied."[359] KB notes also عشق ("cling") and Old South Arabic עשק ("care for").[360]

עתם (Isa 9:18)

Assuming its subject to be ארץ, scholars identify this word with Arabic عتم ("be dark").[361] That verb is a denominative from عتمة ("late") and its meaning, therefore, secondary.[362] Luzzatto's interpretation ("be burnt") would appear to be supported by the Septuagint's συγκεκαυται and the Targum's חרוכת, in light of which Delitzsch suggests reading נצתה.[363] The Peshitta's ܢܘܥ, translates נוע in 2 Sam 15:20, and an appropriate emendation is offered by Tur-Sinai (מֻעַם) while a reading נתעה is justified by the Vulgate's *conturbatus est*.[364] Ehrlich prefers נערתם, while Moran accepts the reading of 1QIsa[a] (נתעם) on the basis of נתעו in Job 4:10.[365] In light of the methods used for the versions, it

---

[358]Regarding the confusion of שׁ and ס see p. 53 above.
[359]Luzzatto (on Gen 26:20) cites *b. Šebu.* 31a; John Skinner (ICC on Gen 26:20) compares Syriac ܒܣܩ which in the ʾetpaʿel means "be hostile." O. Procksch (KAT on Gen 26:20) notes also Sir 7:25, 40:1. Objecting to the inappropriateness of עסק ("be occupied"), RG (on Gen 26:20) emends to עשׁק.
[360]S.v. עשׁק; the semantic development of the root would be "cling with love > cling in strife" (BDB s.v. עשׁק).
[361]J. Blau, "Etymologische Untersuchungen auf Grund des Palastinischen Arabisch," *VT* 5 (1955) 343. On the problem of gender see GKC § 145a.
[362]W. Robertson Smith, "Old Testament Notes," *Journal of Philology* 13 (1885) 62.
[363]DLS, p. 111, and Luzzatto on Isa 9:18 (compare Arabic عتم, Lane, p. 2229). The correct reading of the Targum may, however, be חרובת (Alexander Sperber, *The Bible in Aramaic* [Leiden: E. J. Brill, 1959-73] on Isa 9:18). Smith ("Old Testament Notes," 61) points out that this meaning too is secondary.
[364]TSLS 2. 130 and KB s.v. עתם.
[365]EMK on Isa 9:18 and W. L. Moran, "The Putative Root ʿtm in Is. 9:18," *CBQ* 12 (1950) 153; see F. Nötscher, "Entbehrliches Hapax Legomena in Jesaia," *VT* 1 (1951) 302.

seems highly unlikely that one could prove any of them had a text different from our own, while 1QIsa^a is certainly no less difficult than the received text and quite readily explained as corrupt itself.

פדע (Job 33:24)

Although the context makes the meaning "save" unavoidable, there is no reasonable way for a root פדע to have been generated from פדה.[366] Most moderns therefore emend to פדהו or פרעהו.[367] The former is supported by the use of this root in v. 28 and the similar Hos 13:14, while the choice of the seemingly inappropriate פרע is based on Aramaic and mishnaic usage for "found ransom."[368] Ehrlich suggests that פדעהו is a conflate of both forms.[369] The best-known seeming cognate, Aramaic פדע, is equivalent to Hebrew פצע and not contextually suitable; Arabic فدع ("distort," "deflect") could fit.[370] König compares فدغ ("break," "crush").[371] Tur-Sinai prefers reading עדפהו, while Wetzstein suggests that this is a metathesized cognate of Arabic دفع ("thrust back").[372] A more complex view sees in this word the conjunctive פ and an imperative of a cognate to Arabic ودع (i.e. דע, "allow") so rendering, "Do not let him (go down to the pit)"; as Guillaume notes, "if we read this in Arabic we get the required meaning."[373] Whatever solution one ultimately

---

[366]Dhorme (*A Commentary on the Book of Job* on Job 33:24) suggests that ע may have been added as a mater lectionis in accord with its use for recent Yiddish although this is inappropriate to any date one might suggest for the book of Job.

[367]For manuscripts, see Ginburg's edition of the Bible at Job 33:24; commentaries with such views are ICC, EHAT, HKAT, and KAT.

[368]Dhrome (*A Commentary on the Book of Job*, on Job 33:24) compares also Ps 49:8. There is no basis to James Ross's claim ("Job 33:14-30: The Phenomenology of Lament," *JBL* 94 1975 40) that 11QtgJob (פצהי) supports this reading. That translation is similar to *Tg. Ket.* (פרוק), the Peshiṭta (ܦܘܪܩܢܐ), and even the Vulgate (*dicit libera eum*) and most likely reflects an interpretation or reading based on פדה. See N. H. Tur-Sinai, *The Book of Job* on Job 33:24.

[369]RG on Job 33:24.

[370]Lane, p. 2352.

[371]*Das Buch Hiob Eingeleitet* (Gütersloh: C. Bertelsmann, 1929) on Job 33:24.

[372]TSLS 2. 146.

[373]A. Guillaume, *Studies in the Book of Job* (ALUOS Supplement 2; Leiden: E. J. Brill, 1968) on Job 33:24; on this kind of logic note the re-

chooses, the meaning is circumscribed by vv. 18 and 28 where the occurrence of פדה makes an interpretation of v. 24 based on the same root virtually inevitable in the absence of any convincing alternative.

פוּן (Ps 88:16)

Although included here because it is vocalized as a verb, this word has been taken as various parts of speech. Delitzsch equates it with the Akkadian adverb *appūna* ("moreover").[374] Dahood proposes אָפְנָה on the basis of Prov 20:26 and Ugaritic *ʾapn*, thus rendering אפונה אמיך as "the terrors of your torture wheel."[375] GB compares Arabic افن ("be confused") to justify the Vulgate (*conturbatus*).[376] Most commonly the form is emended to אפוגה ("embarrassed") so as to accord with Ps 77:3.[377] Tur-Sinai prefers אפפוני or אפוני, and Ehrlich suggests אפוזה, claiming that the lack of recurrence should not count against this reading;[378] but if this is so, it is not clear what is to stand against the received text. *NEB*'s "cower beneath thy blows" relies on אנופה which is ascribed to the Vulgate.[379] Forms of פנה are suggested by Dahood (אֶפְנָה) and Briggs (אָפְנָה, "turned back in confusion").[380] Mandelkern notes also a proposal to read אענה.[381] Tur-Sinai argues that אמיך and אפונה are to be seen as variants of an original "your anger."[382] The lack of even vague consensus points clearly to the uncertainty regarding this word.

---

sponse of Menaḥem's students to the methodology of ben Labraṭ: ואלו כל מלה אשר אין לה דמיון אמרנו כי יש לה דומה בלשון ארמית וערבית, נמצאו הלשונות שוות מבלי הבדלה, ולמדנו שאר לשון עברית הנעלם ונהחסר. (S. Stern, *Liber Responsionum* [Vienna: 1870] 96-97).

[374]DP, pp. 135-36; the method seems to satisfy (anticipate?) Cohen's concern that contextually similar usages be sought (see pp. 13-15 above).

[375]AB on Ps 88:16.

[376]S.v. פון.

[377]BDB s.v. פון.

[378]TSLS 2. 433 and A. Ehrlich, *Die Psalmen* on Ps 88:16.

[379]L. H. Brockington, *The Hebrew Text of the Old Testament* (London: Oxford and Cambridge University Presses, 1973) on Ps 88:16.

[380]AB and ICC on Ps 88:16. As in the interpretation of *NEB* cited above, the claim that the versions support these readings seems without foundation.

[381]Mandelkern s.v. פון.

[382]Review of Schlögl, *Die Heiligen Schriften*, in Göttingische Gelehrte Anzeigen 178 (1916) 333.

פנק (Prov 29:21)

There is no question as to the meaning of this word. Cognates are known throughout Aramaic as well as in rabbinic Hebrew and Arabic, all meaning "enjoy, pamper" which fits Prov 29:21 quite readily.[383] The word is attested also in Sir 14:16 where it parallels ענג, the Hebrew root it commonly translates in the Targum.[384] Only the concluding מנון renders this verse difficult.

פסג (Ps 48:14)

Finding a suitable explanation for this word which parallels שיחו לבכם or ספרו ought not be difficult, and yet no truly satisfactory interpretation has emerged. Tur-Sinai mirrors the medieval comparison with פסגה in his interpretation of this word as "be high."[385] Emendations include פסעו and פקדו.[386] Some have compared rabbinic פסג ("cut through"), rendering the biblical form as "pass between."[387] GB notes Akkadian *pasāku*, and Mandelkern relates several initial-פ verbs, all meaning "split" or "move around" (פסג, פשח, פסע, and פסק).[388] Briggs ascribes to the Septuagint (καταδιελεσθε) and Vulgate (*distribuite*) the Hebrew *Vorlage* הפלו.[389] More recently the form has been interpreted as conjunctive פ with סוג ("fence in, repair") or שיג ("examine").[390]

פצם (Ps 60:4)

Dahood treats this word as פ with עָצְמָה ("and it went to pieces").[391] Such reasoning is more complicated than is necessary. Even though it is a

---

[383] KB s.v. פנק.
[384] As in *Tg. Onq.* Deut 28:54.
[385] TSLS 2. 431 treats the form as qal perfect.
[386] B. Duhm, KHC on Ps 48:14 and J. Morgenstern, "Psalm 48," *HUCA* 16 (1941) 20.
[387] Thus BDB (s.v. פסג) "cleft"; Driver ("Notes on the Psalms" *JTS* 43 [1942] 155) compares Arabic فسج ("part legs").
[388] S.v. פסג.
[389] ICC on Ps 48:14.
[390] M. Dahood, AB on Ps 48:14 and "The Language and Date of Psalm 48," *CBQ* 16 (1954) 17-18.
[391] AB on Ps 60:4, comparing the Ugaritic usage of *ṣmt* as parallel to *mḥṣ* in *CTA* 2.IV.9.

hapax legomenon, the meaning is not uncertain. The context refers clearly to upheavals, and appropriate cognates include Aramaic פצם ("cut out") and Arabic فصم ("crack, break").[392]

פרשז (Job 26:9)

This word raises several difficult problems. There are no cognates; even the text is uncertain. Although most texts read שׂ, one edition has שׁ which was preferred by Baer-Delitzsch.[393] Some would emend to פרשׂ; however, פרשׁ means "separate" where פרשׂ ("spread") seems more appropriate. Yannay notes the possibility of a suffixed ז or inserted ר.[394] Others suggest that it is a mixed form based on פרז and פרשׂ.[395] Some regard it as a dissimilated form of פרשש which may itself be secondary.[396]

פשח (Lam 3:11)

The medieval opinion equating this with פשׁח of *Tg. Neb.* 1 Sam 15:33 has persisted into present research, although some prefer comparison with Akkadian *pasâḫu* ("be quiet").[397] Aquila's interpretation, which relates the Hebrew to פסח ("lame") is cited as the basis for emendation by Wiesmann.[398] BHK notes that the Septuagint (κατεπαυσε) may suggest a reading וישביתו.[399] Citing Syrian Arabic فشخ, Guillaume interprets the Hebrew to mean "make to stray."[400]

---

[392] KB s.v. פצם; *AHW* (p. 839) cites also one occurrence of Akkadian *paṣâmu*.

[393] See LXX, Vg., Peshiṭta, and *Tg. Ket.* at Job 26:9. Although the rabbinic פרש רחום שדי זיו does interpret the third letter as שׂ, this cannot be considered decisive for textual matters (see pp. 66-67 above). KD (on Job 26:9) explains the שׂ as the result of dissimilation to avoid the unnatural combination זשׁ.

[394] "Augmented Verbs in Biblical Hebrew," *HUCA* 45 (1974) 92-94.

[395] *BHK* on Job 26:9 and KB s.v. פרשז.

[396] W. Chomsky in QMChomsky, p. 216.

[397] D. Hillers, AB on Lam 3:11; the root occurs also in Syriac (PS pp. 3316-17). The Akkadian cognate is cited by Jakob Barth, *Etymologische Studien*, 9; KB (s.v. פשח) notes that in the D stem this means "leave fallow."

[398] *Die Klagelieder*, on Lam 3:11.

[399] On Lam 3:11.

[400] GHAL 4. 12.

צבט (Ruth 2:14)

The Septuagint's ἐβούνισεν ("pile") is considered by some to be evidence for reading צבר or צבה which is similarly treated in Ruth 2:16.[401] Joüon proposes reading ויצב.[402] There is, however, little reason to doubt the text. The relevance of post-biblical בית צביטה ("handle") was recognized already in the rabbinic period.[403] The root is confirmed by Arabic ضبط and Ugaritic ṣbṭ.[404] These are likely to be related to the complex of cognates represented in Hebrew by צבת.[405] Thus Joüon's observation that צבט is a hapax legomenon and that the Septuagint had a different reading is inadequate reason to eliminate it from the dictionary of biblical Hebrew.[406]

צות (Isa 27:4)

Most scholars regard אציתנו as a form of יצת with the dagesh omitted either through error or because the verb was vocalized as if it were middle weak.[407] Delitzsch regards צות as related to יצת; other cases of middle weak forms of normally prima-yod verbs are known.[408] To Robertson is ascribed the view that one should read אציענה;[409] however, all ancient witnesses support the consonantal text as it stands.[410] The absence of a *dagesh* alone—although not necessarily the result of corruption—is too slim a reed to justify radical reinterpretation.

---

[401] TSPM on Ruth 2.14.

[402] *Ruth, Commentaire Philologique et Exegetique* (Rome: Pontifical Biblical Institute, 1924) 59.

[403] P. 62 above.

[404] GHAL (2. 29) considers צבת to be a weakened form of the same root.

[405] See J. C. Greenfield, "Studies in Aramaic Lexicography I," *JAOS* 82 (1962) 292-94.

[406] "Notes de critique Textuelle," *MUSJ* 6 (1913) 203.

[407] GKB 2. 173 and BL §55c'.

[408] "Philologische Forderungen an die hebräische Lexikographie," *OLZ* 19 (1916) 165, see p. 77 above.

[409] O. Procksch, KAT on Isa 27:4.

[410] 1QIsa^a reads ואציתנה; the later Hebrew root צות ("obey, command") is well-attested throughout Semitic, but does not fit this passage.

צנם **(Gen 41:23)**

The simplest potential cognate is the Talmudic צנומה ("dried bread"), supported also by Aramaic نُصْاٌ ("rock"), which can provide the justification for its connotation of "image, idol."[411] Because of the word's occurrence in Aramaic, which would not have influenced Hebrew at the time Genesis was written, Procksch prefers to compare أصنام ("idol"); others consider the word a late gloss, especially in light of its absence in the Septuagint, Vulgate, and the parallel Gen 41:6.[412] Ball suggests it arose out of confusion with the later צמחות.[413] A form such as this, though no doubt adequately understood, would benefit from independent confirmation of the sort that is available from Ugaritic and Akkadian.

צען **(Isa 33:20)**

The parallel יסע יתדותיו suggests that this verb means "move" or "fall." Ehrlich's emendation יצעה reflects the medieval etymology of this word.[414] Others prefer finding cognates, suggesting Akkadian *ṣênu*, ("load"), Arabic ظعن ("depart"), Old South Arabic ט̄ען, Ethiopic *ṣʿn*, and even Aramaic טען ("carry").[415] In fact, some of these are properly cognate with Hebrew טען ("load") which, however, Nöldeke claims is an Aramaism of the true Hebrew צען.[416] Perles respects the text of this verse sufficiently to "restore" צענו to Zech 10:2b.[417]

צפד **(Lam 4:8)**

In light of its context, a meaning "dry, shriveled" is to be expected for this word, the latter of which is confirmed by Arabic صفد("bind") and rabbinic צפד ("press").[418] Ehrlich, arguing that the rabbinic usage has

---

[411] KB s.v. צנם; Jakob Barth (*Etymologische Studien*, 44) cites an Arabic cognate as well. A Nabatean usage of this root is considered a byform of צלם (*RES* 1128 A.159).

[412] *BHK* and *KAT* on Gen 41:23.

[413] SBOT on Gen 41:23.

[414] RG on Isa 33:20.

[415] See GB, BDB, and KB s.v. צען.

[416] Review of E. Kautzsch, *Die Aramaismen*, ZDMG 57 (1903) 412.

[417] Perles, p. 33; thus it would parallel נסע as in Isa 33:20.

[418] GB, BDB, and KB s.v. צפד. The use in *Pesiq. R.* 38:1 is clearly dependent on Lam 4:8.

Hapax Legomena in Contemporary Scholarship   155

קאם (Hos 10:14)

Unquestionably a form of קום, this word has been included solely because of the atypical א. Some regard it as a mater lectionis for ā;[420] others view it as an Aramaism.[421] For König it is evidence of a tendency to triliteralize an originally biliteral verb.[422] Nyberg compares the Arabic قام ("grasp").[423]

קוש (Isa 29:21)

Often emended to various forms of יקש, this verb is most easily explained as meaning "lay trap."[424] Some suggest that the middle weak form is a variant or alternative vocalization for the initially weak יקש.[425] Despite Guillaume's comparison of قاف ("dog the footsteps of"), there are no appropriate cognates.[426] Nor does the word recur in later Hebrew. It is most likely therefore in light of the available evidence that this is a corruption or variant of the more common יקש.

קסס (Ezek 17:9)

Following the apparent contextual meaning "pluck off," many compare Hebrew קצץ; Cooke compares Arabic قشّ as well.[427] A root *qss* does

---

[419] The verse begins חשך משחור (see HKAT and RG on Lam 4:8).

[420] Alexander Sperber, "Hebrew Based upon Biblical Passages in Parallel Transmission," *HUCA* 14 (1939) 176-77.

[421] T. H. Robinson, HAT on Hos 10:14.

[422] König p. 439; compare וראמה (Zech 14:10).

[423] *Studien zum Hoseabuche* (UUÅ 1935.6; Uppsala: Almqvist & Wiksells Boktryckerie-AB, 1935) 82.

[424] יְקֻשּׁוּ or יְקֻשּׁוּן. See *BHK* and *BHS* on Isa 29:21 and GKB 2. 174. Such a connection is supported by the LXX πρόσκομμα.

[425] BL §586h".

[426] "A Contribution to Hebrew Lexicography," *BSOAS* 16 (1954) 4.

[427] ICC on Ezek 17:9; W. Zimmerli (BKAT on Ezek 17:9) notes the parallel נתק.

רהה (Isa 44:8)

Whatever its etymology, there is no question that this word means "fear."[430] The simplest approach is to emend the form to תיראו, a reading now supported by 1QIsa[a].[431] Guillaume compares Arabic روا ("fear"); other attribute the attested form to ירה on the basis of Arabic ورى.[432] Lagarde prefers the reading תרהבו which, according to Perles, led to our present reading when it was abbreviated תרה'.[433] Driver suggests תדהו which he equates with Arabic دهى ("be afraid") although Barr points out that he has missed the primary force of that verb.[434] Torrey suggests instead reading תִּדָּחוּ ("led astray").[435]

רזם (Job 15:12)

There is very little support for this root. Even the biblical text, its only occurrence throughout Hebrew, is not certain; some manuscripts read ירמזון of which the present text is seen as a metathesis or corruption, and one reads ירמון as does LXX[a].[436] Only Arabic, Mandaic, and Old

---

[428] MD 408; cited cognates are all geminates with emphatic sibilants.
[429] KB s.v. קסס; Immanuel Löw, "Yayin Koses," *REJ* 82 (1926) 167.
[430] This is ensured by the parallel תפחדו.
[431] EMK on Isa 44:8.
[432] Freytag (s.v. ورى) defines this as "be ignorant, stupefied" (compare Lane, p. 2933); the appropriate biblical form would be תרהו. See GHAL 1. 10 and 27.
[433] Perles, p. 33; note the Peshitta's ܬܬܙܝܥܘܢ.
[434] G. R. Driver, "Hebrew Notes on Prophets and Proverbs," *JTS* 41 (1940) 164 and Barr, p. 166 (see Lane, p. 927). The citation of "cognates" in medieval Jewish liturgical texts is not helpful; many hapax legomena were pressed into use for such compositions because of their biblical nuances as understood by the poet and sometimes because of their obscurity; see N. M. Sarna, "Hebrew and Bible Studies in Medieval Spain," in *The Sephardi Heritage* (ed. R. D. Barnett; New York: Ktav, 1971) 1. 323.
[435] C. C. Torrey, *The Second Isaiah* (New York: Charles Scribner's Sons, 1928) on Isa 44:8. See Vg. (*conturbemini*) and Theod μηδὲ πλανᾶσθε).
[436] BY (s.v. רזם) cites only medieval poetry in addition to the biblical occurrence. Although once believed found in the Lachish letters

South Arabic offer even potential cognates.[437] Szold suggests this be seen as a form of רז ("secret").[438]

רטה (Job 16:11)

Some possibilities for this form have been discussed under the heading ירט above to which root this form is often ascribed, usually by suggesting that the attested form should be considered as יְרָטֵנִי.[439] Szold equates such a root with ירד, echoing a medieval view.[440] Others emend to יְרַמֵּנִי.[441]

רטפש (Job 33:25)

This form is thoroughly anomalous. Most Hebrew quadriliterals result either from the reduplication of a biliteral element or the insertion of a common infix. Noting that the preceding word ends with ר, many see the initial letter as a dittography and emend the word to טפש or יטפש.[442] Comparing Syriac ܪܛܦܫ, several scholars are able to explain the quadriliteral form as resulting from an infixed ר, again basing the form on a root טפש.[443] The comparison with Ps 119:30 is alone inadequate justification for this approach.[444] Perles sees in this word a loanword from Akkadian *ritpašu* ("wide"), while Guillaume bases his view on رطب ("soft,

---

(3:5, see N. H. Tur-Sinai ed., *Lachish* I [London: Oxford University Press, 1938] 51 reading—כה רזמ -) this has now been rejected in favor of את עין or את אזן. For manuscript information see *BHK* at Job 15:12. F. Horst (BKAT on Job 15:12) suggests this root also for Sir 27:22.

[437] Arabic رزم ("fatigue," Lane p. 1077; but see R. Dozy, *Supplement aux Dictionnaires Arabes* [Leiden: E. J. Brill, 1967] 254 and N. H. Tur-Sinai, *The Book of Job* on Job 15:12), Mandaic *rzm* ("torment," MD p. 432), and Sabaean *rzm* ("requisition," J. C. Biella, *Dictionary of Old South Arabic*, 484).

[438] *The Book of Job*, on Job 15:12.

[439] BDB and KB s.v. רטה.

[440] *The Book of Job* on Job 16:11; he also compares רטט and מרט. For the medieval view see p. 82 above.

[441] C. J. Ball, *The Book of Job* on Job 16:11.

[442] N. H. Tur-Sinai, *The Book of Job* on Job 33:25, after pointing out with respect to רטפש that "there is no such word."

[443] S. Fraenkel, "Lexicalisches," *ZA* 3 (1888) 55; the word occurs also in Aramaic and later Hebrew (see p. 90 above).

[444] K. Budde, HKAT on Job 33:25; טפש, although also a hapax legomenon, is typically triliteral and supported by various cognates.

tender") with the added Arabic suffix س.[445] Others regard this as a portmanteau word composed of רטב and טפש or Egyptian *rwṯ* ("be green") and פש ("grow large").[446] Duhm reads יחי רטב, while Nichols prefers יָרָה with the Septuagint.[447] Şiproni reads רטב בשרו.[448] To the extent that the following מנער makes a meaning "fat" inappropriate, the actual background for this word has not yet been established; certainly no one has adequately explained the Masoretic text.[449]

רנה (Job 39:23)

Several regard this root as a by-form of רנן.[450] Some support for this may be found in Aramaic רני ("speak, reply").[451] Others prefer reading תרן or תרנה so as to preserve the attested consonants.[452] BDB suggests that the root is onomatopoeic.[453] Tur-Sinai proposes reading תדנה ("approach"); according to Mandelkern, the Targum (תשרי) reflects a Hebrew reading תרמה ("throw").[454]

רפף (Job 26:11)

Various cognates support the general idea of motion—Arabic رف ("wink"), Syriac وفوف ("flap wing"), and وف ("be moved"), the Targum's רפף ("shake"), rabbinic רפף ("churn milk"), Christian Palestinian Aramaic وفوف ("stir"), and Ethiopic *räfärräfä* ("strew plentifully").[455]

---

[445]F. Perles, "Babylonisch-biblische Glossen," *OLZ* 8 (1905) 181; the root would thus be *rapāšu* ("be large"). An analogous case of *t* > *ṭ* in the presence of פ is presented in Hebrew טפסר which corresponds to Akkadian *tupšarru*. GHAL 2. 30.

[446]KD on Job 33:25 and N. Herz, "Egyptian Words and Idioms in the Book of Job," *OLZ* 16 (1913) 346.

[447]KHC on Job 33:25 and H. H. Nichols, "The Composition of the Elihu Speeches," *AJSL* 27 (1911) 158.

[448]"חלופי האותיות ב' פ' במקרא," *Leš* 1 (1927) 55.

[449]Barr p. 221.

[450]C. J. Ball (*The Book of Job* on Job 39:23) compares the pairs הגה-הגג, קצה-קצץ, and Aramaic רנא-רנן.

[451]PS p. 3935, MD p. 436, and *DISO* s.v. רנה (p. 281).

[452]Mitchell Dahood, "Northwest Semitic Philology and Job," 74.

[453]S.v. רנה.

[454]S.v. רנה; see N. H. Tur-Sinai, *The Book of Job* on Job 39:23.

[455]GB, BDB, KB s.v. רפף, also S. R. Driver (ICC) and KD on Job 26:11 and F. Schulthess, *Lexicon Syropalestinum* (Berlin: Georg Reimer, 1903) 196 and LHC p. 66.

רפק (Cant 8:5)

The Arabic رفق ("help") has been cited as a cognate for this form since the medieval period.[456] Tannaitic מרפק ("elbow") and Ethiopic *rpq* ("lean") are also noted as confirming the obvious contextual reference to "lean."[457] Ehrlich finds this verb also in Judg 19:22.[458]

רצד (Ps 68:17)

Although the ancient view of this as composite persists in Malbim's interpretation of it as תרוץ צד ("run by the side of . . .") and Tur-Sinai prefers reading תרעדון, most moderns compare the Arabic رصد ("lie in wait") to derive a meaning "regard enviously."[459] The verb is attested in the Aramaic of the midrash and still earlier in Ben Sira, where the Greek confirms a meaning "lie in wait."[460] It occurs also in Akkadian.[461]

רשם (Dan 10:21)

There is no question as to the meaning or authenticity of this word. It appears also in biblical Aramaic and is thus included as a hapax legomenon by something of a technicality.[462] It is common throughout Aramaic and rabbinic Hebrew as in Arabic.[463] In light of this history as well as its unique occurrence in Daniel, there is ample reason to consider this root an Aramaism with Plöger.[464]

---

[456] See Lane, p. 1125 and p. 91 above.
[457] BDB and KB s.v. רפק and LHC p. 66.
[458] RG on Cant 8:5.
[459] TSPM and M. Malbim on Ps 68:17; see A. A. Anderson, *The Book of Psalms* on Ps 68:17.
[460] Sir 14:32, see also LNHeb 4. 464.
[461] *AHW* p. 959.
[462] Dan 5:24-25, 6:9-14; see p. 20 above.
[463] See PS, p. 3985, MD p. 437, Lane p. 1084, *KAI* 223.C3, 1QH 16:10-11, and Hubert Grimme, *Texte und Untersuchungen zur Ṣafatenisch-Arabischen Religion*, p. 187.
[464] KAT on Dan 10:21; James Montgomery (ICC on Dan 10:21) notes that the LXX τὰ πρῶτα suggests a reading הָרָשִׁים.

שוח (Gen 24:63)

It is ironic that so seemingly simple a passage could cause such confusion and even consternation, leading one scholar not usually given to frustration to remark "the verb is not translatable."[465] The rendering "pray, meditate" by most versions which compare this form with שיח is accepted by KD although Ehrlich notes Isaac had no reason to pray, nor would he be likely to have done so in a field.[466] On the basis of the Peshiṭta's ܠܡܫܠܒ and the similar phrasing in v. 65 (הולך בשדה) some prefer to read לשוט.[467] Blau cites modern Arabic شاخ ("swing arm> stroll") which fits the passage; Ball prefers ساح ("wander") which would, however, require a Hebrew reading לשוש.[468] A similar "emendation" underlies the view of Wernberg-Mǿller who, comparing 1QS 7:15 which he interprets as referring to prayer, derives the form from שוח ("bend down").[469] Von der Ploeg prefers reading 1QS 7:15 as לשוח ("speak") although in context this makes little sense.[470] Tur-Sinai, citing the same passage, explains the verb as "wash with water."[471] Ehrlich emends the biblical form to לרוח.[472]

שחט (Gen 40:11)

This root appears in mishnaic Hebrew and Aramaic as סחט with the contextually appropriate meaning "squeeze."[473] The Akkadian ṣaḫatu is

---

[465] Gerhard von Rad (OTL on Gen 24:63).
[466] KD and RG on Gen 24:63. Only Aq and the Peshiṭta do not concur although Speiser's assertion that they "guess" (AB on Gen 24:63) is too stern a judgment.
[467] BDB s.v. שוח.
[468] J. Blau, "Etymologische Untersuchungen," *VT* 5 (1955) 343-44 and C. J. Ball, SBOT on Gen 24:63.
[469] "A Note on לשוח בשדה in Gen XXIV 63," *VT* 7 (1957) 414; see also Sir 43:10. He suggests the biblical usage refers to lying down; the שׂ would be either an error or dialectic variant. The ancient tradition that this word means "pray" is explained as derived from this meaning despite the clear rabbinic statement to the contrary (see p. 66 above).
[470] "Le 'Manuel de Discipline,'" *Bib Or* 8 (1951) 118.
[471] TSPM on Gen 24:63 and R. Marcus ("Notes on the Dead Sea Manual of Discipline," *JNES* 11 [1952] 209) translates "dig (a hole for excretion)" and compares rabbinic proscriptions regarding the procedure for defecation.
[472] RG on Gen 24:63, comparing Gen 3:8.
[473] BDB s.v. שחט.

used similarly, and Cohen therefore derives both from an original *צחט with the dissimilation of an emphatic accounting for the divergent forms.[474] Guillaume compares Arabic شحط ("fill a vessel").[475]

שפן (Deut 33:19)

Most often this root is seen as a variant of ספן or צפן.[476] Barth compares Arabic شفن ("spy"); Driver prefers Akkadian *sapannu* ("darkness").[477] Bertholet explains the Septuagint (ἐμπορια) as based on the reading שכני.[478] BHK reads instead וצפני, Cassuto ושפע, and Ehrlich יְשָׁפְנוּ.[479] Tur-Sinai suggests חשפון or regarding the phrase as an ellipsis based on שפע ושפוני מטמנים.[480]

שקד (Lam 1:14)

Because of its lack of additional attestation, this word is usually emended. Many prefer to read the graphically identical נִשְׂקַד, revocalizing על to עַל so as to fit both the newly created context and the Septuagint and Vulgate.[481] Others maintain על by reading נקשה.[482] The apparent meaning "bind" is used to support other readings as well. Ehrlich prefers

---

[474]Cohen, p. 35; see F. W. Geers, "The Treatment of Emphatics in Akkadian," *JNES* 4 (1945) 65-67.
[475]GHAL 3. 7.
[476]GB, BDB, KB s.v. שפן; S. Bartina ("Espana, 'Isla de Emporios,'" *Sef* 25 [1965] 72-77) uses this passage and the LXX (ἐμπορια) to explain the origin of the name Spain.
[477]J. Barth, *Wurzeluntersuchungen zum Hebräischen und Aramäischen Lexicon* (Leipzig: J. C. Hinrichs'sche Buchhandlung, 1902) 51 and G. R. Driver, "Problems in Aramaic and Hebrew Texts," AnOr 12, p. 60. M. Dahood proposes the meaning "draw up" or "absorb" ("Deuteronomy 33,19 and *UT* 52:61-63," *Or* 47[1978] 263).
[478]KHC on Deut 33:19.
[479]RG and *BHK* on Deut 33:19; U. Cassuto, "Il Cap. 33 del Deuteronomio e la Festa del Capo d'anno Nell'antico Israele," *RSO* 11 (1928) 246.
[480]TSPM on Deut 33:19; compare Jer 49:10.
[481]See *BHK* on Lam 1:14; F. Perles ("A Miscellany . . . ," *JQR* 2 [1911-12] 127) suggests reading פשעי in light of v. 13.
[482]F. Praetorius, "Threni I,12.14. II,6.13," *ZAW* 15 (1895) 143-44; see 1 Kgs 12:4. *Tg. Ket.* אתיקר is explained similarly. W. Rudolph (KAT on Lam 1:14) suggests reading נקשו עלי.

נקשרו, while Tur-Sinai suggests נעקד.[483] Guillaume compares Arabic شقد ("sleepless").[484]

שקר (Isa 3:16)

Although some texts read מִשְׁקְרוֹת, most moderns resolve this word as it now stands. Especially common is the comparison with Aramaic and Syriac ܣܩܪ ("blink, look at").[485] A few note Arabic شقر ("be red") and Aramaic סיקרא ("red paint") so as to translate "put on paint."[486] Tur-Sinai adds Akkadian tašqirtam tapalu ("put on red paint").[487]

שתם (Lam 3:8)

Context, some manuscripts, and the versions support equating the form as either a variant or corruption with סתם although some would add a prepositional מ to the following תפלתי, the loss of which is easily explained by haplography.[488] Barth resolves the syntax by comparing instead Arabic شمت ("return prayer empty").[489] Tur-Sinai prefers شتم ("despise") while Ehrlich would read שת מתפלתי.[490]

שתר (1 Sam 5:9)

As for most words beginning with שׁ, the first impulse has been to consider the form equivalent to that with intial ס.[491] Most moderns now equate this with Arabic شتر ("cut, split"), Syriac ܨܠܚ ("rip"), and Sabean שתר ("destroy").[492] The Hebrew thus means "break out." Nestle derives the same meaning from the form, treating it as a hitpaʿel of שׂרה.[493]

---

[483] RG on Lam 1:14 and N. H. Torczyner, review of GB in *ZDMG* 70 (1916) 561.
[484] GHAL 2. 33.
[485] *BHK* on Isa 3:16; GB, BDB, KB s.v. שקר.
[486] Concerning this practice see note 200 above (p. 127).
[487] *The Book of Job*, p. 221.
[488] W. Rudolph, KAT on Lam 3:8; see Num 24:3, 15.
[489] *Etymologische Studien*, p. 9.
[490] TSPM and RG on Lam 3:8; compare Ps 102:18 and Job 10:20.
[491] Thus KJV ". . . in their secret parts."
[492] GB, BDB, KB s.v. שתר; see also Ezra 5:12. Robert Gordis ("Studies in the Relationship of Biblical and Rabbinic Hebrew," *Louis Ginzberg Jubilee Volume* [New York: American Academy for Jewish Research, 1945] 187-89) includes also Akkadian šatâru ("tear down").
[493] "Miszellen," *ZAW* 29 (1909) 232.

שאס (Jer 30:16)

Widely regarded as an Aramaized participle for שסס, this root has no attested cognates nor is it used in post-biblical Hebrew. In several editions it is indicated as a kĕtîb for which the qĕrê is שׁסיך, a reading accepted by various modern scholars.[494] Sperber consider the aleph to be a mater lectionis, suggesting this as a middle weak root; indeed, several geminate verbs do seem to occur in middle weak forms.[495] A connection with שסס or שסה is supported by the following משסה.[496]

שיה (Deut 32:18)

The form תֶּשִׁי points to a root שיה for which the chiastic parallelism requires the meaning "forget."[497] König cites Arabic سها ("neglect"); however, the lack of complete consonantal correspondence makes such a comparison suspect.[498] On the basis of the Samaritan תשא there are those who would rather see this as a hifʻil of נשא (i.e. "decree").[499] Guillaume ascribes to BDB a comparison with Arabic آسا ("support").[500] The Samaritan reading and treatment by the Targum (אתנשיתא) as well as the lack of appropriate cognates makes a derivation from נשה ("forget") both attractive and appropriate, whether through reading תִּשֶּׁה or even תֶּשִׁי.[501]

---

[494] GKB 2. 133, GKC p. 180, C. H. Cornhill, SBOT on Jer 30:16 and KB p. 999; for manuscript evidence see C. D. Ginsburg edition of the Bible.

[495] "Hebrew Based upon Biblical Passages in Parallel Transmission," HUCA 14 (1939) 196; the form is marked with the Masoretic note יתיר 'א.

[496] Note the correlation in this verse between בזזיך and בז.

[497] Compare וַיַּחִי (Deut 4:33).

[498] *Hebräisches und Aramäisches Wörterbuch zum Alten Testament* (Leipzig: Dieterich'sche Verlagsbuchhandlung, 1910) 496a.

[499] BHK on Deut 32:18 and GB s.v. שיה.

[500] "A Contribution to Hebrew Lexicography," BSOAS 16 (1954) 5.

[501] For example, Mitchell Dahood, "Hebrew-Ugaritic Lexicography, XI," Bib 54 (1973) 356. Luzzatto (on Jer 18:23) discusses several instances in which yod appears to be superfluous; the yod here is written small. The Vg. (*dereliquisti*) uses a similar translation for נשה on occasion (as in Jer 23:30); regarding the LXX translation, see p. 54 above.

שכה (Jer 5:8)

Judging from the overall meaning of this verse, several scholars see in מַשְׁכִּים a denominative from אשך ("testicle").[502] Aquila and Theodotion seem to have understood מֹשְׁכִים ("pull"),[503] confirming our text, although not the present vocalization. Relying on the same root, Ehrlich translates "attract."[504] Keil compares Ethiopic *sky* ("wander") and Schultens notes an Arabic word meaning "strong."[505] Dahood refers to *CTA* 53:14-15 where he reads *hm.ntk p m‘nk* ("behold we long here for your reply"), deriving *ntk* from *tky*.[506] Ewald compares שוק ("run").[507]

שנס (1 Kgs 18:46)

As a result of numerous semantic parallels there is no question but that this verb means "gird," and so it is rendered by all versions despite the apparent lack of cognates. The sole question for scholars is to find a suitable etymology. The general solution has been to compare the word with שנץ.[508] Guillaume prefers Arabic سنف ("gird up camel") based on a ف-س shift he perceives.[509] Cassuto has found this root in Ugaritic *’tkt rišt lbmth šnst kpt bḥbšh* ("she attached heads to her back, girded hands to her waist," *CTA* 3.2.13).[510] Given the clarity of its biblical context,

---

[502] KB s.v. שכה.
[503] ἔλκοντες; compare Jerome's *trahentes*.
[504] RG on Jer 5:8.
[505] Cited by Luzzatto on Jer 5:8; GB (s.v. שכה) notes also Arabic سكع.
[506] *Ugaritic-Hebrew Philology*, p. 74.
[507] Cited by C. H. Cornhill, SBOT on Jer 5:8.
[508] Compare rabbinic שנץ ("strap"), Syriac ܚܣܡ ("bind"), Arabic شنص ("adhere") noted in Jastrow, p. 1607, Freytag s.v. شنص; note also Peshiṭta Matt 17:14. Šanda (EHAT on 1 Kgs 18:46) compares Egyptian *sndw-t*, and KB (s.v. שנס) cites Coptic *šento* ("apron"). Joüon ("Le Costume d'Elie et celui de Jean Baptiste," *Bib* 16 [1935] 79) notes that the LXX treats this word differently from its translation of חגר, ascribing to it the meaning "press."
[509] GHAL 1. 16.
[510] האלה ענת, pp. 64 and 77; for an alternative view see J. Gray, *The Legacy of Canaan*, VTSup 5, p. 41 note 8, although this is rejected by M. Dahood ("Hebrew-Ugaritic Lexicography XI," *Bib* 54 [1973] 362) and Marvin Pope (review of J. Gray, *The Legacy of Canaan*, JSS 11 [1961] 236).

finding an etymology for this word need hardly be considered pressing. No emendations have been proposed or are needed.

שסף (1 Sam 15:33)

The meaning of this word ("kill") has never been disputed despite the lack of a convincing etymology. All versions and editions concur. So clear is its meaning that it was used during the medieval period to define פשח (Lam 3:11) by which it is rendered in the Targum and Peshiṭta.[511] Driver proposes reading שסע on the basis of Judg 14:5 although Segal objects that that root refers to killing (tearing to pieces) by hand.[512] Others have compared rabbinic שצף ("cut").[513] Thierry suggests that it should be viewed as a šafʿel of סוף, meaning therefore "put an end to."[514] Guillaume compares شسّ ("sunder").[515] The word is used also in *Lam. Rab.* 3:64 which, however, cannot be considered since it is patently derivative from this verse; the word is found also in medieval and modern usage.[516]

ששה (Isa 10:13)

This word is almost universally regarded as a variant spelling of שסה as it appears in many manuscripts.[517] שסה does not, however, appear elsewhere in the pôʿēl. According to Blau the unique spelling is the result of the preceding שׁ. Delitzsch suggests it arose in stages—first שָׁסִתִי was written with שׂ, then שׂוֹשֵׂתִי > שׁישֵׂתִי > שָׁשֵׂיתִי > שָׁשֵׂתִי.[518] The combination of the unusual spelling and form require special attention. Rabin, apparently

---

[511] See p. 93 above.
[512] S. R. Driver, *Notes on the Hebrew Text* . . . , and M. H. Segal, ספרי שמואל (2d ed.; Jerusalem: Kiryat Sepher, 1964) on 1 Sam 15:33.
[513] KB s.v. שסף.
[514] G. J. Thierry, "Remarks on Various Passages of the Psalms," *OTS* 13 (1963) 88.
[515] GHAL 2. 34.
[516] ESh s.v. שסף.
[517] See *BHK* on Isa 10:13 and BL§ 8c; the ancient versions uniformly accept it as having the same meaning as שסה.
[518] DLS, p. 60; see J. Blau, *On Pseudo-Corrections*, 121.

ששא **(Ezek 39:2)**

Although this word's context is inadequate to define its meaning exactly, the general connotation should be one of restoration. On the basis of Ethiopic *ssw* ("proceed"), several interpreters view it as a pilpel form, shortened from *שאשא meaning "lead."[520] Others derive the same translation by reading והשאתיך.[521] Relating the form to נשא, Tur-Sinai proposes reading ונשאתיך, while Dahood sees the text as the šaf'el of the same root.[522] Comparing it to סאסא, Schultess proposed that it be regarded as a shortened form of the onomatopoeic *ša'ša'a* ("call a horse") and that the preceding שובבתיך be related not to שוב, but *šabšab* with the same meaning.[523] Ehrlich omits the word altogether as a corrupt dittography of the preceding.[524] KJV "leave one sixth" reflects the medieval view which equated this with שׁשָּׁה.[525] The interpretation of this word remains very uncertain.

תזז **(Isa 18:5)**

Rabbinic Hebrew נתז has in the causative the appropriate meaning "cut off." Gray therefore emends תַּז to הֵתִיז.[526] The meaning "jump" is justified by reference to the qal of נתז as well as תוז by Procksch.[527] Guillaume refers to Arabic تبّ ("cut off").[528]

---

[519]C. Rabin, "השפעל בעברית ובארמית - מהותו ומוצאו", *EY* 9 (1969) 149.

[520]BDB s.v. ששא and G. A. Cooke, ICC on Ezek 39:2.

[521]KB s.v. ששא.

[522]TSPM on Ezek 39:2 and M. Dahood, "Hebrew-Ugaritic Lexicography XI," *Bib* 54 (1973) 365.

[523]F. Schultess, "Noch einige Zurufe an Tiere," *Zeitschrift für Semitistik* 2 (1924) 16.

[524]EMK on Ezek 39:2.

[525]P. 81 above.

[526]ICC on Isa 18:5.

[527]KAT on Isa 18:5.

[528]GHAL 4. p. 3.

תכה (Deut 33:3)

As a hapax legomenon אָפֻּו is something of an anomaly inasmuch as the identical form occurs in Isa 1:5. It is included here, albeit with some uncertainty, because its context calls for the third person plural, suggesting that the ה may be part of the root. Not only is the form peculiar, but the entire verse is sufficiently uncertain as to eliminate any possibility of consensus in its interpretation. Cognates cited include Arabic تك and وكى ("recline"), Aramaic תכא ("tray") and תיכא ("chain"), Syriac and Arabic *tkk* ("crush"), and a medieval Hebrew usage of תכה ("approach").[529] In addition several emendations have been proposed: תַּכּוּ, התמכו, הָמתכו, יסכו, תומך, and הלכו.[530]

תרגל (Hos 11:3)

Historically the tendency has been to treat this as a denominative of רגל.[531] Such a meaning fits well with the context, and many moderns rely heavily on the passage as evidence for a tifʻel conjugation.[532] The evidence for this view is not, however, strong. Only two other such verbs have been located in Hebrew; however, תרגם is loanword while תתחרה may be denominative.[533] Albright points to a similar form in Akkadian, but it too may be denominative.[534] Conjugated as if they were quadriliteral,

---

[529] According to Lane (p. 2962) these first two are variants of the same root. See E. König (KAT on Deut 33:3), T. Gaster ("An Ancient Eulogy on Israel, Deuteronomy 33_{3-5, 26-29}," *JBL* 66 [1947] 57-58), B. Margulis ("Gen. XLIX 10/Deut. XXXIII 2-3," *VT* 19 [1969] 209), J. T. Milik ("Deux Documents inedits du Desert de Juda," *Bib* 38 [1957] 252), F. Stummer (" אָפֻּו = adpropinquant," in *Alttestamentliche Studien Friedrich Nötscher* [BBB 1; Bonn: Peter Hanstein, 1950] 265-70), F. M. Cross and D. N. Freedman ("The Blessing of Moses," *JBL* 67 [1948] 200), and O. Komlós ("אָפֻּו לְרַגְלֵהּ [Deut. xxxiii 3]," *VT* 6 [1956] 435-36).

[530] U. Cassuto, "Il Cap. 33 del Deuteronomio . . . ," *RSO* 11 (1928) 237; F. M. Cross and D. N. Freedman, "The Blessing of Moses," 200; TSPM, S. R. Driver in ICC, and *BHK* on Deut 33:3.

[531] See *Tg. Neb.* דברית ("lead"); needless to say, if such is the case, the word cannot be considered an absolute hapax legomenon.

[532] For example, GKC p. 153; M. D. Goldman adopts this approach, but relates the word to an Arabic root meaning "sick" in his "Lexicographical Notes on Exegesis (5)," *AusBR* 4 (1954-55) 92.

[533] Barth, p. 279.

[534] W. F. Albright, "Two Letters from Ugarit (Ras Shamrah)," *BASOR* 82 (1941) 48, where he evaluates *tiḫtati* (EA 102:12) as tifʻel

these forms alone do not provide convincing evidence that such a conjugation did exist. KD sees in the attested form a derivative of the hifʿil while Marti would actually read hifʿil here.⁵³⁵ The only other point of view commonly expressed relies on Akkadian *tarkullu* which is related to a root *rgl* ("bind") to yield such translations as "wrap in swaddling" and "bind to yoke."⁵³⁶ Perles, noting that the Akkadian root is properly *rakâsu*, suggests either a dialectic variant or a reflex of popular etymology based on רגל.⁵³⁷ Sellin notes also the dubious possibility of a relation to Arabic رجل ("be quiet"),⁵³⁸ while Goldman understands it to mean "suckle," also on the basis of Arabic.⁵³⁹ NJV renders it "pamper."

תרגם (Ezra 4:7)

Although its exact meaning in this particular text is somewhat uncertain, the word itself is well-known, particularly in Aramaic.⁵⁴⁰ It occurs also in Akkadian and Arabic from which it has entered Western languages.⁵⁴¹ As its sole occurrence is adjacent to the Aramaic section of Ezra, there is little reason not to regard this as an Aramaism. In light of its complex history, one cannot cite this word as evidence for a functioning tifʿel in Hebrew.⁵⁴² Commonly taken to mean "translate," there are any number of other meanings connected with forms of this root, such as "pronounce, explain, render."⁵⁴³ Although תרגם is often explained on the basis of *rgm* known in Akkadian and Ugaritic as "call, speak," Baruch

---

perfect, first person singular from *ḫatû* ("smash"), noting especially the nominal form *taḫtû* ("defeat").

⁵³⁵KD and KHC on Hos 11:3.

⁵³⁶TSLS 1. (2d ed.) 414. J. C. Greenfield has pointed out (written communication) that this is actually a Sumerian loanword in Akkadian.

⁵³⁷"Babylonisch-biblische Glossen," *OLZ* 8 (1905) 183.

⁵³⁸KAT on Hos 11:3.

⁵³⁹M. D. Goldman, "Lexicographical Notes," p. 92.

⁵⁴⁰PS p. 4495, LNHeb 4. 668,. Friedrich Schulthess, *Lexicon Syro-Palestinum* (Berlin: George Reimer, 1903) s.v. رجل.

⁵⁴¹See F. D. H. Zimmern, *Akkadische Fremdwörter als Beweis fur Babylonischen Kultureinfluss* (Leipzig: J. C. Hinrisch'sche Buchhandlung, 1915) 7 and Lane, p. 302.

⁵⁴²Baruch Levine, *Survivals of Ancient Canaanite in the Mishnah* (unpublished dissertation, Brandeis University, 1962) 35.

⁵⁴³Baruch Levine (*Survivals*, 34) and M. Gertner ("Terms of Scriptural Interpretation," *BSOAS* 25 [1962] 17) describe the word's semantic range with appropriate citations.

Levine points out that Akkadian *targumanu* predates *ragâmu*, while elsewhere it coexists in a given dialect only with *rgm* "stone," and not the homographic root meaning "call."[544] Both Gelb and Rabin argue for a non-Semitic origin.[545]

---

[544] B. Levine, *Survivals*, 38.
[545] Chaim Rabin, "Hittite Words in Hebrew," *Or* 32 (1963) 134-35 and I. J. Gelb, "The Word for Dragoman in the Ancient Near East," *Glossa* 2 (1968) 101-2.

8

Summary and Conclusions

Gevirtz has observed that "the unique evokes suspicion,"[1] and in the case of hapax legomena this is most dramatically true. Throughout the ages every effort of biblical exegesis has been to eliminate the uniqueness of such words. The most obvious evidence of such an approach is the practice of emendation whereby a rare word is changed to a more common root; yet even the philological method seeks to identify these with other attested forms, albeit in different languages. The benefits of such methods can scarcely be denied. The more evidence available concerning a word, the better any given occurrence can be understood. Uncertainty is minimized and specific nuances often more clearly recognized. However, there is as well an undercurrent within biblical scholarship which tends to mitigate the assumption that rare words are suspicious. In several cases one hapax legomenon is rejected in favor of another which is deemed more reliable. לעי, for example, is replaced by *BHK* because it is rare with לעז which, too, occurs only once.[2] The difficult רטפש is often replaced with various forms of the hapax legomenon שפט.[3]

Some hapax legomena are not at all in doubt with respect to either their accuracy or their meaning. Often the problems in a verse can be traced not to the hapax legomenon, but rather to a more common word which is difficult in a particular context.[4] Identifying a word as a hapax legomenon does not necessarily provide useful information about it.

---

[1] Stanley Gevirtz, "Of Patriarchs and Puns," *HUCA* 46 (1975) 36.
[2] *BHK* on Isa 33:19.
[3] See p. 157 above.
[4] For example, Ps 32:9.

There is no unique method for dealing with unique words.[5] The available evidence must instead be evaluated from several perspectives. Lacking the corroboration of multiple usage, one must find alternative sources for evaluation; but the methods themselves are equally applicable to more common words.

The analyses of hapax legomena and their treatment in previous chapters makes it possible now to assess the usefulness of various methods proposed for dealing with rare forms. The variety of interpretations offered for a large number of these words demonstrates adequately that the assumption of textual error is without warrant. Though emendations have been proposed for virtually all, in most cases there are also interpretations which leave the attested forms intact, meeting the needs of context while benefiting from the support of the received text. Many such interpretations have achieved a modicum of consensus, although there are words for which no real agreement exists. The fact that a word is rare cannot itself, therefore, support the assertion that it is corrupt. Emendation requires stronger justification.

One criterion for evaluation is a root's conformity to principles of Hebrew phonology. Recognized since the Middle Ages, these principles have been explored in detail by Joseph Greenberg in an exhaustive analysis of the combinatory patterns of Arabic roots with comparison to other Semitic languages.[6] After charting the frequency of consonant combinations in the various possible positions of a triliteral root, Greenberg and the others who have since applied this approach to the biblical lexicon compare the results with the expected frequency of occurrence for each combination to identify the formative principles governing the creation of a language's vocabulary.[7] Using such patterns to assess the probability

---

[5] John Gray (*I & II Kings*, OTL, pp. 589 and 592) identifies both חפא and גדא as hapax legomena, yet emends the latter according to the evidence of the versions while accepting the former on the basis of an Akkadian cognate. In such cases one must wonder concerning the relevance of the fact that a word is a hapax legomenon.

[6] Joseph Greenberg, "Patterning of Root Morphemes in Semitic," *Word* 6 (1950) 162-81; for medieval references see SE, pp. 38-39. The major finding of such studies is that identical and even homorganic consonants tend not to occur in immediate proximity, with the obvious exception of geminate roots.

[7] This approach is applied to the biblical lexicon by Kalevi Koskinen ("Kompatibilität in den dreikonsonantigen hebräischen Wurzeln," *ZDMG* 114 [1964] 16-58) and David E. Y. Sarna and Lawrence H. Schiffman ("A

Summary and Conclusions 173

that an individual root is corrupt or not indigenous to a particular dialect (here Hebrew) is fraught with peril. It cannot be concluded with any certainty that the occurrence of an unexpectedly rare combination is the result of either error or borrowing. The nature of language and statistical distribution is such that some combinations appear infrequently simply because the language tends to avoid such combinations, at least to the extent attested. A pattern may be rare without being wrong. For example, נבה is the only Hebrew root to begin with נ and end with ה (one would expect 6.2 such roots), yet no one doubts its authenticity.

Each pair of consonants in the roots here studied was evaluated separately for "probability in biblical Hebrew" according to the data in the aforementioned studies. All which occur significantly less often than would be expected were reexamined to find those for which this might be of some importance regarding the word itself rather than the phonological principles of ancient Hebrew.[8] One must handle this data with extreme caution. בטל is the only Hebrew verb to end with טל—(one would expect 3.1 such cases); this might be attributed to the word's foreign origin were it not for the fact that several Hebrew roots begin with this sequence.[9] Similarly, the last two letters of צנם do not occur in that sequence in any other biblical verb although nine such cases would be expected, but they are found in some nouns.[10] The results of this kind of evaluation point only to the need for further investigation; they cannot be decisive for

---

Computer Analysis of Biblical Roots" [1968] unpublished). Expected frequency is calculated for any combination *XY* in root positions one and two, for example, by multiplying the number of times *X* occurs in position one times the number of times *Y* occurs in position two and dividing by the total number of roots (J. Greenberg, "Patterning," 163).

[8]For example, if a consonant pattern is expected twenty-five times but occurs only ten, the fact that one of these ten words is a hapax legomenon is not germane whereas a pair that would be expected five times but occurs only once may indicate something unique about the word in which it is found. Similarly, a rare pattern needs no further examination if it is to be expected only a handful of times.

[9] טלל, טלא, and טלה according to the list provided in the study by Sarna and Schiffman ("A Computer Analysis"). Regarding the possibility that the occurrence of בטל in Qoh 12:3 may be due to Aramaic influence, see p. 105 above.

[10]Sarna and Schiffman ("A Computer Analysis") treat צנמות (Gen 41:23) as nominal; the other two nominal roots with the combination נמ are גמל and נמר.

assessing individual words.[11] Moreover, the borderline between improbable and merely unusual patterns is vague and the evidence not always convincing. Few hapax legomena are so phonologically unique as to demand further examination. נלה is the only verb in the Bible with the combination נל despite a theoretical likelihood of there being 12.3 such words.[12] The repeated consonants in עער, עלע, and ששא are also suspicious.[13] קא (in קאם) is attested only one other time (קיא) although it would be expected seven times. In all these cases philological and textual analysis had already suggested the existence of uncertainty. This technique is thus useful to the extent that it corroborates conclusions already proposed, but it does not itself offer new possibilities.

---

[11]Evaluation is hampered by the fact that different methods for dealing with weak roots are used by the two studies on which we must rely, neither of which is truly satisfactory for our purposes. By excluding all weak roots, Koskinen ("Kompatibilität," 19) eliminates a significant body of information, particularly for geminate and final weak verbs in which the relationship of the first two radicals is in no way affected by the root's "irregularity." According to his charts, no verb shares the רנ- pattern found in the hapax legomenon רנה, a conclusion of dubious import since the common geminate רנן was not included; moreover, the combination רנ is attested in several roots, albeit as the second and third radicals (גרן and קרן). Sarna and Schiffman treat all weak roots as if they were biliteral, equating the relationship between two adjacent consonants in a strong root with that attested in a hollow root where the consonants are not immediately adjacent. דוץ is the only root to contain ד and צ in that sequence (one would expect 3.2); but this arrangement may be tolerable only because the two letters are not in direct proximity. In addition to the cases described, the following roots contain "unlikely" combinations of consonants; the figures in parentheses indicate first the actual and then the expected number of occurrences for each relevant pair of consonants: בש-(בשט 1/2.5, ב-ש 0/1.1, -סט 0/1.1, ז-ר(זער 1/2.8), יהר(יה 2/6.1, הד-1/2.4), י-ך(יסך 1/2.6) נתס(-תס 1/2.3, נ-ס 1/2.1), ע-ש(עמש 0/1.2, צען(ען-1/6.5), רה-(רהה 1/2.4), ששה(שש 0/1.5), תזז(תז 1/2.6).
[12]J. Greenberg ("Patterning," 172-73) classes n and l as homorganic although he notes the existence of the similarly unlikely root רנן.
[13]See note 6 above. Using Sarna and Schiffman's data ("A Computer Analysis") one would expect the sequence עע to occur at least eight times and שֹשׁ seven; this latter sequence occurs elsewhere only in שָׁשָׂה. Only eight non-geminate roots there listed have identical consonants in adjacent positions, of which five are hollow (ריר, צוץ, נון, הוה, and שׁוֹשׁ; the others are דדה, שׁשׁא, and ששה).

Summary and Conclusions 175

The versions too provide useful corroborative information. The difficulties in evaluating such data have already been noted.[14] One can never be certain whether an unexpected translation is the result of philological interpretation on the part of ancient translators or a *Vorlage* different from our own Hebrew text. Even witnesses to the Hebrew text itself must be handled cautiously. The Samaritan Pentateuch, Qumran scrolls, and second column of the Hexapla provide ancient attestation for some hapax legomena of which only a proportionately small number differ significantly from our own text.[15] Yet even in these cases such evidence is insufficient to resolve longstanding uncertainty.

The value of context has already been assessed as well.[16] It is the ultimate criterion: whatever meaning one proposes for a word must necessarily fit into its attested context. This is often the basis for emendations which seek a smoother reading, while ignoring many times the possibility that the correct text may be unique. Context alone is only suggestive. The meaning of a word cannot always be correctly deduced from the passage or sentence in which it occurs.

Additional attestations of rare words can serve to reassure critics while broadening the base from which to ascertain nuances and assess semantic range. For biblical hapax legomena such support must come from cognate material. However, it is possible to overestimate the need for such recourse. Cognates may themselves have been originally explained from the supposedly obscure biblical passages, while many hapax legomena are adequately understood from context alone. As Barr points out, such information often serves primarily to make opaque words more transparent, explaining why they mean what they do.[17]

---

[14] Pp. 47-48 above.

[15] Of the twenty-one hapax legomenon verbs here studied which occur in the Pentateuch, only five have significantly variant reading in the Samaritan Pentateuch (ידזם, יסך, ירט, כמס, and שיה). Only six of the twenty-five hapax legomena from Isaiah are attested in Qumran scrolls (אדש, הבר, הזה, נלה, עתם, and רהה) as is יאב in Psalms; the root עות is also supported by 1QH and עוש by Mur XII. The Hexapla provides no variants, while inner-biblical parallels do cast suspicion on four of the verbs here studied (חרג, כרבל, ער, and צנם). This latter finding is difficult to assess since any supportive parallels would have led to the root's exclusion as a dislegomenon (see pp. 28-29 above).

[16] Pp. 92-100 above.

[17] James Barr, "Etymology and the Old Testament," *OTS* 19 (1974) 20-21.

Some cognates are more reliable than others. The closer the "sister" language, the more likely a cognate is to be similar in meaning to its biblical counterpart; Aramaic, for example, is preferable to Ethiopic where the choice is available. On the other hand, the less intimate the cultural relationship between the Bible and speakers of the cognate language, the more likely it is that the related word has not been influenced by the biblical passage itself or its interpretation. The use of biblically rare words in medieval *piyyuṭim* and modern Hebrew is often conditioned by an interpretation of the word's biblical occurrence, limiting the value of these sources for assessing the original meaning or validity of a rare word.[18]

Reliance on metathesis or complicated phonetic shifts reduces the probability of a proposed cognate relationship while increasing the number of possible cognates to the point of absurdity if injudiciously applied. In such cases the ability to present a real case of identical contexts can lend strength to the proposed relationship.[19] Since satisfactory interpretation can often be achieved through other means, such equations seem occasionally gratuitous.

The best confirmation of hapax legomena would be in extrabiblical Hebrew texts from the biblical period. That only one of the verbs here studied is so attested is hardly surprising in light of the dearth of such material.[20] Several of these words do occur in Ben Sirah where there is a minimal risk that the usage is based on the biblical occurrence; a few are found in non-biblical literature from Qumran, and many occur in tannaitic Hebrew.[21] It is sometimes difficult to ascertain whether such usages are

---

[18] N. M. Sarna, "Hebrew and Bible Studies in Medieval Spain," *The Sephardi Heritage* (ed. R. D. Barnett; New York: Ktav, 1971) 333. The use of ܦܩܥ in Syriac is also to be ascribed to this phenomenon, since it is apparently a Hebraism derived from the verb's usage in Esth 8:17 (see Julius Grünthal, *Die Syrische Uebersetzung zum Buche Esther* [Breslau: H. Fleischmann, 1900] 49-50.

[19] This is the value of citing *CTA* 4.7.34-35 to connect the related, though not identical Ugaritic *nṭṭ* with Hebrew נוט (pp. 14-15 above). One cannot, however, assume theoretically cognate roots to be actually related. Only when conditioning factors can be demonstrated, as in the case of Hebrew שחט and Akkadian *šaḫatu* (see p. 160 above) are such arguments convincing.

[20] Only כחל is so supported; דהם and רזם, although once ascribed to inscriptions, now lack such corroboration in light of improved readings (see appropriate sections of chapter VII).

[21] אנס, בטה, חרת, סכת, פנק, רצד, and perhaps עשק and לעב occur

Summary and Conclusions

based on the biblical occurrence; usually the differences in context and even grammatical form are sufficient to minimize the likelihood of actual dependence.[22] These sources, along with Aramaic, seem capable of confirming the largest number of hapax legomena. It is no wonder, therefore, that these words caused so little difficulty for early exegetes.[23] Some interpretations, however, require Arabic or Akkadian evidence; Ugaritic is necessary for the correct understanding of only two hapax legomena verbs.[24]

Cognates are not always available. Although a cognate may be discovered in some still unknown text, it is hard to give credence to those who, ascribing to hapax legomena the aura of unique difficulty, hold out hope for new discoveries to unlock the mysteries of these words. Freedman's expectation that the recent finds at Tell Mardikh, for example, will provide solutions for hapax legomena seems unnecessary.[25] Most hapax

---

in Ben Sirah (טפש) also occurs, but as a gloss). Qumran literature includes אנס, חרת, and עזק. כרבל, סלק, רשם, and perhaps שתר are found in biblical Aramaic. Post-biblical Jewish sources in both Hebrew and Aramaic include evidence of the following roots which does not seem to have been based on the biblical usage: זהם, דוץ, גרד, בלם, בטל, בטה, אנס, אלץ, כסס, כמה, כחל, יאה, יאב, טפש, טעה, טנף, טוש, חתך, חרת, חרג, חטם, עזק, עות, עוש, עגן, עגם, סעה, נבח, מוק, מהל, לעט, לעז, לעב, כרסם, שחט, רשם, רצד, רפק, רפף, קסס, צפד, צנם, צבט, פשח, פצם, פנק, עשק, סלד, מחק, כפש, יבב, חלט, זרב and probably also תרגם, שתר and שקר.

[22] Often the only dependence is that imposed by the modern exegete who tries to find a common origin for both the biblical and non-biblical usage (see S. R. Driver, *A Critical and Exegetical Commentary on the Book of Job*, ICC, 38). The usage of עות in 1QH 8:36 clearly relies on Isa 50:4, and we have already noted that עגונה is close in its application to the apparent meaning of עגן (p. 144 above). An example of grammatical difference is the fact that עזק is used in the qal in 1QH 8:23 whereas it appears in the piʻel in Isa 5:2; similarly סכת is used in the hifʻil in Deut 27:9, but in the nifʻal for Sir 13:23.

[23] See p. 61 above.

[24] In the discussion of chapter VII, Arabic evidence was essential for the interpretation of עבש, נוט, מלץ, מחק, כשה, הדך, דגה, and possibly הכר, זער, and טחח; Akkadian provided crucial information for אבך, חפא, כמס, and בתק (along with Ethiopic) and דהם and צען (along with Arabic) as well as perhaps for נתע and סכת. Ugaritic alone provided cognates for הבר and שנס although its evidence was supportive of the interpretation which other evidence provides for several other verbs.

[25] David Noel Freedman, unpublished report on finds at Tell Mardikh (ca. 1976), 12.

legomena will not be resolved by this material because most have already been explained, if indeed they were ever uncertain, by more mundane methods. As with the esoteric methods of the past, so those of the present are often superfluous.[26] Furthermore, Herdan has shown that many words which occur only once in a selection are rare also in the larger corpus or which it is a part.[27] It may be that some hapax legomena in the Bible are unique occurrences within the body of extant Semitic texts and as such there may always be a small group of words for which אין לו דומה.

Having studied the methods applied to a representative group of apparently absolute hapax legomena, we can now evaluate the significance of a word's being unique on the basis of empirical observation rather than seemingly obvious assumptions. Some of these words are apparently corrupt. עלע and ער are not only inexplicable as they stand, but violate generally respected rules of Hebrew and even Semitic phonology; נלה and שיה also seem to fit into this category.[28] For the time being these can reasonably be regarded as ghost words in the Hebrew lexicon.[29] What is remarkable is that only these among the one hundred forty verbs here studied are obviously and certainly corrupt. A larger group comprises variants and by-forms of otherwise attested roots.[30] Whether

---

[26]This is not to say that they are useless, but that the importance of such tools for understanding recognized hapax legomena is easily exaggerated. Such material may help in identifying new hapax legomena. Compare J. Barr ("Etymology and the Old Testament," *OTS* 19 [1974] 2): "Etymology is particularly important for the identification and elucidation of rare words and *hapax legomena*."

[27]Gustav Herdan, "The Hapax legomena: a real or apparent phenomenon?" *Language and Speech* 2 (1959) 26-36.

[28]שיה is weak in too many respects to have been assessed by the criterion of Hebrew phonology. חספס, רטפש, and most likely פרשז should also be included in this category of unlikely roots inasmuch as their forms deviate significantly from normal Semitic patterns.

[29]For examples in English see W. W. Skeat, "Report on 'Ghost-Words,' or Words Which Have No Real Existence," *Transactions of the Philological Society* (1885-87) 250-74.

[30]Likely constituents of this group are טחח, דוב, בטה, אדש, אדב, רזם, קוש, קאם, צות, עמש, נצא, יעט, יעז, יסך, ימש, יחר, יזם, יהד, שאס, and perhaps בשס, חרת, כפה, כפש, שתם, and תרגל (yielding thus no more than 16 percent of the words here studied). It is, of course, possible that the attested readings of these roots are incorrect and that they should be emended to forms of the more common roots. In any case they are not truly absolute hapax legomena. One must also recognize the pos-

Summary and Conclusions 179

secondary roots or alternative conjugation patterns of known words, these are only apparently-absolute hapax legomena; included so as to ensure an objectively defined category, they are no longer appropriate for treatment in this setting. The largest category contains those hapax legomena whose validity is supported by the discovery of additional usages in ancient Hebrew or cognate tongues.[31] For only a relatively small proportion of hapax legomena is the information available from context or cognates inadequate to provide a clear interpretation.[32] The implications for the methodological principle *lectio difficilior praeferenda est* are thus ambiguous. Better than any theoretical considerations are illustrations such as טנף and נבח which are clear from both context and any number of cognates.

If most hapax legomena are valid Hebrew words, one must ask why their occurrences are so limited. In the Middle Ages accident was the reason cited: these words just happened to be included in the surviving corpus of ancient Hebrew texts. There is much to be said in favor of this assertion, since many hapax legomena are attested independently in Ben Sirah, the Qumran scrolls, and tannaitic literature.[33] Yet statistical evaluation suggests that there is another factor. Accepting Herdan's demonstration that most hapax legomena within a small selection are also rare within the larger corpus from which it is taken, it is probable that many biblical hapax legomena were not common in ancient Hebrew. Poetry tends to include more rare words than does prose, a predictable conclusion for the literature of any language. So, too, do certain writers seem to have a predilection for the less common. One hardly needs a statistical study to recognize that Job has a proportionately large number

---

sibility of rarely attested grammatical forms along with lexical hapax legomena. In this group we might include the prefixing of א and ת to a verbal root as well as the conjugation of a weak root of one type according to the pattern of some other group (for example, אדש, יזם, and תרגל).

[31] See notes 20-24 above. This group includes about half of the verbs studied, depending on whether one includes cases here regarded as probable. An additional seven verbs are clear beyond doubt, but lack cognates (חשל, נחץ, נתס, פדע, רהה, שסף, תזז, and perhaps הדה and ששה).

[32] גוש, נדא, ירט, יזן, טמה, התת, הלא, הכר, הזה, הבו, בלט, שקר, שקד, שפן, שוח, רטה, פסג, פון, עהם, עות, סרף, סמן, סלא, סאסא, תכה, ששא, שכה.

[33] Approximately one-third of the biblical hapax legomena are attested with a similar meaning in post-biblical Hebrew sources not dependent on the biblical occurrence.

of hapax legomena. This is supported also by the relatively large number which appear as B words in biblical poetry, the position scholars consider to be that usually alotted the less common of two synonyms.[34] With no evidence of nonce forms in the verbs here studied, such words cannot be consigned to the category of "freak" or artificial creations. Many, although as legitimate a part of the language and its vocabulary as the most common terms, were probably rare even in antiquity.[35] Some words are doubtless part of a specialized vocabulary.[36] No more than two of the verbs here examined can be considered loan words.[37] The limited number

---

[34] Pp. 44-45 above.

[35] This is not to assert that they were obscure; frequency and simplicity cannot be equated. Some part of their infrequency can also be ascribed to lexical change. Some hapax legomena may be old and even archaic words; others may be new to Hebrew, as through the influence of Aramaic on later Hebrew usage. These Aramaisms are particularly difficult to identify in light of the possibility that words common to Hebrew and Aramaic may be cognates without having been borrowed and conform perfectly to the patterns of Hebrew structure and grammar. Moreover, since cognates to most Hebrew words are known from several languages, it is difficult to identify with any certainty those whose biblical usage is the result of Aramaic influence. For probability to be maximized, such words should be known from only Aramaic sources and found only in biblical texts subject to such influence. Kautzsch (p. 17) recognizes that this is basically an argument from silence. Furthermore, apparent Aramaisms can be found in early biblical passages while being rare in post-exilic books (A. Hurvitz, "The Chronological Significance of 'Aramaisms' in Biblical Hebrew," *IEJ* 18 [1968] 234 and Wagner, pp. 143-44). In any event, the data concerning hapax legomena is too limited to permit identification of any pattern of occurrence (against Wagner, p. 59). Those hapax legomena which may be the result of Aramaic influence are אנס, בטל, סלק, טעה, רשם, תרגם, and perhaps טוש and יאב. (Kautzsch includes also נוט, פסג, and פשח; Wagner, דוב, דוץ, חרת, and מחק. Both agree on מוק, לעז, לעב, כרבל, טנף, and עגן.)

[36] The composition of this category is dependent on the nature of the text to which it is applied. Cult terms are undoubtedly more frequent in the Bible than in ancient Hebrew as a whole, whereas biological and economic terminology are comparatively rare. The effect of some of these factors has been minimized by our primary interest in verbs whereas technical terms are more likely to be nouns.

[37] תרגם and כרבל, although the latter has been Hebraized. That only verbal forms have been treated here in depth is likely responsible for the paucity of loan words which are most often nouns denoting objects or

Summary and Conclusions

of such cases illustrates again the fact that these are not exotic words nor need they be assumed to be non-indigenous to the Hebrew lexicon.

Despite the absence of more extensive evidence from ancient sources, there is no reason to deny that most hapax legomena are to be considered perfectly good Hebrew. All the circumstantial evidence—and it is no more than that—seems time and again to support this contention. These words do not exceed the proportion to be expected according to the principles of frequency distribution known from other languages; they accord well with established principles of Hebrew phonology and are readily explained in their biblical contexts by known cognates, most often from relatively close Semitic dialects. In only a very limited number of cases is the evidence of corruption at all convincing. Nor must hapax legomena be regarded as particularly difficult. Their meanings are no harder to establish than are the methods used to verify them unique. Even some words for which cognates have not been satisfactorily identified are clear beyond question.[38] While all rare words are not self-evident and the possibility of corruption cannot be ignored, roots whose meanings are clear from context even without cognates must be seen alongside well-supported hapax legomena before making blanket assertions.[39] Rareness alone does not prove that a word has been inaccurately transmitted. The general lack of exegetical diversity for many of these words, contrasting perhaps with the variety of explanations used to justify any one interpretation, unequivocally disproves the claim that hapax legomena are exceptionally unclear or that the tradition of their meaning is especially weak.

Hapax legomena are a fact of any body of language. It cannot be overemphasized that this is unrelated to the Bible's antiquity and composite nature. Although the specific percentage is influenced by corpus

---

processes not native to Israel as can be seen from a survey of the various studies in loan words, which deal almost exclusively in nouns, such as Thomas Lambdin, "Egyptian Loan Words in the Old Testament," *JAOS* 73 (1953) 145-55 and M. Ellenbogen, *Foreign Words in the Old Testament* (London: Luzac and Co., 1962).

[38]See note 31 above.

[39]Note the following: טמה "is found only here, so one resorts to emendations" (Anton Blommerde, *Northwest Semitic Grammar and Job*, 83); רפף "is found only here, but its meaning is not in doubt" (H. H. Rowley, CB on Job 26:11); "durch Konjektur das Genuine aus dem AT herausgeworfen und durch Plattheiten ersetz wird" (Friedrich Delitzsch cited by F. Stummer, "תכּו" p. 265.

size and the extent to which inflection is used as a formative principle, it has been quite adequately demonstrated on both empirical and theoretical grounds that hapax legomena constitute the largest category of words in ancient and modern texts of both formal and colloquial style.[40] The large proportion of unique words in the biblical vocabulary is thus a result of statistical necessity, although the lack of a significant amount of additional material in ancient Hebrew has no doubt encouraged the tendency among biblical scholars to seek cognates and propose emendations in such cases.[41] A word need not be doubted or explained away simply because it occurs only once. Instead these words must be assumed, in the absence of counter-indication, to be legitimate and valid parts of the ancient Hebrew vocabulary and treated in the same manner as other words, albeit with the recognition that their limited number of occurrences may reduce the possibility of certainty or even consensus regarding their interpretation.

---

[40] See pp. 31-34 above.
[41] Barr (p. 4) contrasts the methods used to interpret New Testament Greek.

Appendix I

Absolute Hapax Legomena

Prov 23:29	אבוי	2 Kgs 4:42	בצקלון(?)
Ezek 21:20	אבחה	1 Kgs 5:3	ברברים(?)
Qoh 12:5	אביונה(?)	Ezek 27:24	ברומים
Isa 9:17	אבך	Cant 1:17	ברות
Cant 6:11	אגוז	Hos 10:6	בשנה(?)
Job 38:28	אגל	Amos 5:11	בשס
1 Sam 2:33	אדב	Isa 5:6	בתה(?)
Isa 28:28	אדש	Isa 7:19	בתה(?)
2 Chr 32:28	אורות	Ezek 16:40	בתק
Prov 7:16	אטון		
Ezek 40:15	איתון(?)	Job 28:18	גביש
Judg 16:16	אלץ	Ezek 47:13	גה(?)
Prov 30:31	אלקום	Qoh 10:8	גומץ
Jer 42:6	אנו	Job 7:5	גוש
Esth 1:8	אנס	Ezra 1:8	גזבר
Dan 11:45	אפדן(?)	Ezek 5:1	גלב
Isa 41:24	אפע(?)	Job 16:15	גלד
Cant 3:9	אפריון	1 Chr 28:11	גנזך(?)
Deut 14:5	אקו	Isa 27:9	גר
2 Chr 2:6	ארגון	Job 2:8	גרד
Ps 21:3	ארשת		
Jer 50:15	אשיה	Deut 33:25	דבא
Lev 21:20	אשך	2 Kgs 6:25	דביונים
		Gen 48:16	דגה
Zech 2:12	בבה	Jer 14:9	דהם
Ezek 25:7	בג(?)	Lev 26:16	דוב
Esth 1:6	בהט	Job 41:14	דוץ
Lev 13:39	בהק	Ezek 4:9	דחן
Ezek 1:14	בזק	Jer 36:18	דיו
Prov 12:18	בטה	Ps 50:20	דפי
Qoh 12:3	בטל	Esth 1:6	דר
Ps 32:9	בלם		
Amos 7:14	בלס	Hos 8:13	הבהבי(?)
Num 11:5	בצל	Hos 4:18	הבו(?)

Ezek 27:15	הבנים	Ezek 40:15	יאתון (?)
Isa 47:13	הבר	Judg 5:28	יבב
Ezek 42:12	הגינה	Esth 8:17	יהד
Ezek 7:7	הד (?)	Gen 11:6	יזם
Isa 11:8	הדה	Jer 5:8	יזן
Job 40:12	הדך	2 Sam 20:5	יחר
Isa 56:10	הזה	1 Sam 4:13	יך
Ezek 2:10	הי	Gen 36:24	ימם (?)
Job 19:3	הכר	Judg 16:26	ימש
Mic 4:7	הלא (?)	Exod 30:32	יסך
Isa 64:1	המסים	Isa 33:19	יעז
Ezek 23:24	הצן	Isa 61:10	יעט
Ezek 43:15	הראל	Num 22:32	ירט
Ps 62:4	התת	Mic 6:14	ישח
Prov 21:8	וזר	Amos 8:8	כאר
		Ezek 23:40	כחל
Num 6:4	זג	Job 41:11	כידוד
Job 33:20	זהם	Ps 74:6	כילפות
Job 17:1	זעך	Ps 63:2	כמה
Num 11:20	זרא	Deut 32:34	כמס
Job 6:17	זרב	Ezra 4:7	כנת
Ps 72:6	זרזיף	Exod 12:4	כסס
Prov 30:31	זרזיר (?)	Prov 21:14	כפה
		Hab 2:11	כפיס
Isa 19:17	חגא	Lam 3:16	כפש
Isa 48:9	חטם	1 Chr 15:27	כרבל
Job 41:4	חין	Cant 4:14	כרכם
1 Kgs 20:33	חלט	Ps 80:14	כרסם
Lev 11:30	חמט	Esth 1:6	כרפס
Ps 78:47	חנמל	Jer 51:34	כרש
Exod 16:14	חספס	Deut 32:15	כשה
2 Kgs 17:9	חפא	Cant 2:9	כתל
Ps 18:46	חרג (?)		
Lev 11:22	חרגל (?)	Qoh 12:12	להג
Cant 1:10	חרוזים	1 Sam 19:20	להקה
Exod 32:16	חרת	Lev 11:30	לטאה
Deut 25:18	חשל	2 Chr 36:16	לעב
Ps 68:32	חשמן	Ps 114:1	לעז
Dan 9:24	חתך	Gen 25:30	לעט
		Hos 3:2	לתך
Job 9:26	טוש		
Gen 21:16	טחה	Hab 1:9	מגמה (?)
Isa 44:18	טחח	Isa 14:4	מדהבה
Job 18:3	טמה	Isa 1:22	מהל
Cant 5:3	טנף	Ps 140:11	מהמרה
Ezek 13:10	טעה	Ps 73:8	מוק
Ps 119:70	טפש	Cant 7:3	מזג
		Deut 32:24	מזה
Ps 119:131	יאב	Exod 4:2	מזה (?)
Jer 10:7	יאה	Ps 144:13	מזו

Appendix I. Absolute Hapax Legomena

2 Kgs 23:5	מזל	Isa 19:14	ועים
Ps 107:30	מחוז	Joel 4:11	עוש
Judg 5:26	מחק	Isa 50:4	עות
Job 40:18	מטיל	Isa 5:2	עזק
2 Sam 12:31	מלכן	Job 21:24	עטין
Ps 119:103	מלץ	Job 41:10	עטישה
2 Kgs 10:22	מלתחה	Isa 11:15	עים
Ps 58:7	מלתעות	Ps 140:4	עכשוב
Prov 29:21	מנון	Isa 32:4	עלג
Job 15:29	מנלם(?)	Prov 30:15	עלוקה
Deut 22:8	מעקה	Job 39:30	עלע
Job 37:16	מפלש	Neh 4:11	עמש
Isa 10:15	משור	Isa 15:5	ערע
2 Sam 13:9	משרת	Ps 104:12	עפי
Job 19:4	משוגה	Job 39:5	ערוד
Ezek 16:4	משעי	Gen 26:20	עשק
		Isa 9:18	עתם
Isa 56:10	נבח		
Job 38:16	נבך	Job 38:11	פא
2 Kgs 17:21	נדא	Cant 2:13	פגה
Ezek 7:11	נה	Job 33:24	פדע
Ps 99:1	נוט	Ps 88:16	פון
Ps 69:21	נוש	Nah 2:4	פלדות
Esth 7:4	נזק	Dan 8:13	פלמני
1 Sam 21:9	נחץ	Ezek 27:17	פנג
Isa 33:1	נלה(?)	Prov 29:21	פנק
Jer 48:9	נצא	Ps 48:14	פסג
Job 30:13	נתס	Ps 60:4	פצם
Job 4:10	נתע	2 Kgs 23:11	פרוד
		Job 26:9	פרשז
Isa 27:8	סאסא	Judg 3:22	פרשדון
Isa 5:25	סוחה	Job 35:15	פש
2 Kgs 19:29	סחיש	Lam 3:11	פשח
Ps 101:3	סטים	Qoh 8:1	פשר
Deut 27:9	סכת	Isa 3:24	פתיגיל
Lam 4:2	סלא		
Job 6:10	סלד	Ruth 2:14	צבט
Ps 139:8	סלק	Ruth 2:16	צבת
Isa 28:25	סמן	Isa 27:4	צות
Cant 7:9	סנסנים	Isa 5:13	צחה
Isa 51:8	סס	Joel 2:20	צחנה
Ps 55:9	סעה	Jer 29:26	צינוק
Ezek 2:6	סרב	Num 32:24	צנא
Amos 6:10	סרף	Ps 8:8	צנה
Isa 55:13	סרפד(?)	Gen 41:23	צנם
Cant 2:11	סתו	Zech 4:12	צנתר
		Isa 33:20	צען
Joel 1:17	עבש	2 Chr 3:10	צעצעים
Job 30:25	עגם	Lam 4:8	צפד
Ruth 1:13	עגן	2 Chr 2:15	צרך
Isa 64:5	עדה		

Hos 10:14	קאם(?)	Lam 1:14	שקד
Isa 29:21	קוש	Isa 3:16	שקר
Ezek 16:47	קט	Lam 3:8	שתם
Hab 2:16	קיקלון (?)	1 Sam 5:9	שתר
1 Sam 13:21	קלשון		
Job 18:2	קנץ	Jer 30:16	שאס
Ezek 17:9	קסס	Isa 3:18	שביס
Lev 19:28	קעקע	Ps 19:13	שגיאה
Isa 34:15	קפוז	Num 11:5	שומים
Num 11:5	קשאה	Isa 37:30	שחיס
		Deut 32:18	שיה
Isa 44:8	רהה	Jer 5:8	שכה
Job 15:12	רזם	2 Sam 6:7	של
Cant 1:17	רחיט	Ps 68:18	שנאן
Job 16:11	רטה	1 Kgs 18:46	שנס
Jer 49:24	רטט	1 Sam 15:33	שסף
Job 33:25	רטפש	Jer 47:3	שעטה
Esth 8:10	רמכים	Gen 49:17	שפיפון
Job 39:23	רנה	Isa 54:8	שצף
2 Chr 2:15	רפסדות	Jer 31:39	שרמות
Job 26:11	רפף(?)	Isa 10:13	ששה
Cant 8:5	רפק	Ezek 39:2	ששא
Isa 57:20	רפש		
Hab 3:17	רפת	Job 4:18	תהלה
Ps 68:17	רצד	Job 41:21	תותח
Ezra 3:7	רשיון	Isa 18:5	תז
Dan 10:21	רשם	Deut 33:3	תכה(?)
Hos 13:1	רתת	Esth 8:15	תכריך
		Hos 13:5	תלאובות
Job 16:19	שהד	Cant 4:4	תלפיות
Gen 24:63	שוח(?)	Lev 6:14	תפינים
Gen 40:11	שחט	Job 17:6	תפת(?)
Ezek 41:16	שחיף	Hos 11:3	תרגל
Judg 4:18	שמיכה	Ezra 4:7	תרגם
Prov 30:28	שממית	Ezek 47:12	תרופה(?)
Deut 33:19	שפן	Isa 44:14	תרזה

Appendix II

Non-absolute Hapax Legomena

Prov 27:20	אבד	Cant 7:2	אמן
Esth 8:6	אבד	Isa 25:1	אמן
Esth 9:5	אבדן	Esth 2:20	אמנה
Job 9:26	אבה	Job 17:9	אמץ
Num 11:5	אבטח	Zech 12:5	אמצה
Job 35:36	אבי	Lam 2:17	אמרה
Cant 3:6	אבקה	Isa 21:2	אנחתה
Job 39:26	אבר	2 Sam 12:15	אנש
Gen 41:43	אברך	2 Kgs 4:2	אסוך
1 Sam 2:36	אגורה	Qoh 12:11	אספה
Prov 7:18	אהבים	Isa 24:22	אספה
Ps 120:5	אויה	Num 11:4	אספסף
Deut 23:14	אזן	Exod 9:32	אפיל
Isa 19:6	אזנח	Amos 5:20	אפל
Isa 13:21	אח	Prov 25:4	אפן
Ezek 21:21	אחד	Ezek 47:3	אפסים
Job 13:17	אחוה	Isa 54:12	אקדח
Isa 19:3	אטים	Isa 33:7	אראל
Ps 69:16	אטר	Isa 25:11	ארבה
2 Kgs 6:13	איכה	Ezek 27:24	ארוז
1 Sam 21:9	אין	Zeph 2:14	ארזה
Ps 88:5	איל	Isa 44:14	ארן
Ps 22:20	אילות	Num 21:15	אשדה
Prov 27:4	אכזריות	Deut 33:2	אשדת
1 Kgs 19:8	אכילה	Jer 6:29	אשה
Prov 16:26	אכף	Prov 20:20	אשון
Job 33:7	אכף	Isa 49:10	אשמן
Josh 24:26	אלה	Lam 4:5	אשפתה
Gen 37:7	אלם	Gen 30:13	אשר
Isa 47:9	אלמן	Isa 46:8	אשש
Jer 51:5	אלמן	Ezek 41:15	אתוק
Ezek 10:30	אמלה	Hos 2:14	אתנה
Ps 6:3	אמלל		
Neh 3:34	אמלל	Ezek 8:5	באה

Gen 14:10	באר	Ezek 47:13	גה
Job 31:40	באשה	Hos 5:13	גהה
Amos 3:12	בדל	Prov 17:22	גהה
2 Chr 34:10	בדק	Neh 7:3	גוף
Job 37:21	בהיר	Ps 71:6	גזה
Neh 3:36	בוזה	Lev 16:22	גזרה
Nah 2:11	בוקה	Ps 22:10	גח
Esth 1:18	בזיון	Isa 40:4	גיא
Jer 6:27	בחון	Isa 28:28	גלגל
Num 11:28	בחורים	Ezek 27:14	גלום
Isa 23:13	בחין	2 Kgs 2:8	גלם
Isa 32:14	בחן	Ps 139:16	גלם
Isa 30:15	בטחה	Judg 3:16	גמד
Job 12:6	בטחה	Ezek 27:11	גמד
Gen 43:11	בטנה	Ezek 16:5	געל
Jer 6:7	ביר	Gen 6:14	גפר
Ezra 10:1	בכה	Isa 17:6	גרגר
Jer 24:2	בכורה	Jer 41:17	גרות
Gen 50:4	בכית	Ps 31:23	גרז
Isa 60:6	בכר	Prov 19:19	גרל
Jer 2:33	בכרה	Judg 5:21	גרף
Ezra 4:4	בלה	Deut 33:14	גרש
Ezek 41:13	בניה	Ezek 45:9	גרשה
Exod 22:5	בערה		
Jer 38:22	בץ	Job 41:14	דאבה
Mic 2:12	בצרה	Deut 28:65	דאבון
Zech 9:12	בצרון	Lev 11:14	דאה
Jer 17:8	בצרת	Cant 7:10	דבב
Amos 7:14	בקר	Jer 5:13	דבר
Ezek 34:12	בקרה	Deut 33:3	דברה
Lev 19:20	בקרת	1 Kgs 5:23	דברה
2 Sam 20:4	בר	Isa 30:6	דבשת
Isa 32:19	ברד	Nah 3:2	דהר
Ps 69:22	ברות	Amos 4:2	דוגה
Ps 144:6	ברק	Lev 12:2	דוה
Ezek 28:13	ברקת	Num 11:8	דוך
2 Sam 2:29	בתרון	Gen 6:3	דון
		Ps 84:11	דור
Prov 7:13	גאה	Jer 16:16	דיג
Isa 63:4	גאולים	Lev 26:5	דיש
Ps 123:4	גאיון	Deut 14:5	דישון
Neh 13:29	גאל	Deut 23:2	דכה
Lev 13:41	גבח	Ps 93:3	דכי
Job 10:10	גבינה	Deut 28:22	דלקת
Lev 21:20	גבן	Ezek 27:32	דמה
Exod 9:31	גבעל	Isa 38:10	דמי
Jer 48:37	גדדה	Ps 17:12	דמיון
Ezek 5:15	גדופה	Exod 22:28	דמע
Cant 1:8	גדיה	Isa 40:22	דק
Ezek 16:26	גדל	Isa 13:21	דרבן
Ezek 42:12	גדרת	Qoh 12:11	דרבן

Appendix II. Non-Absolute Hapax Legomena

Ps 49:4	הגות	Deut 1:45	זמר
Dan 11:20	הדד	Deut 33:22	זנק
Ezek 30:2	הה	Gen 3:19	זעה
Qoh 10:13	הוללות	Gen 48:10	זקן
Deut 1:41	הון	Isa 60:3	זרח
Neh 12:8	הידה	Dan 1:12	זרע
Prov 31:27	הילכות	Dan 1:16	זרען
Isa 14:12	הילל		
Isa 3:9	הכרה	Job 33:33	חב
Ezek 36:25	הלזו	Deut 33:3	חבב
Job 29:6	הליך	Hab 3:4	חביון
Judg 5:26	הלמות	Prov 23:34	חבל
Ezek 7:11	המהם	Ezek 18:7	חבלה
Isa 14:11	המיה	Job 40:30	חבר
Prov 19:18	המית	Jer 13:23	חברברה
Ezek 5:7	המן	Job 34:8	חברה
Esth 2:18	הנחה	Isa 53:5	חברה
Num 13:30	הסה	1 Chr 9:31	חבתים
Lam 3:49	הפגה	Job 41:22	חדוד
Gen 19:29	הפכה	Isa 38:11	חדל
Prov 21:8	הפכפך	Prov 15:19	חדק
Esth 4:14	הצלה	Mic 7:4	חדק
Jer 44:21	הקטר	Ezek 21:19	חדר
2 Sam 14:11	הרבות	Dan 1:10	חוב
Gen 3:16	הרון	Ezek 18:7	חוב
Hos 14:1	הריה	Job 26:10	חוג
Amos 9:11	הריסה	Isa 29:22	חור
Isa 49:19	הריסות	Isa 19:9	חורי
Isa 19:18	הרס	2 Chr 1:29	חזות
Ezek 24:6	השמעות	Ps 18:2	חזק
2 Kgs 5:18	השתחויה	Num 15:28	חטאה
Ezek 22:22	התוך	Exod 1:19	חיה
Dan 11:23	התחברות	2 Sam 20:3	חיות
1 Kgs 18:27	התל	Job 6:10	חילה
Job 17:2	התלים	Ezek 13:10	חיץ
		Ps 90:10	חיש
Gen 11:30	ולד	Prov 23:29	חכלילות
		Gen 49:12	חכלילי
Gen 30:20	זבד	2 Chr 16:12	חלא
Gen 30:20	זבד	Exod 30:34	חלבנה
Hos 4:19	זבחה	Lev 11:29	חלד
Gen 30:20	זבל	Prov 31:8	חלוף
Hab 3:11	זבלה	Exod 32:18	חלושה
Isa 46:6	זול	Hos 2:15	חליה
Jer 5:8	זון	Job 6:6	חלמות
Ps 124:5	זידון	1 Sam 17:40	חלק
Job 28:17	זכוכית	Dan 11:32	חלקה
Isa 18:5	זלזל	Joel 4:10	חלש
Ps 12:9	זלת	Isa 1:17	חמוץ
Cant 2:12	זמיר	Cant 7:2	חמוק
Ps 140:9	זמם	Isa 30:24	חמיץ

Ezek 16:5	חמלה	Isa 14:23	טאטא
Ps 71:4	חמץ	Ezek 23:15	טבולים
Isa 1:17	חמץ	1 Sam 8:13	טבחה
Judg 15:16	חמרה	Ps 89:45	טהר
Gen 47:26	חמש	Ezek 13:12	טיח
Jer 37:16	חנות	Isa 22:17	טלטל
Gen 50:3	חנטים	Isa 40:11	טלי
Gen 14:14	חניך	Neh 3:15	טלל
Jer 16:13	חנינה	Lam 5:13	טחון
Isa 32:6	חנף	Qoh 12:4	טחנה
Jer 23:15	חנפה	Mic 2:10	טמאה
Isa 30:3	חסות	Lam 2:20	טפוח
Ps 89:9	חסין	Isa 3:16	טפף
Deut 28:38	חסל	Ruth 3:14	טרום
Isa 23:18	חסן	Isa 1:14	טרח
Qoh 1:15	חסרון	Job 37:11	טרח
Job 33:9	חף		
Deut 33:12	חפף	Lev 22:22	יבלת
Ps 64:7	חפש	Jer 39:10	יגב
Lev 19:22	חפש	Job 20:18	יגע
Ezek 27:20	חפש	Qoh 12:12	יגעה
Lev 19:20	חפשה	Jer 12:7	ידדות
Ps 32:4	חרבון	Ps 45:1	ידידות
Deut 28:22	חרחר	Ps 55:23	יהב
Gen 40:16	חרי	Jer 17:8	יובל
Jonah 4:8	חרישי	Ezek 44:18	יזע
Prov 12:27	חרך	Lam 3:26	יחיל
Cant 2:9	חרך	Neh 7:5	יחש
Lev 21:18	חרם	Deut 32:10	ילל
Jer 19:2	חרסית	1 Sam 17:40	ילקוט
Isa 18:6	חרף	Job 42:12	ימימה
Num 6:4	חרצן	Ezek 17:4	יניקה
Jer 17:6	חרר	Isa 34:11	ינשוף
Exod 35:33	חרשת	Ps 87:1	יסודה
1 Kgs 7:33	חשוק	Job 40:2	יסור
Isa 14:6	חשך	Isa 28:17	יעה
Prov 22:29	חשך	Ps 5:19	יעלה
1 Kgs 20:27	חשף	Lam 4:3	יען
2 Kgs 7:33	חשר	Dan 9:21	יעף
2 Sam 22:12	חשרה	1 Sam 14:27	יערה
Gen 35:5	חתה	Jer 4:31	יפח
Ezek 30:21	חתול	Ps 27:12	יפח
Qoh 12:5	חתחת	Ezek 28:7	יפי
Job 38:9	חתלה	2 Chr 32:21	יציא
Gen 38:25	חתמת	1 Kgs 7:24	יצקה
Cant 3:11	חתנה	Job 17:7	יצר
Deut 27:23	חתנת	Isa 30:15	יקוד
Job 9:12	חתף	Job 8:14	יקוט
Prov 23:28	חתף	Hos 9:8	יקוש
Job 6:21	חתת	Jer 31:20	יקיר
		Isa 28:16	יקרה

Appendix II. Non-Absolute Hapax Legomena

Job 39:8	ירוק	Gen 3:24	להט
Num 24:18	ירשה	Exod 7:11	להטים
Ps 55:16	ישימות	Gen 30:37	לוז
1 Kgs 3:6	ישרה	Isa 25:7	לוט
2 Chr 26:17	ישש	1 Kgs 6:8	לול
Job 39:8	יתור	Prov 4:24	לזות
Isa 33:16	יתן	Deut 34:7	לח
Prov 12:26	יתר	Judg 5:8	לחם
		Isa 34:14	לילית
Ps 10:10	כאה	Prov 3:26	לכד
Exod 14:25	כבדות	Neh 13:21	לן
2 Chr 9:18	כבש	Prov 23:2	לע
Isa 22:18	כדור	Isa 28:11	לעג
Exod 21:25	כויה	Job 24:6	לקש
Ps 68:7	כושרה		
Isa 30:9	כחש	Jer 50:26	מאבס
Job 21:20	כיד	Ps 140:9	מאוה
Job 15:24	כידור	Isa 11:8	מאורה
Job 2:20	כיר	Isa 9:18	מאכלת
Prov 31:19	כישור	Job 36:19	מאמץ
Jer 2:2	כלולות	Lev 2:4	מאפה
Deut 28:32	כלות	Josh 24:7	מאפל
Jer 23:50	כלמות	Jer 2:31	מאפליה
Ps 80:16	כנה	Josh 16:9	מבדלה
Jer 10:17	כנעה	Nah 2:11	מבוקה
Isa 30:20	כנף	Num 30:7	מטא
Exod 17:16	כס	Job 28:11	מבכי
Prov 7:20	כסא	Jer 8:18	מבליגית
Ps 81:4	כסה	Ezek 40:2	מבנה
Exod 17:16	כסיה	Ezek 17:21	מברח
Prov 9:13	כסילות	Deut 25:11	מבשים
Jer 10:8	כסל	Ezek 46:23	מבשלה
Ezek 44:20	כסם	Exod 28:14	מגבל
Ezek 17:7	כפנה	Hag 2:19	מגורה
Gen 6:14	כפר	Ps 55:16	מגורם
2 Kgs 6:23	כרה	2 Sam 12:31	מגזרה
Zeph 2:6	כרה	Lam 3:65	מגנה
Isa 66:20	כרכרה	Deut 28:20	מגערה
Lev 5:6	כשיבה	1 Kgs 6:6	מגרעה
Ps 74:6	כשיל	Joel 1:17	מגרפה
Prov 16:18	כשלון	Ezek 27:28	מגרשה
Jer 27:9	כשף	Lam 2:14	מדוח
Ps 68:7	כתבת	Prov 26:28	מדחה
Prov 31:19	כתם	Ps 140:12	מדחפה
Lev 19:28	כתש	Num 11:8	מדכה
		Isa 25:10	מדמנה
Ps 57:5	לבא	Ruth 3:2	מדעת
Num 2:13	לבאה	Prov 12:18	מדקרה
Ezek 16:30	לבה	Deut 2:5	מדרך
Exod 3:2	לבה	Isa 21:10	מדשה
Ezek 19:2	לביה	Prov 27:21	מהלל

Isa 30:10	מהתלה	Ezek 16:3	מכורה
Neh 12:38	מואל	2 Chr 4:21	מכלות
Hab 3:6	מוד	Ps 50:2	מכלל
Deut 1:1	מול	Ezek 27:24	מכללים
Exod 4:26	מולה	1 Kgs 5:25	מכלת
Ezek 41:7	מוסב	Dan 11:43	מכמן
2 Kgs 16:18	מוסך	Isa 51:20	מכמר
Isa 14:31	מועד	Ps 141:10	מכמר
Josh 20:9	מועדה	Isa 19:8	מכמרת
Isa 8:23	מועף	Gen 49:5	מכרה
Ps 66:11	מועקה	Zeph 2:9	מכרה
Lev 6:2	מוקדה	Isa 30:14	מכתה
Ps 68:21	מושעות	Hag 1:13	מלאכות
Job 12:21	מזיח	Cant 5:12	מלאת
Job 38:32	מזר	Job 30:4	מלוח
Job 37:9	מזר	Jer 43:9	מלט
Job 38:32	מזרות	Deut 23:26	מלילה
Isa 19:7	מזרע	Job 18:10	מלכדת
Job 21:24	מח	Judg 3:31	מלמד
Isa 32:2	מחבא	Joel 1:17	ממגרה
1 Sam 23:23	מחבא	Job 38:5	ממד
Isa 3:24	מחגרת	Lev 25:42	ממכרת
Isa 44:13	מחוגה	Prov 17:25	ממר
1 Chr 25:4	מחזיאות	Job 9:18	ממרור
Isa 25:6	מחח	Ezek 8:14	ממשח
Ezek 26:9	מחי	Zeph 2:9	ממשק
Isa 2:19	מחלה	Ps 61:8	מן
2 Chr 24:25	מחליים	Lam 3:63	מנגינה
Ezra 1:9	מחלף	2 Kgs 9:20	מנהג
1 Chr 27:5	מחלקה	Judg 6:2	מנהרה
Ps 55:22	מחמאה	Ps 44:15	מנוד
Ezek 24:21	מחמל	Nah 3:17	מנדר
Job 7:15	מחנק	Isa 65:11	מני
Ps 39:2	מחסום	Deut 33:25	מנעל
Isa 30:26	מחץ	Ps 141:4	מנעם
Ps 95:4	מחקר	2 Sam 6:5	מנענע
2 Kgs 10:27	מחראה	Job 6:14	מס
1 Sam 13:20	מחרשת	Job 37:12	מסבה
Gen 30:37	מחשף	1 Kgs 7:9	מסד
Isa 14:23	מטאטא	Judg 3:23	מסדרון
Isa 14:21	מטבח	Deut 16:10	מסה
Ezek 9:9	מטה	Job 9:23	מסה
Isa 8:8	מטה	Mic 7:4	מסוכה
Prov 24:11	מטה	2 Kgs 11:6	מסח
Exod 35:25	מטוה	1 Kgs 10:15	מסחר
Isa 52:5	מי	Ps 74:9	מסך
2 Sam 17:20	מיכל	Ezek 28:13	מסכה
2 Kgs 16:18	מיסך	Deut 8:9	מסכנות
Prov 30:33	מיץ	Isa 35:8	מסלול
2 Kgs 8:15	מכבר	1 Kgs 10:12	מסעד
Zech 5:11	מכונה	Job 33:16	מסר

Appendix II. Non-Absolute Hapax Legomena

Ezek 20:37	מסרות	Ps 68:27	מקהלה
Isa 4:6	מסתור	Isa 22:11	מקוה
Isa 53:3	מסתר	2 Chr 19:7	מקח
Job 34:26	מעבד	Neh 10:32	מקחה
1 Kgs 7:46	מעבה	Exod 30:1	מקטר
Isa 7:26	מעדה	2 Chr 30:14	מקטרות
Isa 7:25	מעדר	Jer 22:17	מקצה
Isa 8:22	מעוף	Isa 44:13	מקצעה
Hab 2:15	מעור	Qoh 10:18	מקרה
Isa 61:3	מעטה	Deut 33:11	מקרה
Job 21:20	מעטה	Isa 3:24	מקשה
Isa 3:22	מעטפה	Job 39:18	מרא
Isa 17:1	מעי	Lev 1:16	מראה
Neh 8:6	מעל	Ezek 23:32	מרבה
Ps 69:3	מעמד	Isa 33:23	מרבה
Zech 12:3	מעמסה	Ezek 25:2	מרבץ
1 Sam 14:14	מענה	Zeph 2:15	מרבץ
Ps 129:3	מענית	Jer 6:16	מרגוע
Isa 40:11	מעצבה	Prov 26:8	מרגמה
Ps 14:6	מעצור	Isa 8:12	מרגעה
Prov 25:28	מעצר	Josh 22:22	מרד
Isa 42:16	מעקש	1 Sam 20:30	מרדות
Judg 20:33	מערה	Prov 14:10	מרה
Prov 16:1	מערך	Gen 26:35	מרה
2 Chr 28:15	מערמים	Lev 21:20	מרוח
Isa 10:33	מערצה	Qoh 9:11	מרוץ
Job 7:20	מפגע	Esth 2:12	מרוקים
Job 11:20	מפח	Isa 38:21	מרח
Jer 6:29	מפח	Ps 118:5	מרחביה
Prov 25:18	מפיץ	Job 3:5	מרירי
Job 37:16	מפלאה	Deut 32:24	מרירי
2 Chr 35:12	מפלגה	Ezek 21:11	מרירות
Isa 17:1	מפלה	Lev 26:36	מרך
Ps 55:9	מפלט	Ezek 27:24	מרכלת
Prov 8:22	מפעל	Dan 11:27	מרע
Ezek 9:2	מפץ	Jer 8:15	מרפה
Jer 51:20	מפץ	Ezek 34:19	מרפש
Judg 5:17	מפרץ	2 Kgs 16:17	מרצפת
1 Sam 4:18	מפרקת	Cant 5:13	מרקח
1 Chr 19:4	מפשעה	Job 16:13	מררה
Prov 8:6	מפתח	Jer 50:21	מרתים
Isa 16:4	מץ	2 Chr 24:7	מרשעת
1 Sam 14:12	מצבה	2 Chr 19:7	משא
Job 37:12	מצבה	Prov 26:26	משאון
1 Sam 17:6	מצחה	Deut 15:2	משה
Zech 14:20	מצלה	Prov 15:19	משכה
Isa 28:20	מצע	Hab 1:10	משחק
Obad 6	מצפון	Isa 5:5	משוכה
Isa 66:11	מצץ	Judg 5:11	משאב
Isa 41:12	מצת	Lam 1:7	משבת
Ps 26:12	מקהל	Gen 43:12	משגה

Isa 42:24	משוסה	2 Kgs 18:4	נחשתן
Ps 110:3	משחר	2 Kgs 6:9	נחת
Ezek 9:1	משחת	Zeph 1:21	נטיל
Isa 52:24	משחת	Ps 141:12	נטיע
Lev 22:25	משחת	Prov 27:3	נטל
Ezek 47:10	משטיח	Exod 30:34	נטף
Job 38:33	משטר	Job 36:27	נטף
Job 38:31	משכת	Ezek 27:32	ני
Gen 38:24	משלש	Job 16:5	ניד
Neh 8:10	משמן	Lam 1:8	נידה
Isa 11:3	משמע	Ps 72:17	נין
Num 22:24	משעול	Jer 48:44	ניס
Isa 3:1	משען	Isa 1:31	ניצוץ
Isa 3:1	משענה	Job 30:8	נכא
Isa 5:7	משפח	Isa 16:7	נכא
Isa 33:4	משק	Ps 35:15	נכה
Gen 15:2	משק	Job 12:5	נכון
Ezek 4:10	משק	Num 28:15	נכל
Isa 28:17	משקול	1 Sam 4:9	נמבזה
Isa 28:17	משקלת	2 Chr 10:15	נסבה
2 Kgs 21:13	משקלת	Ps 4:7	נסה
Ezek 34:18	משקע	Ps 16:11	נעמות
Num 6:3	משרה	Isa 17:10	נעמן
Isa 25:10	מתבן	Jer 32:30	נערות
Isa 40:22	מתח	Isa 30:30	נפץ
Mal 1:13	מתלאה	Josh 17:15	נפת
Judg 20:48	מתם	Gen 30:8	נפתולים
Judg 9:11	מתק	Judg 3:22	נצב
		Isa 65:4	נצורים
Jer 23:31	נאם	Isa 49:6	נציר
Hos 2:4	נאפוף	Cant 2:12	נצן
Hos 2:12	נבלות	Ezek 28:13	נקב
Isa 59:9	נגהה	Cant 1:11	נקדה
Exod 21:29	נגח	Isa 3:24	נקפה
Job 7:4	נדדים	2 Sam 19:43	נשאת
Ezek 16:33	נדה	Isa 46:1	נשואת
Mic 2:4	נהיה	Gen 32:33	נשה
Isa 1:19	נהלל	2 Kgs 4:7	נשי
Job 3:4	נהרה	Ps 88:13	נשיה
Ps 56:9	נוד	Isa 42:14	נשם
2 Chr 6:41	נוח		
Prov 23:21	נומה	Isa 9:4	סאון
Ps 48:3	נוף	Isa 9:4	סאן
Lam 4:15	נוץ	1 Kgs 12:15	סבה
Job 6:12	נחוש	Judg 8:17	סבך
Ps 5:1	נחילה	Judg 12:5	סבלת
Job 41:12	נחיר	Ps 35:3	סגר
Ps 16:6	נחלת	Prov 27:15	סגריר
Hos 13:14	נחם	Job 10:22	סדר
Cant 1:6	נחר	Cant 7:3	סהר
Job 39:20	נחר	Cant 7:3	סוגה
Jer 8:16	נחרה	Ezek 19:9	סוגר

Appendix II. Non-Absolute Hapax Legomena

Cant 1:9	סוסה	Job 5:16	עלתה
Jer 2:22	סוריה	Mic 1:11	עמדה
Gen 49:11	סות	Exod 21:10	ענה
Ezek 26:4	סחה	Ps 22:25	ענות
Lam 3:45	סחי	Ezek 19:10	ענפה
Ps 91:4	סחרה	Mal 3:21	עסס
Ezek 27:15	סחרה	Ezek 32:10	עפף
Esth 1:6	סחרת	2 Sam 16:13	עפר
Jer 8:7	סיס	Isa 48:5	עצב
Ps 42:5	סך	Isa 58:3	עצב
Nah 2:6	סכך	Lev 3:9	עצה
Qoh 10:6	סכל	Prov 16:30	עצה
Ps 86:5	סלח	Ps 10:10	עצומים
Gen 28:12	סלם	Judg 18:9	עצל
Jer 6:9	סלסלה	Isa 41:21	עצמות
Lev 11:22	סלעם	Judg 18:7	עצר
Jer 51:27	סמר	2 Kgs 10:19	עקבה
Isa 10:33	סעף	Gen 22:9	עקד
Ps 119:113	סעף	Ps 55:4	עקה
1 Kgs 18:21	סעפים	Hab 1:4	עקל
Jer 22:14	ספון	Isa 27:1	עקלתון
Jonah 1:5	ספינה	Lev 25:47	עקר
1 Kgs 6:15	ספן	Isa 19:7	ערה
Ps 34:11	ספף	Isa 5:30	עריפים
2 Chr 2:16	ספר	Jer 22:3	עשוק
Ps 56:9	ספרה	Ezek 27:19	עשות
Ps 71:15	ספרות	Isa 38:14	עשקה
Exod 26:12	סרח	Cant 5:14	עשת
Ezek 31:5	סרעפה	Ps 146:4	עשתון
Deut 32:38	סתרה	Job 12:5	עשתות
		Lev 16:2	עתי
Exod 19:9	עב	Jer 33:6	עתרת
Hab 2:6	עבטיט		
2 Sam 15:28	עברה	Deut 32:26	פאה
Mic 7:3	עבת	Deut 24:20	פאר
Ezek 23:11	עגבה	Isa 10:23	פארה
Isa 47:8	עדין	Neh 3:49	פדיום
Neh 9:25	עדן	Lam 2:18	פוגה
Qoh 4:2	עדנה	Zeph 3:10	פוצי
Lam 2:1	עוב	1 Sam 25:31	פוקה
Ezek 21:32	עוה	Jer 2:19	פחדה
Isa 13:22	עון	Gen 49:4	פחז
Lev 22:22	עורת	Jer 23:32	פחזות
Lam 3:59	עותה	Isa 42:22	פחח
Job 38:32	עיש	Ps 11:6	פחים
Hos 10:9	עלוה	Lev 13:55	פחתת
Isa 5:14	עלז	Num 8:16	פטרה
Prov 27:22	עלי	Jer 46:20	פיה
Ps 12:7	עליל	1 Sam 13:21	פים
Ps 48:15	עלמות	Job 15:27	פימה
Ezek 31:15	עלפה	Nah 2:11	פיק
Hab 3:14	עלצות	Ezek 47:2	פכה

2 Chr 35:5	פלגה	Ezek 32:6	צפה
Job 31:28	פלילי	Ezra 4:15	צפוע
Isa 28:7	פליליה	Lam 4:17	צפיה
Job 9:6	פלץ	Ezek 4:1	צפיע
Ps 72:16	פסה	Isa 22:24	צפיעה
Ps 12:2	פסס	Exod 16:31	צפיחת
Isa 42:14	פעה	Ps 17:14	צפין
1 Sam 13:21	פצירה	Isa 21:5	צפית
Gen 30:37	פצלה	Isa 22:24	צפעה
Jer 37:13	פקדת	Ezek 17:6	צפצפה
2 Kgs 4:39	פקעה	Judg 7:3	צפר
Hos 13:15	פרא	2 Chr 3:15	צפת
1 Chr 26:18	פרבר	1 Sam 26:10	צקון
Joel 1:17	פרדה	Isa 5:28	צר
Jer 2:24	פרה	Ezek 21:3	צרב
Isa 2:20	פרות		
Hab 3:14	פרז	2 Kgs 6:25	קב
Job 30:12	פרחח	Num 25:8	קבה
Amos 6:5	פרט	Isa 57:13	קבוץ
Lev 19:10	פרט	Ezek 22:20	קבצה
Isa 65:4	פרק	Judg 5:21	קדום
1 Sam 27:4	פשע	Isa 50:3	קדרות
2 Sam 20:3	פשע	Ezek 47:8	קדמון
Ezek 13:19	פתות	Mal 3:14	קדרנית
Ps 119:130	פתח	Ezek 23:24	קובע
Prov 9:13	פתיות	Isa 61:1	קוח
Deut 32:5	פתלתל	Lev 26:13	קוממיות
Lev 2:6	פתת	Isa 59:5	קור
		Deut 33:10	קטורה
Num 5:21	צבה	Ezek 46:22	קטרות
Jer 12:9	צבוע	Obad 9	קטל
2 Kgs 10:8	צבור	Job 22:20	קים
Judg 5:30	צבע	Lam 3:63	קימה
Ezra 8:17	צהב	2 Sam 21:16	קים
Job 24:11	צהר	Lev 22:23	קלט
Gen 6:16	צהר	Ezek 22:4	קלסה
Isa 42:11	צוח	2 Kgs 3:25	קלע
Isa 44:27	צולה	Num 21:5	קלקל
Dan 9:25	צוק	Zech 14:6	קפאון
Cant 4:9	צוררן	Isa 38:12	קפד
Isa 58:11	צחצחה	Ezek 7:25	קפדה
Ezek 27:18	צחר	Isa 18:6	קץ
Judg 5:10	צחר	Ps 45:9	קציעה
Jer 16:16	ציד	Joel 1:7	קצפה
Jonah 9:4	ציר	Exod 6:9	קצר
2 Chr 35:13	צלחה	Jonah 3:2	קריאה
2 Kgs 2:20	צלחית	Jer 46:20	קרץ
Judg 7:13	צליל	Num 24:17	קרקר
Jer 2:25	צמאה	Ps 60:6	קשט
Hos 9:14	צמק	Prov 22:21	קשט
Isa 22:18	צנפה	Deut 9:27	קשי
Exod 16:33	צנצנת	Gen 21:20	קשת

Appendix II. Non-Absolute Hapax Legomena

Ref	Heb	Ref	Heb
Job 10:15	ראה	Cant 8:2	רקח
Deut 14:13	ראה	Isa 57:9	רקח
Job 37:18	ראי	Lev 15:8	רקק
Qoh 5:10	ראיות	Ezek 24:5	רתח
Zech 14:10	ראם	Mic 1:13	רתם
Ezek 36:11	ראשה		
Zech 4:7	ראשה	1 Kgs 7:17	שבך
Jer 25:1	ראשני	2 Sam 18:9	שבך
Prov 7:16	רבד	Ps 40:5	שוט
Ps 139:3	רבעי	Judg 9:49	שוך
Deut 28:65	רגז	Judg 9:48	שוכה
Ezek 12:18	רגזה	Isa 28:25	שורה
Ps 68:28	רגמה	Amos 4:13	שח
Ps 55:15	רגש	Ezek 47:5	שחו
Ps 64:3	רגשה	Hos 5:2	שט
Ps 40:6	רהב	Ezra 4:6	שטנה
Ps 90:10	רהבה	Job 20:6	שיא
Cant 1:17	רהיט	1 Kgs 14:4	שיב
Hab 3:10	רום	1 Kgs 18:27	שיג
Mic 2:3	רומה	Num 33:55	שך
Isa 33:3	רוממות	Lam 2:6	שך
Job 26:11	רוף	Job 40:31	שכה
Lev 15:3	רור	Job 38:36	שכו
Isa 24:16	רזי	Isa 2:16	שכיה
Ps 45:2	רחש	Prov 23:2	שכין
Isa 30:24	רחת	Qoh 1:17	שכלות
Job 24:8	רטב	Deut 21:15	שניא
Job 8:16	רטב	Lev 13:4	שערה
Job 37:11	רי	Isa 3:17	שפח
Prov 28:19	ריש	Job 36:18	שפק
Deut 28:56	רך	Job 20:22	שפק
Ezek 27:20	רכבה	Josh 10:20	שרד
Ps 104:3	רכוב	Isa 44:13	שרד
Isa 40:4	רכס	Lev 19:28	שרט
Ps 31:21	רכס	Lev 21:5	שרטת
Ezek 32:5	רמות	Isa 19:9	שריק
Ps 32:7	רן	Jer 2:23	שרך
Ezek 46:14	רס	Gen 49:11	שרקה
Ezek 46:14	רסס		
1 Kgs 5:3	רעי	Prov 1:27	שאוה
Nah 2:4	רעל	Isa 24:12	שאיה
Zech 12:2	רעל	Lev 18:17	שארה
Isa 3:19	רעלה	Lam 3:47	שאת
Job 39:19	רעמלה	Hos 8:6	שבב
Job 15:32	רען	Job 18:5	שביב
Prov 3:8	רפאות	Isa 52:2	שביה
Cant 3:20	רפידה	Isa 47:2	שבל
Jer 47:3	רפיון	Ps 58:9	שבלול
Ps 68:31	רץ	2 Sam 1:9	שבץ
Exod 21:6	רצע	Judg 7:15	שבר
Cant 3:10	רצף	Job 19:29	שדון
Job 41:19	רקבון	2 Kgs 19:26	שדפה

Job 15:31	שו	Isa 3:19	שר
Ps 35:17	שוא	Prov 3:8	שר
Isa 30:15	שובה	Isa 3:19	שרה
Gen 14:5	שוה	Jer 18:16	שרוקה
Job 24:11	שורה	Job 41:18	שריה
Job 22:29	שח	Job 40:16	שריר
Lam 4:8	שחור	Exod 28:22	שרשות
Prov 28:10	שחות	Esth 1:8	שתיה
2 Chr 30:17	שחיטה		
Exod 30:34	שחלת	Ps 119:20	תאבה
Qoh 11:10	שחרות	Lam 3:65	תאלה
Cant 1:6	שחרחר	Judg 14:4	תאנה
Josh 23:13	שטט	Jer 2:22	תאניה
1 Chr 29:2	שיש	Ezek 24:2	תאנים
Isa 49:20	שכלים	2 Chr 22:7	תבוסה
Job 31:22	שכמה	Isa 10:25	תבלית
Job 21:23	שלאנן	Lev 21:20	תבלל
Ps 68:13	שלג	Ps 116:12	תגמל
Isa 16:8	שלחה	Ps 39:11	תגרה
2 Sam 3:27	שלי	Neh 12:31	תהלכה
Deut 28:57	שליה	Ps 137:3	תולל
Isa 6:13	שלכת	Ps 16:5	תומיך
Deut 32:35	שלם	2 Sam 23:8	תחכמני
Ps 91:8	שלמה	2 Kgs 6:8	תחנה
Isa 1:23	שלמן	Prov 29:13	תכך
Ezek 35:7	שממה	Ps 119:96	תכלה
Ps 150:5	שמע	Isa 59:17	תלבשת
Exod 32:25	שמצה	Gen 27:3	תלי
Exod 12:42	שמר	1 Chr 25:8	תלמיד
Ps 141:3	שמרה	Nah 2:4	תלע
Ps 77:5	שמרה	Cant 5:11	תלתל
Ps 132:4	שנת	Ps 58:9	תמס
Prov 23:7	שער	Ezra 9:5	תענית
Jer 29:17	שער	Ps 68:36	תעצמות
Hos 6:10	שערורי	Jer 25:34	תפוצה
Jer 17:13	שערת	Lev 6:14	תפין
2 Sam 17:29	שפה	2 Sam 22:27	תפל
Lev 4:12	שפך	Jer 49:16	תפלצת
Deut 23:2	שפכה	Isa 30:33	תפתה
Isa 32:19	שפלה	Lev 26:37	תקומה
Qoh 10:18	שפלות	Ezek 7:14	תקוע
Deut 33:19	שפע	Ezra 47:17	תקופה
Ps 16:6	שפר	Qoh 6:10	תקיף
Gen 49:21	שפר	Ps 150:3	תקע
Job 26:13	שפרה	Num 32:14	תרבות
Jer 43:10	שפריר	Ezek 48:12	תרומיה
1 Chr 22:9	שקט	Judg 9:31	תרמה
Lev 14:37	שקערורות	Exod 28:4	תשבץ
1 Kgs 7:5	שקף	Job 30:22	תשוה
Gen 42:20	שקת	Lev 5:21	תשומה
Gen 30:38	שקת	1 Sam 9:7	תשורה

Appendix III
Chi-Square Test for Distribution of Hapax Legomena

Book	Total Words	Absolute Hapax Legomena			All Hapax Legomena		
		Expct. Hapax	Actl. Hapax	"D"	Expct. Hapax	Actl. Hapax	"D"
Gen	20,611	19.81	8	7.04	102.91	57	20.48
Exod	16,712	16.07	4	9.07	83.45	37	25.86
Lev	11,950	11.49	7	1.75	59.67	51	1.26
Num	16,413	15.78	7	4.89	81.95	29	34.21
Deut	14,294	13.74	10	1.02	71.37	55	3.75
Josh	10,051	9.66	0	9.66	50.19	8	35.47
Judg	9,884	9.50	6	1.29	49.35	34	4.77
Sam	24,300	23.36	11	6.54	121.33	51	40.77
Kgs	25,420	24.44	9	9.75	126.93	57	38.53
Isa	16,930	16.28	43	43.85	84.53	239	282.28
Jer	21,819	20.98	14	2.32	108.95	83	6.18
Ezek	18,731	18.01	21	0.50	93.53	127	11.98
Hos	2,383	2.29	4	1.28	11.90	23	10.35
Joel	957	0.92	3	4.70	4.78	8	2.17
Amos	2,042	1.96	4	2.12	10.20	13	0.77
Obad	291	0.28	0	0.28	1.45	2	0.21
Jonah	688	0.66	0	0.66	3.44	4	0.09
Micah	1,396	1.34	1	0.09	6.97	11	2.33
Nahum	558	0.54	1	0.39	2.79	9	13.82
Hab	671	0.65	2	2.80	3.35	14	33.86
Zeph	767	0.74	0	0.74	3.83	7	2.62
Hag	600	0.58	0	0.58	3.00	2	0.33
Zech	3,128	3.01	2	0.34	15.62	11	1.37
Mal	876	0.84	0	0.84	4.37	3	0.43
Pss	19,531	18.78	33	10.77	97.52	159	38.76
Prov	6,915	6.65	10	1.69	34.53	70	36.44
Job	8,343	8.02	39	119.67	41.66	149	276.57
Cant	1,250	1.20	14	136.53	6.24	36	141.93
Ruth	1,294	1.24	3	2.50	6.46	5	0.33
Lam	1,542	1.48	6	13.80	7.70	29	58.92
Qoh	2,987	2.87	4	0.44	14.91	21	2.49
Esth	3,045	2.93	8	8.77	15.20	17	0.21
Dan	2,324	2.23	3	0.27	16.60	14	0.41
EzrNh	7,854	7.55	5	0.86	39.22	28	3.21
Chr	24,056	23.13	7	11.25	120.11	39	54.77
TOTAL	300,613		289	419.05		1,501	1,187.93

Calculation of "D" for Hypothetical Books

Hypothetical Book			Words	Expct. Hapax	Actl. Hapax	"D"
1 Samuel			13,264	12.75	7	2.59
2 Samuel			11,036	10.61	4	4.12
1 Kings			13,140	12.63	2	8.95
2 Kings			12,280	11.81	8	1.23
Ezra			2,541	2.44	4	1.00
Nehemiah			5,313	5.11	1	3.31
1 Chronicles			10,744	10.33	2	6.72
2 Chronicles			13,312	12.80	6	3.61
Proto-Isaiah			9,900	9.52	29	39.86
Deutero-Isaiah			4,333	4.17	8	3.52
Trito-Isaiah			2,697	2.60	6	4.45
Psalms:	First Book		5,232	5.03	4	0.21
	Second Book		4,058	3.90	12	16.82
	Third Book		2,780	2.67	5	2.03
	Fourth Book		2,328	2.24	3	0.26
	Fifth Book		5,133	4.93	9	3.36
Elohistic Psalter			5,772	5.55	16	19.68
Job: Prose framework			797	0.77	1	0.07
Speakers:		Job	4,016	3.86	15	32.15
		Eliphaz	826	0.79	5	22.44
		Bildad	252	0.24	2	12.91
		Zophar	367	0.35	0	0.35
		Elihu	1,201	1.15	5	12.89
		God	884	0.85	13	173.67
Jeremiah: Prose			13,269	12.76	4	6.01
Poetry*			8,550	8.22	11	0.94
Joshua 1-11, 22-24			6,451	6.20	0	6.20
Chronicles with hapax legomena repeated in parallel passages restored			24,056	23.13	11	6.36

*For the purposes of this calculation, the following sections of Jeremiah were counted as poetry: 1:5-10; 2:2-3:5; 3:12-13; 3:19-4:9; 4:11-6:30; 7:28-29; 8:4-10:25; 11:15-16, 18-20; 11:22-12:13; 18:13-23; 20:7-18; 21:12-14; 22:6-7, 10, 13-23; 22:28-23:1; 23:5-6, 9-29; 25:30-38; 30:5-31:30; 31:35-37; 33:2-3, 15-16, 20-22; 45:3-51:58.

Appendix IV

Absolute Hapax Legomena Verbs: Index and Glossary

Following are the verbal forms from among the absolute hapax legomena listed in Appendix I; these constitute the sample studied in detail, from which the conclusions in this volume have been drawn. In some cases only the biblical passage, rather than the word itself, is indicated in the text. An asterisk indicates that the word is treated several times on that page.

אבך (Isa 9:17, "whirl up") — 4, 5, 19*, 57, 62, 76, 94, 98, 101-2, 177

אדב (1 Sam 2:33, related to or corruption of דאב/דוב, "languish") — 8, 19*, 49*, 56, 76, 77, 84, 102, 178

אדש (Isa 28:28, form or variant of דוש, "thresh") — 19, 50, 56, 58, 76, 100, 103, 175, 178, 179

אלץ (Judg 16:16, "press, urge") — 19*, 49, 56, 67, 76*, 81, 93*, 94, 103-4, 177

אנס (Esth 1:8, "constrain") — 19*, 20, 49, 56, 63, 84, 104, 176, 177*, 180

בטה (Prov 12:18, variant of בטא, "speak [rashly]") — 50, 56, 58, 81, 84, 104-5, 176, 177, 178

בטל (Qoh 12:3, "cease") — 20, 49*, 56, 58, 84, 105, 173, 177, 180

בלם (Ps 32:9, "restrain") — 3, 23, 57, 62, 84, 105, 171, 177

בלס (Amos 7:14, meaning uncertain) — 5, 56, 57*, 65, 85, 94, 98, 105-6, 179

בשס (Amos 5:11, possibly related to בוס or שסס, context requires a meaning "oppress") — 4, 5, 8, 50, 56, 78, 80, 94, 106-7, 174, 178

בתק (Ezek 16:40, "split") — 5, 47, 57, 79, 82, 85, 93*, 94, 98*, 107, 177

גרד (Job 2:8, "scrape") — 2, 4, 6, 47, 49, 56, 83*, 85, 94, 107, 177

דגה (Gen 48:16, "multiply") — 18*, 50, 55, 56, 57, 58*, 59, 65, 93, 107-8, 177

דהם (Jer 14:9, probably "surprise") — 5, 47, 57, 78, 85, 93, 95, 108, 176, 177

דוב (Lev 26:16, related to דאב, "languish") — 49*, 50, 56, 59, 109, 178, 180

דוץ (Job 41:14, "jump, dance") — 4, 5, 49*, 52-53, 56, 57, 58, 62, 85, 109, 174, 177, 180

הבו (Hos 4:18, form and meaning uncertain) — 50, 74, 76, 109-10, 179

הבר (Isa 47:13, "worship") — 5, 57, 75, 81, 85, 93, 95, 110-11, 175, 177

הדה (Isa 11:8, probably "extend") — 4, 5, 56, 58, 73, 75, 81, 85, 93, 95, 111, 179

הדך (Job 40:12, "tear down") — 5, 50, 57, 75, 85, 95, 111, 177

הזה (Isa 56:10, meaning uncertain) — 5, 54, 57, 75, 85, 93, 94, 95, 112, 175, 179

הכר (Job 19:3, meaning uncertain) — 5, 57, 75, 79, 85, 112, 177, 179

הלא (Mic 4:7, probably "be distant") — 50, 52, 72, 93, 95, 113, 179

התת (Ps 62:4, probably "assault") — 3, 50, 56, 73, 75, 81, 85, 113, 179

זהם (Job 33:20, "despise") — 5, 72, 85, 95, 98, 113-14, 177

זעך (Job 17:1, "be short") — 5, 49*, 56, 58, 77, 83, 95, 114, 174, 177

זרב (Job 6:17, probably "flow") — 57, 63, 76, 82, 85, 95, 98, 114-15, 177

חטם (Isa 48:9, "restrain") — 5, 67, 82, 85, 92, 95, 98, 115, 177

חלט (1 Kgs 20:33, probably "do/state definitely") — 56, 83, 86, 93*, 95, 115, 177

חספס (Exod 16:14, form and meaning uncertain) — 4, 5, 50, 56, 58*, 59, 68, 69, 86, 95, 116, 178

חפא (2 Kgs 17:9, probably "say") — 56, 57, 58, 62, 76, 81, 86, 95, 116, 172, 177

חרג (Ps 18:46, "fear") — 4*, 5, 48, 52, 57, 86, 95, 116-17, 175, 177

חרת (Exod 32:16, "engrave") — 4, 5, 7, 54, 56, 58*, 59, 61-62, 65, 77, 82, 83, 86, 117, 176, 177*, 178, 180

Appendix IV. Index and Glossary

חשל (Deut 25:18, "straggle") — 56, 57, 59, 77, 86, 118, 179

חתך (Dan 9:24, "cut, determine") — 5, 13*-14, 57, 62, 86, 92, 95, 118, 177

טוש (Job 9:26, "fly") — 5, 49*, 53*, 56, 58, 86, 95, 98, 118-19, 177, 180

טחה (Gen 21:16, "shoot") — 18*, 56, 58, 59, 63, 73, 82, 86, 119, 177

טחח (Isa 44:18, form or variant of טוח, "besmear") — 50, 56, 73, 93, 119, 178

טמה (Job 18:3, meaning uncertain) — 2, 49, 54, 57, 76, 86, 120, 179, 181

טנף (Cant 5:3, "soil") — 4, 49*, 56, 58, 62, 86, 120, 177, 179, 180

טעה (Ezek 13:10, "stray") — 6, 49*, 54, 56, 58, 82, 86, 120-21, 177, 180

טפש (Ps 119:70, "be fat") — 5, 49, 56, 86, 95, 98, 121, 157, 171, 177*

יאב (Ps 119:131, "desire") — 4, 5, 56, 74, 95, 98, 100, 121, 175, 177, 180

יאה (Jer 10:7, "befit") — 49, 57, 63, 74, 121-22, 177

יבב (Judg 5:28, "bewail, lament") — 56, 57, 58, 64, 74*, 86, 93, 122, 177

יהד (Esth 8:17, "become/act like a Jew") — 49, 57, 65, 72, 122-23, 174, 176, 178

יזם (Gen 11:6, form or variant of זמם, "devise") — 18*, 56, 58, 59, 74, 79, 93, 123, 175, 178, 179

יזן (Jer 5:8, form and meaning uncertain) — 47, 50, 57, 62, 77, 81, 87, 123-24, 179

יחר (2 Sam 20:5, variant or corruption of אחר, "delay") — 47, 54, 56, 58, 76, 81, 124, 178

ימש (Judg 16:26, variant or corruption of משש, "touch") — 47, 50, 56, 58, 77, 124, 178

יסך (Exod 30:32, form or variant of סוך, "anoint") — 49*, 51, 59, 62, 65, 74, 81, 87, 124-25, 174, 175, 178

יעז (Isa 33:19, probably form or variant of עזז, "be strong") — 5, 51, 57, 62, 74, 78, 82, 125, 171, 178

יעט (Isa 61:10, variant or corruption of עטה, "cover") — 51, 56, 58, 62, 73, 125-26, 178

ירט (Num 22:32, meaning uncertain) — 57, 58, 59, 68, 69, 73, 82, 83, 87, 94, 97, 126, 157, 175, 179

כחל (Ezek 23:40, "paint [eyes with antimony]") — 49, 56, 78, 87, 126-27, 176, 177

כמה (Ps 63:2, "long for") — 3, 4, 5, 51, 63, 65, 87, 93, 95, 127, 177

כמס (Deut 32:34, "store") — 4, 5, 54, 56, 58*, 59, 62, 63, 72, 78, 87, 93, 95, 98, 127-28, 175, 177

כסס (Exod 12:4, "divide") — 49*, 55, 56, 58, 59, 64, 65, 73, 93, 128, 177

כפה (Prov 20:14, "turn aside") — 2, 56, 62, 73, 78, 82, 87, 128-29, 178

כפש (Lam 3:16, probably "tread") — 4*, 53, 82, 87, 96, 129-30, 177, 178

כרבל (1 Chr 15:27, "wrap") — 3, 48, 56, 62, 76, 87, 130, 175, 177, 180*

כרסם (Ps 80:14, "tear/eat away") — 62, 76*, 78, 83, 87, 130-31, 177

כשה (Deut 32:15, "become fat") — 5, 57, 58, 59, 60, 67, 77, 80, 83, 96, 131, 177

לעב (2 Chr 36:16, "mock") — 56, 58, 62, 78, 79, 87, 131-32, 176, 177, 180

לעז (Ps 114:1, "speak unintelligibly") — 49, 56, 82, 87, 132, 171, 177, 180

לעט (Gen 25:30, "eat, swallow voraciously") — 5, 18*, 56, 58, 59, 63, 88, 96, 99, 132, 177

מהל (Isa 1:22, "dilute") — 4, 7, 10, 14, 56, 63, 75, 88, 96, 98, 132-33, 177

מוק (Ps 73:8, "mock") — 49*, 56, 57, 73, 88, 133, 177, 180

מחק (Judg 5:26, "smash, annihilate") — 54, 57, 75, 79, 88, 133, 177*, 180

מלץ (Ps 119:103, "be sweet") — 4, 5, 56, 58, 75, 82, 93, 96, 134, 177

נבח (Isa 56:10, "bark") — 2, 7, 49*, 56, 58, 72, 88, 134, 173, 177, 179

נדא (2 Kgs 17:21, form and meaning uncertain) — 47, 54, 56, 58, 74, 134, 172, 179

Appendix IV. Index and Glossary

נוט (Ps 99:1, "shake") — 5, 8, 14-15, 48-49, 54, 56, 58, 73, 84, 96, 135, 176, 177, 180

נוש (Ps 69:21, form and meaning uncertain) — 3, 51, 57, 76, 135-36, 179

נחץ (1 Sam 21:9, the attested form means "urgent") — 15, 56, 75, 82, 93*, 136, 179

נלה (Isa 33:1, probably corrupt for כלה, "finish") — 51, 57, 76, 88, 96, 100, 136-37, 174, 175, 178

נצא (Jer 48:9, probably related to יצא or נוצה) — 51, 57, 75, 81, 137, 178

נתס (Job 30:13, "destroy") — 5, 57, 80, 137-38, 174, 179

נתע (Job 4:10, probably "crush") — 54, 57, 62, 75*, 78-79, 138-39, 177

סאסא (Isa 27:8, form and meaning uncertain) — 49*, 56, 66, 68, 78, 88, 94, 139, 166, 179

סכת (Deut 27:9, "be silent") — 3, 4, 56, 57, 59, 68, 72, 82, 88, 93, 96, 99, 140, 176, 177*

סלא (Lam 4:2, probably "weigh, be valuable") — 57, 66, 79, 81, 140, 179

סלד (Job 6:10, "jump") — 6, 57, 88, 140-41, 177

סלק (Ps 139:8, "ascend") — 49*, 56, 75, 88, 93, 141, 177, 180

סמן (Isa 28:25, meaning uncertain) — 49, 55, 57, 64, 88, 141-42, 179

סעה (Ps 55:9, "sweep," the root may actually be סוע) — 5, 57, 75, 88, 96, 142, 177

סרף (Amos 6:10, meaning uncertain) — 5, 10, 53*, 57, 80, 96, 99, 142-43, 179

עבש (Joel 1:17, "shrivel") — 5*, 7, 10, 53, 79, 82, 88, 95, 143-44, 177

עגם (Job 30:25, "grieve") — 5, 49, 56, 84, 89, 96, 144, 177

עגן (Ruth 1:13, "hold back") — 5, 54, 56, 62, 63, 84, 89, 144-45, 177*, 180

עוש (Joel 4:11, "aid") — 51, 56, 58, 73, 81, 93*, 96, 98, 145, 175, 177

עות (Isa 50:4, meaning uncertain) — 3, 57, 66, 68, 73, 83, 89, 96, 145-46, 175, 177*, 179

עזק (Isa 5:2, "dig") — 5, 56, 57, 62, 72, 89, 96, 146, 177*

עלע (Job 39:30, corrupt) — 57*, 63, 77, 78, 89, 96, 99, 146-47, 174, 178

עמש (Neh 4:11, probably a variant of עמס, "load") — 53*, 80, 147, 174, 178

ער (Isa 15:5, corrupt) — 3, 4, 28, 48, 52, 57, 73, 77, 89, 147, 174, 175, 178

עשק (Gen 26:20, "contend") — 5, 7, 18*, 21, 49*, 53*, 56, 57, 59, 80, 89, 93*, 147-48, 176, 177

עתם (Isa 9:18, meaning uncertain) — 5, 57, 77, 81, 84, 89, 93*, 97, 98*, 139, 148, 175, 179

פדע (Job 33:24, "save," may be corruption of פדה) — 5, 8, 56, 58, 64, 68, 82, 83, 93, 97, 98, 149-50, 179

פון (Ps 88:16, form and meaning uncertain) — 56, 73-74, 89, 150, 179

פנק (Prov 29:21, "pamper") — 49*, 56, 58, 62, 64, 89, 151, 176, 177

פסג (Ps 48:14, meaning uncertain) — 3, 51, 57, 72, 151, 179, 180

פצם (Ps 60:4, "split") — 4*, 5, 57, 65, 89, 97, 151-52, 177

פרשז (Job 26:9, form uncertain, probably related to פרש, "spread") — 4, 5, 49*, 51, 56, 58, 68, 77, 78, 94, 97, 98*, 152, 178

פשח (Lam 3:11, probably "tear apart") — 49, 53, 56, 64, 80, 90, 151, 152, 177, 180

צבט (Ruth 2:14, "hold out") — 5, 6, 54, 57*, 62, 81, 82, 90, 97, 98, 153, 177

צות (Isa 27:4, form or variant of יצת, "burn") — 51, 66, 74, 75, 153, 178

צנם (Gen 41:23, "be hard") — 4, 5, 18*, 48, 49*, 57, 58, 59, 82, 90, 97, 154, 173, 175, 177

צען (Isa 33:20, "move") — 4*, 5, 7, 57, 68, 74, 81, 90, 97, 154, 174, 177

צפד (Lam 4:8, "shrivel") — 5*, 6, 49*, 62, 90, 93*, 97, 154-55, 177

קאם (Hos 10:14, form of קום, "rise") — 49, 56, 76, 81, 155, 174, 178

קוש (Isa 29:21, variant or corruption of יקש, "lay trap") — 56, 74, 77, 90, 155, 178

Appendix IV. Index and Glossary   207

קסס (Ezek 17:9, probably "become scaly, moldy") — 3, 5, 81, 90, 97, 98, 155-56, 177

רהה (Isa 44:8, "fear" although correct form and root are uncertain) — 4, 5, 49, 52, 55, 81, 90, 97, 100, 156, 174, 175, 179

רזם (Job 15:12, probably corruption or variant of רמז, "wink," if not of רום, "be high") — 2, 5, 49*, 52, 57, 58, 77, 90, 93, 156-57, 176, 178

רטה (Job 16:11, root and meaning uncertain) — 49, 57, 64, 74, 82, 83, 90, 97, 157, 179

רטפש (Job 33:25, form and meaning uncertain, probably corrupt) — 4*, 5, 57, 78, 79, 82, 90, 97, 157-58, 171, 178

רנה (Job 39:23, probably "make sound [rattle]") — 5*, 51, 57, 74, 90, 158, 174

רפף (Job 26:11, "shake") — 64, 74, 78, 91, 158-59, 177, 181

רפק (Cant 8:5, "lean") — 4, 5, 56, 68, 78, 91, 97, 159, 177

רצד (Ps 68:17, "watch enviously") — 3, 4, 5, 8, 57, 68-69, 79, 91, 97, 159, 176, 177

רשם (Dan 10:21, "inscribe") — 20, 49, 51, 57, 62, 91, 159, 177*, 180

שׂוח (Gen 24:63, meaning uncertain) — 18*, 51, 53, 56, 58, 59, 66, 91, 160, 179

שׂחט (Gen 40:11, "squeeze") — 18*, 53, 56, 59, 80, 91, 93*, 160-61, 176, 177

שׂפן (Deut 33:19, meaning uncertain) — 4, 5, 53, 57, 59, 80, 81, 93, 97, 161, 179

שׂקד (Lam 1:14, meaning uncertain) — 4*, 5, 51, 53*, 56, 64, 67, 80, 91, 97, 161-62, 179

שׂקר (Isa 3:16, meaning uncertain) — 5, 53, 55, 56, 67*, 80, 91, 93, 97, 162, 177, 179

שׂתם (Lam 3:8, form uncertain, possibly related to סתם) — 49, 53*, 56, 67*, 69, 80, 162, 178

שׂתר (1 Sam 5:9, "break out") — 49, 53, 56, 80, 93, 162, 177*

שאס (Jer 30:16, probably form of שסס/שסה "plunder") — 47, 57*, 76, 81, 93, 163, 178

שיה (Deut 32:18, probably corrupt for נשה, "forget") — 49*, 51, 54, 56, 59, 60, 62, 64, 167, 175, 178

שכה (Jer 5:8, root and meaning uncertain) — 1, 2, 22, 52, 72, 164, 179

שנס (1 Kgs 28:46, "gird") — 4, 8, 56, 93, 97, 98, 164-65, 177

שסף (1 Sam 15:33, "kill") — 4, 5, 56, 58, 65, 93*, 165, 179

ששׂה (Isa 10:13, root and meaning uncertain) — 2, 3, 53, 56, 58, 80, 165-66, 174, 179

ששׁא (Ezek 39:2, meaning uncertain) — 5, 75, 81, 91, 93*, 98, 139, 166, 174, 179

תזז (Isa 18:5, "cut off") — 5, 6, 52, 57, 80, 91, 98, 166, 174, 179

תכה (Deut 33:3, root and meaning uncertain) — 1, 52, 57, 58, 59, 66, 72, 83, 98, 167, 179, 181

תרגל (Hos 11:3, probably derived from the root רגל, "foot") — 52, 57, 66, 69, 77, 78, 83, 92, 167-68, 178, 179

תרגם (Ezra 4:7, "translate, explain") — 2, 20, 49, 57, 61, 92, 168-69, 177, 180*

Bibliography

Aaron ben Elijah. כתר תורה. Eupatria, 1866-67.

Aaron the Karaite. מבחר ישרים. Gozlow, 1766.

Abrabanel, Isaac. פירוש על התורה. Jerusalem: Arbel Sons, 1964.

_____. פירוש על נביאים וכתובים. Tel Aviv: Elisha, 1970.

_____. פירוש על נביאים ראשונים. Jerusalem: Torah Vadaat, 1956.

Abraham ibn Ezra. *The Commentary of Ibn Ezra on Isaiah.* Ed. M. Friedlander. New York: Philip Feldheim Inc., 1964.

_____. *Commentary on the Canticles.* Ed. H. J. Matthews. London: Trübner and Co., 1874.

_____. אבן עזרא על התורה. Jerusalem: Mossad Harav Kook, 1976.

_____. מאזני הלשון הקדש. Ophibeck: Segalspitz, 1791.

_____. ספר צחות. Ed. Gabriel H. Lippmann. Fürth: D. Zürndorffer, 1827.

_____. שפה ברורה. Ed. Gabriel H. Lippmann. Fürth: D. Zürndorffer, 1839.

_____. שפת יתר. Warsaw: Duberos Tors, 1895.

_____. *Sephat Jether.* Ed. G. H. Lippmann. Frankfurt a. M., 1843.

Abu Ibrahim Isaac ben Barun. יתר הפליטה מן כתאב אלמואזנה בין אלעבראניה ואלערביה. Ed. Pavel Kokovtsov. Petrograd: Eliezer Behrman and Zvi Rabinowitz, 1890.

---

*Standard editions of the Hebrew Bible and ancient versions along with medieval commentaries available only in the Rabbinic Bible have not been included in this listing.

_____. מספרי הבלשנות העברית בימי הביניים in "כתאב אלמואזנה". Ed. Pavel Kokovtsov. Jerusalem: Kedem, 1970.

Ahuviah, Abraham. "כל אשר יבטא האדם - בשבועה," *BM* 28 (1983) 107-10.

Aisleitner, Joseph. *Wörterbuch der Ugaritischen Sprache.* Berlin: Akademie Verlag, 1963.

Albek, Hanoch, ed. הדרש בראשית רבתי. Jerusalem: Mekize Nirdamim and Mossad Harav Kook, 1940.

Albright, William F. "The Assumed Hebrew Stem *skt*, be silent," *JBL* 39 (1920) 166-67.

_____. "The Earliest Forms of Hebrew Verse," *JPOS* 2 (1922) 69-86.

_____. "Two Letters from Ugarit (Ras Shamrah)," *BASOR* 82 (1941) 43-49.

Ali ben Suleiman, *The Arabic Commentary of Ali ben Suleiman the Karaite on the Book of Genesis.* Ed. Solomon L. Skoss. Philadelphia: Dropsie College, 1928.

Allony, Nehemiah. "'אלפאט' נוספים ממשנת שבת ועירובים'," *Leš* 19 (1954) 31-48.

_____. "הקדמת רב סעדיה גאון לספרו 'שבעים מלים הבודדות'" in ספר זיידל. Jerusalem: Kiryat Sepher Ltd., 1962. Pp. 233-52.

_____. "אוצר השקפות קראיות ב'מחברת מנחם' והמלים בערך 'גלבי'," יהודי ספרד 5 (1962) 21-54.

_____. "ירמיה ב'שבעים מלים בודדות' לרס"ג," *BM* 7 (1962) 43-49.

_____. "ישעיה ב'שבעים מלים בודדות' לרס"ג" in ספר טור סיני. Jerusalem: Kiryat Sepher Ltd., 1960. Pp. 279-88.

_____. "כתאב אלסבעין לפטי'ה לרב סעדיה גאון," *Ignace Goldziher Memorial Volume.* Ed. Samuel Löwinger. Jerusalem: Rubin Mass, 1958. 2. 1-47.

_____. ספר דים in "מיכה ב'שבעים מלים בודדות' לרס"ג". Jerusalem: Kiryat Sepher Ltd., 1958. 362-66.

_____. "המלים הבודדות ב'שאלות עתיקות'," *HUCA* 30 (1959) 1-14.

_____. מספרי הבלשנות in "קטע חדש מ'ספר הקרחה' לר' יהודה חיוג'" העברית בימי הביניים. Ed. Pavel Kokovtsov. Jerusalem: Kedem, 1970. Pp. i-ix.

_____. ספר in "שבעים מלים בודדות ב'רסאלה' ליהודה אבן קריש" שמואל ליבין. Jerusalem: Kiryat Sepher Ltd., 1970. Pp. 409-25.

———. "שלושה קטעים חדשים מחיבורי אבן בלעם," *BM* 20-21 (1964) 87-122.

———. "שני קטעים נוספים מהנוסח המקורי של 'שבעים מלים בודדות'," *Sinai* 37 (1955). 245-60.

Altschüller, M. A. "Einige textkritische Bemerkungen zum Alten Testament," *ZAW* 6 (1886) 211-13.

Amusin, J. D. and M. L. Heltzer. "The Inscription from Mesad Hashavyahu," *IEJ* 14 (1964) 148-57.

Andersen, Francis I. and D. N. Freedman, *Hosea*. AB 24. Garden City, NY: Doubleday and Co., 1980.

Anderson, A. A. *The Book of Psalms*. London: Oliphants, 1972.

Ashbel, Dov. "הערות לנבואות עמוס," *BM* 11 (1965) 103-10.

Athenaeus. *The Deipnosophists*. Trans. Charles B. Gulick. LCL. Cambridge, MA: Harvard University Press, 1951.

Avigad, N. "Two Hebrew Inscriptions on Wine-Jars," *IEJ* 22 (1972) 1-9.

Avishur, Y. "Word Pairs Common to Phoenician and Biblical Poetry," *UF* 7 (1975) 13-47.

Bacher, Wilhelm. "לקוטים מספר אבן בחן לר' מנחם בן שלמה" הגרן 4 (1903) 38-58.

Baḥya ben Joseph ibn Paquda. *Duties of the Heart*. Trans. Judah ibn Tibbon and Moses Hyamson. Jerusalem: Boystown Jerusalem Publishers, 1965.

———. ביאור על התורה. Ed. C. D. Chavel. Jerusalem: Mossad Harav Kook, 1966.

Bailey, Richard W. "Statistics and Style: A Historical Survey," in *Statistics and Style*. Ed. L. Dolezel and R. W. Bailey. New York: American Elsevier, 1969. 217-36.

Baird, J. Arthur. "Content-Analysis and the Computer: A Case-Study in the Application of the Scientific Method to Biblical Research," *JBL* 95 (1976) 255-76.

Ball, C. J. *The Book of Genesis*. SBOT 1. Baltimore: Johns Hopkins Press, 1896.

———. *The Book of Job*. Oxford: The Clarendon Press, 1922.

Bar-Asher, Moshe. "צורות נדירות בלשון התנאים," *Leš* 41 (1977) 83-102.

Bardtke, Hans. *Das Buch Esther.* KAT 17[5]. Gütersloh: Gerd Mohr, 1963.

Baron, Salo Wittmayer. *A Social and Religious History of the Jews.* 2d. ed. Philadelphia: Jewish Publication Society of America, 1952-.

Barr, James. *Comparative Philology and the Text of the Old Testament.* Oxford: Clarendon Press, 1968.

_____. "Etymology and the Old Testament," *OTS* 19 (1974) 1-28.

_____. *The Semantics of Biblical Language.* London: Oxford University Press, 1961.

Barth, Jakob. *Etymologische Studien zum Semitischen insbesondere zum Hebräischen Lexicon.* Berlin: H. Itzkowski, 1893.

_____. *Die Nominalbildung in den Semitischen Sprachen.* Leipzig: J. C. Hinrichs'sche Buchhandlung, 1889.

_____. "Das Nominalpräfix na im Assyrischen," *ZA* 2 (1887) 111-17.

_____. "Das passive Qal und seine Participien," in *Jubelschrift zum Siebzigsten Geburtstag des Dr. Israel Hildesheimer.* Berlin: H. Engel, 1890. 145-53.

_____. *Wurzeluntersuchungen zum Hebräischen und Aramäischen Lexicon.* Leipzig: J. C. Hinrichs'sche Buchhandlung, 1902.

_____. "Zur altaramäischen Inschrift des Königs Zkr," *OLZ* 12 (1909) 10-12.

Barthélemy, Dominique. *Les Devanciers d'Aquila.* VTSup 10. Leiden: E. J. Brill, 1963.

Bartina, Sebastián. "España, 'Isla de Emporios,'" *Sef* 25 (1965) 72-77.

Barton, George Aaron. *A Critical and Exegetical Commentary on the Book of Ecclesiastes.* ICC. New York: Charles Scribner's Sons, 1908.

Bartura, A. "לשון למודים לדעת לעות את יעף דבר"," *BM* 28 (1982) 72.

Batten, Loring W. *A Critical and Exegetical Commentary on the Books of Ezra and Nehemiah.* ICC. New York: Charles Scribner's Sons, 1913.

Bauer, Hans, and Pontus Leander. *Historische Grammatik der Hebräischen Sprache des Sprache des Alten Testamentes.* Hildesheim: Georg Olms Verlagsbuchhandlung, 1965.

Baumgartner, Walter, et al. *Hebräisches und Aramäisches Lexikon zum Alten Testament.* 3d ed. Leiden: E. J. Brill, 1967.

Bibliography

Baumstark, Anton. "Neue orientalistische Probleme biblischer Textgeschichte," *ZDMG* 14 (1935) 89-118.

_____. "Pešiṭta und palästinensisches Targum," *BZ* 19 (1931) 257-70.

Bechor Shor, Joseph ben Isaac. פירוש על התורה. Ed. Aaron Jellinek. Leipzig: Wolfgang Gerhard, 1856.

_____. פירוש על התורה. Vol. 4^2. Ed. M. A. Bamberger. Budapest: Katzburg Brothers, 1928.

Bedersi, Abraham. חותם תכנית. Ed. G. I. Polak. Amsterdam: I. Levisson, 1865.

Bee, Ronald E. "The Use of Statistical Methods in Old Testament Studies," *VT* 23 (1973) 257-72.

Beer, Georg. *Exodus*. HAT 3. Tübingen: J. C. B. Mohr (Paul Siebeck), 1939.

Behrmann, Georg. *Das Buch Daniel*. HKAT III 3^2. Göttingen: Vandenhoeck & Ruprecht, 1894.

Ben-Hayyim, Z. *The Literary and Oral Tradition of Hebrew and Aramaic Amongst the Samaritans*. Jerusalem: Bialik Institute, 1957.

Bennett, Paul E. "The Statistical Measurement of a Stylistic Trait in *Julius Caesar* and *As You Like It*," in *Statistics and Style*. Ed. L. Dolezel and R. W. Bailey. New York: American Elsevier, 1969. 29-41.

Benveniste, E. *Textes sogdiens*. Mission Pelliot en Asie Centrale série in-quarto III. Paris: Librarie Orientaliste Paul Geuthner, 1940.

Ben-Yehuda, Eliezer. מלון הלשון העברית. New York: M. Yoseloff, 1960.

Benzinger, I. *Die Bücher der Chronik*. KHC 20. Tübingen: J. C. B. Mohr (Paul Siebeck), 1901.

_____. *Die Bücher der Konige*. KHC 9. Tübingen: J. C. B. Mohr (Paul Siebeck), 1899.

Bergsträsser, G. *Hebräische Grammatik*. Hildesheim: George Olms Verlagsbuchhandlung, 1962.

Bertholet, Alfred. *Das Buch Hesekiel*. KHC 12. Tübingen: J. C. B. Mohr (Paul Siebeck), 1897.

_____. *Die Bücher Esra und Nehemia*. KHC 19. Tübingen: J. C. B. Mohr (Paul Siebeck), 1897.

_____. *Deuteronomium*. KHC 5. Tübingen: J. C. B. Mohr (Paul Siebeck), 1899.

_____. *Hesekiel*. HAT 13. Tübingen: J. C. B. Mohr (Paul Siebeck), 1936.

_____. *Leviticus*. KHC 3. Tübingen: J. C. B. Mohr (Paul Siebeck), 1901.

_____. "Ruth" in *Die fünf Megillot*. KHC 17. Tübingen: J. C. B. Mohr (Paul Siebeck), 1898. 49-69.

Bezold, Carl. *Babylonisch-Assyrisches Glossar*. Heidelberg: C. Winter, 1926.

Biella, Joan Copeland. *Dictionary of Old South Arabic, Sabaean Dialect*. Harvard Semitic Studies 25. Chico, CA: Scholars Press, 1982.

Birot, Maurice. "Textes Economiques de Mari," *RA* 49 (1955) 15-31.

Blau, Joshua. "Etymologische Untersuchungen auf Grund des palaestinischen Arabisch," *VT* 5 (1955) 337-44.

_____. "Hapax Legomena," *Encyclopedia Judaica*. New York: Macmillan, 1971. 7. 1318-19.

_____. "*Hōḇᵃrē šāmājim* (Jes xlvii 13) = Himmelsanbeter?" *VT* 7 (1957) 183-84.

_____. "מחקרים במבנה הפועל המקראי" in ספר זיידל. Ed. Eliezer Eliner. Jerusalem: Kiryat Sepher, 1962. 294-301.

_____. *On Pseudo-Corrections in Some Semitic Languages*. Jerusalem: The Israel Academy of Sciences and Humanities, 1970.

_____. "Über homonyme und angeblich homonyme Wurzeln," *VT* 6 (1956) 242-48.

_____ and Jonas C. Greenfield. "Ugaritic Glosses," *BASOR* 200 (1970) 11-17.

Bloch, Joshua. "The Authorship of the Peshitta," *AJSL* 35 (1919) 215-22.

Blommerde, Anton, C. M. *Northwest Semitic Grammar and Job*. Rome: Pontifical Biblical Institute, 1969.

de Boer, P. A. H. *Research into the Text of I Samuel I-XVI*. Amsterdam: H. J. Paris, 1938.

Böhl, Franz, M. T. *Die Sprache der Amarnabriefe*. Leipzig: August Pries, 1909.

_____. *Wilhelm Gesenius' Hebräisches und Aramäisches Handwörterbuch über das Alte Testament*. 16th ed. Leipzig: F. C. W. Vogel, 1915.

Boling, Robert G. *Judges*. AB 6A. Garden City, NY: Doubleday and Co., 1975.

The Book of Ben Sira. Jerusalem: Academy of the Hebrew Language and the Shrine of the Book, 1973.

Borger, R. "Hiob XXXIX 23 nach dem Qumran-Targum," *VT* 27 (1977) 102-5.

Boström, Otto H. *Alternative Readings in the Hebrew of the Books of Samuel*. Rock Island, IL: Augustana Book Concern, 1918.

Böttcher, Friedrich. *Ausführliches Lehrbuch der hebräischen Sprache*. Leipzig: Johann Ambrosius Barth, 1868.

Braslavi, Joseph. "עמוס - נוקד, בוקר ובולס שקמים'," *BM* 12 (1967) 87-101.

Brederek, Emil. *Konkordanz zum Targum Onkelos*. BZAW 9. Giessen: Alfred Töpelmann, 1906.

Briggs, Charles Augustus and Emilie Grace Briggs. *A Critical and Exegetical Commentary on the Book of Psalms*. ICC. New York: Charles Scribner's Sons, 1906.

Bright, John. *Jeremiah*. AB 21. Garden City, NY: Doubleday and Co., 1965.

Brockelmann, Carl. *Grundriss der Vergleichenden Grammatik der Semitischen Sprachen*. Berlin: Reuther & Reichard, 1908.

_____. *Lexicon Syriacum*. 2d. ed. Halis Saxonum: Max Niemeyer, 1928.

Brockington, Leonard H. *Ezra, Nehemiah and Esther*. CB. London: Thomas Nelson and Sons Ltd., 1969.

_____. *The Hebrew Text of the Old Testament*. London: Oxford and Cambridge University Presses, 1973.

Brown, Francis, S. R. Driver, and Charles A. Briggs. *A Hebrew and English Lexicon of the Old Testament*. Oxford: Clarendon Press, 1962.

Brüll, Adolf. *Das Samaritanische Targum zum Pentateuch*. New York: Georg Olms Verlag, 1971.

Buber, Solomon, ed. ילקוט המכירי על ספר תהלים. Berdyczew: J. Scheftel, 1899.

_____, ed. *Midrasch Mischle*. Vilna, 1893.

_____, ed. מדרש שמואל. Cracow: Joseph Fischer, 1893.

_____, ed. מדרש תהלים המכונה שוחר טוב. Vilna: Ram, 1891.

_____, ed. *Midrasch Tanchuma*. Vilna: Wittwe & Gebrüder Romm, 1885.

Budde, Karl. *The Books of Samuel*. SBOT 8. Baltimore: Johns Hopkins Press, 1894.

_____. *Das Buch der Richter*. KHC 7. Tübingen: J. C. B. Mohr (Paul Siebeck), 1897.

_____. *Das Buch Hiob*. HKAT II^1. Göttingen: Vandenhoeck & Ruprecht, 1913.

_____. *Die Bücher Samuel*. KHC 8. Tübingen: J. C. B. Mohr (Paul Siebeck), 1902.

_____. "Das Hohelied, Die Klagelieder," in *Die fünf Megillot*. KHC 17. Tübingen: J. C. B. Mohr (Paul Siebeck), 1898. 1-48 and 70-108.

_____. "Zu Text und Auslegung des Buches Amos," *JBL* 43 (1924) 46-131 and 44 (1925) 63-122.

Burney, Charles Fox. *The Book of Judges*. New York: Ktav Publishing House, 1970.

_____. *Notes on the Hebrew Text of the Books of Kings*. Oxford: Clarendon Press, 1903.

Burrows, Millar. *The Dead Sea Scrolls of St. Mark's Monastery*. New Haven: American Schools of Oriental Research, 1951.

Campbell, Edward F., Jr. *Ruth*. AB 7. Garden City, NY: Doubleday and Co., 1975.

Canaani, Jacob. אוצר הלשון העברית. Jerusalem: Massada, 1960-.

Cantineau, Jean. *Le Nabatéen*. Paris: Libraire Ernest Leroux, 1930.

Carmignac, Jean. "Précisions apportées au Vocabulaire de l'Hébreu biblique par la guerre des fils de lumière contre les fils de ténèbres," *VT* 5 (1955) 345-65.

Casanowicz, I. M. "Hapax Legomena—Biblical Data," *JE* VI, 226-28.

Caspari, Wilhelm. *Die Samuelbücher*. KAT 7. Leipzig: A. Deichertsche Verlagsbuchhandlung, 1926.

Cassuto, Umberto. "Il Cap. 22 del Deuteronomio e la Festa del Capo d'anno Nell'antico Israele," *RSO* 11 (1928) 233-53.

_____. *A Commentary on the Book of Exodus*. Trans. Israel Abrahams. Jerusalem: Magnes Press, 1967.

_____. *A Commentary on the Book of Genesis*. Trans. Israel Abrahams. Jerusalem: Magnes Press, 1961-64.

_____. האלה ענת. Jerusalem: Mossad Bialik, 1951.

Chajes, H. P. "Notes de Lexicographie Hébraique," *REJ* 44 (1902) 223-29.

Charles, Robert H., ed. *The Apocrypha and Pseudepigrapha of the Old Testament in English*. Oxford: Clarendon Press, 1913.

_____. *A Critical and Exegetical Commentary on the Book of Daniel*. Oxford: Clarendon Press, 1929.

Cheyne, T. K. *The Book of Isaiah*. SBOT 10. Baltimore: Johns Hopkins Press, 1899.

_____. "A New German Commentary on the Minor Prophets," *Exp* 5th series, 6 (1897) 361-71.

Childs, Brevard S. *Exodus, A Commentary*. London: SCM Press, 1974.

Chomsky, William. *David Ḳimḥi's Hebrew Grammar (Mikhlol)*. Philadelphia: Dropsie College, 1953.

_____. "How the Study of Hebrew Grammar Began and Developed," *JQR* 35 (1944-45) 281-301.

_____. "Some Irregular Formations in Hebrew," *JQR* 38 (1947-48) 409-18.

Chude, Fannie. *Hapax Legomena: A Linguistic Study of Words Occurring Once*. Diss., Ph.D., Radcliffe College, 1954.

Cohen, A. "Studies in Hebrew Lexicography," *AJSL* 40 (1924) 153-85.

Cohen, Amos. "שימושי לשון בספרי נביאים," *BM* 11 (1965) 123-28.

Cohen, Boaz. "Quotations from Saadia's Arabic Commentary on the Bible from Two Manuscripts of Abraham ben Solomon," *Saadia Anniversary Volume*. Texts and Studies II. New York: American Academy for Jewish Research, 1943. 75-140.

Cohen, Harold Robert. *Biblical Hapax Legomena in the Light of Akkadian and Ugaritic.* SBLDS 37. Missoula, MT: Scholars Press, 1978.

Condon, E. U. "Statistics of Vocabulary," *Science* 67 (March 16, 1928) 300.

Cook, Stanley A. "The Articles of Dress in Dan. III.21," *Journal of Philology* 26 (1898) 306-13.

Cooke, Albert G. *A Text-Book of North-Semitic Inscriptions.* Oxford: Clarendon Press, 1903.

Cooke, G. A. *A Critical and Exegetical Commentary on the Book of Ezekiel.* ICC. Edinburgh: T. & T. Clark, 1951.

Coppens, J. "La Théophanie de Jud., V,4-5," *ETL* 43 (1967) 528-31.

Cornill, C. H. *The Book of Jeremiah.* SBOT 11. Leipzig: J. C. Hinrichs'sche Buchhandlung, 1895.

Cowley, A. *Aramaic Papyri of the Fifth Century B.C.* Osnabrück: Otto Zeller, 1967.

Cross, Frank Moore, Jr. "Epigraphic Notes on Hebrew Documents of the Eighth-Sixth Centuries B.C.: II. The Murabbaʿât Papyrus and the Letter Found Near Yabneh-Yam," *BASOR* 165 (1962) 34-46.

_____. "Ugaritic Dbʾat and Hebrew Cognates," *VT* 2 (1952) 162-64.

_____ and David Noel Freedman. "The Blessing of Moses," *JBL* 67 (1948) 191-210.

Curtis, Edward Lewis and Albert Alonzo Madsen. *A Critical and Exegetical Commentary on the Books of Chronicles.* New York: Charles Scribner's Sons, 1910.

Dahood, Mitchell J. "Deuteronomy 33,19 and UT 52:61-63," *Or* 47 (1978) 263-64.

_____. "The Etymology of Malṭāʿôt (Ps 58,7)," *CBQ* 17 (1955) 300-303.

_____. "Hebrew-Ugaritic Lexicography III," *Bib* 46 (1965) 311-32.

_____. "Hebrew-Ugaritic Lexicography IV," *Bib* 47 (1966) 403-19.

_____. "Hebrew-Ugaritic Lexicography XI," *Bib* 54 (1973) 351-66.

_____. "The Language and Date of Psalm 48 (47)," *CBQ* 16 (1954) 15-19.

_____. "The Linguistic Position of Ugaritic in the Light of Recent Discoveries," *Sacra Pagina.* Gembloux: Editions J. Duculot, 1959. I. 267-79.

_____. "Northwest Semitic Philology and Job," *The Bible in Current Catholic Thought*. Ed. John L. McKenzie. New York: Herder and Herder, 1962. 55-74.

_____. "The Phoenician Contribution to Biblical Wisdom Literature," *The Role of the Phoenicians in the Interaction of the Mediterranean Civilizations*. Ed. W. A. Ward. Beirut: American University of Beirut, 1968. 123-52.

_____. *Proverbs and Northwest Semitic Philology*. Rome: Pontifical Biblical Institute, 1963.

_____. *Psalms*. AB 16-17A. Garden City, NY: Doubleday and Co., 1966-70.

_____. *Ugaritic-Hebrew Philology*. Rome: Pontifical Biblical Institute, 1965.

_____. "Ugaritic-Hebrew Syntax and Style," *UF* 1 (1969) 15-36.

_____. "Ugaritic Lexicography," *Melanges Eugene Tisserant*. Vatican City: Biblioteca Apostolica Vaticana, 1964. I. 81-104.

Daiches, Samuel. "An Explanation of Isaiah 27,8," *JQR* 6 (1915-16) 399-404.

_____. "Lexikalisches," *ZA* 17 (1903) 91-93.

Dalman, Gustaf H. *Aramäisch-neuhebräisches Handwörterbuch zu Targum, Talmud und Midrasch*. Hildesheim: Georg Olms, 1967.

David Al-Fasī. *The Hebrew-Arabic Dictionary of the Bible Known as Kitāb Jāmiᶜ al-Alfāẓ (Agrōn) of David ben Abraham Al-Fāsī the Karaite*. Ed. Solomon L. Skoss. Yale Oriental Series, Researches XX-XXI. New Haven: Yale University Press, 1936-45.

Delcor, M. "Quelques cas de survivances de vocabulaire nomade en hébreu biblique, Leur Signification," *VT* 25 (1975) 307-22.

Delitzsch, Friedrich. *The Hebrew Language Viewed in the Light of Assyrian Research*. London: Williams and Norgate, 1883.

_____. *Die Lese- und Schreibfehler im Alten Testament*. Berlin: Vereinigung Wissenschaftlichen Verleger, 1920.

_____. "Philologische Forderungen an die hebräische Lexikographie," *OLZ* 19 (1916) 161-73.

_____. *Prolegomena eines neuen hebräisch-aramäischen Wörterbuchs zum Alten Testament*. Leipzig: J. C. Hinrichs'sche Buchhandlung, 1886.

Deller, K. "Zur Terminologie neuassyrischer Urkunden," *WZKM* 57 (1961) 29-42.

Demsky, A. "'Dark Wine' from Judah," *IEJ* 22 (1972) 233-34.

Derenbourg, Joseph, and Hartwig Derenbourg. *Opuscules et traités d'Abou'l-walid Merwan ibn Janah de Cordove*. Paris: L'imprimerie Nationale, 1880.

Dhorme, Edouard P. *A Commentary on the Book of Job*. Trans. H. Knight. London: Thomas Nelson, 1967.

_____. *Le Livres de Samuel*. Paris: Librairie Victor Lecoffre, 1910.

Dietrich, M., O. Loretz, J. Sanmartin. "Zur Ugaritischen Lexikographie XIII," *UF* 7 (1975) 157-69.

Diez-Macho, Alejandro. *Neophyti I*. Madrid: Consejo Superior de Investigaciones Cientificas, 1971.

_____. "Nuevos fragmentos del Targum palestinense," *Sef* 15 (1955) 31-39.

_____. "The Recently Discovered Palestinian Targum: Its Antiquity and Relationship with the Other Targums," VTSup 7 (1959) 222-45.

Donner, Herbert, and W. Röllig. *Kanaänische und aramäische Inschriften*. Wiesbaden: Harrassowitz, 1966-69.

Dozy, Reinhart Pieter Anne. *Supplément aux dictionnaires arabes*. 3d ed. Leiden: E.. J. Brill, 1967.

Driver, G. R. *Aramaic Documents of the Fifth Century B.C.* Rev. ed. Oxford: Clarendon Press, 1957.

_____. "An Aramaic Inscription in the Cuneiform Script," *AfO* 3 (1926) 47-53.

_____. "The Aramaic Papyri from Egypt: Notes on Obscure Passages," *JRAS* (1932) 77-90.

_____. "A Hebrew Burial Custom," *ZAW* 66 (1954) 314-15.

_____. "Hebrew Notes on Prophets and Proverbs," *JTS* 41 (1940) 162-75.

_____. "Hebrew Poetic Diction," VTSup 1 (1953) 26-39.

_____. "Linguistic and Textual Problems: Minor Prophets, II," *JTS* 39 (1938) 260-73.

Bibliography

_____. "L'interprétation du Texte Masorétique à la Lumière de la Lexicographie Hébraïque," *ETL* 26 (1950) 337-53.

_____. "The Modern Study of the Hebrew Language," *The People and the Book*. Ed. A. S. Peake. Oxford: Clarendon Press, 1925. 73-120.

_____. "Notes on the Psalms," *JTS* 43 (1942) 149-60.

_____. "Once Again: Birds in the Bible," *PEQ* 90 (1958) 56-58.

_____. "Problems in Aramaic and Hebrew Texts," *Miscellanea Orientalia Dedicata Antonio Deimel*. AnOr 12. Rome: Pontifical Biblical Institute, 1935. 46-70.

_____. Review of *CAD* vol. Ṣ, *JSS* 9 (1964) 346-50.

_____. "Some Hebrew Medical Expressions," *ZAW* 65 (1953) 255-62.

_____. "Some Hebrew Roots and their Meanings," *JTS* 23 (1922) 69-73.

_____. "Some Hebrew Verbs, Nouns, and Pronouns," *JTS* 30 (1929) 371-78.

_____. "Some Hebrew Words," *JTS* 29 (1928) 390-96.

_____. "Textual and Linguistic Problems of the Book of Psalms," *HTR* 29 (1936) 170-95.

_____, and John C. Miles. *The Babylonian Laws*. Oxford: Clarendon Press, 1960.

Driver, Samuel Rolles. *A Commentary on the Book of Proverbs Attributed to Abraham ibn Ezra*. Oxford: Clarendon Press, 1880.

_____. *A Critical and Exegetical Commentary on the Book of Deuteronomy*. ICC. 3d ed. Edinburgh: T. & T. Clark, 1902.

_____. *A Critical and Exegetical Commentary on the Book of Job*. ICC. Edinburgh: T. & T. Clark, 1921.

_____. *Notes on the Hebrew Text and Topography of the Books of Samuel*. 2d ed. Oxford: Clarendon Press, 1913.

_____. *A Treatise on the Use of the Tenses in Hebrew*. 3d ed. Oxford: Clarendon Press, 1892.

_____, and H. A. White. *The Book of Leviticus*. SBOT 3. Baltimore: Johns Hopkins Press, 1894.

Drower, Ethel, and R. Macuch. *A Mandaic Dictionary*. Oxford: Clarendon Press, 1963.

Duhm, Bernhard. "Anmerkungen zu den Zwölf Propheten," *ZAW* 31 (1911) 1-43, 81-110, 161-204.

_____. *Das Buch Hiob.* KHC 16. Tübingen: J. C. B. Mohr (Paul Siebeck), 1897.

_____. *Das Buch Jeremiah.* KHC 11. Tübingen: J. C. B. Mohr (Paul Siebeck), 1901.

_____. *Das Buch Jesaia.* HKAT III. Göttingen: Vandenhoeck & Ruprecht, 1922.

_____. *Die Psalmen.* KHC 14. Tübingen: J. C. B. Mohr (Paul Siebeck), 1899.

Dukes, Leopold. "Erklärung seltener biblischer Wörter von Saadias Gaon," *Zeitschrift für die Kundes des Morgenlandes* 5 (1844) 115-36.

Du Mesnil du Buisson, Robert. *Inventaire des inscriptions palmyréniennes des Doura-Europos.* Rev. ed. Paris: Librairie Orientaliste Paul Geuthner, 1939.

Dunash ben Labrat. ספר תשובות דונש בן לברט על רב סעדיה גאון. Ed. R. Schröter. Breslau: Schletter'sche Buchhandlung, 1866.

_____. ספר תשובות דונש בן לברט עם הכרעות רבינו יעקב תם. Ed. Herschel Filipowski. London: H. Filipowski, 1855.

Dupont-Sommer, A. "Le Tablette Cuneiforme Araméene de Warka," *RA* 39 (1943) 35-52.

Duran, Profiat. ספר מעשה אפוד. Jerusalem: Makor Ltd., 1970.

Dutripon, F. P. *Concordantiae Bibliorum Sacrorum Vulgate Editionis.* 2d ed. Barri-Ducis, 1868.

Efros, Israel. "Maimonides' Treatise on Logic," *PAAJR* 8 (1937).

Ehrlich, Arnold B. מקרא כפשוטו. New York: Ktav Publishing House Inc., 1969.

_____. *Die Psalmen.* Berlin: M. Poppelauer, 1905.

_____. *Randglossen zum Hebräischen Bibel.* Leipzig: J. C. Hinrichs'sche Buchhandlung, 1908.

Eichrodt, Walther. *Ezekiel, A Commentary.* OTL. Trans. Cosslett Quinn. London: SCM Press, 1970.

Eilers, Wilhelm. "Kyros," *Beiträge zur Namenforschung* 15 (1964) 180-236.

Eissfeldt, Otto. *The Old Testament, An Introduction.* Trans. Peter R. Ackroyd. New York: Harper and Row, 1965.

Eitan, Israel. "The Bearing of Ethiopic on Biblical Exegesis and Lexicography," *JPOS* 3 (1923) 126-43.

_____. "Biblical Studies," *HUCA* 14 (1939) 1-22.

_____. *A Contribution to Biblical Lexicography.* New York: Columbia University Press, 1924.

Eliezer of Beaugency. *Commentaries on the Later Prophets.* Ed. John W. Nutt. London: Joseph Baer and Co., 1879.

_____. *Kommentar zu Ezechiel und den XII Kleinen Propheten.* Schriften des Vereins Mekize Nirdamim III:4. Warsaw, 1913.

Elijah ben Solomon, Gaon of Vilna. ספר אדרת אליהו פירוש על התורה. Tel Aviv: Sinai Publishing, 1963.

_____. ספר אדרת אליהו פירוש על נביאים וכתובים. Tel Aviv: Sinai Publishing, 1963.

Elijah Levita. מתורגמן. Isnae, 1541.

_____. ספר הבחור. Prague, 1789.

_____. ספר ההרכבה. Prague, 1793.

_____. ספר התשבי, לעקסיקאן המבארת לשון התלמוד והמדרשים. New York: Saphrograph Co., 1951.

Ellenbogen, Maximilian. *Foreign Words in the Old Testament, Their Origin and Etymology.* London: Luzac and Co., 1962.

Elliger, Karl. *Leviticus.* HAT 4. Tübingen: J. C. B. Mohr (Paul Siebeck), 1966.

Emerton, J. A. "Unclean Birds and the Origin of the Peshitta," *JSS* 7 (1962) 204-11.

Emmerson, Grace I. "A Fertility Goddess in Hosea IV 17-19?" *VT* 24 (1974) 492-97.

Epstein, Jacob Nahum. מבוא לנוסח המשנה. Jerusalem, 1948.

_____. "Notes on Post-Talmudic-Aramaic Lexicography," *JQR* 12 (1921-22) 299-377.

Even-Shoshan, Abraham. המלון החדש. Jerusalem: Kiryat Sepher Ltd., 1969.

Feldmann, Franz. *Das Buch Isaias.* EHAT 14. Münster: Verlag der Aschendorffscher, 1925.

Felsenthal, B. "Zur Bibel und Grammatik," *Semitic Studies in Memory of Rev. Dr. Alexander Kohut.* Berlin: S. Calvary & Co., 1897. 126-38.

Fenton, Terry L. "Ugaritica-Biblica," *UF* 1 (1969) 65-70.

Field, Fridericus. *Origenis Hexaplorum.* Hildesheim: Georg Olms, 1964.

Finkelstein, Eliezer Aryeh, ed. ספרי דברים. New York: Jewish Theological Seminary of America, 1969.

Fischer, Bonifatius, ed. *Vetus Latina, die Reste der altlateinischen Bibel nach Petrus Sabatier.* Freiburg: Verlag Herder, 1949-.

Fisher, Loren, ed. *Ras Shamra Parallels.* AnOr 49. Rome: Pontifical Biblical Institute, 1972.

Fitzgerald, Aloysius. "The Interchange of *L, N,* and *R* in Biblical Hebrew," *JBL* 97 (1978) 481-88.

Fitzmyer, Joseph A. *The Aramaic Inscriptions of Sefire.* BibOr 19. Rome: Pontifical Biblical Institute, 1967.

_____. *The Genesis Apocryphon of Qumran Cave I.* BibOr 18. Rome: Pontifical Biblical Institute, 1966.

Fleischer, Ezra. "לצביון 'השאלות העתיקות' ולבעית זהות מחברן," *HUCA* 38 (1967) 1-23.

Fohrer, Georg. *Das Buch Hiob.* KAT 16. Gütersloh: Gerd Mohn, 1963.

_____. *Ezechiel.* HAT 13. Tübingen: J. C. B. Mohr (Paul Siebeck), 1955.

Forbes, R. J. *Studies in Ancient Technology.* 2d ed. Leiden: E. J. Brill, 1965.

Fossum, Andrew. "Hapax Legomena in Plato," *American Journal of Philology* 53 (1931) 205-31.

Fraenkel, Siegmund. *Die aramäischen Fremdworter im Arabischen.* Hildesheim: Georg Olms, 1962.

_____. "Lexicalisches," *ZA* 3 (1888) 50-56.

_____. "Zum Sporadischen Lautwandel in den Semitischen Sprachen," *Beiträge zur Assyriologie* 3 (1898) 60-86.

Frankenberg, W. *Die Sprüche.* HKAT II 3[1]. Göttingen: Vandenhoeck & Ruprecht, 1898.

Freedman, David Noel. Report on Excavations at Tell Mardikh. Unpublished, ca. 1976.

Freytag, Georg Wilhelm. *Lexicon Arabico-Latinum.* Halis Saxonum: C. A. Schwetschke et filium, 1830 -37.

Friedmann, Meir. מאיר עין על ספר שופטים. Vilna, 1891.

Friedrich, Johannes. "Göttersprache im hethitischen Schrifttum," *Sprachgeschichte und Wortbedeutung, Festschrift Albert Debrunner.* Bern: Franke, 1954. 135-39.

_____, and Wolfgang Röllig. *Phönizisch-Punische Grammatik.* 2d ed. AnOr 46. Rome: Pontifical Biblical Institute, 1951.

von Gall, August Frhr. *Der Hebräische Pentateuch der Samaritaner.* Giessen: Alfred Töpelmann, 1918.

Galling, Kurt. *Der Prediger.* HAT 18. Tübingen: J. C. B. Mohr (Paul Siebeck), 1969.

Garbini, G. "Note Semitiche," *Ricerche Linguistiche* 5 (1962) 171-81.

Gaster, Theodor. "An Ancient Eulogy on Israel. Deuteronomy 33_{3-5}, 26-29," *JBL* 66 (1947) 53-62.

_____. *The Dead Sea Scriptures.* Rev. ed. Garden City, NY: Anchor Books, 1964.

Gelb, I. J. "The Word for Dragoman in the Ancient Near East," *Glossa* 2 (1968) 93-104.

_____ et al. *Assyrian Dictionary.* Chicago: Oriental Institute of the University of Chicago, 1956-.

Gemser, Berend. *Sprüche Salomos.* HAT 16. Tübingen: J. C. B. Mohr (Paul Siebeck), 1963.

Gerleman, Gillis. *Esther.* BKAT 21. Neukirchen: Verlag des Erziehungsvereins, 1973.

_____. *Ruth, Das Hohelied.* BKAT 18. Neukirchen: Verlag des Erziehungsvereins, 1965.

Gertner, M. "Terms of Scriptural Interpretation: A Study in Hebrew Semantics," *BSOAS* 25 (1962) 1-27.

Gevirtz, Stanley. "The Issachar Oracle in the Testament of Jacob," *EY* 12 (1975) 104*-112*.

_____. "Of Patriarchs and Puns: Joseph at the Fountain, Jacob at the Ford," *HUCA* 46 (1975) 33-54.

_____. "On Canaanite Rhetoric, The Evidence of the Amarna Letters from Tyre," *Or* 42 (1973) 162-77.

_____. "West-Semitic Curses and the Problem of the Origins of Hebrew Law," *VT* 11 (1961) 137-38.

Giesebrecht, F. *Das Buch Jeremia*. HKAT III 2^1. Göttingen: Vandenhoeck & Ruprecht, 1907.

Ginsberg, H. L. "Lachish Notes," *BASOR* 71 (1938) 24-27.

_____. "Lachish Ostraca New and Old," *BASOR* 80 (1940) 10-13.

_____. *The Legend of King Keret*. BASOR Supplementary Studies 2-3. New Haven: American Schools of Oriental Research, 1946.

Ginsburg, Christian D. *Introduction to the Masoretico-Critical Edition of the Hebrew Bible*. New York: Ktav, 1966. 109-13.

_____. *The Massorah Compiled from Manuscripts Alphabetically and Lexically Arranged*. New York: Ktav, 1975.

_____. *The Song of Songs and Coheleth*. New York: Ktav, 1970.

Ginsburger, Moses. *Das Fragmententhargum*. Berlin: S. Calvary, 1899.

_____. *Pseudo-Jonathan*. New York: Georg Olms, 1971.

Ginzberg, Louis. "Beiträge zur Lexicographie des Jüdisch-Aramäischen II," *MGWJ* 78 (1934) 9-33.

Gluck, J. J. "Proverbs XXX 15a," *VT* 14 (1964) 367-70.

_____. "Some semantic complexities in the book of Hosea," *Studies on the Books of Hosea and Amos, Papers Read at the 7th and 8th Meetings of Die O.T. Werkgemeenskap in Suid-Afrika*. 1964-65. 50-63.

Goldberg, Lea. *Das samaritanische Pentateuchtargum*. Bonner Orientalistische Studien 11. Stuttgart: W. Kohlhammer, 1935.

Goldman, M. D. "Lexicographical Notes on Exegesis (5)," *AusBR* 4 (1954/55) 85-92.

Gordis, Robert. *Koheleth, The Man and His World*. 3d ed. New York: Schocken Books, 1968.

_____. *The Song of Songs and Lamentations*. New York: Ktav, 1974.

_____. "Studies in the Relationship of Biblical and Rabbinic Hebrew," *Louis Ginzberg Jubilee Volume*. New York: The American Academy for Jewish Research, 1945. 173-99.

Gordon, Cyrus H. "The Aramaic Incantation in Cuneiform," *AfO* 12 (1937-39) 105-17.

_____. *Introduction to Old Testament Times*. Ventnor, NJ: Ventnor Publishers, 1953.

_____. "Ugaritic ḤRT/ḤIRÎTU Cemetery," *Syria* 33 (1956) 102-103.

_____. *Ugaritic Textbook*. Rome: Pontifical Biblical Institute, 1965.

Goshen-Gottstein, M. H. Review of A. Vööbus *Peschitta und Targumim des Pentateuchs*, *JSS* 6 (1961) 266-70.

Gray, George Buchanan. *A Critical and Exegetical Commentary on Numbers*. ICC. New York: Charles Scribner's Sons, 1903.

_____. *A Critical and Exegetical Commentary on the Book of Isaiah I-XXXIX*. ICC. New York: Charles Scribner's Sons, 1912.

Gray, John. *Joshua, Judges and Ruth*. CB. London: Thomas Nelson and Sons, 1967.

_____. *The KRT Text in the Literature of Ras Shamra*. 2d ed. Leiden: E. J. Brill, 1964.

_____. *The Legacy of Canaan*. Rev. ed. VTSup 5. Leiden: E. J. Brill, 1965.

_____. *I and II Kings, A Commentary*. OTL. London: SCM Press, 1964.

Greenberg, Joseph H. "Patterning of Root Morphemes in Semitic," *Word* 6 (1950) 162-81.

Greenfield, Jonas C. "Lexicographical Notes I," *HUCA* 29 (1958) 203-28.

_____. "Some Glosses on the Keret Epic," *EY* 9 (1969) 60-70.

_____. "Studies in Aramaic Lexicography I," *JAOS* 82 (1962) 290-99.

Grünberg, Samuel. "Exegetische Beiträge," *Festschrift zum 50 jährigen Bestehen des Rabbinerseminars zu Berlin*. Hanover: Orient-Buchhandlung Heinz Lafaire, 1924. 41-95.

_____. "Exegetische Beiträge," *Jeschurun* 10 (1923) 373-86.

Grünthal, Julius. *Die Syrische Uebersetzung zum Buche Esther.* Breslau: H. Fleischmann, 1900.

Guillaume, A. "The Arabic Background of the Book of Job," *Promise and Fulfillment.* Ed. F. F. Bruce. Edinburgh: T. & T. Clark, 1964.

──────. "A Contribution to Hebrew Lexicography," *BSOAS* 16 (1954) 1-12.

──────. "The First Book to Come Out of Arabia," *Islamic Studies* 3 (1964) 151-66.

──────. "Hebrew and Arabic Lexicography, A Comparative Study," *AbrN* 1 (1959-60) 3-35; 2 (1960-61) 5-35; 3 (1961-62) 1-10; 4 (1962-63) 1-18.

──────. *Studies in the Book of Job.* Ed. John Macdonald. ALUOS Supplement 2. Leiden: E. J. Brill, 1968.

Gunkel, Hermann. *Genesis.* HKAT 1. Göttingen: Vandenhoeck & Ruprecht, 1917.

──────. *Die Psalmen.* HKAT II 2^4. Göttingen: Vandenhoeck & Ruprecht, 1926.

Gunther, Robert T. *The Greek Herbal of Dioscorides.* New York: Hafner Publishing Co., 1959.

Guthe, Hermann and L. W. Batten. *The Books of Ezra and Nehemiah.* SBOT 19. Baltimore: Johns Hopkins Press, 1901.

Guyard, M. Stanislas. "Nouvelles notes de lexicographie assyrienne," *JA* series 8, vol. 2 (1883) 184-98.

Halkin, A. S. "The Medieval Jewish Attitude toward Hebrew," *Biblical and Other Studies.* Ed. Alexander Altmann. Cambridge, MA: Harvard University Press, 1963. 233-48.

Hammershaimb, E. "On the so-called *infinitivus absolutus* in Hebrew," in *Hebrew and Semitic Studies Presented to Godfrey Rolles Driver.* Oxford: Clarendon Press, 1963. 85-94.

──────. *The Book of Amos, A Commentary.* Trans. John Sturdy. Oxford: Basil Blackwell, 1970.

Harper, William Rainey. *A Critical and Exegetical Commentary on Amos and Hosea.* ICC. Edinburgh: T. & T. Clark, 1905.

Harris, Zellig Sabbettai. *A Grammar of the Phoenician Language.* New Haven: American Oriental Society, 1936.

Hart, Alfred. "Vocabularies of Shakespeare's Plays," *Review of English Studies* 19 (1943) 128-40.

Har-Zahav, Ṣvi. הוצאת מחברות לספרות :Tel Aviv .דקדוק הלשון העברית, 1951-55.

Hartman, Louis F., and Alexander A. DiLella. *The Book of Daniel.* AB 23. Garden City, NY: Doubleday and Co., 1978.

Hatch, Edwin, and Henry A. Redpath. *A Concordance to the Septuagint.* Oxford: Clarendon Press, 1897.

Haupt, Paul. "Assyr. *daggasse,* Mineralfarben," *OLZ* 16 (1913) 492-94.

_____. "Babylonian Elements in the Levitic Ritual," *JBL* 19 (1900) 55-81.

_____. "Critical Notes on Esther," *AJSL* 24 (1908) 97-186.

_____. "Elul and Adar," *ZDMG* 64 (1910) 703-14.

_____. "The Etymology of Mohel, Circumciser," *AJSL* 22 (1906) 249-56.

Ḥayyuj, Judah. *Two Treatises on Verbs Containing Feeble and Double Letters by R. Jehuda Ḥayug of Fez.* Ed. John W. Nutt. London: Asher and Co., 1870.

_____. מספרי הבלשנות העברית בימי in "יתר הפליטה מן כתאב אלנתף" הבינים. Ed. Pavel Kokovtsov. Jerusalem: Kedem, 1970.

Held, Moshe. "The Root *zbl/sbl* in Akkadian, Ugaritic and Biblical Hebrew," *JAOS* 88 (1968) 90-96.

_____. "Studies in Biblical Homonyms in the Light of Akkadian," *JANESCU* 3 (1970) 46-55.

Heller, Chaim. *Untersuchungen über die Peschîtta.* Berlin: M. Poppelauer, 1911.

Henslow, George. "Egyptian Figs," *Nature* 47 (December 1, 1892) 102.

Herdan, Gustav. "The Hapax legomena: a real or apparent phenomenon," *Language and Speech* 2 (1959) 26-36.

_____. *Language as Choice and Chance.* Groningen: P. Noordhoff Ltd., 1956.

_____. "The Patterning of Semitic Verbal Roots Subjected to Combinatory Analysis," *Word* 18 (1962) 262-68.

_____. *Quantitative Linguistics*. London: Butterworths, 1964.

Herdner, Andree. *Corpus des tablettes en cunéiformes alphabétiques*. Paris: Imprimerie Nationale, 1963.

Hermann, Johannes. *Ezechiel*. KAT 11. Leipzig: A. Deichertsche Verlagsbuchhandlung, 1924.

_____. "אדאד Jes 27$_8$ und שאשא Hes 39$_2$," *ZAW* 36 (1916) 243.

Hertzberg, Hans Wilhelm. *I and II Samuel, A Commentary*. Trans. J. S. Bowden. London: SCM Press Ltd., 1964.

_____. *Der Prediger*. KAT 17^4. Gütersloh: Gerd Mohn, 1963.

Herz, N. "Egyptian Words and Idioms in the Book of Job," *OLZ* 16 (1913) 343-46.

Hille. "Ueber den Gebrauch und die Zusammensetzung der orientalischen Augenschminke (الكحل)," *ZDMG* 5 (1851) 236-42.

Hillers, Delbert R. *Lamentations*. AB 7A. Garden City, NY: Doubleday and Co., 1972.

Hirschfeld, Hartwig. *Literary History of Hebrew Grammarians and Lexicographers*. London: Oxford University Press, 1926.

Hölscher, Gustav. *Das Buch Hiob*. HAT 17. Tübingen: J. C. B. Mohr (Paul Siebeck), 1952.

Hoffmann, D. *Mechilta de-Rabbi Simon b. Jochai*. Frankfurt a.M.: J. Kauffmann, 1905.

_____. *Midrasch Tannaim zum Deuteronomium*. Berlin: H. Itzkowski, 1908.

Hoffmann, Georg. "Aramäische Inschriften aus Nerab bei Aleppo. Neue und alte Götter," *ZA* 11 (1896-97) 207-92.

_____. "Versuche zu Amos," *ZAW* 3 (1883) 87-126.

Holma, Harri. *Die Namen der Körperteile im Assyrisch-Babylonischen*. Leipzig: Otto Harrassowitz, 1911.

Holzinger, H. *Exodus*. KHC 2. Tübingen: J. C. B. Mohr (Paul Siebeck), 1900.

_____. *Genesis*. KHC 1. Tübingen: J. C. B. Mohr (Paul Siebeck), 1898.

_____. *Numeri.* KHC 4. Tübingen: J. C. B. Mohr (Paul Siebeck), 1903.

_____. "Sprachcharakter und Abfassungszeit des Buches Joel," *ZAW* 9 (1889) 89-131.

Hommel, Fritz. "Das Samech in den minäo-sabäischen Inschriften," *ZDMG* 46 (1892) 528-38.

_____. "The Word הברו in Isaiah xlvii,13," *Exp Tim* 12 (1900-1) 239.

Hoonacker, A. Van. "Joel 1,17," *RB* 1 (1904) 374-76.

Horatius Flaccus, Quintus. *Satires, Epistles and Ars Poetica.* LCL. Trans. H. Rushton Fairclough. Cambridge, MA: Harvard University Press, 1955.

Horst, Friedrich. *Hiob.* BKAT 16. Neukirchen: Verlag des Erziehungsverein, 1968.

_____. "Nahum bis Maleachi," in *Die Zwölf Propheten.* HAT 14. Tübingen: J. C. B. Mohr (Paul Siebeck), 1964.

Hospers, J. H. "The Present-Day State of Research on the Pešiṭtā (since 1948)," in *Verbum* (Festschrift H. W. Obbink). Utrecht: Drukkerij en Vitgeuerig V/H Kemink EN Zoon, N.V., 1964. 148-57.

Humbert, Paul. "בולס שקמים (Amos VII,14)," *OLZ* 20 (1917) 296-98.

Hunzinger, Claus-Hunno. "Fragmente einer älteren Fassung des Buches Milḥamâ aus Höhle 4 von Qumrān," *ZAW* 69 (1957) 131-51.

Hurvitz, A. "The Chronological Significance of 'Aramaisms' in Biblical Hebrew," *IEJ* 18 (1968) 234-40.

Hyatt, J. Philip. *Commentary on Exodus.* London: Oliphants, 1971.

Isaiah of Trani. נימוקי חומש לרבינו ישעיה. Ed. C. D. Chavel. Jerusalem: Mossad Harav Kook, 1972.

_____. In ספר ברכה משולשת. Ed. J. Gad. London: L. Honig and Sons Ltd., 1959.

_____. ספר עשרה מאורות in פירוש חמש מגילות לרבינו ישעיה זצוק"ל הגדולים. Ed. J. Gad. Johannesburg: Pacific Press Ltd., 1952. 96-103, 108-110, 127-35.

_____. פירוש איוב in תקות אנוש. Ed. Israel Schwartz. Berlin: Louis Gerschel Verlagsbuchhandlung, 1868. Pp. 39-67.

_____. פירוש רבינו ישעיה הראשון מטראני. Jerusalem: Ktav Vesefer, 1965.

Isenberg, Sheldon. "On the Jewish Palestinian Origins of the Peshitta to the Pentateuch," *JBL* 90 (1971) 69-83.

Jacob, B. "Das hebräische Sprachgut im Christlich-Palästinischen," *ZAW* 22 (1902) 83-113.

Jacob ben Reuben the Karaite. ספר העשר. Gozlow, 1766.

Jastrow, Marcus. *A Dictionary of the Targumim, the Talmud Babli and Yerushalmi, and the Midrashic Literature*. New York: Jastrow Publishers, 1967.

Jean, Charles François, and Jacob Hoftizer. *Dictionnaire des inscriptions sémitiques de l'ouest*. Leiden: E. J. Brill, 1960.

Jellinek, Adolph. *Bet ha-Midrasch*. 3d ed. Jerusalem: Wahrmann Books, 1967.

_____, ed. *Commentarien zu Esther, Ruth und den Klageliedern von Menachem b. Chelbo, R. Tobia b. Elieser, R. Josef Kara, R. Samuel b. Meir, und einem Ungenannten*. Leipzig: Leopold Schnauss, 1855.

Jenni, Ernst, and Claus Westermann. *Theologisches Handwörterbuch zum Alten Testament*. Munich: Chr. Kaiser Verlag; Zurich: Theologische Verlag, 1976.

Jensen, P. *Assyrisch-Babylonische Mythen und Epen*. Keilinschriftliche Bibliothek. Ed. Eberhard Schrader, VI part I. Berlin: Reuther and Reichard, 1900.

Johnston, Christopher. "Two Assyrian Letters," *JAOS* 15 (1893) 311-17.

Jonah ibn Janaḥ. ספר הרקמה. Ed. M. Wilensky. Berlin: האקדמיה למדעי היהדות, 1928.

_____. *Sepher Haschoraschim. Wurzelwörterbuch der Hebräischen Sprache von Abulwalid Merwan ibn Ganah*. Amsterdam: Philo Press, 1969.

Joseph ibn Aknin. התגלות הסודות. Ed. A. S. Halkin. Jerusalem, 1964.

Joseph ben Abba Mari ibn Kaspi. אדני כסף. Ed. Isaac Last. London: I. Narodiczky, 1911.

_____. *Sharshoth Kesef. The Hebrew Dictionary of Roots by Joseph ibn Caspi*. Ed. Isaac Last. Jerusalem: Makor Ltd., 1970.

Joüon, Paul. "Le Costume d'Elie et celui de Jean Baptise, Etude Lexicographique," *Bib* 16 (1935) 75-81.

_____. "Notes de critique Textuelle," *MUSJ* 6 (1913) 184-211.

_____. "Notes de Lexicographie Hébraïque," *Bib* 6 (1925) 417-23.

_____. *Ruth, Commentaire Philologique et Exégétique*. Rome: Pontifical Biblical Institute, 1924.

Judah ibn Balʿam. "The Arabic Commentary of Abu Zakariya Yaḥa (Judah ben Samuel) ibn Balʿam on the Twelve Minor Prophets." Ed. Samuel Poznanski. *JQR* 15 (1924-25) 1-53.

_____. "ספר הפעלים שהם מגזרת השמות," in מספרי הבלשנות העברית בימי הבינײם. Ed. Pavel Kokovtsov. Jerusalem: Kedem, 1970.

_____. "Arabischer Kommentar zum Buche Jeremia von Jehuda ibn Balʿam," in *Festschrift zu Ehren des Dr. A. Harkavy*. Ed. Jakob Israelsohn. St. Petersburg, 1908. Pp. 273-308.

_____. *Gloses d'Abou Zakariya Yahia ben Bilam sur Isaïe*. Ed. J. Derenbourg. Paris: A. Durlacher, 1892.

_____. "העתק פירוש ספר שופטים לרבי יהודה אבן בלעם משפת ערבית," (Trans. M. Guttstein), in ספר עשרה מאורות גדולים. Ed. J. Gad. Johannesburg: Pacific Press Ltd., 1952. Pp. 38-45.

Judah ibn Quraish. ספר אגרת. Trans. Moshe Katz. Tel Aviv: Dvir Co., 1950.

_____. רסאלה. Ed. J. J. L. Barges and D. B. Goldberg. Paris: B. Duprat and D. Maisonneuve, 1857.

Kahle, Paul E. *The Cairo Geniza*. Oxford: Basil Blackwell, 1959.

_____. "Fragmente des samaritanischen Pentateuchtargums, herausgegeben und erläutert," *ZA* 16 (1902) 79-101 and 17 (1903) 1-22.

_____. *Masoreten des Westens*. Stuttgart: W. Kohlhammer, 1930.

_____. *Textkritische und Lexikalische Bemerkungen zum Samaritanischen Pentateuchtargum*. Halle: W. Drugulin, 1898.

Kaiser, Otto. *Isaiah 1-12. A Commentary*. OTL. Trans. R. A. Wilson. London: SCM Press Ltd., 1972.

_____. *Isaiah 13-39. A Commentary*. OTL. Trans. R. A. Wilson. London: SCM Press Ltd., 1974.

Kamphausen. *The Book of Daniel*. SBOT 18. Leipzig: J. C. Hinrichs'sche Buchhandlung, 1896.

Kapelrud, Arvid S. "Joel 1,17," *NorTT* 45 (1944) 285-92.

_____. *Joel Studies*. UUÅ 1948: 4. Uppsala: A. B. Lundequistska Bokhandeln, 1948.

Kasowski, Chaim Josua. אוצר לשון האונקלוס. Jerusalem, 1940.

Kaufmann, David. "Das Wörterbuch Menahem Ibn Saruks nach Codex Bern 200," *ZDMG* 40 (1886) 367-409.

Kaufmann, Yehezkel. ספר שופטים. Jerusalem: Kiryat Sepher, 1968.

Kautzsch, Emil. *Die Aramaismen im Alten Testament*. Halle: Max Niemeyer, 1902.

_____. *Gesenius' Hebrew Grammar*. Trans. A. E. Cowley. Oxford: Clarendon Press, 1910.

Keil, C. F., and F. Delitzsch. *Biblical Commentary on the Old Testament*. Trans. James Martin and Francis Bolton. Grand Rapids: W. B. Eerdmans Publishing Company, 1951.

Keimer, Ludwig. "Eine Bemerkung zu Amos 7,14," *Bib* 8 (1927) 441-44.

Kennedy, James. *The Note-Line in the Hebrew Scriptures*. Edinburgh: T. & T. Clark, 1930.

Kirschner, Bruno. "Hapax Legomena," *Jüdisches Lexikon*. Berlin: Jüdischer Verlag, 1930. 2. 1429.

Kittel, Rudolph. *The Books of Chronicles*. SBOT 20. Baltimore: Johns Hopkins Press, 1895.

_____. *Die Bücher der Chronik*. HKAT 16[1]. Göttingen: Vandenhoeck & Ruprecht, 1902.

_____. *Die Bücher der Könige*. HKAT I[5]. Göttingen: Vandenhoeck & Ruprecht, 1900.

_____. *Die Psalmen*. KAT 13. Leipzig: A. Deichertsche Verlagsbuchhandlung, 1929.

Klar, Benjamin. "הנוסח המקורי של 'פתרון שבעים מלות בודדות'," in הוצאת מחברת לספרות, 1954. Pp. 259-75. מחקרים ועיונים. Tel Aviv:

Klein, Michael. *The Fragment Targums of the Pentateuch According to their Extant Sources*. Rome: Biblical Institute Press, 1980.

Knobel, August. *Die Bücher Exodus und Leviticus Erklärt.* KHAT. Leipzig: S. Hirzel, 1857.

Knudtzon, Jørgen Alexander. *Die El-Amarna Tafeln.* Aalen: O. Zeller, 1964.

Köbert, R. "Das Koranische 'ṭagut,'" *Or* 30 (1961) 415-16.

Köhler, Ludwig. "Vom alttestamentlichen Wörterbuch," *MGWJ* 78 (1934) 1-6.

_____, and Walter Baumgartner. *Lexicon in Veteris Testamenti Libros.* Leiden: E. J. Brill, 1958.

König, Eduard. *Das Buch Hiob Eingeleitet.* Gütersloh: C. Bertelsmann, 1929.

_____. *Das Deuteronomium.* KAT 3. Leipzig: A. Deichertsche Verlagsbuchhandlung, 1917.

_____. *Hebräisches und Aramäisches Wörterbuch zum Alten Testament.* Leipzig: Dieterich'sche Verlagsbuchhandlung, 1910.

_____. *Historisch-Kritisches Lehrgebäude der Hebräischen Sprache.* Leipzig: J. C. Hinrichs'sche Buchhandlung, 1881.

Kohn, Samuel. "Die samaritanische Pentateuchübersetzung nach der Ausgabe von Petermann und Vollers," *ZDMG* 47 (1893) 626-97.

_____. *Samaritanische Studien.* Breslau: Verlag von der Schletter'schen Buchhandlung, 1868.

_____. "Zur Sprache, Literatur und Dogmatik der Samaritaner," *Abhandlungen für die Kunde des Morgenlandes* 5 (1876) no. 4.

Koleditzky, Shachne, ed. ספרי להתנא האלהי רבי שמעון בן יוחאי. Jerusalem: Mossad Harav Kook, 1948.

Komlós, O. "אֲכוּ לְרַגְלֶךָ (Deut xxxiii 3)," *VT* 6 (1956) 435-36.

Kopf, L. "Arabische Etymologien und Parallelen zum Bibelwörterbuch," *VT* 8 (1958) 161-215.

Koskinen, Kalevi. "Kompatibilität in den dreikonsonantigen hebräischen Wurzeln," *ZDMG* 114 (1964) 16-58.

Kraetzschmar, Richard. *Das Buch Ezechiel.* HKAT III 3^1. Göttingen: Vandenhoeck & Ruprecht, 1900.

Kraus, F. R. *Ein Edikt des Königs Ammi-ṣaduqa von Babylon.* Leiden: E. J. Brill, 1958.

Kraus, Hans-Joachim. *Klagelieder*. *BKAT 20*. Neukirchen: Verlag des Erziehungsvereins, 1968.

_____. *Psalmen*. BKAT 15. Neukirchen: Verlag des Erziehungsvereins, 1960.

Krauss, Samuel. "Saadya's Tafsir of the Seventy *Hapax Legomena* Explained and Continued," in *Saadya Studies*. Ed. Erwin I. J. Rosenthal. Aberdeen: Manchester University Press, 1943. Pp. 47-77.

Küchenmeister, Friedrich. "Einige Bemerkungen zu Uebersetzungen der Probebeibel," *ZWT* 29 (1886) 107-8.

Küchler, Friedrich. *Beiträge zur Kenntnis der Assyrisch-Babylonischen Medizin*. Leipzig: J. C. Hinrichs'sche Buchhandlung, 1904.

Kuhn, Karl Georg. "Nachträge zur *Konkordanz zu den Qumrantexten*," *RevQ* 4 (1963-64) 163-234.

_____, and Albert-Marie Denis et al. *Konkordanz zu den Qumrantexten*. Göttingen: Vandenhoeck & Ruprecht, 1960.

Kuhnig, K. Willibald. *Nordwestsemitische Studien zum Hoseabuch*. Rome: Biblical Institute Press, 1974.

Kupper, J. R. *Correspondance de Kibri-Dagan*. ARM III. Paris: Imprimerie National, 1950.

Kutscher, E. Y. *The Language and Linguistic Background of the Isaiah Scroll (1QIs^a)*. Leiden: E. J. Brill, 1974.

_____. "למילון המקראי," *Leš* 21 (1957) 251-58.

_____. מלים ותולדותיהן, Jerusalem: Kiryat Sepher, 1965.

de Lagarde, Paulus Anton, ed. *Hagiographa Chaldaice*. Leipzig: B. G. Teubner, 1873.

_____. *Mitheilungen*. Goettingen: Dieterichsche Sortimentsbuchhandlung, 1884.

_____. *Übersicht über die im Aramäischen, Arabischen und Hebräischen übliche Bildung der Nomina*. Osnabrück: Otto Zeller Verlag, 1972.

Lambdin, Thomas O. "Egyptian Loan Words in the Old Testament," *JAOS* 73 (1953) 145-55.

Lambert, Mayer, and Louis Brandin. *Glossaire hébreu-francais du xiiie siecle*. Paris: Ernest Leroux, 1905.

Lambert, W. G. *Babylonian Wisdom Literature.* Oxford: Clarendon Press, 1960.

Landberg, C. G. *Glossaire Datinois.* Leiden: E. J. Brill, 1942.

Landsberger, B., "Die Gestalt der semitischen Wurzel," in *Atti del XIX Congresso Internazionale degli Orientalisti* 1935. Pp. 450-52.

Lane, Edward William. *An Arabic-English Lecixon.* London: Williams and Norgate, 1863-93.

Langdon, S. *The Babylonian Epic of Creation.* Oxford: Clarendon Press, 1923.

Lauha, Aarre. *Kohelet.* BKAT 19. Neukirchen-Vluyn: Neukirchener Verlag des Erziehungsvereins GmbH, 1978.

Lee, Samuel, ed. *Vetus Testamentum Syriace.* London: Impensis ejusdem Societis, 1823.

Leslau, Wolf. *Ethiopic and South Arabic Contributions to the Hebrew Lexicon.* Berkeley, CA: University of California Press, 1958.

_____. "Ethiopic Denominatives with Nominal Morphemes," *Le Muséon* 75 (1962) 139-75.

_____. *Hebrew Cognates in Amharic.* Wiesbaden: Otto Harrassowitz, 1969.

_____. *Lexique Soqotri (Sudarabique Moderne).* Paris: Librairie C. Klincksieck, 1938.

Levi ben Gershon. פירוש על חמש מגלות. Königsberg, 1860.

Levine, Baruch A. *Survivals of Ancient Canaanite in the Mishnah.* Diss., Ph.D., Brandeis University, 1962.

Levy, Alfred. *Das Targum zu Koheleth (nach südarabischen Handschriften).* Breslau: Buchdruckerei: H. Fleischmann, 1905.

Levy, Jacob. *Chaldäisches Wörterbuch über die Targumim und einen grossen Theil des rabbinischen Schriftthums.* Leipzig: Baumgärtners Buchhandlung, 1867.

_____. *Neuhebräisches und chaldäisches Wörterbuch über die Talmudim und Midraschim.* Leipzig: F. A. Brockhaus, 1876-89.

Lewy, Julius. "The Problems Inherent in Section 70 of the Bisutun Inscription," *HUCA* 25 (1954) 169-208.

Lidzbarski, Mark. *Altsemitische Texte.* Giessen: Alfred Töpelmann, 1907.

_____. *Ephemeris für Semitische Epigraphik.* Giessen: J. Ricker'sche Verlagsbuchhandlung, 1900-15.

Liebermann, Saul. *Hellenism in Jewish Palestine.* New York: The Jewish Theological Seminary of America, 1950.

_____. *Tosefta Ki-fshuṭah.* New York: Jewish Theological Seminary of America, 1955.

_____, and Y. Kutscher. "חרגין, חרמין וחגרין," *Leš* 27 (1962) 34-39.

Lipinski, Edouard. "Juges 5,4-5 et Psaume 68,8-11," *Bib* 48 (1967) 185-206.

_____. *La Royauté de Yahwé dans la Poésie et le Culte de l'Ancien Israel.* Brussels: Paleis der Academien, 1968.

Löhr, Max. *Die Klagelieder des Jeremias.* HKAT III 2^2. Göttingen: Vandenhoeck & Ruprecht, 1906.

Löw, Immanuel. "Bemerkungen zu Nöldeke's Anzeige von Bickel, Kalilag und Damnag," *ZDMG* 31 (1877) 535-40.

_____. "Bemerkungen zu *OLZ* 1909, Sp. 11," *OLZ* 12 (1909) 115-16.

_____. *Die Flora der Juden.* Hildesheim: Georg Olms, 1967.

_____. Review of J. Preuss, *Biblisch-Talmudische Medizin, OLZ* 15 (1912) 555-59.

_____. "Yayin Koses," *REJ* 82 (1926) 165-67.

Loewenstamm, Samuel E. "Ugarit and the Bible I," *Bib* 56 (1975) 103-19.

_____, and J. Blau. *Thesaurus of the Language of the Bible.* Jerusalem: Bible Concordance Press, 1957-.

Lokotsch, Karl. *Etymologisches Wörterbuch der Europäischen (Germanischen, Romanischen und Slavischen) Wörter Orientalischen Ursprungs.* Heidelberg: Carl Winter's Universitätsbuchhandlung, 1927.

Loretz, Oswald. *Das Althebräische Liebeslied.* Neukirchen-Vluyn: Butzon & Bercker Kevelaer, 1971.

Luckenbill, Daniel David. *Ancient Records of Assyria and Babylonia.* Chicago: University of Chicago Press, 1926-27.

Luzzatto, Samuel David. פירושי שד"יל ז"ל על ירמיה, יחזקאל, משלי ואיוב. Lemberg: A. I. Menkes, 1876.

Bibliography

_____. פירוש שד"יל (ר' שמואל דוד לוצאטו) על חמשה חומשי תורה. Tel Aviv: Dvir, 1965.

_____. פירוש שד"יל על ספר ישעיה. Tel Aviv: Dvir, 1970.

Maag, Victor. *Text, Wortschatz und Begriffswelt des Buches Amos.* Leiden: E. J. Brill, 1951.

McKane, William. *Proverbs, A New Approach.* OTL. London: SCM Press Ltd., 1970.

McKenzie, John L. *Second Isaiah.* AB 20. Garden City, NY: Doubleday and Co., 1968.

McPherson, William B. "The Words *Sôrāh* and *Nismɑn* in Isaiah xxviii,25," *Johns Hopkins University Circulars* 22 (1902) 87-91.

Malbim, Meir Leibush. אוצר פירושים על תנ"ך מקראות גדולות, סדרא א' פירוש המלבי"ם. Jerusalem: Pardes, 1956.

Mandelkern, Solomon. *Veteris Testamenti Concordantiae.* Jerusalem: Schocken, 1967.

Mani, Aaron Soliman Elijah. העברית לאור הערבית. Jerusalem: Raphael Chaim Hakohen Ltd., 1957.

Marazuela, Teofilo Ayusa. *La Vetus Latina Hispana.* Madrid, 1953-.

Marcus, Joseph. "A Fifth Ms. of Ben Sira," *JQR* 21 (1931) 223-40.

Marcus, R. "Notes on the Dead Sea Manual of Discipline," *JNES* 11 (1952) 205-11.

Margoliouth, J. P. *Supplement to the Thesaurus Syriacus of R. Payne Smith, S.T.P.* Oxford: Clarendon Press, 1927.

Margulis, B. "Gen XLIX 10/Deut. XXXIII 2-3," *VT* 19 (1969) 202-10.

Marti, Karl. *Das Buch Daniel.* KHC 18. Tübingen: J. C. B. Mohr (Paul Siebeck), 1901.

_____. *Das Dodekapropheton.* KHC 13. Tübingen: J. C. B. Mohr (Paul Siebeck), 1904.

_____. *Das Buch Jesaja.* KHC 10. Tübingen: J. C. B. Mohr (Paul Siebeck), 1900.

Martinazzoli, Franco. *Hapax Legomenon.* Rome: Gismondi, 1953-57.

Mauchline, John. *1 and 2 Samuel.* CB. London: Oliphants, 1971.

Mays, James Luther. *Amos, A Commentary.* OTL. London: SCM Press Ltd., 1969.

_____. *Hosea, A Commentary.* OTL. London: SCM Press Ltd., 1969.

_____. *Micah, A Commentary.* OTL. Philadelphia: Westminster Press, 1976.

McCarter, P. Kyle, Jr. *1 Samuel.* AB 8. Garden City, NY: Doubleday and Co., 1980.

Meek, Theophile James. *Hebrew Origins.* New York: Harper & Row, 1960.

Meissner, B. "Das Antimongebirge," *OLZ* 17 (1914) 52-55.

Melamed, Ezra Zion. מפרשי המקרא. Jerusalem: Magnes Press, 1975.

Melamed, Raphael Hai. *The Targum of Canticles.* Philadelphia: Dropsie College, 1921.

Menaḥem ibn Saruk. מחברת מנחם. Ed. Z. Filipowski. London, 1854.

Menasce, J. "Mots d'emprunt et Noms propres Iraniens dans les nouveaux documents Araméens," *BiOr* 11 (1954) 161-62.

Merx, Adalbert. *Die Prophetie des Joel und ihre Ausleger.* Halle: Buchhandlung des Waisenhauses, 1879.

מדרש תנחומא. Berlin: Horeb, 1923.

Milik, J. T. "Un Contrat Juif de l'an 134 après J.-C.," *RB* 61 (1954) 182-90.

_____. "Deux Documents inédits du Désert de Juda," *Bib* 38 (1957) 245-68.

_____. "'Prière de Nabonide' et autres écrits d'un cycle de Daniel," *RB* 63 (1956) 407-15.

Mill, John Stuart. *A System of Logic Ratiocinative and Inductive.* 8th ed. New York: Harper & Brothers, 1890.

Montgomery, James. *A Critical and Exegetical Commentary on the Book of Daniel.* ICC. Edinburgh: T. & T. Clark, 1927.

_____. *The Samaritans.* Philadelphia: John C. Winston Co., 1907.

_____, and Henry Snyder Gehman. *A Critical and Exegetical Commentary on the Books of Kings.* Edinburgh: T. & T. Clark, 1951.

de Moor, Johannes C. *The Seasonal Pattern in the Ugaritic Myth of Ba‘lu.* Neukirchen-Vluyn: Butzon & Bercker Kevelaer, 1971.

Moore, Carey A. *Esther.* AB 7B. Garden City, NY: Doubleday and Co., 1971.

Moore, George F. *A Critical and Exegetical Commentary on Judges.* ICC. Edinburgh: T. & T. Clark, 1895.

Morag, Shlomo. "רובדי קדמות, עיונים לשונים במשלי בלעם," *Tarbiz* 51 (1981) 1-24.

Moran, William L. "The Putative Root ‘tm in Is. 9:18," *CBQ* 12 (1950) 153-54.

_____. "Ugaritic *ṣiṣuma* and Hebrew *ṣîṣ*," *Bib* 39 (1958) 69-71.

Mordtmann, J. H., and D. H. Müller. *Sabäische Denkmaler.* Vienna: Karl Gerold's Sohn, 1883.

Morgenstern, Julian. "Psalm 48," *HUCA* 16 (1941) 1-95.

Moscati, Sabatino, ed. *An Introduction to the Comparative Grammar of the Semitic Languages.* Wiesbaden: Otto Harrassowitz, 1964.

Moses ben Isaac ben Ha-Nasia. ספר השוהם. Ed. Benjamin Klar. Jerusalem: Mekize Nirdamim, 1946.

Moses ben Maimon. משנה עם פירוש רבינו משה בן מימון. Jerusalem: Mosad Harav Kook, 1963.

Moses ben Naḥman. ספר איוב. New York: L. Perlow, n.d.

_____. פירוש הרמב"ן על שיר השירים. Ed. M. Bernman. N.D.

_____. פירוש התורה לרבינו משה בן נחמן (רמב"ן). Ed. C. D. Chavel. Jerusalem: Mosad Harav Kook, 1962-66.

_____. פירושים הרמב"ן על נביאים וכתובים. Jerusalem: Boys Town, 1963.

Moses ibn Gikatilla. "Arabische Uebersetzung und arabischer Kommentar zum Buche Hiob von Mose ibn Chiquitilla," in *Festschrift zu Ehren des Dr. A. Harkavy.* Ed. Wilhelm Bacher. St. Petersburg, 1908. Pp. 273-308.

Moses ibn Ezra. *Kitab al-Muḥāḍara wal-Mudhākara.* Ed. A. S. Halkin. Jerusalem: Mekize Nirdamim, 1975.

Moses ibn Habib. דרכי נעם עם מרפא לשון. Rodelheim: Heidenheim & Baschwitz, 1806.

Mosteller, Frederick, and David Wallace. "Inference in an Authorship Problem," *Journal of the American Statistical Association* 58 (1963) 275-309.

Müller, August, and E. Kautzsch. *The Book of Proverbs.* SBOT 15. Baltimore: Johns Hopkins Press, 1901.

Muller, Charles. "Lexical Distribution Reconsidered: The Waring Herdan Formula," in *Statistics and Style.* Ed. L. Dolezel and R. W. Bailey. New York: American Elsevier Publishing Co., 1969. Pp. 52-56.

_____. "Le MOT, unité de texte et unité de lexique en statistique lexicologique," *Travaux de Linguistique et de Literature* I (1963) 155-73.

Muss-Arnolt, Wilhelm. *A Concise Dictionary of the Assyrian Language.* Berlin: Reuther and Reichard, 1905.

Myers, Jacob M. *Ezra Nehemiah.* AB 14. Garden City, NY: Doubleday and Co., 1965.

_____. *I-II Chronicles.* AB 12-13. Garden City, NY: Doubleday and Co., 1965.

Nathan ben Jehiel. ספר ערוך השלם. Ed. A. Kohut. Jerusalem: Makor Ltd., 1969.

Nauck, Wolfgang. "Lex insculpta (חוק חרות) in der Sektenschrift," *ZNW* 46 (1955) 138-40.

Naveh, J. "A Hebrew Letter from the Seventh Century B.C.," *IEJ* 10 (1960) 129-39.

Nestle, Eberhard. *Marginalien und Materialien.* Tübingen: J. J. Heckenhauen'sche Buchhandlung, 1893.

_____. "Miscellen," *ZAW* 16 (1896) 321-27.

_____. "Miscellen," *ZAW* 20 (1900) 164-71.

_____. "Miscellen," *ZAW* 29 (1909) 230-34.

_____. *Septuagintastudien VI.* Stuttgart: Stuttgarter Vereins-Buchdruckerei, 1911.

Neubauer, Karl Wilhelm. "Erwägungen zu Amos 5_{4-15}," *ZAW* 78 (1960) 292-316.

Neubauer, M. Adolphe. "Abraham Ha-Babli, 'Appendice à la Nature sur la lexicographie Hébraique," *JA* 6th series, 2 (1863) 195-216.

Nichols, Helen Hawley. "The Composition of the Elihu Speeches," *AJSL* 27 (1911) 97-186.

Nöldeke, Theodor. *Beiträge zur Semitischen Sprachwissenschaft.* Strassburg: Karl J. Trübner, 1904.

_____. *Mandäische Grammatik.* Darmstadt: Wissenschaftliche Buchgesellschaft, 1964.

_____. *Neue Beiträge zur Semitischen Sprachwissenschaft.* Strassburg: Karl J. Trübner, 1910.

_____. Review of E. Kautzsch, *Die Aramaismen im Alten Testament,* *ZDMG* 57 (1903) 412-20.

_____. Review of *Morgenlandische Forschungen, ZDMG* 29 (1875) 322-34.

_____. Review of George Hoffmann, ed., *Opuscula Nestoriana Syriace, ZDMG* 35 (1881) 491-501.

_____. "Untersuchungen zur semitischen Grammatik," *ZDMG* 37 (1883) 525-40.

Nötscher, F. "Entbehrliches Hapax legomena in Jesaia," *VT* 1 (1951) 299-302.

Noth, Martin. *Exodus, A Commentary.* OTL. Philadelphia: The Westminster Press, 1962.

_____. *Die Israelitischen Personennamen im Rahmen der gemeinsemitischen Namengebung.* BWANT 3:10. Stuttgart: W. Kohlhammer Verlag, 1928.

_____. *Könige.* BKAT 9. Neukirchen-Vluyn: Verlag des Erziehungvereins, 1968.

_____. *Leviticus, A Commentary.* OTL. London: SCM Press Ltd., 1965.

_____. *Numbers, A Commentary.* OTL. London: SCM Press Ltd., 1968.

Nowack, W. *Die Kleinen Propheten.* HKAT III 4. Göttingen: Vandenhoeck & Ruprecht, 1922.

_____. *Richter, Ruth u. Bücher Samuelis.* HKAT I^4. Göttingen: Vandenhoeck & Ruprecht, 1902.

Nutt, John W. *A Sketch of Samaritan History, Dogma, and Literature.* London: Trübner and Co., 1874.

Nyberg, H. S. *Studien zum Hoseabuche.* UUÅ 1935.6. Uppsala: Alquist & Wiksells Boktryckerie-AB, 1935.

Oesterley, William O. E. *The Psalms.* London: SPCK, 1955.

del Olmo, Gregorio. "Notas Criticas al Texto Hebreo de Jr 14-17," *Claretianum* 11 (1971) 283-358.

Olshausen, Justus. *Lehrbuch der Hebräischen Sprache.* Braunschweig: Friedrich Vieweg und Sohn, 1861.

Oort, H. "Kritische Aanteekeningen op Jez 40-66," *Theologisch Tijdschrift* 25 (1891) 461-77.

Orlinsky, Harry M. "The Masoretic Text: A Critical Evaluation," in Christian D. Ginsburg, *Introduction to the Masoretico-Critical Edition of the Hebrew Bible.* New York: Ktav, 1966. i-xxxvii.

Palache, Jehuda Leon. *Semantic Notes on the Hebrew Lexicon.* Trans. R. J. Z. Werblowsky. Leiden: E. J. Brill, 1959.

Paterson, J. A. *The Book of Numbers.* SBOT 4. Baltimore: Johns Hopkins Press, 1900.

Paton, Lewis Bayles. *A Critical and Exegetical Commentary on the Book of Esther.* ICC. New York: Charles Scribner's Sons, 1908.

_____. "A Text-Critical Apparatus to the Book of Esther," in *Old Testament and Semitic Studies in Memory of William Rainey Harper.* Chicago: University of Chicago Press, 1908. 2. 1-52.

Paul, S. M. "Classification of Wine in Mesopotamian and Rabbinic Sources," *IEJ* 25 (1975) 42-44.

Payne-Smith, Robert. *Thesaurus Syriacus.* Oxford: Clarendon Press, 1879-1901.

Peiser, F. E. "Miscellen," *ZAW* 17 (1897) 347-51.

Perez, Maaravi. "הטיפול במלים יחידאות בשורשן בפירושי ר' יהודה אבן בלעם," *Lešˇ* 45 (1981) 213-32.

Perles, Felix. *Analekten zur Textkritik des Alten Testaments.* Munich: Theodor Ackermann, 1895.

_____. *Analekten zur Textkritik des Alten Testaments.* Neue Folge. Leipzig: Gustav Engel, 1922.

_____. "Babylonisch-biblische Glossen," *OLZ* 8 (1905) 125-29.

_____. "Babylonisch-talmudische Glossen," *OLZ* 8 (1905) 381-85.

Bibliography

_____. "A Miscellany of Lexical and Textual Notes on the Bible," *JQR* 2 (1911-12) 97-132.

_____. Review of Friedrich Delitzsch, *Das Buch Hiob*, *OLZ* 6 (1903) 251-52.

_____. "Zu Sachaus *Aramäischen Papyrus und Ostraka*," *OLZ* 14 (1911) 497-503.

פסיקתא רבתי דרב כהנא. Vilna, 1913.

Petermann, H., and C. Vollers. *Pentateuchus Samaritanus*. Berolini: W. Moeser, n.d.

Peters, Curt. "Peschitta und Targumim des Pentateuch," *Le Museon* 48 (1935) 1-54.

_____. "Pešiṭta-Psalter und Psalmentargum," *Le Museon* 52 (1939) 275-96.

Peters, Norbert. *Das Buch Job*. EHAT 21. Münster: Verlag des Aschendorffschen Verlagsbuchhandlung, 1928.

Pinsker, Simḥah. לקוטי קדמוניות. Vienna: A. Della Tarre, 1860.

Plinius, Secundus C. *Natural History*. Trans. H. Rackham. LCL. Cambridge, MA: Harvard University Press, 1949.

van der Ploeg, J. "Le 'Manuel de Discipline,'" *BibOr* 8 (1951) 113-26.

_____, and A. S. van der Woude. *Le Targum de Job de la grotte XI de Qumrân*. Leiden: E. J. Brill, 1971.

Plöger, Otto. *Das Buch Daniel*. KAT 18. Gütersloh: Gerd Mohn, 1965.

_____. *Die Klagelieder*. HAT 18. Tübingen: J. C. B. Mohr (Paul Siebeck), 1969.

Pope, Marvin H. *Job*. AB 15. Garden City, NY: Doubleday and Co., 1965.

_____. *Song of Songs*. AB 7C. Garden City, NY: Doubleday and Co., 1977.

_____. Review of H. Gese et al., *Die Religionen Altsyriens, Altarabiens und der Mandäer*, *UF* 3 (1971) 375-76.

_____. Review of John Gray, *The Legacy of Canaan* (VTSup 5), *JSS* 11 (1961) 228-41.

Porteous, Norman W. *Daniel.* OTL. Philadelphia: Westminster Press, 1965.

Poznanski, Samuel, ed. *Eine Hebräische Grammatik aus dem XIII Jahrhundert.* Berlin: S. Calvary and Co., 1894.

_____. *Mose b. Samuel Hakkohen ibn Chiquitilla.* Leipzig: J. C. Hinrichs'sche Buchhandlung, 1895.

Praetorius, F. "Threni I,12.41. II,6.13," *ZAW* 15 (1895) 143-46.

_____. "Threni III,5.16," *ZAW* 15 (1895) 326.

Prijs, Leo. *Die Grammatikalische Terminologie des Abraham ibn Esra.* Basel: Sepher-Verlag, 1950.

Procksch, Otto. *Die Genesis.* KAT 1. Leipzig: A. Deichertsche Verlagsbuchhandlung, 1924.

_____. *Jesaia I.* KAT 9. Leipzig: A. Deichertsche Verlagsbuchhandlung, 1930.

The Prophets, Nevi'im. Philadelphia: The Jewish Publication Society of America, 1978.

Qara, Joseph. "Der Commentar des R. Joseph Kara zu Job," *MGWJ* 5 (1856) 223-29, 268-78, 343-51, 469-75; 6 (1857) 70-73, 182-84, 270-74, 350-57, 463-70; 7 (1858) 255-63, 345-58.

_____. "ליקוטים מפירושיו של ר' יוסף קרא לישעיה," in ספר היובל לפרופיסור שמואל קרויס. Ed. Alexander Kristenfoler. Jerusalem: Rubin Mass, 1936. Pp. 110-16.

_____. פירוש ירמיה מר' יוסף ב"ר שמעון קרא. Ed. Aryeh Leib Schlossberg. Paris: A. Durchlacher, 1881.

_____. פירוש על קהלת. Ed. H. R. Einstein. Berlin, 1886.

_____. פירוש רבי יוסף קרא על מגלת אסתר. Ed. Solomon Buber. Breslau, 1901.

_____. פירוש ר' יוסף קרא על נביאים ראשונים. in *Jahrbuch der Judisch Literaischen Gesellschaft.* Ed. Simon Eppenstein. Jerusalem: Makor Ltd., 1972.

Qimḥi, David. *The Commentary of David Kimhi on Isaiah.* Ed. Louis Finkelstein. New York: Columbia University Press, 1926.

_____. *The Commentary of Rabbi David Kimhi on Hosea.* Ed. Harry Cohen. New York: Columbia University Press, 1929.

Bibliography

_____ . הפירוש השלם על תהלים. Ed. Abraham Darom. Jerusalem: Mossad Harav Kook, 1971.

_____ . תקות אנוש in פירוש איוב. Ed. Israel Schwartz. Berlin: Louis Gerschel Verlagsbuchhandlung, 1868. Pp. 127-45.

_____ . פירושי רבי דוד קמחי (רד"ק) על התורה. Ed. משה קמלהר. Jerusalem: Mossad Harav Kook, 1970.

_____ . *Rabbi Davidis Kimchi Radicum Liber sive Hebraeum Bibliorum Lexicon cum Animadversionibus Eliae Levitae*. Ed. Jo. H. R. Biesenthal and F. Lebrecht. Berlin: G. Bethge, 1847.

_____ . ספר מכלול שחבר דוד קמחי זצ"ל עם נמוקים שהוסיף אליהו אשכנזי. Ed. I. Rittenberg. Jerusalem, 1966.

Qimḥi, Joseph. תקות אנוש in פירוש איוב. Ed. Israel Schwartz. Berlin: Louis Gerschel Verlagsbuchhandlung, 1868. Pp. 127-45.

_____ . *Sepher Ha-galuy von R. Joseph Kimchi*. Ed. H. J. Matthews. Berlin: Mekize Nirdamim, 1887.

_____ . *Sepher Sikkaron Grammatik der Hebräischen Sprache von R. Joseph Kimchi*. Ed. Wilhelm Bacher. Berlin: Mekize Nirdamim, 1888.

Qimḥi, Moses. תקות אנוש in פירוש איוב. Ed. Israel Schwartz. Berlin: Louis Gerschel Verlagsbuchhandlung, 1868. Pp. 69-126.

_____ . ספר מהלך (שבילי הדעת) עם ביאור ר' אלי' בחור. Hamburg: Lazer, 1785.

Rabin, Chaim. *Ancient West-Arabian*. London: Taylor's Foreign Press, 1951.

_____ . "Etymological Miscellanea," *ScrH* 8 (1961) 384-400.

_____ . "The Historical Background of Qumran Hebrew," *ScrH* 4 (1958) 144-61.

_____ . "Hittite Words in Hebrew," *Or* 32 (1963) 113-39.

_____ . "Judges V,2 and the Ideology of Deborah's War," *JJS* 6 (1955) 125-34.

_____ . "מלים בודדות," *EM* 4, 1066-70.

_____ . "השפעל בעברית ובארמית - מהותו ומוצאו," *EY* 9 (1969) 148-58.

_____ . "התיתכן סמנטיקה מקראית?" *BM* 7 (1962) 17-27.

_____ . *The Zadokite Documents*. 2d ed. Oxford: Clarendon Press, 1958.

von Rad, Gerhard. *Deuteronomy, A Commentary*. OTL. London: SCM Press Ltd., 1966.

_____. *Genesis, A Commentary*. OTL. London: SCM Press Ltd., 1972.

Radday, Yehudah T. *The Unity of Isaiah in the Light of Statistical Linguistics*. Hildesheim: Dr. H. A. Gerstenberg, 1973.

Reider, Joseph. "Contributions to the Scriptural Text," *HUCA* 24 (1952-53) 85-106.

_____. "Etymological Studies in Biblical Hebrew," *VT* 2 (1952) 113-20.

_____. "Etymological Studies in Biblical Hebrew," *VT* 4 (1954) 276-95.

_____. *An Index to Aquila*. VTSup 12. Leiden: Brill, 1966.

_____. "Some Notes to the Text of the Scriptures," *HUCA* 3 (1926) 109-16.

Renan, Ernest. *Histoire Générale et Système Comparé des Langues Sémitiques*. 5th ed. Paris: Calmann Levy, 1878.

Reuchlin, Johannes. *De Rudimentis Hebraicis*. New York: Georg Olms Verlag, 1974.

Richter, Elise. "Über Homonymie," in *Festschrift für Universitäts-Professor Hofrat Dr. Paul Kretschmer*. Beiträge zur Griechischen und Lateinischen Sprachforschung. Vienna: Deutscher Verlag für Jugend und Volk, Ges. M. B. H., 1926. Pp. 167-201.

Rieder, David. התרגום הארמי המכונה תרגום יונתן בן עוזיאל על חמשה חומשי תורה. Jerusalem: Sloman, 1974.

Rinaldi, P. Giovanni. "Nota," *Bibbia e Oriente* 8 (1966) 306.

Roberts, Bleddyn J. *The Old Testament Text and Versions*. Cardiff: University of Wales Press, 1951.

Robinson, Henry Wheeler, ed. *The Bible in its Ancient and English Versions*. Oxford: Clarendon Press, 1954.

Robinson, Theodore H. "Hosea bis Micha," in *Die Zwölf Kleinen Propheten*. HAT 14. Tübingen: J. C. B. Mohr (Paul Siebeck), 1964.

Rosenthal, Franz. *A Grammar of Biblical Aramaic*. Wiesbaden: Otto Harrassowitz, 1961.

_____. *Die Aramaistische Forschung*. Leiden: E. J. Brill, 1964.

Rosenthal, Judah. "שאלות עתיקות בתנ"ך," *HUCA* 21 (1948) 29-54.

Ross, James F. "Job 33:14-30: The Phenomenology of Lament," *JBL* 94 (1975) 38-46.

Rothstein, J. W. "Zur Kritik des Deboraliedes und die Ursprüngliche Rhythmische Form desselben," *ZDMG* 56 (1902) 697-728.

_____, and Johannes Hänel. *Das Erste Buch der Chronik*. KAT 18[2]. Leipzig: A. Deichertsche Verlagsbuchhandlung, 1927.

Rowley, H. H. *Job*. CB. London: Thomas Nelson and Sons, 1970.

Rudolph, Wilhelm. *Das Buch Ruth, Das Hohe Lied, Die Klagelieder*. KAT 17. Gütersloh: Gerd Mohn, 1962.

_____. *Chronikbücher*. HAT 21. Tübingen: J. C. B. Mohr (Paul Siebeck), 1955.

_____. *Esra und Nehemia*. HAT 20. Tübingen: J. C. B. Mohr (Paul Siebeck), 1949.

_____. *Hosea*. KAT 13[1]. Gütersloh: Gerd Mohn, 1966.

_____. "Hosea 4,15-19," in *Gottes Wort und Gottes Land (Festschrift H. W. Hertzberg)*. Ed. H. G. Reventlow. Göttingen: Vandenhoeck & Ruprecht, 1965. Pp. 193-98.

_____. *Jeremia*. HAT 12. Tübingen: J. C. B. Mohr (Paul Siebeck), 1958.

Rundgren, Frithuof. "Semitische Wortstudien," *Orientalia Suecana* 10 (1961) 99-136.

Ružička, Rudolf. *Konsonantische Dissimilation in den Semitischen Sprachen*. Beiträge zur Assyriologie und Semitischen Sprachwissenschaft VI, 4. Leipzig: J. C. Hinrichs'sche Buchhandlung, 1909.

Saʿadiah ben Joseph. *Commentary on Ezra and Nehemiah by Rabbi Saadiah*. Ed. Henry J. Matthews. Jerusalem: Makor Ltd., 1970.

_____. *Haʾegron, Kitāb ʾuṣūl al-Shiʿr al-ʿibrāni by Rav Sēʿadya Gaʾon*. Ed. Nehemiah Allony. Jerusalem: The Academy of the Hebrew Language, 1969.

_____. Ed. שמעון חמש מגילות . . . מקרא, תרגחם, תפסיר (ערבית). בן שמואל נג'אר. 1970.

_____. איוב עם תרגום ופירוש. Ed. Yosef Qafiḥ. Jerusalem: Makor Ltd., 1973.

_____. *Oeuvres Completes de R. Saadia Ben Iosef al-Fayyoumi*. Ed. Joseph Derenbourg. Paris: Ernest Cerous, 1893.

_____. ספר באור תשעים מלות בודדות בתנ"ך. Ed. Solomon A. Wertheimer. Jerusalem, 1931.

_____. פירושי רבינו סעדיה גאון על התורה. Ed. Yosef Qafiḥ. Jerusalem: Mossad Harav Kook, 1963.

_____. תהלים עם תרגום ופירוש. Ed. Yosef Qafiḥ. New York: Alexander Kohut Memorial Foundation, 1966.

Saʿadiah ibn Danan. "Fragment du Lexique de Saadia ibn Danan" (Ed. W. Bacher). *REJ* 41 (1900) 268-72.

Salonen, Erkki. *Über das Erwerbsleben im Alten Mesopotamien*. Studia Orientalia XI. Helsinki, 1920.

Samuel ben Meir. *Commentar zu Kohelet und dem Hohen Liede*. Ed. Adolph Jellinek. Leipzig: Leopold Schnauss, 1855.

_____. פירוש התורוה. Ed. David Rosin. New York: OMP Publishing Company, 1949.

Šanda, A. *Die Bücher der Könige*. EHAT 9. Münster: Verlag der Aschendorffschen Verlagsbuchhandlung, 1911.

_____. "Zu Job 4,10," *BZ* 2 (1904) 121.

Sanders, J. A. "Palestinian Manuscripts 1947-1972," in *Qumran and the History of the Biblical Text*. Ed. F. M. Cross and S. Talmon. Cambridge, MA: Harvard University Press, 1975. Pp. 401-13.

Sarna, David, E. Y., and Lawrence H. Schiffmann. "A Computer Analysis of Biblical Roots." Unpublished. 1968.

Sarna, Nahum M. "Hebrew and Bible Studies in Medieval Spain," in *The Sephardi Heritage*. Ed. R. D. Barnett. New York: Ktav, 1971. I. 323-66.

_____. Review of M. Sokoloff, *The Targum to Job from Qumran Cave XI*, *IEJ* 26 (1976) 151-52.

Sawyer, John F. A. "Root Meanings in Hebrew," *JSS* 12 (1967) 37-50.

Scharbert, Josef. *Der Schmerz im Alten Testament*. BBB 8. Bonn: Peter Hanstein Verlag, 1955.

Schechter, Solomon. *Aboth de Rabbi Nathan*. Vienna: Mauritii Knöpflmacher, 1887.

Scheiber, Alexander. "Fernere Fragmente aus שאלות עתיקות" *HUCA* 36 (1965) 227-59.

Bibliography

_____. "Unknown Leaves from שאלות עתיקות," *HUCA* 37 (1956) 291-303.

Schloessinger, Max. "Hapax Legomena—In Rabbinic Literature," *JE* VI, 228-29.

Schmidt, Hans. *Die Psalmen.* HAT 15. Tübingen: J. C. B. Mohr (Paul Siebeck), 1934.

Schoenfelder, J. M. *Onkelos und Peschittho.* Munich: J. J. Lentner, 1869.

Schulthess, Friedrich. *Homonyme Wurzeln im Syrischen.* Berlin: Reuther & Reichard, 1900.

_____. *Lexicon Syropalestinum.* Berlin: Georg Reimer, 1903.

_____. "Noch einige Zurufe an Tiere," *Zeitschrift für Semitistik* 2 (1924) 14-19.

_____. Review of J. Barth, *Wurzeluntersuchungen, Göttingische Gelehrte Anzeigen* 164 (1902) 665-75.

Schulz, Alfons. *Die Bücher Samuel.* EHAT 8. Münster: Verlag der Aschendorffschen Verlagsbuchhandlung, 1919.

Schwally, Friedrich. *Idioticon des Christlich Palästinischen Aramaeisch.* Giessen: J. Richer'sche Buchhandlung, 1893.

_____. "Die Reden des Buches Jeremia gegen die Heiden. XXV.XLVI-LI," *ZAW* 8 (1888) 177-217.

Schwarz, Günther. "Jesaja 50_{4-5a} Eine Emendation," *ZAW* 85 (1973) 356-57.

Scott, R. B. Y. *Proverbs, Ecclesiastes.* AB 18. Garden City, NY: Doubleday and Co., 1965.

Segal, Moses Hirsch. יסודי הפונטיקה העברית. Jerusalem: J. Junovitch, 1928.

_____. ספרי שמואל. 2d ed. Jerusalem: Kiryat Sepher, 1964.

Sellin, Ernst. *Die Zwölfprophetenbuch.* KAT 12. Leipzig: A. Deichertsche Verlagsbuchhandlung, 1929-30.

Sforno, Obadiah. באור יקר על חמשה חומשי תורה הנקרא ספורנו. Warsaw: W. Drukarni P. Lebensohne, 1856.

_____. באור על התורה. Czernowitz, 1858.

Shy, Hadassa. "Leš 33 (1969) 196-207, 280-96. אלמרשד אלכאפי לר' תנחום הירושלמי",

Siegfried, C. *Esra, Nehemia und Esther.* HKAT I 6². Göttingen: Vandenhoeck & Ruprecht, 1901.

──────. *The Book of Job.* SBOT 17. Leipzig: J. C. Hinrichs'sche Buchhandlung, 1893.

──────. *Der Prediger, Die Hohenliede.* HKAT II 3². Göttingen: Vandenhoeck & Ruprecht, 1898.

Silverstone, A. E. *Aquila and Onkelos.* Manchester: Manchester University Press, 1931.

Şiproni, A. "חלופי האותיות ב' פ' במקרא," *Leš* 1 (1927) 53-55.

Skeat, W. W. "Report Upon 'Ghost Words' or Words Which Have No Real Existence," *Transactions of the Philological Society* (1885-87) 350-74.

Skinner, John. *A Critical and Exegetical Commentary on Genesis.* ICC. 2d ed. Edinburgh: T. & T. Clark, 1930.

Skoss, Solomon L. "A Chapter on Permutation in Hebrew from David ben Abraham Al-Fāsi's Dictionary 'Jamiꜥ al-Alfāẓ,'" *JQR* 23 (1932-33) 1-43.

Smith, Henry Preserved. *A Critical and Exegetical Commentary on the Books of Samuel.* ICC. Edinburgh: T. & T. Clark, 1899.

Smith, John M. P., William Hayes Ward, and Julius A. Bewer. *A Critical and Exegetical Commentary on Micah, Zephaniah, Nahum, Habakkuk, Obadiah and Joel.* ICC. New York: Charles Scribner's Sons, 1911.

Smith, W. Robertson. "Old Testament Notes," *Journal of Philology* 13 (1885) 61-66.

Snaith, N. H. *Leviticus and Numbers.* CB. London: Thomas Nelson and Sons, 1967.

von Soden, Wolfram. *Akkadisches Handwörterbuch.* Wiesbaden: Otto Harrassowitz, 1965-81.

──────. "n als Wurzelaugment im Semitischen," *Wissenschaftliche Zeitschrift Martin-Luther-Universität Halle* 17 (1968) Studia Orientalia in Memoriam Caroli Brockelmann. Pp. 175-84.

Soggin, J. Alberto. *Judges.* OTL. Philadelphia: Westminster Press, 1981.

Sokoloff, Michael. *The Targum to Job from Qumran Cave XI.* Ramat-Gan: Bar-Ilan University, 1974.

Bibliography

Solomon ben Isaac (Rashi). פרשנ-דתא והוא פירוש רש"י על נ"ך. Ed. Isaac Maarsen. Jerusalem: Makor Ltd., 1972.

_____. רש"י על התורה. Ed. A. Berliner. Jerusalem: Feldheim Publishers, 1960.

_____. "Rashi's Commentary on the Song of Songs" (ed. Judah Rosenthal) in *Samuel K. Mirsky Jubilee Volume.* New York: Jubilee Committee, 1958. Pp. 130-88.

Solomon ibn Gabirol. "שני שירים לר' שלמה בן גבירול," in *Jubelschrift zum Neunzigsten Geburtstag des Dr. L. Zunz.* Ed. J. Egers. Berlin: Louis Gerschel, 1884. Pp. 192-96.

Solomon ibn Parḥon. "Commentar des Salomon Parchon zu Jesaia," *MGWJ* 11 (1862) 344-50, 391-96, 430-35; 12 (1863) 61-71, 108-10, 149-53, 269-73.

_____. מחברת הערוך. Ed. Salomo G. Stern. Jerusalem: Makor Ltd., 1970.

Solomon of Urbino. *Ohel Moed, Hebräische Sinonima.* Ed. Jonas Willheimer. Vienna: Georg Brög, 1881.

Speiser, E. A. *Genesis.* AB 1. Garden City, NY: Doubleday and Co., 1964.

Sperber, Alexander. "Hebrew Based upon Biblical Passages in Parallel Transmission," *HUCA* 14 (1939) 153-249.

_____. "Hebrew Based upon Greek and Latin Transliterations," *HUCA* 12-13 (1937-38) 103-274.

_____. *The Bible in Aramaic.* Leiden: E. J. Brill, 1959-73.

_____. "Peschitta und Onkelos," in *Jewish Studies in Memory of George A. Kohut.* Ed. S. W. Baron and A. Marx. New York: Alexander Kohut Memorial Foundation, 1935. Pp. 554-64.

Sprengling, M. "Joel 1,17a," *JBL* 38 (1919) 129-41.

Stade, Bernhard. *Lehrbuch der Hebräischen Grammatik.* Leipzig: F. C. W. Vogel, 1879.

_____, and Friedrich Schwally. *The Books of Kings.* SBOT 9. Baltimore: Johns Hopkins Press, 1904.

Starcky, J. "Un Contrat Nabatéen sur Papyrus," *RB* 61 (1954) 161-81.

Stern, Salomo Gottlieb. *Liber Responsionum.* Vienna, 1870.

Steuernagel, Carl. *Deuteronomium und Josua.* HKAT 1³. Göttingen: Vandenhoeck & Ruprecht, 1900.

Stoebe, Hans Joachim. *Das Erste Buch Samuelis.* KAT 8¹. Gütersloh: Gerd Mohn, 1973.

Strack, Hermann L. *Introduction to the Talmud and Midrash.* New York: Harper & Row, 1965.

Streck, M. "Kerbelā," in *Festschrift Eduard Sachau.* Ed. G. Weil. Berlin: Georg Reimer, 1915. Pp. 393-405.

Stummer, Friedrich, "גָּבַּ = adpropinquant," *Alttestamentliche Studien Friedrich Nötscher.* BBB 1. Bonn: Peter Hanstein, 1950. Pp. 265-70.

Sukenik, E. L. *The Dead Sea Scrolls of the Hebrew University.* Jerusalem: Magnes Press, 1955.

Szold, Benjamin. *The Book of Job.* Baltimore: H. F. Siemers, 1886.

Tacitus, Cornelius. *The Histories.* LCL. Trans. Clifford H. Mouce. Cambridge, MA: Harvard University Press, 1952.

Tal, Abraham. *The Samaritan Targum of the Pentateuch, A Critical Edition.* Tel Aviv: Tel Aviv University, 1980-81.

Tanḥum Yerushalmi. "Aus dem Wörterbuch Tanchum Jeruschalmi's" (ed. Wilhelm Bacher), in *Jahresbericht der Landes Rabbinerschule in Budapest* 26 (1903).

_____. ספר אלמרשד אלכאפי. Ed. Baruch Toledano. Tel Aviv, 1961.

_____. "Ein Fragment aus dem Psalmen-Commentar des Tanḥûm aus Jerusalem," *ZAW* 23 (1903) 287-325.

Tene, David. "Linguistic Literature, Hebrew," *Encyclopedia Judaica.* New York: Macmillan, 1971. XVI. 1352-1401.

Theophrastus. *Enquiry into Plants.* Trans. Arthur Hort. New York: G. P. Putnam's Sons, 1916.

Thierry, C. J. "Remarks on Various Passages of the Psalms," *OTS* 13 (1963) 77-97.

Thomas, D. Winton. "The root אהב 'love' in Hebrew," *ZAW* 57 (1939) 57-64.

Thompson, Catherine M. "Table of Percentage Points of the χ^2 Distribution," *Biometrika* 32 (1941-42) 187-91.

Bibliography

Tomback, Richard S. *A Comparative Semitic Lexicon of the Phoenician and Punic Languages.* SBLDS 32. Missoula, MT: Scholars Press, 1978.

The Torah. Philadelphia: The Jewish Publication Society of America, 1962.

Torrey, Charles C. *Ezra Studies.* New York: Ktav, 1970.

_____. "New Notes on Some Old Inscriptions," *ZA* 26 (1912) 77-92.

_____. *The Second Isaiah: A New Interpretation.* New York: Charles Scribner's Sons, 1928.

Tournay, R. (no title). *RB* 71 (1964) 147.

_____. "Relectures Bibliques Concernant La Vie Future et l'Angélologie," *RB* 69 (1962) 481-505.

Tov, Emmanuel. "On 'Pseudo-Variants' Reflected in the Septuagint," *JSS* 20 (1975) 165-77.

Toy, C. H. *The Book of Ezekiel.* SBOT 12. Leipzig: J. C. Hinrichs'sche Buchhandlung, 1899.

_____. *A Critical and Exegetical Commentary on the Book of Proverbs.* ICC. New York: Charles Scribner's Sons, 1899.

_____. *Quotations in the New Testament.* New York: Charles Scribner's Sons, 1884.

Tur-Sinai (Torczyner) N. H. "בעקבות הלשון והספר," *Leš* 23 (1958) 1-34.

_____. "בשולי המלון של אליעזר בן-יהודה," *Leš* 13 (1944) 95-119.

_____. "Biblische Miszellen," in *Festschrift Adolph Schwarz.* Berlin: R. Löwit Verlag, 1917. Pp. 55-62.

_____. *The Book of Job.* Jerusalem: Kiryat Sepher, 1957.

_____. *Die Bundeslade und die Anfänge der Religion Israels.* Berlin: Philo Verlag, 1930.

_____. הלשון והספר. Jerusalem: Bialik Institute, 1948-55.

_____. "Hapax Legomena," *Encyclopedia Judaica.* Berlin: Verlag Eschkol A.-G., 1931. 7. 997-1000.

_____. *Lachish I.* London: Oxford University Press, 1938.

_____. "דביר 2 (1922) 61-91, "למחקר הלשון והמקרא".

_____. "Presidential Address," *JPOS* 16 (1936) 1-8.

_____. פשוטו של מקרא. Jerusalem: Kiryat Sepher Ltd., 1962.

_____. Review of N. U. Schlögl, *Die Heiligen Schriften des Alten Bundes* in *Göttingische Gelehrte Anzeigen* 178 (1916) 305-38.

_____. Review of GB in *ZDMG* 70 (1916) 555-62.

Ullendorff, Edward. *Ethiopia and the Bible.* London: British Academy, 1968.

_____. "Ugaritic Marginalia II," *JSS* 7 (1962) 339-51.

Ungnad, A. Review of M. J. E. Gautier, *Archives d'une Famille de Dilbat* in *OLZ* 13 (1910) 156-61.

Viroleaud, M. Charles. "Les Nouveaux Textes Mythologiques de Ras Shamra," *Académie des Inscriptions & Belles-Lettres, Comptes Rendus* (1962) 105-13.

_____. "Le Nouveaux Textes Mythologiques et Liturgiques de Ras Shamra," *Ugaritica* V (MRS 16, 1968) 544-606.

_____. "Un Poéme Phénicien de Ras-Shamra," *Syria* 12 (1931) 193-224.

Vogelstein, Hermann. *Die Landwirtschaft in Palästina zur Zeit der Mišnâh.* Berlin: Mayer & Muller, 1894.

Vogt, E. "Ostracon Hebraicus Saec 7 A.C.," *Bib* 42 (1961) 135-36.

Volz, Paul. *Jesaia II.* KAT 9. Leipzig: A. Deichertsche Verlagsbuchhandlung, 1932.

_____. *Der Prophet Jeremia.* KAT 10. Leipzig: A. Deichertsche Verlagsbuchhandlung, 1928.

Vööbus, Arthur. *Peschitta und Targumim des Pentateuchs.* Papers of the Estonian Theological Society in Exile 9. Stockholm: ETSE, 1958.

Vycichl, Werner. "Ägyptische-semitische Anklänge," *ZÄS* 84 (1959) 145-47.

Wagner, Max. *Die Lexikalischen und Grammatikalischen Aramaismen im Alttestamentlichen Hebräisch.* BZAW 96. Berlin: Alfred Töpelmann, 1966.

Wechter, Pinchas. *Ibn Barun's Arabic Works on Hebrew Grammar and Lexicography.* Philadelphia: The Dropsie College for Hebrew and Cognate Learning, 1964.

Weil, Gérard E., ed. *Massorah Gedolah*. Rome: Pontifical Biblical Institute, 1971.

_____. "Prolegomena," to S. Frensdorff *The Massorah Magna*. New York: Ktav, 1968.

Weiser, Artur. *The Psalms, A Commentary*. OTL. Trans. Herbert Hartwell. London: SCM Press Ltd., 1962.

Wellhausen, Julius. *The Book of Psalms*. SBOT 14. Baltimore: Johns Hopkins Press, 1895.

_____. *Die Kleinen Propheten übersetzt und erklärt*. 4th ed. Berlin: Walter de Gruyter, 1963.

_____. *Reste Arabischen Heidentums*. 2d ed. Berlin: Georg Reimer, 1897.

_____. *Skizzen und Vorarbeiten* V. Berlin: Georg Reimer, 1893.

_____. *Der Text der Bücher Samuelis*. Göttingen: Vandenhoeck & Ruprecht, 1871.

Wernberg-Møller, P. *The Manual of Discipline*. STDJ 1. Leiden: E. J. Brill, 1957.

_____. "A Note on לָשׂוּחַ בַּשָּׂדֶה in Gen XXIV 63," *VT* 7 (1957) 414-16.

_____. "Prolegomena to a Re-examination of the Palestinian Targum Fragments of the Book of Genesis Published by P. Kahle, and their Relationship to the Peshitta," *JSS* 7 (1962) 253-66.

_____. "Some Observations on the Relationship of the Peshitta Version of the Book of Genesis to the Palestinian Targum Fragments," *ST* 15 (1961) 128-80.

Westermann, Claus. *Genesis*. BKAT 1. Neukirchen: Verlag des Erziehungsvereins, 1974.

Wetzstein, D. "Ueber אנוש Ps 69,21," in Franz Delitzsch, *Biblischer Commentar über die Psalmen*. 4th ed. Leipzig: Dorffling und Franke, 1883. Pp. 883-90.

Wevers, John W. *Ezekiel*. CB. London: Thomas Nelson and Sons, 1969.

Whatmough, Joshua. *Poetic, Scientific and Other Forms of Discourse*. Berkeley: University of California Press, 1956.

Whitaker, Richard E. *A Concordance of the Ugaritic Literature*. Cambridge, MA: Harvard University Press, 1972.

Wiener, Harold M. "The Text of 1 Samuel II 33," *JPOS* 8 (1928) 63.

Wiesmann, Hermann. *Die Klagelieder*. Frankfurt a.M.: Philosophisch-theologische Hochschule Sankt Georgen, 1954.

Wildberger, Hans. *Jesaia*. BKAT $10^{1,2}$. Neukirchen: Verlag des Erziehungsvereins Neukirchen-Vluyn, 1972-78.

Wildeboer, G. "Der Prediger, Das Buch Esther," in *Die Fünf Megillot*. KHC 17. Tübingen: J. C. B. Mohr (Paul Siebeck), 1898.

_____. *Die Sprüche*. KHC 15. Tübingen: J. C. B. Mohr (Paul Siebeck), 1897.

Wilensky, Michael. "דביר" 2 (1923) ",ספר שפה ברורה לר' אברהם אבן עזרא". 274-302.

Wilson, R. Dick. "Aramaisms in the Old Testament," *Princeton Theological Review* 23 (1925) 234-66.

Winckler, Hugo. "Arabisch-Semitisch-Orientalisch," *MVAG* 6 (1901) 151-374.

Wohl, Schaje. *Das Palästinische Pentateuch Targum*. Zwickaui Sae, 1935.

Wolff, Hans Walter. *Hosea*. BKAT 14^1. Neukirchen: Verlag des Erziehungsvereins, 1965.

_____. *Joel und Amos*. BKAT 14^2. Neukirchen: Verlag des Erziehungsvereins, 1969.

Wright, T. J. "Amos and the 'Sycamore Fig,'" *VT* 26 (1976) 362-68.

Wright, William. *Lectures on the Comparative Grammar of the Semitic Languages*. New York: Macmillan and Co., 1890.

The Writings, Kethubim. Philadelphia: The Jewish Publication Society of America, 1982.

Wurthwein, Ernst. *Ruth, Das Hohelied, Esther*. HAT 18. Tübingen: J. C. B. Mohr (Paul Siebeck), 1969.

_____. *The Text of the Old Testament*. Trans. Peter R. Ackroyd. Oxford: Basil Blackwell, 1957.

Yadin, Yigael. *The Scroll of the War of the Sons of Light Against the Sons of Darkness*. Oxford: University Press, 1962.

Yahuda, A. S. "Bagdadische Sprichwörter," in *Orientalische Studien Theodor Nöldeke*. Giessen: Alfred Töpelmann, 1906.

_____. "Hapax legomena im Alten Testament," *JQR* 15 (1902-3) 618-714.

Yalon, Hanoch. "הערה," *Leš* 3 (1931) 307.

_____. "לדעת לעות את יעף דבר," *Leš* 30 (1965) 248.

_____. מבוא לנקוד המשנה. Jerusalem: Bialik Institute, 1964.

_____. ילקוט שמעוני, צילום הדפוס הראשון שאלוניקי רפ"א - רפ"ז 1968. ספרית מקורות. Jerusalem:

Yannay, Igal. "Augmented Verbs in Biblical Hebrew," *HUCA* 45 (1974) 71-96.

_____. "פעלים מרובי - עיצורים בלשון העברית," *Leš* 38 (1973-74) 118-30, 183-94.

_____. *The Quadriradical Verb in the Hebrew Language*. Diss., Ph.D., University of California, Los Angeles, 1970.

Yeivin, S. "The Judicial Petition from Meẓad Ḥashavyahu," *BibOr* 19 (1962) 3-10.

Yellin, David. "הוראות נשכחות לשרשים עבריים," *Leš* 1 (1928) 5-26.

_____. תולדות התפתחות הדקדוק העברי. Jerusalem: Qohelet Ltd., 1945.

Yule, G. Udny. *The Statistics of Literary Style*. Cambridge: Cambridge University Press, 1944.

Zaborski, Andrezej. "Prefixes, Root-Determinatives and the Problem of Biconsonantal Roots in Semitic," *Folia Orientalia* 11 (1969) 307-13.

Zapletal, Vincenz. *Das Buch der Richter*. EHAT 7. Münster: Verlag des Aschendorffschen Verlagsbuchhandlung, 1923.

Zelson, Louis G. "Les *Hapax Legomena* du Pentateuque Hebraique," *RB* 36 (1927) 243-48.

Zeraḥya ben Yiṣḥaq ben Sheʾaltiel of Barcelona. תקות אנוש in פירוש איוב. Ed. Israel Schwartz. Berlin: Louis Gerschel Verlagsbuchhandlung, 1868. Pp. 167-293.

Ziegler, Joseph. "Beiträge zum griechischen Dodekapropheton," in *Sylloge, Gesammelte Aufsätze zur Septuaginta*. Göttingen: Vandenhoeck & Ruprecht, 1971. Pp. 71-138.

van Zijl, Peter J. *Baal, A Study of Texts in Connection with Baal in the Ugaritic Epics*. AOAT 10. Neukirchen-Vluyn: Verlag Butzon & Bercker Kevelaer, 1972.

Zimmerli, Walther. *Ezechiel.* BKAT 13. Neukirchen: Verlag des Erziehungsvereins, 1969.

Zimmern, Friedrich D. H. *Akkadische Fremdwörter als Beweis für Babylonischen Kultureinfluss.* Leipzig: J. C. Hinrichs'sche Buchhandlung, 1915.

Zipf, George Kingsley. *Selected Studies of the Principle of Relative Frequency in Language.* Cambridge, MA: Harvard University Press, 1932.

www.ingramcontent.com/pod-product-compliance
Lightning Source LLC
Chambersburg PA
CBHW050343230426
43663CB00010B/1965